urned on c

Preventing and Responding to Student Suicide

of related interest

Supporting Transgender and Non-Binary Students and Staff in Further and Higher Education Practical Advice for Colleges and Universities
Dr Matson Lawrence and Dr Stephanie Mckendry
ISBN 978 1 78592 345 6
eISBN 978 1 78450 673 5

Supporting College and University Students with Invisible Disabilities
A Guide for Faculty and Staff Working with Students with Autism,
AD/HD, Language Processing Disorders, Anxiety, and Mental Illness
Christy Oslund
ISBN 978 1 84905 955 8
eISBN 978 0 85700 785 8

Suicide Prevention Techniques
How a Suicide Crisis Service Saves Lives
Joy Hibbins
ISBN 978 1 78592 549 8
eISBN 978 1 78450 949 1

Responding After Suicide
A Practical Guide to Immediate Postvention
Andrea Walraven-Thissen
ISBN 978 1 78592 561 0
eISBN 978 1 78450 958 3

After the Suicide
Helping the Bereaved to Find a Path from Grief to Recovery
Einar Plyhn, Gudrun Dieserud, Kari Dyregrov
ISBN 978 1 84905 211 5
eISBN 978 0 85700 445 1

We Get It
Voices of Grieving College Students and Young Adults
Heather L. Servaty-Seib, Bethany Gower, Diane Brincat, David Fajgenbaum
ISBN 978 1 84905 752 3
eISBN 978 0 85700 977 7

PREVENTING and RESPONDING to STUDENT SUICIDE

EDITED BY
Sharon Mallon and Jo Smith

Foreword by Rosie Tressler, OBE

Jessica Kingsley Publishers
London and Philadelphia

First published in Great Britain in 2022 by Jessica Kingsley Publishers
An Hachette Company

I

Copyright © Sharon Mallon and Jo Smith 2022
Foreword copyright © Rosie Tressler, OBE

A CIP catalogue record for this title is available from the British Library
and the Library of Congress

ISBN 978 1 78775 418 8
eISBN 978 1 78775 419 5

Printed and bound in Great Britain by CPI Group

Jessica Kingsley Publishers' policy is to use papers that are natural, renewable and
recyclable products and made from wood grown in sustainable forests. The logging
and manufacturing processes are expected to conform to the environmental
regulations of the country of origin.

Jessica Kingsley Publishers
Carmelite House,
50 Victoria Embankment,
London, EC4Y 0DZ, UK

www.jkp.com

Contents

Section 2: Responses to Risk

Part 2: Responding to Student Death by Suicide

Foreword

It is a real honour, and a somewhat daunting prospect, to introduce *Preventing and Responding to Student Suicide*. I've been reflecting on what I can add to the thoughtful work of this excellent array of authors, headed up by the inspiring duo of Jo Smith and Sharon Mallon.

I first met Jo as she was starting her work at the University of Worcester and I've been endlessly impressed by what she, Sharon and their various collaborators in this book and beyond have kick-started in the higher education sector. Having a single-minded focus on 'suicide-safer' institutions wasn't always 'popular' but it is what has been needed. The contributors to this book have between them helped thousands more people to hear the message that suicide is preventable, that it is not inevitable and that there is always someone there to help.

When I first sat down to read the manuscript for this collection, I felt both eager to learn and, being honest, also a little apprehensive. In my role as CEO of Student Minds, the UK's student mental health charity, I have met far too many people that either have experience of living with distress, the experience of being bereaved by suicide or been involved in postvention in education settings. Indeed, we heard from thousands of students, professionals and academics during our development of the University Mental Health Charter, and this topic was a key area many of the attendees of our consultation exercise across the UK wanted space to discuss. Sometimes this conversation reminds me of difficult personal feelings too. I have known how powerful connection, non-judgemental listening and validation can be to someone in difficult times.

Indeed, this is one of the most emotive topics on which to write a book. And it is exactly because it is such an emotive topic that it is so crucial we listen to students and the available evidence. This comprehensive book is written with compassion and understanding, with a rigorous focus on the latest evidence. The team have managed to make a complex field accessible, and crucially to ask and answer the questions that matter most. Like me, I'm sure it will leave you feeling informed and hopeful.

Writing this Foreword during the Covid-19 pandemic and during another lockdown period also gives this work a timely lens. Throughout the pandemic, I've overseen the Student Space programme, where our partnership of organizations has supported thousands of students. I've been reading about the number of people whose personal situations have become more precarious over this period, with employment data highlighting that under 30s are being most impacted. Whilst every situation is unique and complex, given what we know about the connection between financial pressure and suicide, and the data analysis presented in this book, we really must do what we can to prevent problems and be ready to offer timely support. We must do our bit in the sector of course, but we too need to see government policy to support those most impacted by this difficult period in society's history. I'm hopeful that the government will act now for our youngest generations.

Something else to bring specific attention to are the multiple references across the chapters of this book that draw attention to the increased suicidal ideation in students who come from communities that still experience discrimination or oppression in our society. Whilst we must do all we can to create brave and compassionate cultures in education, we can't stop there. We must follow the lead of our Students' Union colleagues – who do much to build student belonging but also to advocate – and use every ounce of the influence we have to speak up for all groups that experience oppression, discrimination and inequality in society.

Do look after yourself while you're reading this insightful book, dip in and out of the chapters, utilize the practical resources and, most importantly, connect with others and tell them about it. We absolutely can build a community of people across Higher and Further Education that will sustain this single-minded commitment demonstrated by the authors of this book. The careful configuration of this book indicates what is needed to prevent student deaths by suicide – this is about sustaining a concerted collaborative effort, both across university and college departments with strategic planning to deliver a whole-university approach and across sectors to join up thinking across the education, health and third sector. All of us together have an important role to play – everyone in our community matters and we can build back better together.

Rosie Tressler OBE, CEO, Student Minds

Dedication

To my PhD supervisor and long-term mentor Professor Nicky Stanley.
Thank you for believing in me.
Sharon Mallon

For Clare and Nick, who shared with me their compelling, emotive
narrative of grief and loss of their son, James, while studying at a UK
university (www.jamesplace.org.uk), and Professor David Green, CBE,
Vice Chancellor at University of Worcester, for bringing us together.
This unexpected meeting triggered my involvement in a continuing
narrative around student suicide prevention and a personal commitment
to endeavour to change the story for students like James, their families,
peers, staff within HE and FE, and the institutions they are part of.
Jo Smith

Editorial

JO SMITH AND SHARON MALLON

This editorial sets out the specific contextual challenges of student suicide in further education (FE) and higher education (HE) and outlines the approach of this edited collection in helping to address these challenges.

Introduction

In recent years, there has been increasing concern about suicide among HE students. Although data (Gunnell *et al.* 2020; ONS 2018) suggest the rates of suicide among this group are considerably lower than rates in their age-matched non-student counterparts in the general population, research over the past decade has identified particular risks associated with aspects of student life that may contribute to some deaths (Li, Dorstyn and Jarmon 2019). In addition, the rate of mental health problems and suicide among students has risen dramatically over the last ten years (Gunnell *et al.* 2020).

There is now considerable evidence highlighting the impact a death by suicide can have on staff and students. Of particular concern to those working at campus-based institutions is the potential for copycat deaths and the contagion effect of suicide, where one death by suicide may trigger another. Media reports that highlight clusters of suicide within HE or FE can have a devastating impact on the staff and students who work and study there and may also have consequences for the wider reputation of the institution, affecting subsequent student recruitment. In addition to the immediate impact of a death by suicide, there is now concern about the longer-term impact a suicide can have on academic, clinical and support staff, who may have had to support others or deal with suicide-related issues in the course of their working roles.

For these reasons, it is widely accepted by practitioners and academics within these sectors that suicide-specific prevention and response plans, that manage both individual risk and plan institutional-level responses, should be given priority. However, despite this awareness, many institutions remain unprepared and there continues to be a degree of fear about managing suicide risk and responses even among caring, compassionate and committed staff. Our sense, as experienced researchers and practitioners in this field, is that despite recent efforts, suicide continues to be a challenging topic and some of this inaction results from deep-seated concerns about 'doing the wrong thing'. This can work in combination with a lack of knowledge about how to manage suicide within the context of an HE or FE college setting.

This book aims to address the gap by providing a comprehensive overview from leading experts in the field, each of whom can provide insights into particular problems associated with suicide within higher and further education institutions. It will examine a range of issues associated with suicide risk, prevention and postvention among staff and students. We take this broad approach because we consider that the issues of suicide prevention and postvention are indivisible, both in their effects and their responses. The book will highlight some of the unique support needs of the staff and student communities in regard to suicide and offer examples of effective responses that operate both at the individual and at an institutional level. It will also provide details of how institutions can work most effectively with other agencies, including statutory and voluntary sector partners and other community-based practitioners.

Chapters are based on the most up-to-date research in these areas, drawing on evidence from the UK and other relevant global arenas. The discussion of each area takes into account the current structural context of HE and FE within the UK. Contributors examine issues associated with student suicide as they pertain to the HE and FE sector and provide practical detail of how institutions can effectively plan and manage their suicide prevention and postvention responses. We hope it will be an invaluable resource for all those working to support vulnerable students, their peers, family members and staff who may all be affected by issues associated with student suicide.

Rationale: Why focus a whole book on HE and FE student suicide?

In the UK, three-quarters of all young people aged 16–19 years attend school sixth forms, sixth form colleges and further education colleges.

Since 2010, significant funding reductions have affected staff pay, teaching provision and capacity to support students (Dominiguez-Reig and Robinson 2019). At the same time, in September 2019, the latest Higher Education Initial Participation Rate (HEIPR) data (DfE 2019) showed that 50 per cent of young adults in the UK are now going into HE, although this figure includes 7 per cent studying for HE degrees at FE colleges, 10 per cent studying for higher technical qualifications, 8 per cent studying part-time and 20 per cent who enter HE during their 20s (Brant 2019).

HE and FE institutions are both, therefore, in the business of educating significantly large numbers of young people in the UK. At the same time, there is now evidence and concern about increases in mental health difficulties experienced by young people during further education years (Eskin *et al.* 2016; Thorley 2017). There is also concern that the increasing pressures students face in transition to and during FE and HE studies have the potential to adversely impact on their mental health and wellbeing (Stanley *et al.* 2009). More specifically, suicide is now the leading cause of death globally for young people in this age group (WHO 2018). In the last five years, there has been increasing concern voiced about HE student suicide in the UK (Coughlan 2018; UUK and PAPYRUS 2018). Similar concerns about student suicide have been identified in other countries, including the US, Sweden and Japan (American Foundation for Suicide Prevention 2021; Lageborn *et al.* 2017; Uchida and Uchida 2017). This book reviews the available research evidence and guidance from the UK and internationally to inform efforts to understand and intervene to prevent suicide in young people enrolled in FE and HE.

Evidence for student suicide

Public interest in student suicide has heightened in the last few years, fuelled by media reporting of student suicides in individual institutions (Marzano *et al.* 2018) and in response to national data which apparently showed an increase in deaths by suicide in full-time students in England and Wales between 2001 and 2016 (ONS 2016). Indeed, Jeremy Hunt (2017), then Secretary of State for Health, urged universities to respond to this apparent steep rise in student suicides. On face value, this data did indeed raise questions about HE environments and whether they may be deleterious to the mental health of students, with speculation focusing on various potential contributory factors including student fees, and academic and social media pressures. However, the data did not take into account the rising student population over the same period or look more critically at rates (per 100,000) relative to age-matched non-student peers. In 2018, the ONS negotiated with the Higher Education Statistics Agency (HESA) responsible for the collection, analysis and dissemination of quantitative information about higher education in the UK to link national student records with coroners' verdict data. They published new data showing much lower rates for HE student populations compared with age-matched peers across all age groups. suggesting that higher education environments may instead be intrinsically more protective than harmful.

Student suicide prevention

Notwithstanding this new ONS data, student suicide is still a profoundly impactful phenomenon which can potentially occur from time to time in any FE or HE institution. Any student death will impact on their wider community; it is the end of a life at an age where death is not expected, of someone who is typically at the start of their adult life and brings with it the end of their hopes and ambitions, while those left behind have to come to terms with all that will never be realized. A death by suicide is particularly devastating for family, friends and peers and can have a profound and far-reaching impact on students, staff and the wider institutional community. It is an event which most institutions' senior leaders dread in relation to its potentially adverse impact on reputation and subsequent student recruitment, as it can be constructed as an implied organizational failure to intervene and adequately protect students studying under their watch.

Are student deaths by suicide potentially preventable? Internationally, including in the UK, within mental health services, particularly inpatient care settings, there is a growing 'zero suicide' movement which promotes a proactive strategy to identify and care for all those who may be at risk of suicide, rather than only reacting when individuals have reached a crisis point (Brodsky, Spruch-Feiner and Stanley 2018). It emphasizes a joined-up strategy supported by strong leadership, improved training, better screening and use of the latest data and research to reduce suicide incidence. It also challenges old ideas about stigma and complacency that deaths by suicide are necessarily inevitable or acceptable. Increasingly, zero suicide proponents in the UK have begun to argue for a reform in attitudes and approaches beyond healthcare, including universities (Usborne 2017), to prevent suicide or to aspire to do so.

What would adopting a zero suicide mindset mean for HE and FE colleges? Certainly, it would involve access to in-house support services for those in distress and clear referral pathways into statutory primary and secondary mental health care with effective joined-up working relationships to facilitate transition between them. However, given that many students take their lives without contacting any specialist services, this would also require wider whole organization initiatives including institutional safeguarding, peer support initiatives, suicide prevention training and building vigilant and supportive communities (DePury 2018; UUK and PAPYRUS 2018).

There is also much that FE colleges and HE institutions can do immediately to improve how they respond to deaths by suicide. National Public Health England (PHE) guidance on suicide prevention planning and avoiding contagion/clusters has been developed. It is informed by the latest research evidence on suicide prevention efforts internationally, as well as learning from and employing evidence-based training and resources from other sectors that could be adapted and used in HE and FE settings. In the UK, there are now also published bespoke suicide prevention toolkits for HE (UUK and PAPYRUS 2018) and colleges (PAPYRUS 2018), as well as a student suicide postvention toolkit and support process called *Step by Step* (Samaritans 2013).

However, there remains significant variation in student suicide prevention practice across the FE and HE sectors in the UK. There are many academic and administrative staff, as well as those with more obvious student support roles, who, at some point in their working lives, will be required to offer support to a student who may be struggling or advice to a concerned peer, family member or colleague. They may not have received any direct competency training addressing what may be helpful or effective to say or do in this particular circumstance (National Collaborating Centre for Mental Health 2018) or have access to any specific guidance or bespoke resources to guide them effectively in this task. Consequently, many students can fail to receive informed support or benefit from simple, non-specialist early intervention that may successfully prevent a later crisis and a subsequent suicide attempt.

Some key issues in relation to this book

- *Suicide and self-harm.* This book will focus specifically on student suicide in HE and FE communities. Suicide is defined as 'death by intentional self-harm and deaths of undetermined intent by individuals aged 10 and over' (HQIP 2017). A suicide attempt is defined as 'an act of self-harm in which the person intended to die, and believed that the means and method of the attempt would be fatal'. The relationship between self-harm and suicide is complicated. Although people who self-harm are significantly more likely to die by suicide, or to harm themselves using more serious methods than the general population who do not self-harm, people may have many motivations for self-harm and are not always intent on dying (Klonsky, Victor and Saffer 2014). Suicidal intent may not be evident early on, but often emerges over time (Townsend *et al.* 2016). Therefore, although serious self-harm can be both a precursor and risk factor for suicide, we do not intend to specifically address the topic of student self-harm or associated interventions other than where these may directly relate to a suicide prevention strategy.

- *A specific focus on suicide prevention.* Prevention-focused approaches in mental health are more cost-effective than crisis treatment approaches, and the growing rates of mental health problems and suicide in the HE and FE student populations cannot reasonably be stemmed by treating individuals one at a time. There are already many books and resources focused on addressing the broader wellbeing and mental health of students. As this is the first book that we are aware of that specifically and uniquely focuses on suicide in an educational setting rather than a healthcare context, the focus here will be more directly on student suicide prevention and postvention. Existing books and resources can vary greatly in terms of content, approach, delivery and the weight and quality of evidence from which they have been derived. Our intention with this book is to draw on the most up-to-date research, involving leading suicide prevention researchers and HE practitioners. The recommendations that emerge from the bespoke evidence-based interventions are directly appropriate to student suicide prevention in HE and FE settings.

- *What do we mean by 'risk' and 'responses to risk'?* When considering suicide prevention, it may seem sensible to attempt to identify students who may be particularly vulnerable and 'at risk', or when intervening with a student expressing suicidal ideas or behaviours to try to assess their current level of risk to themselves. The use of a standardized risk assessment tool may also be proposed as a method of screening whole student populations for risk, or as a way of an organization demonstrating that risks have been appraised and protocols have been followed and documented. However, while there are many factors associated with risk, evidence indicates that our ability to accurately predict risk is limited and that formal risk assessment tools and scales lack predictive value (Quinlivan *et al.* 2017; Steeg *et al.* 2018). This means that it is possible to both overestimate and underestimate the actual risk of suicide in an individual student or across a student population at a given moment in time. The approach taken in this book is one which will consider what is currently known about student suicide risk factors, triggers and particular characteristics that may increase vulnerability to suicide in the context of current suicide risk theory. However, the emphasis across the book will be on engaging the young person in a personally meaningful dialogue that helps them to consider their difficulties, the context in which these difficulties arise and the resources available to help keep them safe. Assessment of risk needs always to be combined with strategies centred around risk management, including safeguarding, safety planning, reducing access to lethal means and interventions to keep the young person safe.

- *What do we mean by suicide prevention?* Primary prevention prevents something from occurring in the first place, before a student shows any change in their mental health or wellbeing or starts help-seeking. Universally applied preventative measures have the greatest potential to have a positive effect on a whole student population and are least stigmatizing. In the context of FE or HE, universal interventions designed to help all students include interventions such as reducing alcohol consumption or illicit drug use, addressing loneliness and encouraging social connectedness, combating stigma around mental health and help-seeking through media and community campaigns. They include reducing potential precipitating factors such as facilitating a positive transition to FE and HE studies from school/home, reducing academic stress and financial burden, designing supportive policies and processes (e.g. 'fitness to study' and withdrawal and suspension processes) as well as addressing predisposing factors such as levels of social support, coping style, resilience and other protective factors. They also include specific measures to maintain the wellbeing and mental health of known potentially vulnerable groups such as LGBTIQ, looked after and international students.

Secondary prevention involves early recognition and intervention to restore health. It can include actions such as encouraging help-seeking and engagement, reducing stigma, improving knowledge and coping skills, and preventing collateral damage in terms of disruption to relationships or academic and social functioning. Tertiary prevention is about crisis treatment and interventions, and trying to reduce distress and restore previous health, academic and social functioning in individuals who are actively suicidal (intent and/or behaviour) at a point in time or, from time to time, over the course of their studies. This book will consider all three types of prevention interventions, with chapters looking at whole institution initiatives for students and staff (Chapters 10, 11 and 12) through to talking to someone who is actively suicidal and safety planning (Chapter 15).

- *What do we mean by postvention?* This refers to interventions aimed at supporting student peers and staff who have been directly affected by a death by suicide. These interventions can take the form of individualized support for those close to the student – for example, friends and housemates and personal tutors. It might also refer to interventions offered within the HE or FE organization as a whole, where groups of individuals such as students studying the same course, course staff, as well as members of clubs, societies and teams in which the student may have been involved, are offered support and the opportunity to express their feelings regarding the death of a fellow student or colleague. As with exposure to any traumatic event, many individuals may be able to draw on their own strengths and support networks. However, the death by suicide of a young person is rare, untimely and outside the experience of most young people, and the event may generate significant support needs and public interest that can benefit from an organized response.

- *Evidence-based suicide prevention and postvention interventions.* Student suicide is a relatively novel research field. Until recently, the majority of studies in the UK and US were largely epidemiological, carried out in individual HE institutions. Many evidence gaps exist in the broader suicide prevention literature generally and specifically in relation to HE and particularly FE student suicide prevention and postvention. This book distils the latest and best research evidence about the topic. It also identifies what we don't know in terms of evidence gaps and provides examples where wider suicide prevention literature and national policy and practice developments may be appropriately applied to an HE and FE context.

  Despite the research evidence, information about student suicide prevention and postvention (PAPYRUS 2018; UUK and PAPYRUS 2018) has not necessarily effectively influenced decision making or been routinely applied in HE and FE practice. The problem of research dissemination and uptake becomes considerably more complex when trying to influence the thinking of a more diverse group than just health practitioners working in HE and FE, such as administrative staff, policy leaders and decision makers. Summarizing good quality research evidence is a necessary first step, but not necessarily a sufficient one to change institutional behaviour and ensure that something is actually used and implemented in practice.

  A key barrier to effective student suicide prevention is the social system and cultural context of HE and FE where different ideologies (values, beliefs), institutional structures, interests and incentives can apply. These can influence the way people think and work, constraining both adequate resourcing and effective implementation of suicide prevention initiatives (see Chapters 10 and 13). Simply supplying good quality research evidence is not sufficient in itself to motivate people to change their behaviour. We need also to understand these educational settings, where problems have to be solved quickly and cost effectively, and where staff are dealing with multiple other problems and perspectives. Decision makers, especially those working in institutions concerned with fiscal restraint, increasingly also want to ensure effective outcomes from any new investment. This can be tricky to evidence in the field of suicide prevention where obvious success outcomes may be less tangible. Collaborative models that explicitly involve students, staff, health practitioners, researchers and policy makers working in HE and FE, as well as external community partners, also need to be encouraged. Equally, creating national forums for exchanging ideas and information between HE and FE institutions in an organized and meaningful way, and developing effective mechanisms for busy practitioners and decision makers, as well as researchers, to access and exchange information quickly and easily, is essential. It would help to grow a HE and FE community of knowledge around developing effective and efficient student suicide prevention practices.

What are the aims of this book?

Our book takes a comprehensive and detailed evidence-based approach specifically to the topic of student suicide. It incorporates the best current evidence and draws on practice innovations, in the context of limited resources, with chapters from a wide range of practitioners and leading academics in the field. It expands on published toolkits by drawing on relevant theories in relation to risk, provides an understanding of specific risks for students and draws on recent research evidence specific to an HE and FE context as well as a broader international suicide prevention context. In addition, it provides detailed accounts of what to do in practice, supported by real clinical examples from current HE and FE practice.

The aims of this book are to persuade individuals and institutions that student suicide prevention and postvention are important and key components of 21st century FE and HE support. We have invited key suicide prevention pioneers, working within HE and suicide prevention more broadly, to contribute chapters drawing on the best available latest research evidence to help us understand student suicide and factors that may contribute to it. Early chapters consider how we can reconfigure and mobilize existing services, personnel (academic, support and facilities staff and students themselves) and whole institutions to engage in a student suicide prevention agenda. We conclude the book by outlining best practice evidence-based interventions to most effectively support students, family members, staff and whole institutions in a concerted student suicide prevention endeavour.

Who is the book intended for?

This book will be of interest to anyone working or studying in an FE or HE context in the UK or internationally. It is intended to be relevant to academic and professional staff in HE and FE (and potentially school sixth form settings too) as well as practitioners working in student support, mental health and counselling services, primary care, NHS and public health services. And it targets staff from voluntary sector and charitable organizations who may be looking for ways to best support educational institutions in their endeavours to prevent student suicide. The book may also be of direct practical benefit to a student struggling with suicidal ideas or behaviours, and their peers or family members who may be trying to support them. Through its specific focus on student suicide, it is additionally designed to support suicide researchers and epidemiologists trying to understand this niche area of suicide prevention and to identify gaps in current knowledge and evidence for future research studies.

Chapter contributors are from a range of professional backgrounds including psychiatry, psychology, nursing, social work and counselling. The content is informed by their own research work and practical experiences supporting young people who at times may be suicidal and their families, supporting staff or whole institution interventions.

Overview

Each chapter begins with a brief overview of its primary theme and overall purpose, including the key objectives. These will aid the reader in identifying what they can expect to gain by engaging with the chapter material. The authors explore why a particular problem/issue/theme is important. They also identify key learning and practical recommendations that can be implemented by those working in the sector, including directing readers to other resources where further guidance can be obtained.

Approach

This book's approach is to:

- be accessible but not overly informal

- make reference to, and be informed by, relevant scholarly literature. This includes conceptual and research-based work in relation to student suicide in FE and HE, as well as more broadly, from the field of suicide prevention

- provide comprehensive coverage of issues that influence and impact on student suicide

- explore practical and pragmatic suggestions in relation to what services might best look like, who is best placed to intervene, acknowledging limits on resources and time

- be UK-centric, drawing primarily from HE and FE contexts, but also drawing upon international studies and evidence where relevant or where UK data is unavailable

- be interdisciplinary and collaborative both in authorship and intended readership.

Structure

Part 1: Understanding and Preventing Suicide Among Students

Part 1 focuses on risk and responses to risk and is designed to improve our understanding in relation to preventing student suicide and making the case for addressing student suicide in both HE and FE contexts. The first section, on risk, draws on evidence from student suicide research, and international suicide prevention research more broadly, to explore what we currently know about risk generally and as it may specifically relate to a student population. The second section outlines responses to risk, considering whole institution and individual interventions.

We begin with two key overview chapters looking at suicide in an HE and FE context respectively (Chapters 1 and 2).

Chapter 1 considers the problem of suicide in the HE sector, beginning with a brief overview of suicide, before examining in depth the literature on student suicide within the UK, including recent data on the size of the problem.

Chapter 2 provides an overview of the issue of suicide in the FE sector, drawing on evidence from the available literature on student suicide within this sector, identifying suicide prevention resources for FE and supported by practical experience narratives from two FE colleges in the UK.

SECTION 1: RISK

The next seven chapters (3–9) consider student suicide risk, exploring factors that may contribute to suicidal risk starting with early risk factors for later suicidality in students (Chapter 3), policy perspectives (Chapter 4), the role of social media (Chapter 5), and current risk theory (Chapter 6). We also include a chapter on transitions into FE and HE, where we may need to frontload support to help students manage emerging challenges (Chapter 7). We end this section on risk with two chapters exploring perfectionism (Chapter 8) and contagion/copycat risk (Chapter 9).

Chapter 3 explores early suicide risk factors in students. It draws on research evidence from the University of Ulster, identifying the prevalence of suicidal ideation and behaviour in a large student cohort. It explores the role that early childhood trauma experiences and parenting style may play in relation to later risk for suicide.

Chapter 4 considers the policy context of HE student suicide and outlines government-led initiatives to support suicide prevention in the HE sector. It also considers legal aspects in relation to duty of care, confidentiality and involving family members in suicide prevention.

Chapter 5 considers the influence of social media on suicidal behaviour among students. It explores both the positive and negative aspects of suicide-related online behaviour, exploring how young people use the internet to interact with others and explore online help. It also examines how social media use can negatively impact on an individual's suicidal thinking.

Chapter 6 provides an overview of the theoretical perspectives on suicide to potentially explain how individuals move down the pathway, from first thinking about suicide to ultimately attempting to take their own lives. Three recent theories of suicide positioned within the ideation-to-action framework are described, and fictional case studies are used to illustrate these different models and processes.

Chapter 7 provides a summary of one of the major risk factors identified in a UK study of student suicide – transitions. In-depth case-based analysis, in conjunction with theory from the suicide literature, explores some of the mechanisms by which this might create additional risk in the student population. Strategies institutions might employ to counteract this risk are described.

Chapter 8 explores the potential links between perfectionism and suicide among students and reviews recent findings in relation to perfectionism and how this might contribute towards student suicide. Specific clinical aspects of perfectionism in a student who has suicidal ideation and how staff might respond to these within FE or HE settings are explored.

Chapter 9 unpacks suicide suggestion among the student population and explicates the most up-to-date evidence in relation to suicide clusters and contagion. Our current understanding of the mechanisms of action of this phenomenon are used to provide practical suggestions about how these may be countered in a student population.

SECTION 2: RESPONSES TO RISK

We have laid out responses to risk in the next seven chapters, looking at different levels of prevention: whole institution approaches, including barriers and facilitators influencing suicide prevention interventions (Chapters 10, 11 and 12), helpful interventions at an individual level between friends and family and within FE, HE and the role of the NHS (Chapters 13 and 14), parents' perspectives (Chapter 15) and supporting students who may be actively suicidal using safety planning (Chapter 16).

Chapter 10 examines recent research evidence in relation to successful student suicide prevention and sets out a model for HE student suicide prevention drawing on international models, research evidence and published practice guidance. It provides a higher education institution (HEI) case study example where student suicide prevention strategies have been successfully implemented and embedded into practice.

Chapter 11 provides a framework for training staff to recognize warning signs and refer students who may be at risk of taking their own lives. It considers the literature on whole institution and gatekeeper training in HE and suicide prevention training generally and describes a whole institution suicide prevention 'Three Minutes to Save a Life' HE training model from the University of Wolverhampton.

Chapter 12 illustrates how the University Mental Health Charter (Hughes and Spanner 2019) can be used to inform a framework to support student mental health and wellbeing. Using examples from the University of Bristol, it shows how good practice principles recommended by the Charter can be used to inform the development of student support services.

Chapter 13 presents material that can help inform staff, peers and family members to talk to someone they suspect may be considering suicide or is having suicidal thoughts. It includes practical ideas about how to safely ask questions about suicide, as well as suggestions on how to protect the individual in the short term while next steps are considered.

Chapter 14 uses a student case study to consider how the needs of a student in crisis may be supported within FE and HE. It draws on HE case examples to explore how institutions can work in partnership with other agencies to enable navigation and access to external primary care and specialist mental health support services for students.

Chapter 15 considers parents' perspectives and examines the role and experiences of parents in relation to student suicide. It discusses emerging models that seek to ensure that parents are consulted about students at risk, including those that facilitate new ways of managing the issue of confidentiality.

Chapter 16 considers how we can best support individuals who are actively suicidal (ideation and behaviour) using safety planning. It provides evidence on the benefits of safety planning and identifies useful resources that can assist staff to work with students to develop and implement safety plans.

Part 2: Responding to Student Death by Suicide

Part 2 focuses on responding to a student death by suicide. It considers the key role of student services (Chapter 17) and the postvention support needs of and interventions with families (Chapter 18), students (Chapter 19) and staff (Chapter 20). It includes a broad chapter that explores our current understanding of and responses to a suicide bereavement (Chapter 21) and moves on to explore findings from research which inform postvention support models (Chapter 22). The final chapter in this section (Chapter 23) considers communication with particular reference to handling internal and external media communications.

Chapter 17 considers a student services perspective and its key role in relation to student suicide. Responses in relation to a real-life case of student suicide are described, drawing out the lessons learnt for the application of policy into practice.

Chapter 18 explores responses to family needs. While personal stories of loss will all be unique, research from the UK and elsewhere is combined with a personal narrative of losing a son to suicide at university to highlight best practice for responding to a family's needs.

Chapter 19 focuses on the needs of students and the university response to a student suicide. It considers key factors in an HE and FE context, the objectives of a death response plan (DRP) and suggests ways of supporting students in the immediate aftermath and beyond.

Chapter 20 presents findings from recent research on the experiences of staff in UK HEIs following a student death by suicide. It identifies key recommendations to help inform HEIs and FE colleges about the kinds of postvention support needs that staff may have following a student suicide.

Chapter 21 considers our understanding of suicide bereavement and the unique issues associated with a bereavement by suicide and what this type of death means for those who are left behind.

Chapter 22 outlines a model for suicide postvention in higher education and explores how institutions may plan to ensure timely interventions that are appropriate to the particular circumstances of any suicide.

Chapter 23 covers the latest evidence in relation to media reporting about suicide and provides examples of how universities might effectively engage with the media to ensure coverage is responsible and sensitive to the needs of the bereaved.

Concluding comments

The intention of this book is to provide a specific focus on an emotive topic of increasing concern for students, families, institutions, national and local media, government, public institutions and voluntary sector bodies. The aim was to gather the best available evidence from research and clinical practice innovations in one place. While acknowledging that both research and practice in this sector are still at a developmental stage, our intended purpose is to provoke and inspire all those who work in FE and HE. We hope it helps to move us further forward in addressing student suicide risk, prevention and postvention practice in an HE and FE context.

Acknowledgements

We would like to acknowledge and thank all of our chapter authors for their support and enthusiasm in contributing to this book and for delivering their respective chapters in a timely manner, despite the challenges that Covid-19 created for us all. We would like to thank Jessica Kingsley Publishers for their encouragement at every stage and without whose practical support this book would not have been published.

References

American Foundation for Suicide Prevention (2021) *State Laws: Suicide Prevention on University and College Campuses*. Accessed on 29/06/21 at: https://afsp.org/university-and-college-campus-suicide-prevention [Higher Education issue brief].

Brant, P. (2019) *It's Not (Yet?) True That Half of Young People Go to University*. Oxford: Higher Education Policy Institute (HEPI). Accessed on 28/03/21 at: www.hepi.ac.uk/2019/10/09/its-not-yet-true-that-half-of-young-people-go-to-university

Brodsky, B.S., Spruch-Feiner, A. and Stanley, B. (2018) The zero suicide model: applying evidence-based suicide prevention practices to clinical care. *Frontiers in Psychiatry 9*, 33. doi: 10.3389/fpsyt.2018.00033

Coughlan, S. (2018) Student suicide increase warning. *BBC News*, 13 April.

Department for Education (DfE) (2019) *Participation Rates in Higher Education: Academic Years 2006/2007–2017/2018 (Provisional)*. London: DfE.

De Pury, J. (2018) *Understanding Student Suicide*. London: Universities UK.

Dominiguez-Reig, G. and Robinson, D. (2019) *16–19 Education Funding: Trends and Implications*. London: Education Policy Institute.

Eskin, M., Sun, J.M., Abuidhail, J., Yoshimasu, K. *et al.* (2016) Suicidal behavior and psychological distress in university students: a 12-nation study. *Arch Suicide Res. 20*, 3, 369–388.

Gunnell, D., Caul, S., Appleby, L., John, A. and Hawton, K. (2020) The incidence of suicide in university students in England and Wales 2000/2001–2016/2017: record linkage study. *Journal of Affective Disorders 261*, 113–120.

Health Quality Improvement Partnership (HQIP) (2017) *National Confidential Inquiry into Suicide and Homicide by People with Mental Illness: Annual Report October 2017*. London: HQIP.

Hughes, G. and Spanner, L. (2019) *The University Mental Health Charter*. Leeds: Student Minds.

Hunt, J. (2017) Steep rise in student suicides must be tackled. *Times Higher Education*, 20 September.

Klonsky, E.D., Victor, S.E. and Saffer, B.Y. (2014) Nonsuicidal self-injury: what we know, and what we need to know. *Canadian Journal of Psychiatry 59*, 565–568.

Lageborn, C.T., Ljung, R., Vaez, M. and Dahlin, M. (2017) Ongoing university studies and the risk of suicide: a register-based nationwide cohort study of 5 million young and middle-aged individuals in Sweden, 1993–2011. *BMJ Open 7*, 3, e014264.

Li, W., Dorstyn, D. and Jarmon, E. (2019) Identifying suicide risk among college students: a systematic review. *Death Studies 44*, 7, 450–458.

Marzano, L., Fraser, L., Scally, M., Farley, S. and Hawton, K. (2018) News coverage of suicidal behaviour in the United Kingdom and the Republic of Ireland. *Crisis 39*, 5, 386–396.

National Collaborating Centre for Mental Health (2018) *Self-Harm and Suicide Prevention Competence Framework: Community and Public Health*. Accessed on 28/03/21 at: www.rcpsych.ac.uk/docs/default-source/improving-care/nccmh/self-harm-and-suicide-prevention-competence-framework/nccmh-self-harm-and-suicide-prevention-competence-framework-public-health.pdf?sfvrsn=341fb3cd_6

Office for National Statistics (ONS) (2016) *Student Suicides in Those Aged 18 years and Above, by Sex and Usual Place of Residence Indicator, Deaths Registered in England and Wales between 2001 and 2015*. London: ONS.

Office for National Statistics (ONS) (2018) *Estimating Suicide among Higher Education Students, England and Wales: Experimental Statistics*. London: ONS.

PAPYRUS (2018) *Building Suicide-Safer Schools and Colleges: A Guide for Teachers and Staff*. Warrington: PAPYRUS.

Quinlivan, L., Cooper, J., Meehan, D., Longson, D. *et al.* (2017) Predictive accuracy of risk scales following self-harm: multicentre, prospective cohort study. *British Journal of Psychiatry 210*, 429–436.

Samaritans (2013) *Help When We Needed It Most: How to Prepare for and Respond to a Suspected Suicide in Schools and Colleges*. Ewell, Surrey: Samaritans.

Stanley, N., Mallon, S., Bell, J. and Manthorpe, J. (2009) Trapped in transition: findings from a UK study of student suicide. *British Journal of Guidance & Counselling* 37 4, 419–433.

Steeg, S., Quinlivan, L., Nowland, R., Carroll, R. *et al.* (2018) Accuracy of risk scales for predicting repeat self-harm and suicide: a multicentre, population-level cohort study using routine clinical data. *BMC Psychiatry 18*, 113.

Thorley, C. (2017) *Not by Degrees: Improving Student Mental Health in the UK's Universities*. London: IPPR.

Townsend, E., Wadman, R., Sayal, K., Armstrong, M. *et al.* (2016) Uncovering key patterns in self-harm in adolescents: Sequence analysis using the Card Sort Task for Self-harm (CaTS). *Journal of Affective Disorders 206*, 161–168.

Uchida, C. and Uchida, M. (2017) Characteristics and risk factors for suicide and deaths among college students: a 23-year serial prevalence study of data from 8.2 million Japanese college students. *The Journal of Clinical Psychiatry 78*, 4, e404–e412.

Universities UK (UUK) and PAPYRUS (2018) *Suicide Safer Universities*. Accessed on 28/03/21 at: www.universitiesuk.ac.uk/policy-and-analysis/reports/Documents/2018/guidance-for-universities-on-preventing-student-suicides.pdf

Usborne, S. (2017) The bold new fight to eradicate suicide. *The Guardian*, 1 August 2017.

World Health Organization (WHO) (2018) *Suicide*. Accessed on 28/03/21 at: www.who.int/news-room/fact-sheets/detail/suicide

PART 1

Understanding and Preventing Suicide among Students

CHAPTER 1

The Problem of Suicide in the Higher Education Institution Sector

JOANNA MCLAUGHLIN AND DAVID GUNNELL

Overview

This chapter will provide an overview of the issue of suicide in the HEI sector. It begins with a brief summary of the epidemiology of suicide before examining in depth the literature on student suicide within the UK, including recent data on the size of the problem.

Brief summary of the epidemiology of suicide
Introduction
HOW BIG IS THE PROBLEM?

Suicide is one of the most frequent causes of premature death in young people. The suicide rate in those aged 20–24 in the UK is 11.2 per 100,000 (ONS 2019b). In the UK, suicide rates amongst young people have been increasing in recent years (Figure 1.1). The suicide rate for young females (up to 24 years old) is at its highest rate since 1981 (ONS 2019b). National mortality statistics show that the leading cause of death in males aged 10–49 and in females aged 10–34 in England is suicide and injury or poisoning of undetermined intent (ONS 2019a). Rising rates are likely to reflect the general increase in poor mental health in young people, particularly females (Bould *et al.* 2019; McManus *et al.* 2016). It should be noted that the statistics presented here do not include the period of the Covid-19 pandemic, and its effects on mental health and suicide remain to be seen.

The determination that a death is by suicide is the role of the region's coroner in England, Northern Ireland and Wales, and of the Procurator

Fiscal in Scotland. For all deaths given a verdict of suicide, a coroner makes this decision having ruled out all other possible explanations. Some deaths considered by researchers and clinicians to be probable suicides receive 'narrative' conclusions from coroners rather than other 'short form' conclusions, such as accident, suicide or homicide. Where the coroner's conclusion does not make clear whether or not the death was self-inflicted and/or there was no clear evidence that the act was carried out with suicidal intent, the Office for National Statistics (ONS) code these as 'accidental deaths'. There is further discussion on the coroner's determination of 'intent' later in this chapter.

Evidence from the UK indicates that trends in student suicide deaths reflect patterns seen in the wider population, so it is likely that if suicide rates amongst young people in general continue to rise, they will also increase amongst students (Gunnell *et al.* 2020).

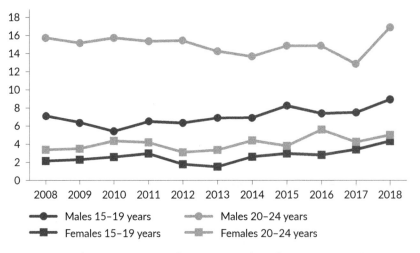

Figure 1.1: Suicide rate per 100,000 for young people in the UK 2008–2018

Source: Office for National Statistics (ONS) (2019b) Suicides in the UK: 2018 Registrations. London: ONS.

The National Statistics definition of suicide is based on International Classification of Diseases (ICD) codes X60–X84 and Y10–Y34

WHAT CAUSES SUICIDE?

The causes of suicide are complex, and death is rarely due to a single issue. Three-quarters of suicides occur in men. Other risk factors for suicide are well documented including older age, self-harm, mental illness, substance misuse, bullying, physical and sexual abuse, poor educational attainment and socioeconomic deprivation. There is evidence that easy access to high lethality means for suicide (e.g. bridges or chemicals) and media reporting of suicides also increase the risk of suicide (Turecki and Brent 2016). Around one-third of those who die by suicide are in current or recent contact with psychiatric services and around half have previously self-harmed (HQIP 2017).

ARE STUDENTS DIFFERENT?

In recent years, there have been increasing concerns about the mental health of higher education students and deaths by suicide in this setting. Media attention has been intense with high levels of reporting of suicide deaths in a number of university settings. Students experience similar risk factors for suicide as the rest of the population, but in addition to these, some stressors are more specific to student life – for example, the transition to personal and financial responsibility on moving to a higher education institution (HEI), altered levels of family contact and support, academic pressures and exposure to new cultures around alcohol and drugs. This can mean there are other more student-specific risk factors to consider in addition to those typical for the rest of the population, and these may be an important focus for suicide prevention efforts in this sector.

'Clustering' refers to a situation in which more suicides than expected occur in terms of time, place or both. A suicide cluster usually includes three or more deaths. However, two suicides occurring in a specific community, or setting and time period, should also be taken very seriously in terms of possible links (or contagion), particularly in the case of young people (PHE 2019).

Clustering of suicidal behaviour is more common in young people (<25 years) than adults. Clusters in the HEI setting have not been widely reported upon in academic literature, though the first in-depth UK study of student suicide found evidence that in a small number of cases studied, students' behaviour was clearly influenced by another death (Stanley *et al.* 2009). As institutional environments for young people, universities have the potential to be vulnerable to being the setting for clusters, making it very important for connections between deaths to be detected and acted upon if possible (Hawton *et al.* 2019). The last chapter of this section (Chapter 9) focuses specifically on the considerations for clusters of deaths by suicide in HE and FE settings.

AIMS OF THIS CHAPTER

This chapter will cover the epidemiology and trends in suicide in the UK in order to answer the question 'How big is the problem of suicide in the UK HEI sector?' Aside from the numbers of deaths by suicide, this chapter provides information on other elements that are important in considering the problem to identify patterns and opportunities for intervention and prevention:

- the demographics of students that die by suicide (gender, ethnicity, age, disability)

- information on the nature of their studies (type and stage of study)

- details of the deaths (method, timing and location of suicide)

- risk factors for suicide present in the deceased; these are numerous but include:

    - general population risk factors (male, being older, mental ill health, previous self-harm, alcohol and substance misuse, bullying and abuse, socioeconomic deprivation)

    - more student specific risk factors (academic and financial difficulties, social isolation, being in a period of transition)

Exploration of the literature on the size and nature of the problem
Incidence of suicide in UK HEIs and trends over time

Data from the ONS shows that 1330 students died by suicide between 2000/01 and 2016/17 in England and Wales. The number of suicides in the most recent period for which data is available (the 12 months ending July 2017) is 95. Two-thirds were male and the median age at death was 26 years. Undergraduates accounted for 83 per cent of the HE student suicides (1109 deaths) and postgraduates accounted for 17 per cent (221 deaths) (ONS 2018).

There are indications that the rate of suicide for university students in England and Wales has increased in recent years (Figure 1.2) (Gunnell *et al.* 2020), just as it has in the wider population (Bould *et al.* 2019). Nevertheless, as shown in Figure 1.3, the rate of suicide is lower amongst students than in the general population of similar ages.

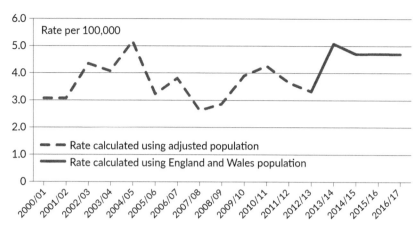

Figure 1.2: Rate per 100,000 of university student suicides by year: deaths registered in England and Wales, 2000/01 to 2016/17, amongst students aged 18 years and over

Source: Office for National Statistics (ONS) (2018) Estimating Suicide among Higher Education Students, England and Wales: Experimental Statistics. London: ONS.

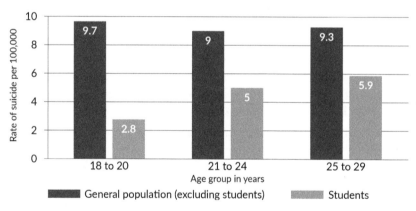

Figure 1.3: Rate of suicide per 100,000 by age group in the general population (not including university students) and in university students, deaths registered in England and Wales, between the 12 months ending July 2013 and the 12 months ending July 2017 combined

Source: The incidence of suicide in university students in England and Wales 2000/2001–2016/2017: record linkage study (Gunnell et al. 2020)

The overall rate in students is 4.4 deaths per 100,000 students compared with 11.6 deaths per 100,000 general population. The rate in males shows the greatest difference, with a rate of 6.6 in the student population compared with 18.0 in the general population. In females, the rate in students (2.7) was almost half that of the general population (5.2).

The average age of the general population is of course higher than that of the student population, which presents some difficulty in comparing the two populations directly; Figure 1.3 shows the comparison in rates for different age groups.

Comparison with other countries

There are relatively few academic articles on the epidemiology of deaths by suicide in HEI students. Aside from UK studies, the most comprehensive recent data comes from the USA (Schwartz 2006; Silverman *et al.* 1997; Westefeld *et al.* 2005) and Japan (Uchida and Uchida 2017). A recent meta-analysis of studies of suicide attempt prevalence reports that internationally 3 per cent of university students had made an attempt at suicide and almost a quarter had expressed suicidal ideation (Mortier *et al.* 2018).

The World Health Organization *World Mental Health Surveys International College Student Initiative* has published data drawn from first year students at 19 colleges across 8 countries. A report from this data shows that the proportion of students who made a suicide attempt in the preceding 12 months ranged from 15.4 per cent in those with high mental health co-morbidity to 0.1 per cent of students with no lifetime mental health disorders (Auerbach *et al.* 2019). We can conclude from these studies that suicide in HEI students is an international issue affecting many thousands of students, with particular links to students' existing mental health. Furthermore, whilst suicide attempts amongst students are relatively common, death by suicide is rare.

Presence of risk factors

Published and in-press literature has identified a number of risk factors associated with suicide in students. These are listed in Table 1.1. We can't be sure that any of these risk factors have a role in actually causing death by suicide (as the temporality can be uncertain between developing the risk factor and developing suicidal intent). Nevertheless, it is important to be aware of the links as this may allow identification of high-risk groups of students who may benefit from targeted intervention and help.

Risk ratios (which show the risk of the presence of each factor in students that died by suicide compared to in the general HEI student population in the UK) have been reported in academic literature in some cases. These suggest that students that died by suicide were 2.4 times as likely to have been male, 1.9 times as likely to be in their second or later year of study and 2.3 times as likely to be aged over 30 (Gunnell *et al.* 2020).

Table 1.1: Risk factors associated with suicide in higher education students

Risk factor	
General	Male
	Age over 30
	Drug or alcohol misuse
	Personal life difficulties including relationship break-up or bereavement
	Prior self-harm or suicide attempts
	Previous or current contacts with secondary care mental health services for psychiatric illness
	Chronic or life-limiting physical illness
	LGBT sexual orientation
	Sleep disturbance and insomnia
Student specific	Year of study – second year or later at undergraduate level
	Level of study – undergraduate
	In receipt of a bursary or other financial assistance
	Academic difficulties
	Social isolation

Sources for student specific risk factors: Gunnell et al. 2020; HQIP 2017; McLaughlin and Gunnell 2020; ONS 2018; Shaddick, Dagirmanjian and Barbot 2015; University of Manchester 2017; Westefeld et al. 2005

The factors listed in the 'general' section are all well-recognized risk factors for suicide in the general population (Turecki and Brent 2016). Academic and university-specific factors associated with suicide in university students are also of importance, but few studies have reported on these factors, and published case series often include small numbers of cases and lack comparison risk factor data from the wider student population. Concerns over academic achievement have clear relevance to students: a 1995 study of deaths by suicide at Oxford University found two-thirds of the 21 students that died had been worried about academic achievement or their course, and suggested that improving means of alleviating academic stress could help to prevent suicides (Hawton *et al.* 1995). Data from Japan indicate that students within later years of study who need to repeat years or who took academic leave of absence were at heightened risk of suicide (Uchida and Uchida 2017). A recent case series of 37 university student deaths by suicide in the UK provides further evidence for the role of academic difficulties (McLaughlin and Gunnell 2020). Three factors were particularly strongly related to risk: suspension of studies, repeating a year and changing course; 18 students (48.6%) that died by suicide had at least one of these factors recorded, compared to a prevalence in the wider student population of <5 per cent.

A psychological autopsy study of UK university student suicides in 2000–2005 suggested that it may in fact be the *experience of transition* for these students that had been a significant factor and academic difficulties were reported for half the deaths (n=10), though the definitions of the transition period were very broad (Stanley *et al.* 2009).

A recent systematic review has suggested that there is evidence that sleep disturbance and insomnia are a risk factor for suicide in students (Russell *et al.* 2019), raising these as further issues of interest in our efforts to address risk in the UK student population.

ARE STUDENTS THAT DIE BY SUICIDE GENERALLY KNOWN TO HEALTH AND WELLBEING SERVICES?

Non-help-seeking is a common issue amongst people who die by suicide; around two-thirds of those that die by suicide in the general population are not known to mental health services at the time of their death (Luoma, Martin and Pearson 2002). Reasons include perception that treatment is not needed, perceived stigma and thinking that nothing can be done to resolve their problems (Gulliver, Griffiths and Christensen 2010). An additional barrier facing students is that they may feel reluctant to consult university services due to fears over their perceived fitness to study (Czyz *et al.* 2013).

A recent analysis of student suicides in England and Wales suggested that around 17 per cent occurred in those who had been in current or recent contact with NHS psychiatric services (Gunnell *et al.* 2020). This low figure is in keeping with that reported in other countries: 16 per cent of students in Japan had a psychiatric diagnosis (Uchida and Uchida 2017) and only around a quarter of US student suicides were counselling service clients (Schwartz 2006).

A UK case series (McLaughlin and Gunnell 2020) found that at least 41 per cent of the students that died by suicide had contact with the NHS for reasons of mental health at some point in their lifetime, though this contact was not always recent. Sharing of data between the NHS and student wellbeing services is not routine and so students may be known to one service but not another, even following significant incidents such as attempts at suicide.

A challenge for students with pre-existing serious mental illness is the transfer of care provider when they relocate from home to their new university setting (initially on moving away from home or repeatedly during holiday periods). This may occur at the same time as they make the transition from Child and Adolescent Mental Health Services into Adult Services. Poor communication between services has been identified as a further barrier to information sharing to highlight students at risk (National Health Service 2019).

ARE THERE ALWAYS WARNING SIGNS?

Several students in the UK case series had no evident flags of concern or contributory factors for their suicide (McLaughlin and Gunnell 2020). This type of occurrence is also reflected in a recent national study of suicide in young people where 29 per cent of deaths (n=84) were deemed 'out of the blue' (University of Manchester 2017), and as already mentioned above there may be no history of contact with mental health services in many cases of death by suicide. This indicates that despite best efforts to use the presence of risk factors to identify students in need of support, reliance on these factors would fail to identify all students at risk of suicide.

Method of suicide

The methods of suicide used by students differ very little from those used by people of the same age in the general population. Hanging accounts for around half of suicide deaths, and 17 per cent are by poisoning and 3 per cent by drowning. The recent analysis of student suicides in England and Wales noted that death by jumping was somewhat higher in students than in the general population (8.2% vs. 4.2%) (Gunnell *et al.* 2020). As most students will be based in an urban setting, this may explain the higher use of jumping due to easier access to high buildings.

In the UK case series, no students obtained means for suicide from university premises, which was important to note as there is often concern that the university setting with access to chemicals or the design of accommodation could contribute to deaths. Precautionary principles dictate that guidance on making teaching and residential spaces safer by reducing access to means remains sensible, for example by including additional safety measures if student residences are in multi-storey buildings.

Timing of suicide

At present, there is no clear pattern in the timing of student suicides by season or academic term, though this may be because few studies have had sufficient statistical power to investigate this issue. ONS statistics identified a peak in student deaths by suicide in the month of January (Gunnell *et al.* 2020). Perhaps surprisingly, studies from the UK and Japan indicate there is no evidence of a heightened risk of suicide during the first year of study – this might be considered the time of greatest social change and risk of isolation for new students (Gunnell *et al.* 2020; Uchida and Uchida 2017).

Location of suicide

Geographical location of deaths by suicide is rarely reported on. The recent UK case series found that many of the deaths occurred away from the university itself: nineteen (51%) occurred away from the university city, generally in or near to the student's own/family home (McLaughlin and Gunnell 2020). This finding is important as the voluntary or involuntary suspension of a student's studies, or their informal absence from the university to return home once they have been identified as experiencing difficulties, may not be as protective as it may be hoped. Deaths away from the university setting also have implications for university suicide response teams' access to timely information and inquest results.

Are numbers of suicide deaths in students likely to rise in coming years?
Rising suicide rates in all young people and changes in student demographics

As discussed in the introduction, rates of mental ill health and suicide are rising in the general population of young people and this rise is likely to be reflected in the subgroup of young people that are the student population. It is also likely that student suicide numbers in future years will increase as the HEI student population itself increases. Figure 1.4 shows the steady rise in the number of HEI students in the UK.

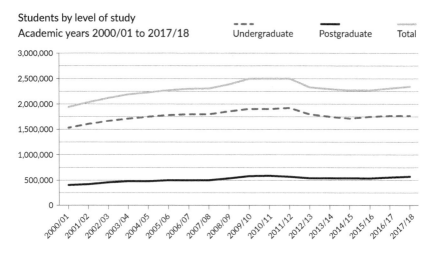

Figure 1.4: Trends in the number of HEI students in the UK
Source: HESA (Higher Education Statistics Agency) 2019

Changes in participation in higher education over time mean trends in deaths by suicide amongst students may be confounded by changes in age and socioeconomic composition of the student population. The agenda for widening participation in the UK seeks to increase access to higher education for people from socioeconomically disadvantaged backgrounds, from minority groups and for people with disabilities (DfE 2019). These demographic changes in the student population are likely to mean more students from higher risk groups join the population and, therefore, the rate of suicide may increase even if there is no alteration in the student environment.

Problems of categorizing students – are all HEIs the same?

HEI students are not a homogenous group. Students may study at university or college, or at a distance through online learning, study full time or less than full time and may live independently or continue to live in their family homes. Any distinctions in risk factors between these groups are not yet clear, but it is likely that differences do exist and that needs vary depending on circumstances.

Estimates for numbers and trends of deaths by suicide in students rely on the information concerning the occupation of the deceased that is provided by the informant on the death certificate. This is problematic as less than full time students may be invisible if their main occupation is listed without mention of their student status. Conversely, some deaths attributed to students are likely to be in recently graduated students that are yet to enter the work force. Record linkage studies using Higher Education Statistics Agency data with ONS mortality data help to overcome these issues (Gunnell *et al.* 2020).

Changes in coroners' conclusions over time

In July 2018, the standard of proof used by coroners in England and Wales to determine whether a death was suicide changed (Appleby *et al.* 2019). Previously, a 'criminal standard' was applied, meaning that the coroner required evidence 'beyond all reasonable doubt' that a death was suicide. Since July 2018, a 'civil standard' has been applied by coroners, meaning that it must be shown on the balance of probability that:

- the death occurred because of a deliberate act by the deceased

- in doing so and at all relevant times, the deceased intended the consequence would be death.

While this change does not account for the rise in rates of suicide in young people seen over the last decade, it may lead to an increase in the number of deaths classified as suicide from 2018 onwards. The ONS will monitor and report the impact of this change on its data, although the impact of the change will not be clear until we have more data. It seems likely that numbers of suicide will appear higher than they would have done in the past and this is something that any HE or FE setting should note in trying to determine the success of their suicide prevention efforts.

Implications and applicability

This chapter has highlighted the following key points:

1. The rate of suicide for university students in England and Wales has increased in recent years. Nevertheless, *the rate of suicide is lower amongst students than in the general population of similar ages and rises in suicide are also seen in the general population.*

2. *Overall numbers of suicides in students are likely to rise in coming years* due to rising student numbers, lower thresholds for categorizing deaths as suicides and rising rates of suicide and mental ill health in young people as a whole.

3. *Surveillance for rapid identification of suspected clusters is important* as HEI settings are known to be vulnerable (see Chapter 10) and a rapid response may offset the risk of further deaths.

4. *The majority of students who die by suicide are not known to NHS or HEI health and wellbeing services*; prevention strategies are needed to reach those not in contact with such services.

5. *We are already aware of many risk factors seen in students who die by suicide and these offer opportunities to better identify students who may benefit from targeted prevention and intervention.*

6. *Some risk factors are specific to the HEI setting and must be strongly considered in prevention efforts: suspension of studies, repeating a year and changing course.*

7. *There is a need for better data*; case series with data linkage across health, wellbeing, university, coroner/police records and others offer the fullest picture, but there are significant barriers to achieving this and they are not done routinely or shared between institutions at present.

Author biographies

Dr Joanna McLaughlin is an academic clinical fellow at the University of Bristol and a specialty registrar in public health in the South West Deanery of Health Education England. She has a research interest in suicide prevention in higher education and wider work in decreasing inequalities in healthcare.

Professor David Gunnell is Professor of Epidemiology at the University of Bristol, UK. He is a public health physician and epidemiologist with a long-standing research interest in the aetiology and prevention of suicide and in improving population mental health.

References

Appleby, L., Turnbull, P., Kapur, N., Gunnell, D. and Hawton, K. (2019) New standard of proof for suicide at inquests in England and Wales. *BMJ 366*, l4745.

Auerbach, R.P., Mortier, P., Bruffaerts, R., Alonso, J. *et al.* (2019) Mental disorder comorbidity and suicidal thoughts and behaviors in the World Health Organization World Mental Health Surveys International College Student initiative. *Int J Methods Psychiatr Res. 28*, 2, e1752.

Bould, H., Mars, B., Moran, P., Biddle, L. and Gunnell, D. (2019) Rising suicide rates among adolescents in England and Wales. *The Lancet 394*, 10193, 116–117.

Czyz, E., Horwitz, A., Eisenberg, D., Kramer, A. and King, C. (2013) Self-reported barriers to professional help seeking among college students at elevated risk for suicide. *J Am Coll Health 61*, 7, 398–406.

Department for Education (DfE) (2019) *Widening Participation in Higher Education: 2019*. London: DfE. Accessed on 28/03/21 at: www.gov.uk/government/statistics/widening-participation-in-higher-education-2019

Gulliver, A., Griffiths, K.M. and Christensen, H. (2010) Perceived barriers and facilitators to mental health help-seeking in young people: a systematic review. *BMC Psychiatry 10*, 113.

Gunnell, D., Caul, S., Appleby, L., John, A. and Hawton, K. (2020) The incidence of suicide in university students in England and Wales 2000/2001–2016/2017: record linkage study. *Journal of Affective Disorders 261*, 113–120.

Hawton, K., Hill, N., Gould, M., John, A., Lascelles, K. and Robinson, J. (2019) Clustering of suicides in children and adolescents. *The Lancet Child & Adolescent Health 4*, 1, 58–67.

Hawton, K., Simkin, S., Fagg, J. and Hawkins, M. (1995) Suicide in Oxford University students, 1976–1990. *British Journal of Psychiatry 166*, 44–50.

Healthcare Quality Improvement Partnership (HQIP) (2017) *National Confidential Inquiry into Suicide and Homicide: Annual Report 2017*. London: HQIP. Accessed on 28/03/21 at: www.hqip.org.uk/resource/national-confidential-inquiry-into-suicide-and-homicide-annual-report-2017/#.XOUvV4lKiUl

Higher Education Statistics Agency (HESA) (2019) Who's studying in HE? Accessed on 28/03/21 at: www.hesa.ac.uk/data-and-analysis/students/whos-in-he

Luoma, J.B., Martin, C.E. and Pearson, J.L. (2002) Contact with mental health and primary care providers before suicide: a review of the evidence. *Am J Psychiatry 159*, 6, 909–916.

McLaughlin, J. and Gunnell, D. (2020) Suicide deaths in university students in a UK city between 2010 and 2018 – case series. *Crisis*. DOI: 10.1027/0227-5910/a000704

McManus, S., Bebbington, P., Jenkins, R. and Brugha, T. (2016) Adult Psychiatric Morbidity Survey: Survey of Mental Health and Wellbeing, England, 2014. Accessed on 28/03/21 at: https://digital.nhs.uk/data-and-information/publications/statistical/adult-psychiatric-morbidity-survey/adult-psychiatric-morbidity-survey-survey-of-mental-health-and-wellbeing-england-2014

Mortier, P., Cuijpers, P., Kiekens, G., Auerbach, R. *et al.* (2018) The prevalence of suicidal thoughts and behaviours among college students: a meta-analysis. *Psychol Med 48*, 4, 554–565.

National Health Service (2019) *South West Clinical Senate Council: Student Mental Health*, NHS SW Clinical Senate. Accessed on 28/03/21 at: https://swsenate.nhs.uk/wp-content/uploads/2019/10/2019-18-07-Senate-Recommendations-Student-Mental-Health-FINAL.pdf

Office for National Statistics (ONS) (2018) *Estimating Suicide among Higher Education Students, England and Wales: Experimental Statistics*. London: ONS. Accessed on 28/03/21 at: www.ons.gov.uk/peoplepopulationandcommunity/birthsdeathsandmarriages/deaths/articles/estimatingsuicideamonghighereducationstudentsenglandandwalesexperimentalstatistics/previousReleases

Office for National Statistics (ONS) (2019a) *Deaths Registered in England and Wales 2018*. London: ONS. Accessed on 28/03/21 at: www.ons.gov.uk/peoplepopulationandcommunity/birthsdeathsandmarriages/deaths/bulletins/deathsregistrationsummarytables/2018

Office for National Statistics (ONS) (2019b) *Suicides in the UK: 2018 Registrations*. London: ONS. Accessed on 28/03/21 at: www.ons.gov.uk/peoplepopulationandcommunity/birthsdeathsandmarriages/deaths/bulletins/suicidesintheunitedkingdom/2018registrations#suicide-patterns-by-age

Public Health England (PHE) (2019) *Suicide Prevention: Identifying and Responding to Suicide Clusters*. London: Public Health England. Accessed on 28/03/21 at: www.gov.uk/government/publications/suicide-prevention-identifying-and-responding-to-suicide-clusters

Russell, K., Allan, S., Beattie, L., Bohan, J., MacMahon, K. and Rasmussen, S. (2019) Sleep problem, suicide and self-harm in university students: a systematic review. *Sleep Med Rev 44*, 58–69.

Schwartz, A. (2006) College student suicide in the United States: 1990–1991 through 2003–2004. *J Am Coll Health 54*, 341–352.

Shaddick, R., Dagirmanjian, B. and Barbot, B. (2015) Suicide risk among college students: the intersection of sexual orientation and race. *Crisis 36*, 6, 416–423.

Silverman, M. M., Meyer, P. M., Sloane, F., Raffel, M. and Pratt, D. M. (1997) The big ten suicide study: a 10-year study of suicides on midwestern university campuses. *Suicide and Life-Threatening Behaviour 27*, 285–303.

Stanley, N., Mallon, S., Bell, J. and Manthorpe, J. (2009) Trapped in transition: findings from a UK study of student suicide. *British Journal of Guidance & Counselling 37*, 4, 419–433.

Turecki, G. and Brent, D. (2016) Suicide and suicidal behaviour. *Lancet 387*, 10024, 1227–1239.

Uchida, C. and Uchida, M. (2017) Characteristics and risk factors for suicide and deaths among college students: a 23-year serial prevalence study of data from 8.2 million Japanese college students. *J Clin Psych 78*, e404–e412.

University of Manchester (2017) *Suicide by Children and Young People. National Confidential Inquiry into Suicide and Homicide by People with Mental Illness (NCISH)*. London: Healthcare Quality Improvement Partnership.

Westefeld, J., Homaifar, B., Spotts, J., Furr, S., Range, L. and Werth, J. (2005) Perceptions concerning college student suicide: data from four universities. *Suicide and Life-Threatening Behavior 35*, 6, 640–645.

CHAPTER 2

Suicide Prevention in Further Education (FE)

KATE PARKER AND JO SMITH

Overview

This chapter:

- considers the problem of student suicide as it relates to further education (FE) and explains why a specific focus on FE is important

- describes the current status of suicide prevention in FE and, using case study examples, considers potential interventions and identifies bespoke resources

- explores the policy, funding, research and practice implications of taking a student suicide prevention agenda forward in FE.

The FE context and student cohort

FE refers to the education students receive following completion of GCSEs at secondary school. The sector is wide-ranging, with many different types of institutions, including general FE colleges, sixth-form colleges and independent training providers. According to the Association of Colleges (AoC) (2019a), the membership body for colleges in England, there were 244 colleges with 2.2 million students in England in the 2019–2020 academic year. This includes 168 FE colleges and 51 sixth-form colleges. Of those, 1.4 million were adults (19+), 669,000 were 16- to 18-year-olds, 69,000 were 16- to 18-year-old apprentices and 13,000 were 14- to 15-year-olds. The average age of a student attending FE college is 29 years. In terms of equality, diversity and inclusion, 26 per cent of 16- to 18-year-olds and 33 per cent of adults were from an ethnic minority background. Forty-six per cent of 16- to 18-year-olds and 54 per cent of adult students were female. Twenty-three per cent of 16- to 18-year-olds and 14 per cent of adult students had learning difficulties or a disability (AoC 2019a). This reveals the diversity of the FE student population in age, ethnic origin and disability.

The total number of FE colleges exceeds that of HE institutions in England (n=165, based on HESA, the Higher Education Statistics Agency, student records for 2018–2019), and the total number of FE students in England is only marginally less than the 2.38 million students recorded as studying at UK HE institutions (HESA 2020). Given these high FE student numbers, we might predict similar suicide incidence rates to HE in an FE student population. However, FE student suicide data has never been disaggregated from suicide rates for students, or those of children and young people. Additionally, it has not been linked to records of FE provision collected by the Department for the Economy, Northern Ireland (DfeNI) or the Office for Students (OfS) in England. Consequently, we do not currently know if rates of student suicide at FE colleges are comparable with those of HE students. We also do not know if the incidence of FE student suicide has increased in line with trends observed in HE students and young people in the wider population (Gunnell *et al.* 2020). These issues will be explored in more detail later in this chapter. First, we will explore the broader issues of mental health in this population of students.

FE student mental health and support provision

Poor mental health of FE students is a growing public policy concern (AoC 2015, 2017a). A survey of members about the incidence of mental health issues amongst students (AoC 2015) found two-thirds of respondents saying that the number of students with mental health difficulties had 'significantly increased' in the previous three years. Another survey in 2017 revealed that these problems continued to worsen, with 85 per cent of colleges that responded to the survey (n=105, 32% of all colleges in England) reporting a further increase in the incidence of mental health issues since 2015 (AoC 2017a). This included issues with student self-harm, suicidal ideation and suicide attempts. Seventy-four per cent noted that they had referred students experiencing mental health crises to Accident and Emergency (A&E) in the previous academic year with an average of 6.6 (range 1–30) referrals per college (AoC 2017b). A recent national youth mental health 'My World 2' survey in Ireland (Dooley *et al.* 2019) specifically sampled 'seldom heard groups' including almost 300 young people in FE colleges. The FE sample was more anxious, more likely to report having a long-term health difficulty, more likely to have made a suicide attempt and reported lower support from family and friends than age-matched peers. Data on the mental health of FE students is consistent with prevalence rates in UK HE students (Pereira *et al.* 2020; Thorley 2017).

Mental health difficulties are associated with a number of negative outcomes including academic underperformance (Hysenbegasi, Hass and Rowland 2005) and increased risk of dropping out of college (Unite Students 2016). 'The transition from school to an FE college presents new opportunities and challenges, including academic, financial and social pressures', and it is common for mental health problems to arise whilst students are adjusting to these transitions (Harris 2019, p.27). A prospective cohort study (Bewick *et al.* 2010) found heightened levels of psychological distress in students, particularly during semester one, but at no time throughout the course of their studies did distress levels fall to pre-registration levels.

Services offered within FEs may typically include individual or group counselling. A Department for Education survey in 2017 (Marshall *et al.* 2017) reported that more than nine out of ten schools and colleges provided in-house counselling services from their own educational budget. According to an online survey of UK student counselling services, there has been an increase in demand for student support services over a three-year period in FE and HE sectors, predominantly for high-intensity support (Broglia, Millings and Barkham 2018). This increased demand is set within a context of government funding reductions which led to closure of student counselling services in many FE colleges (Caleb 2014).

According to a survey of 142 colleges by the *Times Education Supplement* (Parker 2020a), 17,481 students were seeing a college counsellor or accessing mental health support regularly. The data showed that the number of staff in roles with dedicated mental health responsibilities had more than doubled in three years from 372 in 2016, to 914 in 2019. The number of FE staff with mental health first-aid training, or another form of mental health awareness training, had also substantially increased in the same period, from 571 to 4668. More than 120 of the colleges offered a counselling service for their learners.

Colleges often refer students to external support providers such as child and adolescent mental health services (CAMHS). The number of external referrals from colleges for mental health related problems doubled in two years from 1592 in 2016 to 3201 in 2018 (Parker 2020a). However, the Education Policy Institute (EPI; Crenna-Jennings and Hutchinson 2019) found one in four young people referred to specialist mental health services, such as CAMHS, were rejected for treatment. The most common reasons for rejection were that the referrals did not meet eligibility criteria because the young person was older than the cut-off age for accessing CAMHS or the referring problem was not deemed serious enough to meet CAMHS access thresholds. The authors commented that it was unclear what support was given to young people whose referrals were rejected.

FE colleges' struggles with finances have been well documented. The sector, which has historically been referred to as the 'Cinderella sector' due to neglect in terms of both funding and resources, has seen a boost in both funding and recognition in recent years (Parker 2020b). Education secretary Gavin Williamson was vocal in his support for the sector, outlining the need for FE reform in a speech to the Social Market Foundation (Williamson 2020). The sector received a £400m funding boost in September 2020 after a long campaign by sector leaders to raise the base rate of funding for 16- to 18-year-olds. However, the Institute for Fiscal Studies' annual report on education spending in England (Britton *et al.* 2020) suggested this is likely to be eroded due to a huge rise in student numbers, stimulated in response to the Coronavirus pandemic starting in 2020 and that colleges could still be set for a real-term fall in funding per student. In 2020, 32 colleges faced financial 'notices to improve' issued by the Education and Skills Funding Agency (2020). As budgets decrease, so does the capacity to increase spend on supporting student mental health.

Despite the troubling financial situation in the sector, mental health provision in colleges has been a focus for investment over several years. In 2015, Public Health England published a document with eight areas of action which would lead to effective 'whole institution' practice by a college in addressing student wellbeing, emotional and mental health support needs (Public Health England 2015). Additionally, in 2015, £1.25bn was invested in the 'Future in Mind' programme (DH and NHS England 2015). The programme's aim was to transform children and young people's mental health services. Local areas were asked to set out their strategy to do so, and 122 local transformation plans were developed nationally. However, analysis by EPI (Frith 2016) found only a quarter of FE colleges were aware of the existence of a local transformation plan in their area. The report concluded that health services need to work more effectively with FE colleges.

In 2017, the National Union of Students (NUS) reported on findings from an FE student roundtable about mental health provision in FE and identified key drivers of poor mental health including social media, sexuality, workload and poor careers guidance (NUS 2017). The report noted that many of the students who struggled to access mental health support related this to stigma surrounding mental health in FE. Cuts to college funding and long waiting lists were also identified as barriers to accessing support. The NUS outlined what students believe good mental health provision should look like and provided good practice examples from FE colleges. It also included a charter for mental health provision in FE colleges, developed with and for students.

In 2019, the Centre for Mental Health published *Making the Grade* (Abdinasir 2019), which said that UK education departments needed to ensure colleges were properly funded and resourced to allow them to foster a positive and nurturing learning environment. In the same year, the AoC published a mental health and wellbeing charter (2019b) which included a set of principles FE colleges can sign up and commit to in promoting good mental health in both students and staff. By mid-December 2020, the Association reported that 172 colleges (out of the total 244) had signed up to these charter principles.[1]

Suicide and self-harm in an FE setting

It is well established that suicide rates and suicide-related behaviours are low for adolescents but increase in the late teens following the onset of puberty, in parallel with a similarly steep increase in the prevalence of mental illnesses (Kutcher, Wei and Behzadi 2017). A gender paradox also exists whereby suicide rates are more than double among boys but girls have higher rates of suicidal ideation and attempted suicide (Cash and Bridge 2009). In recent years, suicide has become the most common cause of death for young people in the UK and the second leading cause of death in 15- to 29-year-olds globally (WHO 2018). Suicide and self-harm among young people are recognized as a public health priority with

---

[1]   www.aoc.co.uk/colleges-signed-mental-health-charter

opportunities to enhance suicide prevention within educational settings being highlighted (HM Government 2019). In recent years, specific concerns have been raised about student mental health, self-harm and their associated risk for suicide (UUK 2018). A cross-national study which investigated the prevalence of suicidal behaviour and psychological distress in a large sample of university students from 12 countries using a self-report questionnaire (Eskin *et al.* 2016) showed almost 29 per cent had considered suicide at some point in their lives and 7 per cent reported attempting suicide. A meta-analysis of 36 studies (Mortier *et al.* 2017) similarly identified that suicidal thoughts and behaviour (STB) were common among college students and generally higher for females compared with males.

In 2019, Gunnell *et al.* (2020) linked data on suicide mortality rates collected by the ONS with student records collected by HESA, the Higher Education Statistics Agency for England and Wales. Students in secondary schools and FE colleges were excluded. The study provided a comprehensive overview of HE student death trends, characteristics, methods used and seasonal distribution compared to an age-matched general population over 15 years. They found student suicide rates had risen and almost doubled, but overall the rate of HE student suicide was less than half that recorded in an age-matched general population. The study found suicide rates increased with age and rates for males were almost double those for females, reflecting similar trends in the general population. Risk of suicide was lower amongst black students than other ethnic groups. There appeared to be a higher risk of suicide in the second year of undergraduate study and during January, with lowest risk during the summer vacation period. In relation to methods used, jumping was more prevalent in the student group. Knowledge of commonly used suicide methods in a student population is important to devise prevention strategies which have been shown to be effective, such as restriction of access to means of suicide. There have been no similar comparable national studies on the rate of student suicide specifically in FE settings and we don't know if serious self-harm and suicide in FE students is also increasing. We also cannot necessarily assume that we might observe similar findings with an FE student population whose socio-demographic characteristics and living circumstances may be different from those of a typical HE student population.

Research has also explored risk factors associated with student life and study. The strongest risk factor for suicide is a previous suicide attempt. Self-harm has peak incidence in young people where females are a high-risk group with the highest rates (McManus *et al.* 2016) and is a significant, persistent risk factor for future suicide, increasing lifetime risk by 50 to 100 times. Self-harm rates have been shown to be rising for young people, particularly females. One study (McManus and Gunnell 2020) using data on young people aged 16–24 years from three UK National Psychiatric Morbidity Surveys carried out in 2000, 2007 and 2014 compared students (including FE college students) with non-students and found no difference in overall prevalence of suicide attempts or non-suicidal self-harm (NSSH) between the two groups. They also reported a rise in NSSH between 2007 and 2014 for both students and non-students.

Data from the World Health Organization World Mental Health Surveys (Mortier *et al.* 2018) have shown that STBs are common among first-year students, particularly students who have a non-heterosexual orientation or a heterosexual orientation with some same-sex attraction. These groups were most likely to transition from ideation to plans and/or attempts. Other vulnerability factors and stressors that have been identified relate to transition, academic demands, social isolation and financial pressures (Centre for Mental Health 2019). The National Confidential Inquiry into 145 suicides by young people aged under 20 years in England (NCI 2016) identified that 53 per cent were in education, 15 per cent were experiencing academic pressures and 29 per cent were facing exams or exam results at the time of their death. Fifty-four per cent had a previous history of self-harm and 27 per cent had expressed thoughts of suicide in the previous week. Social isolation or withdrawal were reported in 25 per cent. Suicide-related internet use was an antecedent in 23 per cent of deaths. Exam pressures and self-harm were more common in females who died. Forty-one per cent were in contact with mental health services, although 43 per cent had no known contact with any support services.

In summary, there is an absence of quality data and national studies on suicide and suicide attempt rates in FE institutions. Robust national data on FE student suicide is required to support a focus on and investment in suicide prevention in FE colleges combined with routine monitoring of suicide and suicide attempts at a local and national level to support and evidence effective FE suicide prevention strategies. There is also potential learning that can be accessed from exploring lived experiences of suicide attempt survivors. Middlesex University launched a national survey in 2019 to learn from FE and HE students' lived experiences of attempted suicide (Smit 2019). This will, we hope, provide unique and important data to inform more effective suicide prevention strategies in FE settings.

Suicide prevention in FE

By 6 April 2021, 180 colleges had signed up to the FE Mental Health Charter[2] (AoC 2019b), suggesting that the majority of colleges appear to be taking active steps to promote student mental health. This is important as it addresses the potential precursors and risk factors of suicidal ideation. However, it is unclear if student suicide prevention will be explicitly included in the commitment. This is also true of earlier published guidance on mental health provision in FE (CYPMHC 2021; NUS 2017). The lack of sector-specific data does not help in pressing this need, as without a clear indicator that student suicide is a significant issue of concern, many FE colleges may fail to recognize the importance of making specific provision to prevent student suicide.

Practical steps that FE colleges can take to prevent student suicides

In order to be effective, college-based suicide prevention and intervention programmes need to be systematic, multi-focused and comprehensive, involving the whole organization (Abdinasir 2019; Malley, Kush and Bogo 1994). Programmes need to span a continuum from well before the point of a potential suicide, to specific interventions before a potential suicide, during a suicidal crisis and following a suicide (Kush 1991). The programme needs to be seen as an integral and ongoing element of FE student support. Senior leadership support and an identified lead responsible for the implementation of a college suicide prevention strategy is key (Abdinasir 2019; CYPMHC 2021).

Existing published student suicide prevention guidance (JED Foundation 2019; PAPYRUS 2018; UUK and PAPYRUS 2018) identifies a number of common factors including whole community suicide awareness training, institutional safeguarding practice, support for at-risk students, crisis helpline information, restricting access to means and postvention planning. The guidance emphasizes the importance of enabling factors,

---

2　Figures updated by the Association of Colleges on 6 April 2021

notably senior leadership support, a whole college approach, a written formal suicide policy and prevention strategy which incorporates early intervention, crisis and postvention support and universal prevention strategies including embedding mental health topics and suicide prevention discussions into the curriculum.

There are many interventions that can be introduced by colleges that do not necessarily place a strain on budgets. These include free online mental health awareness training from the Charlie Waller Memorial Trust that targets FE non-specialist staff, and free online suicide prevention training modules from the Zero Suicide Alliance for college teaching and support staff (see 'Useful organizations and suicide prevention resources for FE' below). As colleges offer tutor-time for students, there is already dedicated time within the college timetable that could be utilized for addressing vulnerability factors and stressors relevant to suicide prevention. That said, rather than a series of isolated uncoordinated interventions, a whole college approach, which includes the support of teaching and support staff as well as students, and which is underpinned by a written suicide policy, is likely to be key to any successful college suicide prevention strategy (Malley et al. 1994).

Suicide clusters are a phenomenon that happen more often in young people aged 25 years old or younger and tend to occur in certain community and institutional settings, including colleges (Hawton et al. 2020). Risk factors for cluster suicides include exposure to a suicide death, particularly among young bereaved adults (Pitman et al. 2016), perceptions around suicide and STB being more common among peers, vulnerable adolescents being friends with the deceased and social media networks which can speed the spread of information in close knit communities (Hawton et al. 2020). Consequently, any college suicide prevention strategy needs to be aware of the potential risk of suicide contagion and clusters (Chapter 9) and ideally have prepared a postvention protocol documenting the agreed response to a suspected suicide (see Chapters 17 and 22). A key postvention strategy is identifying and supporting students who may be bereaved, affected and vulnerable (see Chapter 19) but should also include support for staff who may be equally affected by a student suicide (see Chapter 20).

Evidence for the effectiveness of FE suicide prevention

Although existing student suicide prevention guidelines (JED Foundation 2019; PAPYRUS 2018; UUK and PAPYRUS 2018) are evidence based, their effectiveness has not yet been formally evaluated and there are no studies into their efficacy in FE student suicide prevention. A systematic review of the global literature on two commonly applied school-based suicide prevention programmes in Canada (Kutcher *et al.* 2017) found no evidence for their effectiveness in preventing youth suicide and concluded, despite much enthusiasm, that they remain largely unproven. Another recent global review of systematic reviews into what works to improve student mental health and wellbeing by the What Works Centre for Wellbeing (Worsley, Pennington and Corcoran 2020) specifically identified 'students attending FE colleges in [the] UK' and 'suicide prevention' as areas where there was currently limited evidence available. As far as we are aware, only one large multicentre, cluster-controlled trial in ten European Union countries, which used a curriculum-based intervention linked to gatekeeper-type training and access to mental health care provision for youth identified as at risk, has demonstrated promising findings in relation to reducing the number of suicide attempts and severe suicidal ideation in school-based adolescents (Wasserman *et al.* 2015). There are a number of potentially effective FE student suicide prevention programmes currently being implemented which require formal evaluation to establish their efficacy. Research is required, both qualitative and quantitative, to clearly establish what works, what does not work and what may cause harm in relation to FE student suicide prevention.

Useful organizations and suicide prevention resources for FE

While FE-specific resources are limited, there are a number of organizations and resources that FE colleges can access to assist in relation to student suicide prevention and responding to a suspected suicide:

- The **Association of Colleges** (www.aoc.co.uk) has published a Mental Health and Wellbeing Charter (AoC 2019b) which FE colleges can sign up to. It has also produced a short publication on *Mental Health in FE: Strategic Engagement between Colleges and Different Parts of the Health Service.*

- **Big Dog, Little Dog** (www.bdld.org.uk) is a mental health enterprise that has launched three new qualifications (levels 2–4) specifically on suicide prevention. The aim is for apprentices, trainees and other frontline workers to complete a level 2 or 3 course as part of their training (Parker 2020c).

- The **Charlie Waller Memorial Trust** (https://charliewaller.org) has an e-learning mental health training platform specifically for non-specialist FE college staff in security, careers, libraries and academic and pastoral support who offer day-to-day support to students. The e-learning includes a module which covers signs to look out for and how to talk to students at risk or in crisis. The Trust has also produced booklets on mental health topics including guidance for school staff and parents on coping with self-harm.

- **MindEd** (www.minded.org.uk) provides free educational resources on young people's mental health and online training specifically adapted for those working in FE. It also offers advice and useful links for families concerned about a young person's mental health.

- **PAPYRUS** (www.papyrus-uk.org) has published a guide to support teachers and college staff in *Building Suicide-Safer Schools and Colleges* (PAPYRUS 2018). The free guide provides college staff with an understanding of the most effective strategies to implement to create a suicide-safer environment. It includes information on how to draft a suicide prevention policy. PAPYRUS also offers an advice service for professionals and young people and runs a national helpline, HOPELINEUK, for young people at risk of suicide and those who are worried about a young person at risk of suicide.

- **Public Health England** (www.gov.uk/government/organisations/public-health-england) produced a helpful guide that can be usefully applied in an FE context, *Identifying and Responding to Suicide Clusters and Contagion: A Practice Resource* (www.gov.uk/government/publications/suicide-prevention-identifying-and-responding-to-suicide-clusters).

- **Samaritans** (www.samaritans.org) has published *Help When We Needed It Most* (2013), which guides school and college staff through an eight-point plan in response to a suspected student suicide. Samaritans also offer a Step by Step service to colleges to assist leadership teams to prepare for and respond to a suspected suicide in college.

- **Student Minds** (www.studentminds.org.uk) has produced two transitions guides for students. *Know before You Go* is an e-resource for Year 12 and 13 students and staff to support transition from college to university. *Transitions* provides helpful tips for navigating university life including time management, relationships, identity, finances, sexual activity, mental illness, suicide and addictions.

- **The Jed Foundation** (www.jedfoundation.org) has published its *Comprehensive Approach* (2019), seven key steps to promote mental health and prevent suicide for teens and young adults (www.jedcampus.org/our-approach).

- **Universities UK** (www.universitiesuk.ac.uk) with PAPYRUS has developed a *Suicide-Safer Universities* toolkit; much of the content is relevant to FE colleges.

- The **Zero Suicide Alliance** (www.zerosuicidealliance.com) has short online suicide prevention training modules in two formats: the Gateway Module 'Let's Talk' provides a brief (5–10 minutes) introduction to suicide awareness, while 'Suicide Awareness' provides more in-depth training (20–25 minutes) to give skills and confidence to support someone considering suicide.

FE college suicide prevention good practice examples

Many FE colleges have a specific focus on student suicide prevention. Strategies developed by two colleges are described below.

East Coast College

East Coast College in Yarmouth and Lowestoft has several initiatives to support students who are at risk of suicide. When students first apply and enrol at the college, they can indicate if they struggle with poor mental health and disclose specific issues to a member of staff. These students are then given extra support with transition into college life. The wellbeing team have a close relationship with the local council and have regular meetings about local suicide triggers. For example, if there is a high number of universal credit applications waiting to be reviewed, the college keeps a close eye on those who they know to already be struggling financially, and if there is a rise in homelessness, they look for students who may have been displaced. Potential stress triggers are covered during tutorial times, when students are advised where they can go to get further support for themselves or peers. Safeguarding data is reviewed monthly, as are specific cases to look for gaps in support or where provision can be strengthened. The college has increased the use of restorative approaches and has trained ambassadors to speak to their peers about friendship issues.

Staff training is reviewed in line with safeguarding data, and personal development training opportunities for staff include mental health first aid. All duty principals have received an introduction to mental health training as well as more specific training around emotional intelligence, conflict handling and using appropriate language when talking about mental health and suicide. The safeguarding team have received training in suicide prevention. The college fills out risk assessments with students identified as at risk of self-harm or a suicide attempt. These risk assessments give students a sense of control and provide staff with an insight into what students are feeling and any plans they might have in relation to self-harm or suicide. Staff try to work collaboratively with the student to maintain their personal safety and stop any plan from being successfully completed – for example, de-activating the exit on a student's college card with their agreement so that they can only leave the building when accompanied by others and alerting the safeguarding team, or giving a student a route around college that avoids a certain toilet in which they have self-harmed previously.

Activate Learning

Activate Learning is one of the biggest college groups in England. It has a strong focus on mental health and specifically suicide prevention. The group has a dedicated mental health and wellbeing team with eight full-time members of staff. Thirty-six other members of staff across the college have been trained as mental health first aiders.[3] The college has worked extensively with external organizations to build staff expertise in mental health and suicide prevention. For example, Samaritans have delivered mental health and suicide prevention training to staff. The college has

---

3   See https://mhfaengland.org

worked with the mental health charity Mind to implement their Five Steps to Wellbeing programme: connect, be active, take notice, learn and give.[4]

The team have worked extensively with staff and students to give them confidence to have conversations about suicide. Staff understand it is best to be clear and concise when raising suicide with a student, and are trained to ask, 'Do you want to die? Or do you not want to feel like this anymore?' Activate have also set up a suicide bereavement network, in which students are actively involved. The focus at Activate is on making learners feel connected and understood so that when a student discloses feelings about suicide, the support services team are immediately alerted and the level of risk is established. A support plan is put in place for students which may include a referral for external support – for example, an emergency referral to local crisis support services in a case of immediate risk – or for internal help and support – for example, booking them in for regular support from a college nurse or counsellor.

If a student attempts suicide, a range of support is put in place for them on their return to college. Members of the wellbeing team contact parents to ask them what support they would like to receive and will visit the student at their home to agree a transition plan to support their college return. When the student returns to college, a support plan is created with the student that lists any external support they are already receiving and what support they would like to receive from the college. Support can range from providing 'exit cards' so they can leave lessons if they start to feel overwhelmed to having a regular check-in with a college counsellor, where frequency of contact can be daily, weekly or bi-weekly, depending on the student's identified level of support need.

Concluding remarks

The Centre for Mental Health (2019) recommended statutory health education in all colleges. If this was to be successfully introduced, it would necessitate mental health first aid training for all college teaching staff. Safeguarding and wellbeing teams should also receive suicide prevention training to ensure they have the tools and confidence to support students at risk effectively.

Colleges should be held to account for student mental health support

---

4   www.mind.org.uk/workplace/mental-health-at-work/taking-care-of-yourself/
    five-ways-to-wellbeing

provision and should be required to have a mental health policy in place which specifically mentions suicide prevention. There should also be recognition that colleges cannot be solely responsible for the mental health of young people in their care. Local authorities need to work with colleges to ensure they are engaged with, and included in, local transformation plans. This will ensure colleges are adequately supported by external agencies, particularly local primary and secondary mental health, as well as crisis support services.

There is much work to be done; we need to be able to measure the impact of action taken by FE colleges to assess how successful suicide prevention initiatives have been. We also need to identify gaps in provision of FE support and training and encourage reflection as to what works and what could work better. There also needs to be more accurate data on the rate of suicide among the FE college population. This would serve to profile the issue with FE colleges, education authorities and external partners. Crucially, it would give more accurate information about the scale of the problem and whether rates are increasing that may require concerted targeted intervention to reduce suicide risk and incidence in young people currently attending FE colleges in the UK.

Author biographies

Kate Parker is an FE reporter with the *Times Educational Supplement* (TES). She has been a journalist at the TES for five years, having previously been an online and social media writer.

Professor Jo Smith was Project Lead for the University of Worcester 'Suicide-Safer' student suicide prevention initiative (2014–2020) and co-author of an 'International Declaration on Zero Suicide in Healthcare' (2015). She was on national working groups which produced UUK (2017) *#Stepchange: Mental Health in Higher Education*, UUK (2018) *Minding Our Future* and UUK and PAPYRUS (2018) *Suicide-Safer Universities*.

References

Abdinasir, K. (2019) *Making the Grade: How Education Shapes Young People's Mental Health.* London: Centre for Mental Health.

Association of Colleges (AoC) (2015) *Survey of Students with Mental Health Conditions in Further Education.* London: Association of Colleges.

Association of Colleges (AoC) (2017a) *Survey of Students with Mental Health Conditions in Further Education.* London: Association of Colleges.

Association of Colleges (AoC) (2017b) *Colleges Forced to Refer Students with Mental Health Issues Directly to A&E*. London: Association of Colleges.

Association of Colleges (AoC) (2019a) *College Key Facts 2019–20*. London: Association of Colleges.

Association of Colleges (AoC) (2019b) *Mental Health and Wellbeing Charter*. London: Association of Colleges.

Bewick, B., Koutsopoulou, G., Miles, J., Slaa, E. and Barkham, M. (2010) Changes in undergraduate students' psychological well-being as they progress through university. *Studies in Higher Education 35*, 6, 633–645.

Britton, J., Farquharson, C., Sibeita, L., Tahir, I. and Waltmann, B. (2020) *2020 Annual Report on Education Spending in England*. London: Institute for Fiscal Studies.

Broglia, E., Millings, A. and Barkham, M. (2018) Challenges to addressing student mental health in embedded counselling services: a survey of UK higher and further education institutions. *British Journal of Guidance & Counselling 46*, 4, 441–455.

Caleb, R. (2014) Uni counselling services challenged by ongoing demand. *Guardian Online*, 27 May.

Cash, S.J. and Bridge, J.A. (2009) Epidemiology of youth suicide and suicidal behavior. *Current Opinion in Pediatrics 21*, 5, 613–619.

Centre for Mental Health (2019) *Finding Our Own Way*. London: Centre for Mental Health and Charlie Waller Memorial Trust.

Children and Young People's Mental Health Coalition (CYPMHC) (2021) *Promoting Children and Young People's Emotional Health and Wellbeing: A Whole School and College Approach*. London: Public Health England.

Crenna-Jennings, W. and Hutchinson, J. (2019) *Access to Child and Adolescent Mental Health Services in 2019*. London: Education Policy Institute.

Department of Health (DH) and NHS England (2015) *Future in Mind: Promoting, Protecting and Improving our Children and Young People's Mental Health and Wellbeing*. London: Department of Health.

Dooley, B., O'Connor, C., Fitzgerald, A. and O'Reilly, A. (2019) *My World Survey 2: The National Study of Youth Mental Health in Ireland*. Dublin: UCD and Jigsaw.

Education and Skills Funding Agency (2020) *Colleges and Higher Education Institutions Notices to Improve*. London: Education and Skills Funding Agency.

Eskin, M., Sun, J.M., Abuidhail, J., Yoshimasu, K. *et al.* (2016) Suicidal behavior and psychological distress in university students: a 12-nation study. *Arch Suicide Res 20*, 3, 369–388.

Frith, E. (2016) *Progress and Challenges in the Transformation of Children and Young People's Mental Health Care*. London: Education Policy Institute.

Gunnell, D., Caul, S., Appleby, L., John, A. and Hawton, K. (2020) The incidence of suicide in university students in England and Wales 2000/2001–2016/2017: record linkage study. *Journal of Affective Disorders 261*, 113–120.

Harris, A. (2019) *Finding Our Own Way: Mental Health and Moving from School to Further and Higher Education*. London: Centre for Mental Health.

Hawton, K., Hill, N., Gould, M., John, A., Lascelles, K. and Robinson, J. (2020) Clustering of suicides in children and adolescents. *The Lancet Child and Adolescent Health 4*, 1, 58–67.

Higher Education Statistics Agency (HESA) (2020) *Higher Education Student Statistics: UK, 2018/19 – Student Numbers and Characteristics*. Cheltenham: HESA. Accessed on 29/04/21 at: www.hesa.ac.uk/news/16-01-2020/sb255-higher-education-student-statistics

HM Government (2019) *Cross-Government Suicide Prevention Workplan*. London: Gov.UK.

Hysenbegasi, A., Hass, S. and Rowland, C. (2005) The impact of depression on the academic productivity of university students. *The Journal of Mental Health Policy and Economics 8*, 145–151.

Jed Foundation (2019) *JED: Emotional Health and Suicide Prevention for Teens and Young Adults*. New York: The Jed Foundation.

Kush, F.A. (1991) A descriptive study of school-based adolescent suicide prevention/intervention programs: program components and the role of the school counselor. *Dissertation Abstracts International 52*, 1692A.

Kutcher, S., Wei, Y. and Behzadi, P. (2017) School- and community-based youth suicide prevention interventions: hot idea, hot air, or sham? *Canadian Journal of Psychiatry 62*, 6, 381–387.

Malley, P., Kush, F. and Bogo, R. (1994) School-based adolescent suicide prevention and intervention programs: a survey. *The School Counselor 42*, 2, 130–136.

Marshall, L., Wishart, R., Dunatchik, A. and Smith, N. (2017) *Supporting Mental Health in Schools and Colleges: Quantitative Survey*. London: Department for Education.

McManus, S. and Gunnell, D. (2020) Trends in mental health, non-suicidal self-harm and suicide attempts in 16–24-year old students and non-students in England, 2000–2014. *Soc Psychiatry Psychiatr Epidemiol 55*, 125–128.

McManus, S., Bebbington, P., Jenkins, R. and Brugha, T. (eds) (2016) *Mental Health and Wellbeing in England: Adult Psychiatric Morbidity Survey 2014*. Leeds: NHS Digital.

Mortier, P., Auerbach, R.P., Alonso, J., Bantjes, J. *et al.* (2018) Suicidal thoughts and behaviors among first-year college students: results from the WMH-ICS Project. *Journal of the American Academy of Child and Adolescent Psychiatry 57*, 4, 263–273.

Mortier, P., Cuijpers, P., Kiekens, G., Auerbach, R.P. *et al.* (2017) The prevalence of suicidal thoughts and behaviours among college students: a meta-analysis. *Psychological Medicine 48*, 4, 554–565.

National Confidential Inquiry into Suicide and Homicide by People with Mental Illness (NCI) (2016) *Suicide by Children and Young People in England*. Manchester: University of Manchester.

National Union of Students (NUS) (2017) *Further Education and Mental Health Report: A Report on Experiences of Further Education Students and Mental Health in 2017*. London: National Union of Students.

PAPYRUS (2018) *Building Suicide-Safer Schools and Colleges: A Guide for Teachers and Staff*. Preston: PAPYRUS.

Parker, K. (2020a) 17k college students receive regular counselling. *TES*, 23 January.

Parker, K. (2020b) Gavin Williamson: 'I want to make the FE sector sing'. *TES*, 3 March.

Parker, K. (2020c) 'If we educate people on suicide, we will save lives'. *TES*, 10 September.

Pereira, S., Early, N., Outar, L., Dimitrova, M. *et al.* (2020) *University Student Mental Health Survey 2020: A Large Scale Study into the Prevalence of Student Mental Illness within UK Universities*. London: The Insight Network.

Pitman, A., Osborn, D., Rantell, K. and King, M. (2016) Bereavement by suicide as a risk factor for suicide attempt: a cross-sectional UK-wide study of 3432 young bereaved adults. *BMJ Open 6*, e009948.

Public Health England (2015) *Promoting Children and Young People's Emotional Health and Wellbeing: A Whole School and College Approach*. London: Public Health England.

Samaritans (2013) *Help When We Needed It Most: How to Prepare for and Respond to a Suspected Suicide in Schools and Colleges*. London: Samaritans.

Smit, J. (2019) Suicide in university students in England and Wales. *The Mental Elf*, 17 December.

Thorley, C. (2017) *Not by Degrees: Improving Student Mental Health in the UK's Universities*. London: IPPR.

Unite Students (2016) *Student Resilience: Unite Students Insight Report*. Bristol: Unite Students.

Universities UK (UUK) (2018) *A Case for Action*. London: Universities UK.

Universities UK (UUK) and PAPYRUS (2018) *Suicide Safer Universities*. Accessed on 28/03/21 at: www.universitiesuk.ac.uk/policy-and-analysis/reports/Documents/2018/guidance-for-universities-on-preventing-student-suicides.pdf

Wasserman, D., Hoven, C., Wasserman, C., Wall, M. *et al.* (2015) School based suicide prevention programmes: the SEYLE cluster randomised controlled trial. *Lancet 385*, 1536–1544.

Williamson, G. (2020) *Speech from The Rt Hon Gavin Williamson MP – Secretary of State for Education*. London: Social Market Foundation.

World Health Organization (WHO) (2018) *Suicide*. Geneva: WHO. Accessed on 16/12/20 at: www.who.int/news-room/fact-sheets/detail/suicide

Worsley, J., Pennington, A. and Corcoran, R. (2020) *What Interventions Improve College and University Students' Mental Health and Wellbeing? A Review of Review-Level Evidence*. London: What Works Centre for Wellbeing.

Risk

CHAPTER 3

Student Suicide Risk

Factors Affecting Suicidal Behaviour in
Students in Northern Ireland

MARGARET MCLAFFERTY AND SIOBHAN O'NEILL

Overview

This chapter:

- discusses the prevalence of suicidal behaviour among first-year undergraduate students in Northern Ireland and the associated risk factors such as gender, age and sexual orientation

- identifies the profiles of childhood adversities in this cohort and explores associations between these adversity typologies and suicidal behaviour

- explores the role of adaptive emotion regulation strategies in reducing suicidal behaviour following negative childhood experiences, including childhood adversities and unhelpful parenting practices

- establishes whether an interaction between current stress levels and negative childhood experiences impacts on the development of suicidal behaviour, and ascertains predictors of effective coping among undergraduate students.

Introduction

In recent years there has been growing concern about the increase of mental health problems and suicidal behaviour among university students. While some studies have revealed comparable rates of suicidal behaviours among students and non-students (McManus and Gunnell 2020), others have found that the rates are lower among college students than same-aged peers (Mortier *et al.* 2018a). Nevertheless, suicide is a preventable death and the rates remain alarming. For example, the number of registered suicides for full-time students over the age of 18 in England and Wales increased from 75 in 2007 to 112 in 2011, to 134 in 2015 (ONS 2017).

The World Health Organization (WHO) World Mental Health International College Student Initiative (WMH-ICS) has revealed high rates of self-harm and suicidal thoughts, plans and attempts among college students globally (Auerbach *et al.* 2019; Mortier *et al.* 2018b). Analyses of this large-scale, cross-national study revealed that 32.7 per cent of college students reported lifetime suicidal thoughts, 17.5 per cent had a suicide plan and 4.3 per cent previously attempted suicide (Mortier *et al.* 2018b). In the same study more than a half of the students who indicated they had suicidal thoughts transitioned to a suicide plan, and nearly a quarter of those with a suicide plan transitioned to a suicide attempt. Such findings highlight the importance of expanding the knowledge base on the factors associated with student suicidal behaviour to inform suicide prevention interventions for this population.

Northern Ireland (NI) has the highest suicide rates in the United Kingdom (Samaritans 2019). A review of the research on suicidal behaviour in NI found deprivation and inequality are the main predictors of area-level variation (O'Neill and O'Connor 2020). The region's recent history of violence, known as 'the Troubles', was directly linked to the high suicide rates. The review also reflected on the indirect impact of the legacy of the conflict, inequality and the effects of transgenerational trauma, whereby parental trauma and mental illness increase the risk of suicidal behaviour in their offspring. Overall, this review highlighted the need to adopt a lifespan approach to suicide prevention by addressing the risk factors in specific population sub-groups (O'Neill and O'Connor 2020).

Until recently, little was known about suicidal behaviour, and risk and protective factors, among university students in the region. In 2015, researchers at Ulster University had the opportunity to undertake a large-scale study into student mental health and suicidal behaviour among undergraduate students. This study, known as the Ulster University Student Wellbeing Study, led by Professor Siobhan O'Neill, was conducted as part of the cross-national WMH-ICS.

This chapter reports the study's findings on self-harm and suicidal behaviour among students commencing Ulster University in NI.

Associated risk factors are explored, including demographic factors such as gender, age and sexual orientation. It also considers the role of childhood adversities and other negative early life experiences, such as parental over-control, over-protection and over-indulgence, in relation to later risk of suicidal behaviour. Finally, protective factors, such as the role of adaptive emotion regulation strategies, coping skills and social support, are examined. The chapter concludes by considering how the findings from Ulster University may transfer to other parts of the UK and how those with an interest in student wellbeing can work together to reduce the risk of suicidal behaviour among students in higher education.

Ulster University Student Wellbeing Study

The first wave of the Ulster University Student Wellbeing Study (UUSWS) commenced in September 2015, during registration week, on the four Ulster University campuses across NI. The online survey developed by the WMH-ICS was fully completed by 739 undergraduate students, aged 18 or over, who were commencing university for the first time. The average age of participants was 21. The sample consisted of 462 females, 274 males and three students who identified as 'other'. To ensure the accuracy of the figures, the data were weighted using the gender and age characteristics of the first-year student population at Ulster University. See McLafferty *et al.* (2017) for further details about the methodology employed.

Prevalence rates of self-harm and suicidal behaviour among university students

Self-harm and suicidal thoughts, plans and attempts were assessed using items from the Self-Injurious Thoughts and Behaviour Interview, the SITBI (Nock *et al.* 2007). The study revealed that 18.5 per cent of students reported suicidal behaviour in the previous 12 months, and 31 per cent reported suicidal behaviour at any time in their life (O'Neill *et al.* 2018). Almost a third of students had serious suicidal thoughts in their lifetime. Nearly a fifth of students (19.6%) had made a suicide plan and 7.7 per cent had attempted suicide, with 15 students reporting a suicide attempt in the year prior to starting university. Of those who attempted suicide, almost a half reported that they had made more than one suicide attempt.

Almost a fifth of students (19.6%) said that they had engaged in self-harm. Of these, 5.1 per cent reported that they self-harmed once or twice,

7.5 per cent did it three to ten times, 2.9 per cent between 11 and 30 times, and 2.9 per cent over 30 times (O'Neill *et al.* 2018). Of great concern, a strong link was found between self-harm and suicidal thoughts, plans and attempts, with 122 of the students who self-harmed also reporting suicidal ideation; 91 had a suicide plan and 43 attempted suicide. This corroborates other findings from the WMH-ICS (Kiekens *et al.* 2018).

An automated alert was built into the online survey, with those who reported moderate levels of suicidal behaviour (N=257) being sent an email outlining support services available in the university and the local community. High-risk students (N=84), who indicated that they had suicide plans or had attempted suicide, were contacted by phone by the university counselling service to ensure that they were aware of available support, and they were offered the option of making an appointment with the university student support services.

Risk and protective factors
DEMOGRAPHIC VARIABLES ASSOCIATED WITH SUICIDE IN STUDENTS
The UUSWS revealed several factors that were associated with suicidal behaviour and self-harm. Previous studies have reported that sexual orientation is a major risk factor for suicidal behaviour. For instance, the LGBT Ireland Report, conducted by researchers at Trinity College Dublin (Higgins *et al.* 2016), found extremely high rates of suicidal behaviour among LGBTI (lesbian, gay, bisexual, transgender, transsexual, intersex) young people in the Republic of Ireland (ROI). In the 19–25 age group, an age when many are attending third-level education, 43 per cent reported that they had engaged in self-harm, while 63 per cent had seriously considered suicide.

Students who identified as non-heterosexual (gay or lesbian, bisexual, asexual, not sure, other) in the UUSWS were much more likely to experience suicidal behaviour than students who described themselves as heterosexual. Representing 9 per cent of the student population, non-heterosexual students were more than five times more likely to engage in suicidal thoughts, plans or attempts, and nearly six times more likely to self-harm, than their heterosexual peers. A large-scale study (N=3340) conducted by the Union of Students in Ireland (USI) revealed that many non-heterosexual students felt let down by mental health services, with the focus often being on their sexual orientation rather than their psychological problems (Price, Smith and Kavalidou 2019).

Almost a quarter of females revealed that they engaged in self-harm in comparison to 13 per cent of males. Moreover, females were much more likely to engage in self-harm to a greater extent than males, with 5.7 per cent of females self-harming 30 times or more, in comparison with 1.7 per cent of males. Female students were also more likely to report lifetime suicidal thoughts (35.9%) than males (24.3%) as well as suicide plans (21.6% versus 16.5%) and attempts (9% versus 5.5%). It should be noted, however, that the lower rates of suicidal behaviour revealed for male students might be related to the fact that males may be more likely to die on a first suicide attempt (O'Neill and O'Connor 2020).

The study revealed that the average age of onset for suicidal behaviour was 15.7 years. With so many students commencing university with pre-existing suicidal thoughts, plans and attempts, it is vital that universities are adequately equipped to deal with these issues. Age differences were found for self-harm and suicidal behaviour, with students under 21 more likely to self-harm, while older students were more likely to have attempted suicide. Given the strong link between self-harm and future suicidal behaviour (Kiekens *et al.* 2018) it is important to identify those who self-harm and provide adequate support in order to reduce the risk of escalating behaviour.

It is also important to address mental health problems and substance disorders, since comorbidity with suicidal behaviour is common. In addition to the elevated prevalence rates of self-harm and suicide thoughts, plans and attempts found in the UUSWS, high rates of psychological and substance problems were evident (McLafferty *et al.* 2017). Almost a quarter of this cohort met the criteria for depression, while over a fifth had generalized anxiety disorder. Moreover, approximately one in ten students met the criteria for alcohol dependence and the figure was 3.1 per cent for drug dependence.

ADVERSE CHILDHOOD EXPERIENCES

Suicidal behaviour has also been found to be related to childhood adversities, particularly those related to maladaptive family functioning, such as parental mental illness, criminality and substance problems, family violence, neglect or physical and sexual abuse (McLafferty *et al.* 2016; O'Connor and Nock 2014; O'Neill *et al.* 2015). Furthermore, O'Connor and Nock (2014) reported that suicidal behaviour increases depending on the number of adversities experienced.

While there are many population-based studies on the effect of childhood adversities, there has been less focus on how such experiences impact on the university student population. In recent years, universities in the UK set out to improve the proportions of students entering college from disadvantaged populations. There is therefore potentially a greater risk of negative childhood experiences among cohorts in recent years. A range of studies have shown that parental mental health problems and exposure to other childhood adversities, such as domestic violence, are associated with suicidal behaviour in college students (Blasco *et al.* 2019; You *et al.* 2014).

The UUSWS team analysed the impact of 13 adverse childhood experiences which occurred before participants reached the age of 18: serious parental mental health problems and alcohol or drug problems; parental suicidal behaviour and involvement in criminal activity; domestic violence; physical punishment and physical abuse; insults received repeatedly and emotional abuse; inappropriate touching and sexual abuse; serious neglect; and doing chores which were dangerous or age inappropriate. Latent Profile Analysis (LPA) revealed three population subgroups, as shown in Figure 3.1.

The baseline or low-risk profile, which accounted for 87.1 per cent of the sample, comprised students who experienced few adversities. The moderate-risk profile, which consisted of 10.4 per cent of the sample, was characterized by moderate levels of adversity. Individuals in the high-risk profile, which accounted for 2.5 per cent of the sample, had the highest levels of adverse childhood experiences, especially those related to maltreatment such as physical punishment and physical abuse, family violence, neglect and emotional abuse.

In comparison to individuals with a low-risk profile, students who experienced moderate rates of childhood adversity were more likely to have a range of mental health problems and suicidal ideation, plans and attempts. Individuals with a high-risk profile were on average eight and a half times more likely to engage in suicide ideation and have suicide plans and were nearly eight times more likely to have attempted suicide. Furthermore, those who experienced the highest levels of adversity were more than five and a half times more likely to engage in self-harm. Similar findings were revealed in another WMH-ICS study, with those who reported three or more early traumatic experiences being more than five times more likely than the low-risk group to engage in repetitive non-suicidal self-injury (Kiekens *et al.* 2018).

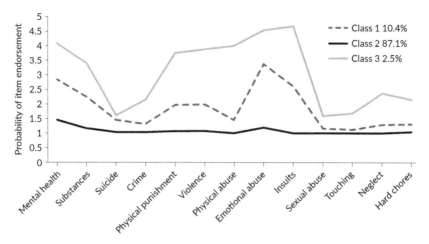

Figure 3.1: Latent profile plot of childhood adversity indicators (source O'Neill *et al.* 2018)

Note: class 1 = moderate risk, class 2 = low risk, class 3 = high risk

NEGATIVE PARENTING PRACTICES

Parenting practices can also impact on suicidal behaviour. Parental over-control, over-protection or over-indulgence may prevent a person from developing essential skills to cope with stress and negative life events. For instance, those who have been over-indulged often have problems with self-control and self-regulation, and lack self-reliance, resilience and coping skills. Having over-controlling or overly protective parenting can also be detrimental. There have been many definitions of this type of parenting in recent years, such as 'helicopter' parenting. Studies have found that children of helicopter parents are more likely to have psychological problems and have low levels of life satisfaction (Schiffrin *et al.* 2014), which may be related to them feeling incompetent and lacking the ability to cope on their own. This may partially account for the increase in mental health problems and suicidal behaviour among university students and young people in general.

EMOTION REGULATION STRATEGIES

While several risk factors were explored, potential protective factors were also examined, such as using adaptive emotion regulation strategies. 'Emotion regulation refers to the process by which we influence which emotions we have, when we have them, and how we experience and express them' (Gross 2002, p.282). Two main types of strategy are used: reappraisal and suppression (Gross 2002), with elevated levels of reappraisal and low levels of suppression found to be adaptive. If good emotion regulation skills can be developed, they may help a person to deal with life stressors, thereby reducing the risk of psychopathology and suicidal behaviour.

The UUSWS revealed that students with adaptive emotion regulation strategies, especially those who used low levels of suppression, were less likely to have psychological problems or engage in suicidal behaviour following negative childhood experiences. However, students who experienced parental over-control were more likely to use high levels of suppression, which can be maladaptive. The study highlights, therefore, that parental over-control can have both a direct and indirect impact, as it not only impacts directly on psychopathology and suicidal behaviour, but it also has an indirect effect since it reduces the likelihood of a person using adaptive emotion regulation strategies.

STRESS AND COPING

The ability to cope or manage stress has been linked to a range of mental health problems and suicidal behaviour. The link between stress, coping and suicidal behaviour was examined using data obtained from the UUSWS (McLafferty *et al.* 2019). Strong associations were revealed between coping and self-harm and suicidal behaviour, with those with poorer coping skills at a much greater risk. It is important therefore to identify protective factors which may enhance coping skills.

The impact of parental over-control, over-indulgence and over-protection on psychopathology, self-harm and suicidal behaviour when stress levels were high was assessed (McLafferty *et al.* 2019). Those who experienced over-control and over-indulgence were more likely to have a mental health problem or engage in self-harm or suicidal behaviour. In particular, over-control was related to self-harm, while those who were over-indulged were more likely to have suicidal thoughts, plans or attempts. The findings may be related to them trying to take some control over their lives or not being able to cope when faced with stressors.

Parental over-control and over-indulgence were significant predictors of poorer coping, which may be related to lower levels of resilience and self-esteem. Childhood adversities, however, were not significant predictors of coping strategies. Some would suggest that those who experience some adversity may develop resilience and skills to deal with stressors, which may account for these findings. Several protective factors were also revealed, with those who had social support or adaptive emotion regulation strategies more likely to have good coping skills.

Addressing these issues

The current study identifies numerous risk and protective factors which can assist students during their transition into university. Such findings may help universities to address the increasing rate of psychopathology and suicidal behaviour found in the student population. The University Mental Health Charter includes a number of recommendations for addressing student suicidal behaviour (Hughes and Spanner 2019). The report proposes that universities need to have effective practices, training and processes in place, provide support and appropriate interventions, support students in reporting problems and provide a safe environment.

It should be remembered that student dynamics have changed recently as a result of widening access to third-level education, with increasing numbers of students from diverse social and cultural back-grounds (Thorley 2017). Universities should be particularly mindful of the needs of those from disadvantaged families, many with low so-cio-economic status, as studies have found that students who struggle financially have significantly higher rates of mental health problems and suicidal behaviour (Bruffaerts *et al.* 2010; Eisenberg *et al.* 2007). Furthermore, they may have experienced elevated levels of childhood adversities and other negative childhood experiences, which, as has been shown, can impact on suicidal behaviour across the lifespan.

The findings from the UUSWS have important implications not only for universities but also for policy makers, clinical practitioners and those involved in designing and implementing programmes to help those who experienced childhood adversities and negative parenting practices. Many people are aware that childhood adversities can be very detrimental. It is important, however, to highlight to parents that practices such as over-control, over-protection or over-indulgence may also have a very negative impact.

While high rates of mental health disorders and suicidal behaviour were revealed in the first-year student population at Ulster University, only a half of those identified as having a problem reported that they had received treatment in the form of psychological counselling or medication for an emotional problem (Ennis *et al.* 2019). This rate, however, at 51 per cent, was much better for those who endorsed both suicidal behaviour and a psychological problem than the rate reported for those with a mental health disorder alone, with only a fifth receiving treatment which could have a detrimental impact on their wellbeing. It is of great importance, therefore, to encourage help-seeking among this vulnerable population.

Anti-stigma campaigns and events which encourage students to seek help should be promoted within university settings. Peer-led initiatives such as 'Mind Your Mood' at Ulster University[1] are showing promising results in relation to help-seeking, but further work is needed.

Since the study found that non-heterosexual students had very elevated rates of mental health problems and suicidal behaviour, it is very important to provide adequate support to help reduce the risk rather than focusing on their sexual orientation as was reported by Price *et al.* (2019). WMH-ICS studies recommend that university support services need to develop outreach strategies and varied cultural competencies to address the needs of students (Auerbach *et al.* 2019; Mortier *et al.* 2018a), especially those from minority groups. Mindfulness-based programmes are also recommended for developing good emotion regulation strategies (Hayes *et al.* 2019), and resilience-building programmes should be encouraged. The majority of universities run a number of programmes and provide support services and counselling to assist students during their time at university.

Conversely, given the limited resources available to universities to help tackle these issues, new cost-effective prevention, intervention and treatment programmes are recommended, such as guided online CBT-based interventions (Bolinski *et al.* 2018). Ulster University commenced a new project in 2019, known as the Student Psychological Intervention Trial (SPIT), to test the effectiveness of such an online intervention, developed by Professor Pim Cuijpers and Professor Heleen Ripers and other collaborators from Vrije Universiteit (VU) Amsterdam (Bolinski *et al.* 2018; Karyotaki *et al.* 2019).

Conclusions and practical recommendations to readers

The UUSWS revealed high prevalence rates of suicidal behaviour among university students in NI. Social support, good emotion regulation and coping skills were found to be of benefit. Several risk factors for suicidal behaviour such as gender, age, sexual orientation and adverse childhood experiences were identified. The studies highlight the importance of protecting young people from adverse early life experiences and developing parent–child relationships from an early age. Campaigns and programmes which highlight the importance of maintaining healthy boundaries and promoting autonomy among young people would also be advantageous.

---

1   www.ulster.ac.uk/mindyourmood

Resilience-building programmes which promote the development of adaptive coping and emotional regulation are also recommended. It should be remembered that emotion regulation and coping strategies are learned from parents and caregivers via social modelling. If caregivers have difficulty managing their own emotions and coping with stressors, their maladaptive coping strategies may transcend to their children.

It is, therefore, important that we consider these risk factors when planning services to support students with mental illness and suicidal behaviour. As many students are entering further education with pre-existing psychological problems, it is important to promote programmes which may help them develop protective factors in primary and secondary school settings. Recently, a new resilience-building programme, 'Hopeful Minds'[2], which has been showing promising results globally, has been developed and piloted in NI. The 'Youth Aware of Mental Health' (YAM) programme, which encourages students to work together to solve problems and develop empathy and coping skills, has also been found to be very beneficial, leading to reductions in suicidal behaviour (Wasserman *et al.* 2015).

There are many opportunities within further education settings to promote positive mental health and reduce the risk of suicidal behaviour. Early detection, intervention and treatment are of utmost importance. For example, Blasco *et al.* (2019) recommend strategies to increase a sense of membership among students that may help prevent suicides. Student support services on campuses play a key role. However, a whole university approach is recommended, involving a collaboration between support services, the students' union, student administration, academic and support staff, and students themselves.

It should be noted that the research discussed in this chapter was based in one university in Northern Ireland, and the findings may therefore not be representative of students from other universities or higher education institutions. It is important therefore to consider how these findings may transfer to other parts of the UK and what this might mean for universities and practitioners. The best results are achieved through collaborative work. In the UK, initiatives such as the Student Mental Health Research Network (SMaRteN) have been established to help expand the knowledge base and develop a network of researchers with an interest in student wellbeing. Such initiatives bring researchers and others with an interest in student mental health and wellbeing together, and by collaborating,

---

2   https://schoolsforhope.org

and sharing knowledge and best practices, psychological problems and suicidal behaviour may be reduced in the student population.

Author biographies

Dr Margaret McLafferty is a research associate in student mental health at Ulster University, Northern Ireland. She helped coordinate a large-scale longitudinal study to identify risk and protective factors for mental health and suicidal behaviour among Ulster University students, conducted as part of the WHO World Mental Health International College Student Initiative.

Professor Siobhan O'Neill is Professor of Mental Health Sciences at Ulster University and Interim Mental Health Champion for NI. Her current research programmes focus on childhood adversities and trauma-informed practice, and the transgenerational transmission of trauma.

References

Auerbach, R.P., Mortier, P., Bruffaerts, R., Alonso, J. *et al.* (2019) Mental disorder comorbidity and suicidal thoughts and behaviors in the World Health Organization World Mental Health Surveys International College Student initiative. *International Journal of Methods in Psychiatric Research 28*, 2, e1752.

Blasco, M.J., Vilagut, G., Alayo, I., Almenarad, J. *et al.* (2019) First-onset and persistence of suicidal ideation in university students: a one-year follow-up study. *Journal of Affective Disorders 256*, 192–204.

Bolinski, F., Kleiboer, A., Karyotaki, R., Bosmans, J.E. *et al.* (2018) Effectiveness of a transdiagnostic individually tailored Internet-based and mobile-supported intervention for the indicated prevention of depression and anxiety (ICare Prevent) in Dutch college students: study protocol for a randomised controlled trial. *Trials 19*, 1, 118.

Bruffaerts, R., Demyttenaere, K., Borges, G., Haro, J.M. *et al.* (2010) Childhood adversities as risk factors for onset and persistence of suicidal behaviour. *The British Journal of Psychiatry 197*, 1, 20–27.

Eisenberg, D., Gollust, S.E., Golberstein, E. and Hefner, J.L. (2007) Prevalence and correlates of anxiety, and suicidality among university students. *American Journal of Orthopsychiatry 77*, 4, 534–642.

Ennis, E., McLafferty, M., Murray, E., Lapsley, C. *et al.* (2019) Readiness to change and barriers to treatment seeking in college students with a mental disorder. *Journal of Affective Disorders 252*, 428–434.

Gross, J.J. (2002) Emotion regulation: affective, cognitive and social consequences. *Psychophysiology 39*, 281–291.

Hayes, D., Moore, A., Stapley, E., Humphrey, N. *et al.* (2019) Promoting mental health and wellbeing in schools: examining mindfulness, relaxation and strategies for safety and wellbeing in English primary and secondary schools: study protocol for a multi-school, cluster randomised controlled trial (INSPIRE). *Trials 20*, 640.

Higgins, A., Doyle, L., Downes, C., Murphy, R. *et al.* (2016) *The LGBT Ireland Report: National Study of the Mental Health and Wellbeing of Lesbian, Gay, Bisexual, Transgender and Intersex People in Ireland.* Dublin: GLEN and BeLonG To.

Hughes, G. and Spanner, L. (2019) *The University Mental Health Charter*. Leeds: Student Minds.

Karyotaki, E., Klein, A.M., Riper, H., de Wit, L. *et al.* (2019) Examining the effectiveness of a web-based intervention for symptoms of depression and anxiety: study protocol of a randomised controlled trial. *BMJ Open 9*, 5, e028739.

Kiekens, G., Hasking, P., Boyes, M., Claes, L. *et al.* (2018) The associations between non-suicidal self-injury and first onset suicidal thoughts and behaviors. *Journal of Affective Disorders 239*, 171–179.

McLafferty, M., Armour, C., Bunting, B., Ennis, E. *et al.* (2019) Coping, stress and negative childhood experiences: the link to psychopathology, self-harm and suicidal behaviour. *Psych J 8*, 3, 293–306.

McLafferty, M., Armour, C., O'Neill, S., Murphy, S., Ferry, F. and Bunting, B. (2016) Suicidality and profiles of childhood adversities, conflict related trauma and psychopathology in the Northern Ireland population. *Journal of Affective Disorders 200*, 97–102.

McLafferty, M., Lapsley, C.R., Ennis, E., Armour, C. *et al.* (2017) Mental health, behavioural problems and treatment seeking among students commencing university in Northern Ireland. *PLoS One 12*, 12, e0188785.

McManus, S. and Gunnell, D. (2020) Trends in mental health, self-harm and suicide attempts in 16 to 24-year old students and non-students in England, 2000–2014. *Social Psychiatry and Psychiatric Epidemiology 55*, 125–128.

Mortier, P., Auerbach, R.P., Alonso, J., Axinn, W.G. *et al.* (2018a) Suicidal thoughts and behaviors among college students and same-aged peers: results from the World Health Organization World Mental Health Surveys. *Social Psychiatry and Psychiatric Epidemiology 53*, 3, 279–288.

Mortier, P., Auerbach, R.P., Alonso, J., Bantjes, J. *et al.* (2018b) Suicidal thoughts and behaviors among first-year college students: results from the WMH-ICS Project. *Journal of the American Academy of Child and Adolescent Psychiatry 57*, 263–273.

Nock, M.K., Holmberg, E.B., Photos, V.I. and Michel, B.D. (2007) Self-Injurious Thoughts and Behaviors Interview: development, reliability, and validity in an adolescent sample. *Psychological Assessment 19*, 309–317.

O'Connor, R.C. and Nock, M.K. (2014) The psychology of suicidal behaviour. *Lancet Psychiatry 1*, 73–85.

O'Neill, S. and O'Connor, R. (2020) Suicide in Northern Ireland: epidemiology, risk factors, and prevention. *The Lancet 7*, 6, 538–546.

O'Neill, S., Armour, C., Bolton, D., Bunting, B. *et al.* (2015) *Towards a Better Future: The Trans-Generational Impact of the Troubles on Mental Health*. Belfast: CVSNI.

O'Neill, S., McLafferty, M., Ennis, E., Lapsley, C. *et al.* (2018) Socio-demographic, mental health and childhood adversity risk factors for self-harm and suicidal behaviour in college students in Northern Ireland. *Journal of Affective Disorders 239*, 58–65.

Office for National Statistics (ONS) (2017) Suicides among full-time students, as defined by National Socio-Economic Class (NS-SEC) classification, deaths registered in England and Wales between 2001 and 2016. Accessed on 21/04/21 at: www.ons.gov.uk/peoplepopulationandcommunity/birthsdeathsandmarriages/deaths/adhocs/007478suicidesamongfulltimestudentsasdefiniedbynationalsocioeconomicclassnssecclassificationdeathsregisteredinenglandandwalesbetween2001and201

Price, A., Smith, H.A. and Kavalidou, K. (2019) *USI National Report on Student Mental Health in Third Level Education*. Dublin: Union of Students in Ireland.

Samaritans (2019) Suicide facts and figures: Suicide statistics and trends for the UK and Republic of Ireland. Accessed on 29/04/2021 at: www.samaritans.org/ireland/about-samaritans/research-policy/suicide-facts-and-figures

Schiffrin, H.H., Liss, M., Miles-McLean, H., Geary, K.A., Erchull, M.J. and Tashner, T. (2014) Helping or hovering? The effect of helicopter parenting on college students' wellbeing. *Journal of Child and Family Studies 23*, 548–557.

Thorley, C. (2017) *Not by Degrees: Improving Student Mental Health in the UK's Universities*. London: IPPR.

Wasserman, D., Hoven, C., Wasserman, C., Wall, M. *et al.* (2015) School based suicide prevention programmes: the SEYLE cluster randomised controlled trial. *Lancet 385*, 1536–1544.

You, Z., Cheng, M., Yang, S., Zhou, Z. and Qin, P. (2014) Childhood adversity, recent life stressors and suicidal behavior in Chinese college students. *PLoS One 9*, 3, e86672.

CHAPTER 4

Student Suicide

The Policy Context

DIANA BEECH, SALLY OLOHAN AND JAMES MURRAY

Overview

This chapter provides:

- an understanding of the political context in England from 2018 onwards, which encouraged further progress on preventing student suicides

- knowledge of various policy initiatives that arose within the higher education (HE) sector during this time

- an appreciation of progress made, in the sector at large and within individual HE institutions, plus an understanding of unresolved issues in this area.

Introduction

This chapter will outline how student suicide became a policy priority for the Westminster Government over the course of 2018 and has led to more focused activity and targeted initiatives across the HE sector to prevent student suicide over the ensuing years. Since HE is a devolved matter in the United Kingdom, this chapter will principally examine the effects of national policy developments on institutional responses in England. It will explore how they have provided the impetus for the sector to devise frameworks through which we have since come to better understand student suicide, mitigate risk and intervene when students get into difficulty.

Taking as its starting point the Cabinet reshuffle that took place in early 2018 and the prominent cases of student suicides at Bristol

University that spring, this chapter traces how the Westminster Government was inspired to intervene to prevent further student deaths. It specifically explores how former Universities and Science Minister, Sam Gyimah, took up the cause as his own in his 11 short months in office. Despite inadvertently wading into a minefield of issues around confidentiality and consent, it traces how he raised the need for step-change in the way student suicide prevention is handled, both across the English HE sector and in government more generally.

By considering the various policy mechanisms and levers that have since emerged as a result of increased ministerial attention on the topic of student suicides, this chapter will survey the impact these have had on sector-wide responses to suicide prevention, as well as inspired the development of individual institutional initiatives. It will also summarize the lessons learned by the sector and explore what further measures are needed. The chapter ends with some reflections on what more can be done to improve safeguarding in the sector in the future.

Ministers matter

It is often said that politics are personal. Political leaders may be drawn to work with others due to personal compatibility and camaraderie. In the same way, politicians may also feel compelled to act on a certain issue if it aligns with their personal belief-set and convictions. When Prime Minister Theresa May appointed Sam Gyimah to the post of Minister of State for Universities, Science, Research and Innovation on 9 January 2018 in a reshuffle widely believed to facilitate her planned review of post-18 education, he came to office with the express intention of looking out for the interests of students. In fact, in his first major speech delivered on 28 February 2018, Gyimah set out his ambition to be 'not just a universities minister, but also a minister for students' (Gyimah 2018a). For him, this involved 'placing a laser-like focus on students' and he set out his intention 'to engage directly with students and listen to their hopes and concerns' (ibid.). This he largely did over the ensuing months through his '#SamOnCampus' tour of universities, which involved him visiting HE institutions across England to answer students' questions on a wide range of topical issues.

It was also during his February speech that Gyimah first expressed the controversial opinion that 'universities need to act *in loco parentis*' – meaning 'in the place of the parent', the implication being that HE institutions should take on some of the duty of care and responsibilities of a parent or guardian. The new minister suggested that HE institutions should 'be there for students offering all the support they need' to enable them to get the most out of their university experience and to help them during their transition to HE (ibid.). He stressed that work on student mental health needs to increase and that 'the provision and understanding of the pressures on students needs to evolve' (ibid.).

At the time of the speech, Gyimah's words provoked criticism from the HE sector for assuming all students are young people trying to adjust to life away from their parental home. This is certainly not the case at 'post-92' universities in London, for example, whose student bodies comprise many mature and commuting students. Gyimah's statement also implies that students' parents are part of the solution and not the problem, which, again, may not always be the case – especially where students may be struggling to escape domestic abuse, forced marriages or other challenging family circumstances.

Some sector commentators at the time pointed out, too, the danger that viewing universities as being *in loco parentis* risks constraining students' wider freedoms. In a blog published in the week following Gyimah's speech, David Malcolm, who was then Head of Policy and Campaigns at the National Union of Students, explained how the concept of being *in loco parentis* has historically 'manifested itself in a broadly paternalistic attitude to students' and could pave the way, if enshrined in law, for students being treated like children, risking wider restrictions and limitations on their rights (Malcolm 2018). Gyimah may never have intended to suggest that HE students should not be legally adult. However, his decision to focus on student mental health and wellbeing issues undoubtedly brought to the fore questions about the duty of care universities have to their students.

It was not long before Sam Gyimah's commitment to student mental health was tested when news emerged in the spring of 2018 from the University of Bristol about the 'sudden and unexpected' death of first-year English student Ben Murray, who had become the third student to take his own life at the university in three weeks and the tenth student to die at the university since October 2016 (Weale 2018). A further two students from the Bristol-based University of the West of England (UWE) were also reported to have taken their own lives around the same period, with a total of 14 UWE students later found to have died by suicide since the start of the decade (Horgan 2019).

At the annual 'Festival of HE' hosted by the University of Buckingham, which took place on 14 June that year, Gyimah was visibly moved to hear Ben Murray's father talk about how his son had been carrying pain and anxiety around with him for the six months leading up to his death and the minister heard his appeal to the sector to make student mental health 'a strategic issue of importance' (Inge 2018). In response, Gyimah reiterated his initial call for universities to be *in loco parentis* in cases where concerns exist that 'life-threatening situations of care' might be at stake (ibid.). He also shrugged off criticism of 'infantilising students' and explained he saw his duty as minister as being to 'fully empower universities' – that means 'where we respect people's rights as adults but make sure we are doing everything in terms of duty of care towards these young people' (ibid).

From that moment on, Gyimah became a minister driven to turn the tide against student suicides. His conviction was no doubt further bolstered by the figures released by the Office for National Statistics (ONS) later that month, which appeared to confirm a rise in suicide rates among students in England and Wales, with 95 students confirmed as having died by suicide in the 12 months leading to July 2017 (ONS 2018). This equated to 4.7 suicides per 100,000 students. Although this number was lower than the suicide rate across the general population in corresponding age groups that year, it was still high enough to prompt Gyimah to call out the 'sobering stats' on social media, declaring that it was 'time to redouble our efforts on mental health support at universities' (Gyimah 2018b). Just three days later, he issued an ultimatum to England's vice-chancellors that student mental health must be considered 'a top priority for the leadership of all our universities' (DfE 2018a).

Gyimah's words were not without substance either. On 28 June, the minister hosted a summit in Bristol with university leaders, student representatives and mental health charities to announce the establishment of the first voluntary University Mental Health Charter, intended to encourage early prevention and intervention in student mental health issues across the sector. Gyimah warned that failing to improve mental health provision in England's universities risked 'failing an entire generation of students' (ibid.). Even though he acknowledged the HE sector had been grappling over duty of care issues for some time, he expressed concern that it was still 'too easy for students to fall between the cracks' (ibid.).

Indeed, the HE sector had long been aware of the complex legal and moral responsibilities on universities when it comes to determining their duty of care over students. In 2015, the Association of Managers of Student Services in HE (AMOSSHE) had agreed that 'there is a balance between what the university should do as a legal minimum' to protect the health, safety and welfare of its students and 'what they could do based on a university's perceived moral obligation to look after and support its students' (AMOSSHE 2015). The group recommended that the sector 'produce a framework on duty of care' to 'help create a feeling of consistency across the sector' while still 'giving freedom within the framework for universities to stamp their own mark on the support they provide' (ibid.).

In September 2017, the representative body for UK HE, Universities UK (UUK), published the first iteration of this framework – the *Stepchange* framework – which made clear the reputational and risk issues to universities of not making students' mental health a strategic priority. A year later, on 5 September 2018, UUK followed up on this general framework by publishing the *Suicide-Safer* guidance in conjunction with the UK's national charity dedicated to the prevention of young suicide, PAPYRUS. The guidance includes specific advice on developing institutional suicide prevention strategies and best practice for responding to student suicides (UUK 2018).

So, when the start of the new academic year 2018/19 arrived and Minister Gyimah began reiterating warnings to vice-chancellors to prioritize student support, the HE sector was already thinking about tackling student suicides and progressing support for mental health. In an article published in the *Huffington Post* in the run up to Freshers' Week, Gyimah called on vice-chancellors to use 'all means in their power to safeguard students from harm' (Gyimah 2018c). He also sent a letter to heads of HE institutions in England urging them to assess institutional approaches to student wellbeing and to engage personally in the consultation process for the new University Mental Health Charter. He added that there could be 'no negotiation on this' (DfE 2018b).

In his correspondence to institutional leaders, Gyimah was careful to encourage a collaborative, 'whole-institution' approach to wellbeing, calling on vice-chancellors to 'ensure a diverse range of voices are heard, including academics, mental health practitioners, social activity organizers, accommodation providers and domestic staff' (ibid.). He also encouraged a 'system-wide approach' to the problem in an attempt to establish high standards and deliver positive change right across the sector, not just within individual institutions (ibid.).

Gyimah's vocal lobbying on this issue appears to have been noted by Downing Street. On 9 October, to mark World Mental Health Day, Prime Minister Theresa May appointed her first UK Minister for Suicide Prevention, Jackie Doyle-Price (UK Government 2018). As minister, Doyle-Price was tasked with overseeing the implementation of the new cross-government suicide prevention workplan, which included a commitment to follow through on the work Gyimah had started on the University Mental Health Charter, on transitions issues and on cross-sector working towards the development of guidance for universities on preventing student suicides (HM Government 2019, pp.32–33).

Just two days later, on 11 October, the regulator for HE in England, the Office for Students (OfS), launched a £6 million 'Challenge Competition' to help universities and colleges generate new approaches to mental health issues. This funding came on top of the £1.5 million that the OfS had already awarded to 17 projects in March 2018, alongside Research England, to support the wellbeing and mental health of postgraduate researchers (PGRs) through the 'PGR Catalyst Fund'. It also came in addition to the 'SMaRteN' national research network, launched on 6 September 2018 with the express intention of improving understanding of student mental health. Equipped with four years of funding, SMaRteN seeks to fill the void of evidence in the HE sector as to what interventions work, and build 'an evidence base to support evidence-based approaches' (SMaRteN 2018). Taken together, these projects show that policymakers and sector leaders were now serious about making positive changes to the way student mental health issues are handled.

The road ahead

The following month, on 30 November 2018, Gyimah, the Universities Minister who had overseen and encouraged many of these developments, resigned from government over concerns about the Prime Minister's withdrawal deal from the European Union. The then Secretary of State for Education, Damian Hinds, took on the baton in December 2018 and wrote to the Chair of a UUK roundtable on student mental health, asking the sector 'to maintain the focus built up in recent months' (DfE 2018c).

In his letter to the roundtable, the Education Secretary asked universities 'to do more to reach out to students' emergency contacts when it is clear that they are at risk of a mental health crisis' (ibid.). Aware that very few universities at the time were giving students the chance to 'opt-in' to allow their institutions to share their personal details with parents or guardians should their mental health cause serious concern, he challenged UUK to produce new advice to give students 'every possible opportunity to choose to receive care from families and trusted friends alongside the support they get from student welfare teams and the NHS' (ibid.). In March 2019 the Education Secretary established a new taskforce – the Education Transitions Network, which included a focus on enabling students to look after their mental health and wellbeing (DfE 2019).

The new Universities Minister, Chris Skidmore, used University Mental Health Day 2019 to speak to representatives from the charity Student Minds to understand how the University Mental Health Charter was progressing. A few weeks later, he acknowledged that there were 'plenty of students in our universities and colleges struggling with hidden disabilities like poor mental health and anxiety' and went on to promise he would meet the government's Suicide Prevention Minister to explore ways to 'improve the provision of student mental health even further, particularly around the continuation of care during term and out of term' (Skidmore 2019).

Yet, with Prime Minister Theresa May's influence waning and the government's capacity to deal with anything other than the UK's withdrawal from the European Union severely hampered, little further progress on student mental health was made from within government circles. In July 2019, Theresa May was replaced as Prime Minister by Boris Johnson, Damian Hinds was succeeded as Education Secretary by Gavin Williamson and Chris Skidmore was replaced by Jo Johnson, who became Universities Minister for the second time in a little over 18 months. New administrations also bring with them new priorities. So, with the personal backing of the former Prime Minister gone from the role of Suicide Prevention Minister, the post was effectively deprioritized, although the responsibilities were nominally passed on to the incumbent Minister for Mental Health, Suicide Prevention and Patient Safety, Nadine Dorries.

Under the Johnson Government, the HE sector has effectively had to make progress on suicide prevention and mental health support with very little top-down government pressure. Despite this, the University Mental Health Charter was published in December 2019 – just over 18 months since its initial conception. Designed following an intensive period of research and consultation, the Charter highlights the risks related to suicide in an HE setting and sets out principles of good

practice which encourage universities to 'do what they can to max-
imise student autonomy' but also offer reassurance that institutions
can override student wishes and contact others without consent if it
is 'clearly justifiable and in the best interests of the student' (Hughes
and Spanner 2019, p.42). Although, to this day, adhering to the Charter
remains a voluntary exercise, it was always hoped the Charter would act
as a quality improvement mechanism to strengthen intra-institutional
support for student mental health issues, as well as recognize universities
with exceptional approaches through a parallel Charter Award Scheme.

In light of lessons learned during the development of the Charter,
UUK also refreshed its *Stepchange* framework in May 2020. The main
changes to the relaunched guidance include a new focus on a 'whole-university approach', emphasized by Minister Gyimah in 2018, and an equal
focus on staff wellbeing alongside that of students (UUK 2020). In an
article published to mark the relaunch, Professor Julia Buckingham, UUK
President and Vice-Chancellor and President of Brunel University London, acknowledged that 'there is much good work to share and celebrate
across our sector' but that universities now have 'to sustain this strategic
focus' (Buckingham 2020).

The publication of two programme evaluations later that year certainly helped to keep the sector aware of the need to continue making
progress in this area. First, the evaluation of the OfS Mental Health
Challenge Competition, published in September 2020, confirmed that
the scheme had generated value and that 'partnership working is helping
to pull in greater expertise', thereby encouraging HE institutions to
continue working with different partners and services 'to reduce the
number of students slipping through the gap' (Wavehill 2020, p.29).
Second, the programme evaluation for the Catalyst Fund-funded scheme
supporting the wellbeing of PGRs published a month later, in October
2020, recommended, amongst others, that 'UUK and other stakeholders
should consider how existing networks can be utilised to support future
work relating to PGR mental health and wellbeing and the sharing of
effective practice' (Vitae 2020, p.5).

In the suicide prevention space, multiple HE institutions can be
seen to have embraced these recommendations of shared working and
forging partnerships outside the HE sector. Some examples include the
Framework for Developing a Suicide Safer University from the University
of Liverpool, which includes a commitment to engage with relevant
regional stakeholders (University of Liverpool 2019), and the *Suicide*

Prevention and Response Plan from Bristol University, which draws on broader UK research as well as 'lived experiences in Bristol' (University of Bristol 2018, p.3).

Real life stories, real life challenges

Through stories told by bereaved families and recommendations of policymakers, HE agencies and government ministers, the sector has learned what factors could have made a difference in preventing loss of life. These factors and the key policy recommendations that flow from them have been debated, challenged and at times misunderstood. As a result, although much insight has been gained since 2018, evidence of sector-wide impact of the various imperatives and initiatives is lacking. There is still much progress to be made in ensuring compassionate, sensitive and joined-up practice to keep students safe.

James Murray is one of a few bereaved parents whose reflections have been influential in bringing about required change. As detailed earlier in this chapter, James' son Ben sadly died in May 2018 whilst a first-year student at Bristol. James' brave and moving accounts of various systemic issues surrounding his son's death (as illustrated in Hart 2020) have challenged universities to reflect on their interactions with vulnerable young people.

Worryingly, it is estimated that 3 per cent of the student population have attempted suicide (Mortier *et al.* 2018). The intentions of the sector and individual HE providers to provide a caring and compassionate learning environment for students are not questioned; however, the level of 'care' required to prevent deaths is something that not all universities are operationally capable of achieving. Some do not have the necessary people, processes, systems and culture in place; without these, suicide prevention will not be possible, and the tragic loss of lives will sadly persist.

Sensitive systems

The stories of student deaths by suicide often highlight missed opportunities to identify risk. Reflecting on Ben's death, James Murray talks about a 'jigsaw', with the different 'pieces' living within disparate institutional 'touchpoints' – be these separate e-mail chains or records unshared between schools, faculties, accommodation services or student unions. This prevents universities from seeing the full picture. James acknowledges, 'It is up to each university to determine its own level of preventative care, but it is our conviction that this single view of a student should exist in all universities and should be updated in real-time to help avert crisis.'

The issues he highlights pertain to organizational structures within universities. Only one in three people who die by suicide are known to mental health services (UUK 2018). Universities are large and complex organizations, where academic interactions with students and students' relationships with other aspects of their experience, such as residential life, student services or administration offices, can run along entirely separate parallel lines. A student noted by a lecturer for failing to attend lectures, for example, may not instantly raise any alarm bells. But if we can connect this to the notes of their residential manager, who has observed they have stopped keeping their room in a hygienic state, and to the accounts office, which has recorded an overdue bill, a picture of personal vulnerability emerges. If there is no system for this information to be pieced together, there is the very real risk that a university may miss an opportunity to escalate concerns, to assess risk and to help that student understand that there are people who will help – and to give hope.

A Regulation 28 Report to Prevent Future Deaths (PFD) was one of the outcomes of the inquest into Ben Murray's death (Courts and Tribunals Judiciary 2019). A PFD is issued when a coroner believes there is a risk of future deaths occurring in similar circumstances unless action is taken. In this case, the PFD included matters raised with the Department for Education, concerning: sharing of good practice on wellbeing intervention and suicide prevention; encouraging disclosure of mental health concerns; supporting the transition of young students into HE and providing good pastoral support in this regard; and ensuring that 'lessons learned' reviews are undertaken after student deaths. Some of the sector-level initiatives established since 2019 could be regarded as an attempt to address these concerns, but the reach and impact of these developments is still to be evidenced.

People and data

Universities are trying to make change. One emerging structural approach is the introduction of trained and qualified student support practitioners (wellbeing advisers, student support advisers, etc.) who work alongside personal tutors, and residential life and other specialist services, such as counselling, financial support and academic administration, to provide outreach, triaging and safeguarding assessment of concerns. These roles often require mental health or social care practitioner qualifications. They typically provide early intervention and preventative actions in cases where students are identified as possibly being at risk – either because of the student experience (e.g. if they were previously in local authority care, estranged from family or homeless) or where there are indicators of concern. A number of universities have also developed systems that will detect such indicators. The OfS Challenge Competition funding programme, for example, includes collaborative projects to create data systems, building on existing learning analytics systems, to help identify potential wellbeing risk factors for students and assist interventions.

A culture of compassion

Interventions to protect vulnerable students will be easier to progress in universities where compassion is a core value in leadership and ways of working. A university with compassion at its core will encourage colleagues to move from reactive to proactive and compassionate practices, empowering them to intervene in situations of concern about others, without fear of blame or criticism. Table 4.1 sets out the behaviours, systems and practices that might be observed in universities as they evolve towards a 'culture of compassion'.

Table 4.1: Compassionate universities. Where is your university in its cultural evolution?

	Reactive	Proactive	Compassionate
Confident information sharing	Safety is important and we share if 'vital interests' are involved. Staff held back by privacy concerns	Staff trained to signpost to support services if they have 'serious concerns'	All staff and students happy and confident in sharing to ensure early intervention
Safer policies, processes and procedures	We have written rules and procedures. Staff may struggle to follow them by the letter	Safer policies introduced – e.g. face-to-face dismissal, student-at-risk meetings, sensitive debtor letters	Continuous training empowers whole university to act safely and instinctively

Joined-up technology	A view of the student can be compiled from various systems but post-incident	'Whole student' view always available with rules to alert staff to talk to students	Predictive analytics helps staff 'nudge' students with progression or crisis risk
Learning from the past	Incidents not investigated save for report to coroner. Bad news may be kept hidden	Leaders open to bad news, but focus is on statistics versus learning from the incident	Bad news actively sought. Serious incident reviews ensure learning from statistics and stories

Crisis intervention

Data has the power to help 'spot the signs' at scale and lead us to conversations. It's the conversations that make the difference. In cases of significant risk, universities often struggle with the challenges of what level of care they should assume and manage. As articulated earlier in this chapter, the topic of information sharing and misunderstood references to universities acting *in loco parentis* have troubled the sector and confused some universities on the actions they should take if they are seriously worried about the visibly declining wellbeing of a student. In addition, there are various interpretations of safeguarding duties. One guide for HE governors on safeguarding issues acknowledges that safeguarding in HE can cover 'wider ethical or pastoral responsibilities where it may be possible to help to safeguard the welfare of children and adults at risk of abuse or neglect' (Advance HE 2018), but it does not explicitly refer to issues of significant student wellbeing concern. Although they may not be bound by the same requirements as statutory agencies, in practice, universities are increasingly applying a broader interpretation of safeguarding in their interventions with students who, although may not fall into categories of 'vulnerable adults', may at times be regarded as being 'adults who are vulnerable' at a specific point of personal or mental health crisis.

Most universities ask for next of kin or emergency contact information from students. It would be reasonable to assume therefore that, by collecting this information, the organization has developed a framework in which it might use it. The critical discussions over GDPR (General Data Protection Regulation) concerns that followed Gyimah's recommendation to the sector to act *in loco parentis* would suggest that many universities are not clear why they are asking for this information and the circumstances in which they would use it. Nevertheless, research undertaken by James Murray in 2020 (unpublished at the time of writing) revealed that at least 25 universities in England had implemented 'opt-in' schemes to gain 'consent at registration' to contact nominated friends or family in the event the university has serious concerns and cannot reach the student.

There are specific situations where it may be helpful to involve a student's nominated emergency contact to assist a student in crisis in a sensitive, compassionate and lawful way. These include situations where, despite best endeavours, the student is not engaging with internal and statutory support and remains at risk. To achieve a supportive outcome for the student, it is essential that appropriately trained senior staff with safeguarding responsibilities assess all available indicators of risk. It is also important that these professionals are consultative and confident in assessing these risk indicators and can apply expert judgement on the most responsible actions that the organization can take to 'widen the safety net' for the student, including involving statutory services and others trusted by the student who may be able to intervene in a supportive way. Any action to inform emergency contacts should be undertaken in the context of a crisis intervention policy that sets out how the university will explain to students at the point of enrolment (or other relevant disclosure point) why this information is being requested and how it will identify who has the authority to assess whether others should be alerted to concerns.

The guiding principles in sensitive interactions with students and their trusted others should always be to act with compassion and in the best interests of the student. By alerting someone who cares about the student, has the capacity to assist and the means to do so, risks can be reduced, hope restored, and a life full of promise and ambition may very well be saved.

Conclusion and practical recommendations

This chapter has shown how in 2018 a renewed focus on suicide prevention from the government coincided with sector efforts to improve interventions to prevent student deaths. The government's focus has since changed, as ministers have come and gone; however, much of this work is still ongoing and conversations around appropriate support and safeguarding in the sector continue. The Covid-19 pandemic in 2020 spotlighted the need for safeguarding in HE to be broad and focused on the 'whole lives' of students – including their practical and emotional needs.

The various initiatives established since 2018 to address challenges in supporting and protecting students now require careful review and evaluation to ensure that good practice principles are implemented consistently across the sector. The step change in practice implemented to help the most vulnerable will help all students to succeed. We therefore need to keep making efforts to 'piece together the jigsaw' and bring together data from different strands of students' lives via 'whole university' approaches, dedicated wellbeing advisers and progress in analytics dashboards. Above all, we need to encourage the development of compassionate universities – with the right values at their core, communicated and lived by leaders who foster a culture of sensitive and appropriate interventions.

Author biographies

Dr Diana Beech was Policy Adviser in the Department for Education to three successive Ministers of State for Universities, Science, Research and Innovation, namely Sam Gyimah, Chris Skidmore and Jo Johnson. She is now Chief Executive Officer of London Higher, the representative body for over 40 London universities and HE colleges.

Sally Olohan MBE was formerly Head of Student Support Services at Nottingham Trent University and member of the Mental Wellbeing in HE Working Group. She has advised on wellbeing process development at Falmouth University FX Plus and was Interim Student Health and Wellbeing Manager at the University of East London in 2018. She is now Head of Student Support and Residential Life at the University of Westminster.

James Murray is the father of Ben Murray, who took his own life in 2018 at the age of 19, while studying at Bristol University. Since Ben's death, James has championed early alert and intervention systems. James believes that better information sharing within universities (and with trusted third parties) is vital to helping students in distress.

References

Advance HE (2018) *Getting to Grips with Safeguarding*. Accessed on 27/01/21 at: www.advance-he. ac.uk/knowledge-hub/getting-grips-safeguarding

AMOSSHE (2015) *Where's the Line? How Far Should Universities Go in Providing Duty of Care for Their Students?* Report of Policy Breakfast from 29 May 2015. Accessed on 16/12/20 at: www.amosshe.org.uk/futures-duty-of-care-2015

Buckingham, J. (2020) The new Stepchange is an opportunity to renew our efforts on mental health. *wonkhe*, 21 May 2020. Accessed on 11/12/20 at: https://wonkhe.com/blogs/the-new-stepchange-is-an-opportunity-to-renew-our-efforts-on-mental-health

Courts and Tribunals Judiciary (2019) Prevention of Future Deaths notice: Benjamin Murray, 16 May 2019. Accessed on 27/01/21 at: www.judiciary.uk/publications/benjamin-murray

Department for Education (DfE) (2018a) New package of measures announced on student mental health, 28 June 2018. Accessed on 08/12/20 at: www.gov.uk/government/news/new-package-of-measures-announced-on-student-mental-health

Department for Education (DfE) (2018b) Minister Gyimah: universities must ensure their mental health services are fit for purpose, 16 September 2018. Accessed on 08/12/20 at: https://dfemedia.blog.gov.uk/2018/09/16/minister-gyimah-universities-must-ensure-their-mental-health-services-are-fit-for-purpose

Department for Education (DfE) (2018c) Further intervention on student mental health, 4 December 2018. Accessed on 09/01/21 at: www.gov.uk/government/news/further-intervention-on-student-mental-health

Department for Education (DfE) (2019) Government creates new student mental health taskforce, 17 March 2019. Accessed on 09/01/21 at: www.gov.uk/government/news/government-creates-new-student-mental-health-taskforce

Gyimah, S. (2018a) A Revolution in Accountability. Speech given at the Office for Students launch conference, 28 February 2018. Accessed on 07/12/20 at: www.gov.uk/government/speeches/a-revolution-in-accountability

Gyimah, S. (2018b) Twitter post, 25 June 2018. Accessed on 09/12/20 at: https://twitter.com/samgyimah/status/1011174200801980416

Gyimah, S. (2018c) With a new year upon us, universities must ensure their mental health services are fit for purpose. *Huffington Post UK*, 16 September 2018. Accessed on 08/12/20 at: www.huffingtonpost.co.uk/entry/university-mental-health_uk_5b9e00i0e4b013b0977b7fd9

Hart, A. (2020) The father fighting for change at universities after losing his son to suicide. *Independent*, 5 October 2020. Accessed on 27/01/21 at: www.independent.co.uk/independentpremium/bristol-student-suicide-ben-murray-university-mental-health-ucas-b744977.html

HM Government (2019) *Cross-Government Suicide Prevention Workplan* (2019) Accessed on 09/12/20 at: https://assets.publishing.service.gov.uk/government/uploads/system/uploads/attachment_data/file/772210/national-suicide-prevention-strategy-workplan.pdf

Horgan, C. (2019) Report shows over half of UWE students who died by suicide had asked the uni for help. *The UWE Tab*, 12 April 2019. Accessed on 08/12/20 at: https://thetab.com/uk/uwe/2019/04/12/report-shows-over-half-of-uwe-students-who-died-by-suicide-had-asked-the-uni-for-help-9632

Hughes, G. and Spanner, L. (2019) *The University Mental Health Charter*. Accessed on 10/12/20 at: www.studentminds.org.uk/uploads/3/7/8/4/3784584/191208_umhc_artwork.pdf

Inge, S. (2018) Minister renews call for universities to be 'in loco parentis'. *Times Higher Education*, 14 June 2018. Accessed on 08/12/20 at: www.timeshighereducation.com/news/minister-renews-call-universities-be-loco-parentis

Malcolm, D. (2018) 'As much freedom as is good for them' – looking back at in loco parentis. *wonkhe*, 7 March 2018. Accessed on 16/12/20 at: https://wonkhe.com/blogs/much-freedom-good-looking-back-loco-parentis

Mortier, P., Cuijpers, P., Kiekens, G., Auerbach, R.P. *et al.* (2018) The prevalence of suicidal thoughts and behaviours among college students: a meta-analysis. *Psychological Medicine* *48*, 4, 554–565.

Office for National Statistics (ONS) (2018) *Estimating Suicide among Higher Education Students, England and Wales: Experimental Statistics*. London: ONS. Accessed on 08/12/20 at: www. ons.gov.uk/peoplepopulationandcommunity/birthsdeathsandmarriages/deaths/articles/ estimatingsuicideamonghighereducationstudentsenglandandwalesexperimentalstatistics/ 2018-06-25

Skidmore, C. (2019) Chris Skidmore: A STEP Further for Students. Speech delivered at wonk-he's Secret Life of Students event, 25 March 2019. Accessed on 10/01/21 at: www.gov.uk/ government/speeches/chris-skidmore-a-step-further-for-students

SMaRteN (2018) About SMaRteN. Accessed on 11/12/20 at: www.smarten.org.uk/about.html

UK Government (2018) PM pledges action on suicide to mark World Mental Health Day, 9 October 2018. Accessed on 09/12/20 at: www.gov.uk/government/news/ pm-pledges-action-on-suicide-to-mark-world-mental-health-day

University of Bristol (2018) *University of Bristol Suicide Prevention and Response Plan*. Accessed on 11/12/20 at: www.bristol.ac.uk/university/media/strategies/suicide-prevention-response-plan.pdf

University of Liverpool (2019) *Framework for Developing a Suicide Safer University*. Accessed on 11/12/20 at: www.liverpool.ac.uk/media/livacuk/Framework,for,Developing,a,Suicide, Safer,University,.pdf

UUK (2018) *Suicide-Safer Universities*, 5 September 2018. Accessed on 08/12/20 at: https://issuu. com/universitiesuk/docs/guidance-for-sector-practitioners-0/1?ff&e=15132110/64400960

UUK (2020) *Stepchange: Mentally Healthy Universities*. Accessed on 11/12/20 at: www. universitiesuk.ac.uk/policy-and-analysis/reports/Documents/2020/uuk-stepchange-mhu. pdf#page=12

Vitae (2020) *Catalyst Fund: Supporting Mental Health and Wellbeing for Postgraduate Research Students. Programme Evaluation*, October 2020. Accessed on 10/01/21 at: https://re.ukri. org/documents/2020/catalyst-fund-programme-evaluation

Wavehill (2020) *Evaluation of the OfS Mental Health Challenge Competition. Early Findings Report*, August 2020. Accessed on 10/01/21 at: https://officeforstudents.org.uk/media/0a1306e9-0c95-4fc2-82e4-7ae62056cacf/mhcc_earlyfindingsreport.pdf

Weale, S. (2018) University of Bristol confirms sudden death of first-year student. *The Guardian*, 10 May 2018. Accessed on 07/12/20 at: www.theguardian.com/uk-news/2018/may/10/ university-of-bristol-confirms-sudden-death-of-first-year-student

CHAPTER 5

The Influence of Social Media on Suicidal Behaviour among Students

RACHEL COHEN AND LUCY BIDDLE

Overview

This chapter aims to give readers:

- an overview of the main themes emerging from existing literature concerning students and young adults' use of the internet and social media and how this may influence suicidal behaviour

- an insight into how theory in media and audience studies can provide a more nuanced understanding of young people's social media use in relation to suicidal feelings

- an illustration of risky suicide-related internet use amongst students, drawing on in-depth qualitative data

- an appreciation of the implications for practitioners and areas for further research.

Introduction

Between 2007 and 2009, the county of Bridgend in South Wales, UK, experienced one of the largest youth suicide clusters of modern times. Twenty-six suicides occurred, mostly amongst young people and all but one using the same method of suicide. Although never substantiated, the deaths were linked to an 'internet suicide cult' on the social networking site 'Bebo'. This brought emerging concerns about the impact of the internet and social media on young people into sharp focus and prompted suggestions that clinicians should take an 'internet history' from young patients presenting with mental health concerns (Cooney and Morris 2009). Cases of 'cybersuicide' – suicides influenced/informed by the online world – have since amassed, being reported in both the popular and academic press. More recent years have witnessed new concerns provoked by the huge expansion of social media in reach and sophistication. Contemporary issues linked to poor mental health and suicide risk include cyberbullying, online gambling, 'fear of missing out' (FOMO), and suicide challenge games, such as the 'Blue Whale Challenge', which are purported to incite suicidal behaviour.

While the online world presents risks for all ages, these are especially pertinent for young people – the 'digital natives' who have grown up with internet technology and for whom it is an inseparable (rather than acquired) part of their existence. In the UK, nearly two-thirds of 15–24-year-olds report being 'hooked' on their mobile phone, with half checking it within five minutes of waking (Ofcom 2015). Social media has been offered as one possible explanation for recent rises in rates of suicide in adolescents (Bould *et al.* 2019).

Empirical evidence has not kept pace with levels of panic and concern but highlights the need to recognize young people as more than passive recipients who are impacted upon, viewing them instead as users who engage with *and generate* online content in complex ways (e.g. Das 2019). Further, it is acknowledged that the online world can also be helpful for young people experiencing suicidal thoughts. The internet may assist suicide prevention by facilitating emotional expression, accessing 'hard to reach' populations – such as LGBTQ groups who may avoid real world help due to fear of stigma (Lucassen *et al.* 2018) – and by delivering emotional support, self-help tools, peer support and online therapy (Marchant *et al.* 2017). These beneficial effects, however, are not without complexity.

In this chapter, we review literature relevant to the concerns outlined above, identifying key themes and areas requiring better understanding. We explore the complexities of social media use among young people, and how these relate to suicidal behaviour. We also consider theoretical approaches facilitating a more nuanced understanding of this. The chapter draws on recent in-depth qualitative research to present a student case study of risky suicide-related internet use and concludes by discussing implications for practitioners.

Existing literature: an overview of current debates and understanding

Debates about whether internet and social media use among young adults are helpful or harmful tend to dominate literature in the field, much of which is organized around this binary opposition. Despite considerable concern about potential harms, greater acknowledgement is now given to more positive aspects. An emerging theme is an emphasis on the complexities of the relationship between the internet/social media and today's digital native generation.

Research focusing explicitly on student populations in this context appears relatively limited and conducted mostly outside of the UK, for instance Mexico (Jasso-Medrano and Lopez-Rosales 2018), Taiwan (Hong et al. 2014), USA (Moreno et al. 2015) and Turkey (Orsal et al. 2013). Most of it is quantitative in nature, and typically finds positive associations between 'risky' (e.g. Moreno et al. 2015), 'problematic' (Odaci and Kalkan 2010) or 'addictive' (e.g. Orsal et al. 2013) internet use and depression or mental health problems. Some studies have made further distinctions in this respect – for example, by emphasizing that excessive internet use, characterized by lengthy duration and high frequency, is usually understood as non-pathological (Jasso-Medrano and Lopez-Rosales 2018), whereas 'addictive' behaviour patterns have been linked to depression (Donnelly and Kuss 2016).

Other research suggests social networks are a risk factor for suicide among young users, but this generally refers to 'extreme' (e.g. pro-suicide) online communities, rather than the use of social networks in general (Luxton, June and Fairall 2012). It is, therefore, important to consider not only the ways in which young people engage with social media, but also the range and type of social media networks that they use. While certain pathways (e.g. forums, pro-suicide websites) may present an increased risk (Daine et al. 2013) in terms of self-harming behaviour and suicidality, networks such as those used primarily for socialization present less of a concern (Jasso-Medrano and Lopez-Rosales 2018). The communicative possibilities provided by social media are, however, complex and ambivalent and understood to carry both positive and negative traits. The relationship between social media use and social 'connectedness' for young people has been described as paradoxical – that is, whilst using social media facilitates the formation of online communities, it can also bring about feelings of alienation and ostracism (Allen et al. 2014).

Research also indicates that young people experiencing suicidal ideation often communicate this via social media (Cheng *et al.* 2015). Since expressions of emotional distress can sometimes help to reduce it, some studies emphasize that these potential benefits of social media use should not be overlooked (Chan *et al.* 2017). Belfort, Mezzacappa and Ginnis (2012) found that young people who attend emergency departments following an incident of self-harm are increasingly using Facebook, Twitter and other platforms beforehand to communicate their distress, especially to a peer, rather than to an adult, highlighting the importance of better understanding the role of social media use during times of emotional crisis. However, a systematic review of studies exploring the potential for social media to be used for suicide prevention found that although suicide communications may provide opportunities for others to intervene, challenges remain around controlling user behaviour, accurately assessing risk and the possibility of contagion (Robinson *et al.* 2017). This led to the conclusion that more research is required into the safety and efficacy of social media as a tool for suicide prevention.

Marchant *et al.* (2017) explored such complexities further in a systematic review that included 51 articles, incorporating quantitative and qualitative evidence and a broad range of internet mediums (e.g. social media, forums, blogs, dedicated self-harm sites and general internet use). Although 18 studies reported negative influences – and only 11 reported a positive influence – 17 found internet use to have a 'mixed' influence on self-harm and suicidal behaviour in young people. The authors concluded that the potential benefits of online behaviour, such as reducing social isolation, outreach, crisis support and the provision of therapeutic services, need to be further explored and more comprehensively mobilized (Marchant *et al.* 2017, p.2).

Such complexities highlight the need to move beyond merely identifying the *direction of causality* in relation to internet/social media use and suicidal behaviour among young people, although this still 'remains unclear' (Sedgwick *et al.* 2019, p.534). Sedgwick *et al.* found that although problematic internet use does increase the risk of suicide attempts among young people, a more nuanced understanding of these risks is needed. Their review draws attention to the heterogeneous ways in which internet and social media use are classified in existing research, and recommends that longitudinal studies be conducted, in order to more adequately comprehend *how* social media and internet use are related to suicidality in today's younger generations.

Other researchers note the importance of acknowledging possible relationships between study design and perceived outcome (e.g. Daine *et al.* 2013). Where qualitative and mixed-methods studies tend to report positive findings regarding the influence of internet use, quantitative ones typically report negative findings. Marchant *et al.* argue that this disparity may be partly explained by acknowledging that quantitative data 'are failing to capture the complexity' (Marchant *et al.* 2017, p.20) of the matter and may be especially biased towards the measurement of particular outcomes and effects – the positive effects of interventions, for instance, or the negative effects of internet addiction. These observations substantiate the need for ongoing study designed to capture the nuances of the relationships between social media use and suicidal thinking among young people and for consideration of the longer-term significance and implications of this.

Awareness is increasing about the potential value of online support for young people experiencing suicidal crisis. Recognizing that young people often prefer to seek help from peers, recent research has explored the potential to educate young people to talk safely about suicide online and to develop suicide prevention messages they can deliver via social media. As well as providing engaging help, such education may assist young people to feel confident about providing emotional support to others (Robinson *et al.* 2017).

Theoretical approaches

Questions of identity are perhaps more important than ever in the internet age. Digital technologies make it possible for us to create 'multiple selves' (Bauman 2004, p.15), and opportunities for the performance and transformation of self have arguably become 'nearly limitless' (Dervin and Abbas 2009, p.3). Social scientific conceptualizations of self and identity help to theorize the complex ways in which people engage with the online world as part of their everyday lives. The reflexive project of the self (Giddens 1991) describes how self-identity is actively produced over time. From this perspective, internet and social media use serves as a means of self-interpretation, allowing us to conduct ongoing 'identity work'. By shifting the focus away from ideas about the internet 'having an impact' on users, a more nuanced appreciation is possible of how and why young people engage with various social media networks. The extent to which identity and self are intertwined with internet use can also be understood in relation to 'technologies of the self': processes that 'permit individuals to effect by their own means or with the help of others a certain number of operations on their own bodies, souls, thoughts, conduct and way of being' (Martin *et al.* 1988, p.18).

Psycho-cultural approaches to media audience studies acknowledge that internet users are active participants, or 'produsers' (Hills 2014, p.185) in choosing and using social media in particular ways, and for a range of purposes. These theoretical frameworks can help to better understand the complexities of social media use, by recognizing the role of culture in mental and social life, whilst also focusing on affective experience and the role of emotions (Bainbridge and Yates 2014). This helps to broaden the scope of concern beyond establishing 'positive' or 'negative' outcomes of social media use, recognizing that although new technologies offer 'the promise of affection, conversation and a sense of new beginnings' (Turkle 2008, p.125), they also – paradoxically – captivate users, potentially 'dragging irrational selves into addiction and compulsion' (Turkle 2008, p.125).

A cross-disciplinary theoretical approach is, therefore, helpful in moving beyond media 'effects' towards understanding of the 'essential tensions' between the media and everyday life (Silverstone 1994). From this perspective, we are better equipped to explore how social media networks form 'an integral part and an extension of [young people's] lives, increasing their communication and social relationships, but also leading to problems and unhealthy habits of use' (Jasso-Medrano and Lopez-Rosales 2018, p.184).

Case study: qualitative insights into risky suicide-related internet use in young people

Research often fails to engage first-hand with the online users that it studies, resulting in an inability to explore the full complexity of use, or the meanings ascribed to it. One of the authors' (LB) own large-scale study made a unique contribution in this regard. The study comprised 1) surveys to measure the prevalence and patterning of suicide-related internet use, including a survey of young people aged 21 years (Mars *et al.* 2015) recruited from the Avon Longitudinal Study of Parents and Children (ALSPAC) (Boyd *et al.* 2013); and 2) in-depth interviews with over 60 participants (with a range of characteristics) exploring the nature and impact of their suicide-related internet use (Biddle *et al.* 2018).

The study's survey data highlighted that young people commonly resort to the online world for information and dialogue about suicide. In a population sample of approximately 4000 young people, 22.5 per cent reported some suicide-related internet use ranging from 'coming across' material to actively searching for suicide content (Mars *et al.* 2015). Amongst those who also reported having attempted suicide (n=248), 70 per cent reported some suicide-related internet use, almost 1 in 2 had deliberately searched for suicide content using a search engine (1 in 5 looking for information about how to harm themselves) and 1 in 3 had discussed their suicidal feelings on social media. Engagement with the online environment was, thus, an integral aspect of the suicide-related illness behaviour of highly distressed young people.

Types of suicide-related use

Sixty qualitative interviews were conducted with young people in the community (aged 21–23 years), hospital patients (18 years +) and adults recruited through the UK suicide prevention charity Samaritans (18 years +). All participants reported suicidal feelings and use of the internet in relation to these feelings. Findings revealed two different types of suicide-related internet use among participants relating to degree of suicidal intent: lower severity 'pessimistic browsing' and higher severity 'purposeful planning'.

Pessimistic browsing

Where individuals experienced ambivalent suicidal feelings, their online activity was also mixed as they tried to make sense of their feelings and looked for others to relate to. They explored suicide as an option while also looking for coping strategies, peer support or help, and so browsed a broad range of content. Their online navigation was disorganized, comprised a haphazard trail through links and hashtags, and involved flitting between helpful and pro-suicide content; through blogs, vlogs, news reports, 'Q&A' sites, help sites, and trawling the stories and dialogue of others who had engaged in suicidal behaviour: 'You'll go down another route, then another, then you start following links and sort of read something, then open a new tab, then look into that, and yeah, just learning different ways to die.' Such browsing behaviour escalates and becomes addictive, gaining momentum as mood dips: 'Every day I would Google "suicide", just as a thing. I guess it was a bit of an obsession.' As indicated in our introduction, this behaviour poses risks. Conclusions from the study data were as follows:

- Individuals may stumble unintentionally upon graphic content about suicide methods.

- Browsing becomes increasingly pessimistic with individuals drawn to negative content, making it difficult to maintain a positive frame of mind and displacing help-seeking intentions.

- Online discourse unhelpfully normalizes suicide and self-harm, sanctioning this as an acceptable, unproblematic (or glamourized) response to distress.

Such online activity maintained suicidal feelings rather than bringing resolution:

> I'd be online talking with all these people and just getting more and more morbid and down and in gruesome chats... It made my battling this stand still because I got so engrossed in the negative stuff... I think I would have been six months to a year further ahead in my treatment than where I am now.

Pessimistic browsing was especially prevalent within the narratives of young people, relating to the fact they were already persistent online users, connected to a wide range of social media and accustomed to 'living life on their phone'. Targeting by online services meant they could come across suicide content without looking. At the same time, a search for such content was also an everyday action. Epitomizing these ideas, one 19-year-old described looking for suicide content as 'a regular thing' she would 'look at alongside grocery lists and directions to classes'.

Purposeful planning

Individuals with intention to pursue suicide as a course of action used the internet with the clear purpose of researching how to do this. Their searching was deliberate and strategic, to source information on possible suicide methods, technical instructions for effective implementation, evaluation of methods according to criteria such as speed and pain, and ways of accessing means for suicide online (e.g. drugs). These higher severity users were less likely to socialize online and showed a clear preference for informational content, which they used to supplement ideas expressed in the lived experience accounts and general conversation posted by other users discussing suicidal behaviour in forums or on chat pages. They also deduced information from web pages not intended to inform about suicide, including professional medical literature. Typically, help content was ignored or avoided. Such internet use could result in high-intent individuals (including young people and students) implementing suicide attempts guided by information gathered online.

Below, we present a case study of lower severity use, illustrating the ambivalent nature of social media and internet use in relation to suicidality, as experienced by Anna, a student.

ANNA

Anna was a 21-year-old student, completing an access course to enable entry to university. She had received counselling for depression at age 18, but when her feelings resurfaced she began to explore suicide online and across social media. This started with broad, non-directive searching and browsing either through Google: 'I used to literally just type in like "suicide" and just see what came up'; or on social media using hashtags: 'I used to just like type in depression on the [hash]tags and then you come up with all these people who post and pictures about depression and I used to spend hours reading through them.' Anna became drawn to content discussing 'ways to kill yourself', despite describing some of this as 'really shocking'. For example, she reported learning how she would need to cut to 'slit her wrists' effectively. She commented that information is 'easy to find' because 'you've got all these messed-up people like me, posting whatever they want'. Attempting to counterbalance such material, Anna would also Google 'self-help' but would often 'jump straight back to looking at suicide'.

Communicating about distress on a range of social media platforms became a key feature of Anna's online activity, since this provided an environment where she felt able to express her feelings openly in a way not possible in the 'real world'. She blogged and posted extensively and was buoyed where others liked or re-posted her posts. Referencing a particular post on suicide, Anna explained feeling, 'I was like "wow", like people get it, people understand me.' Anna's online behaviour began to disrupt her routines:

> I could stay online until about three, four o'clock in the morning and then get up and go to college for 9. I'd be on it at all hours...[when] you should be trying to get to sleep, not looking up God knows what.

Nevertheless, she perceived the online world as reassuring and therapeutic, not least because it was available in the early hours when 'real-world' support from medical services, friends or family could be inaccessible.

While maintaining that her internet use had been helpful, during the interview

Anna reflected on this past behaviour and a complex picture emerged, in which she also recognized how user-generated content could justify, normalize and in turn perpetuate self-harm:

> You can obviously look back with a bit more perspective when you're not actually in it...you can find like a hundred posts like glorifying suicide or embracing self-harm and if you're in that mindset...it makes you feel like that's acceptable for you to do it too...but as soon as you're trying to recover its really unhelpful because you sort of slip back... I think you forget that it's not actually right to be depressed and it shouldn't be acceptable.

In this respect, Anna expressed concern about how some of her own posts may have affected others.

Anna also reflected on the self-identity she had created through her social media posts. While she found the initial writing 'therapeutic', its permanence on her personal feed was not helpful when she tried to move on:

> You sort of re-read it and you're like 'oh yeah, I do feel like that' – rather than being like 'ah, I'm not like that anymore'. Whereas if you talk about it, you say it and [it's] gone. You don't like re-hash it... I go and say things to the counsellor and then they are gone. You don't have to deal with it again. That's why I ended up deleting all my [social media platform] accounts once I got to that next sort of level of being better. It was like 'right, I just need to clear this from my life'.

Anna's case illustrates the difficulty of disentangling the 'help versus harm' debate that prevails in current knowledge about young people's internet/social media use and shows how this binary distinction may limit the scope of understanding. In Anna's case, social media platforms helped her experience a sense of social connection and provided an outlet for self-expression. Whilst these valuable processes proved supportive during a vulnerable time – and may have prevented a worse emotional crisis – they simultaneously threatened to hinder her recovery, by virtue of their permanence as part of her online identity and normalization from within an online subculture.

Importantly, the case study also shows that Anna's attempts to obtain online help for her suicidal feelings were eclipsed as she browsed online and encountered other content. This highlights the need for online support services that engage younger internet users in a timely way. The wider qualitative study, of which Anna's case is one feature, indicated widespread dissatisfaction with online suicide help and that some young people feel there is a lack of age-appropriate, interactive help and moderated opportunities for peer support (Biddle *et al.* 2020). Our 2019 review of online support services (under preparation) confirms a lack of UK online help provision that is specifically tailored to young people experiencing suicidal crisis, although important advances have been made, such as new text crisis lines like SHOUT (www.giveusashout. org).

Implications for practitioners and directions for further research

Given the extent to which digital technology use is now an inherent part of young people's everyday lives, there is a need to address this during mental health consultations and risk assessment. Practitioner awareness about the role of social media use in young people's lives needs to be improved, and the complexity of their online behaviour should be more comprehensively acknowledged and understood. Practitioners may be well placed to contribute to the safeguarding of young people in a digital world. Promoting digital citizenship and the use of safe chat guidelines, especially around suicide,[1] are immediate examples of where this may be possible. Prescribing endorsed mental health apps, suggesting social media breaks or otherwise incorporating personalized online safety practices into crisis plans constitute other possible responses. However, this does require practitioners to engage in dialogue with young people about their digital lives, and recent studies suggest that training within the clinical context for how to manage concerns about social media and mental health is currently lacking (Hill, Hill and Kim 2019). This should be an area for suicide prevention training to improve practitioner confidence.

Digital technologies are used in many areas of healthcare. In relation to mental health, there already exist a range of apps to facilitate self-assessment and self-monitoring. Health professionals in other medical fields – arthritis and diabetes, for example – now use technological platforms as a means of working more collaboratively with patients in helping to manage illness. 'Telemental health' (telepsychiatry and other psychological services) has been described as 'unquestionably effective' (Hilty *et al.* 2013, p.451), comparing favourably to in-person

---

[1]   For example, see www.orygen.org.au/chatsafe

care and offering a valuable complement to other primary care services. Competence in using resources such as encrypted secure messaging technologies for the purposes of collaborative care could also usefully be improved. Amidst the 2020 Covid-19 pandemic, many practitioners began delivering therapeutic help online, highlighting the valuable potential of digital technology for young people's mental health treatment.

Social media itself is a continually developing phenomenon. There are significant challenges for researchers and practitioners in keeping pace with these changes. Nevertheless, the potential of social media to provide a positive influence on the lives of young people and students today deserves continued investigation.

Acknowledgements

This work was supported in part by the Elizabeth Blackwell Institute for Health Research at the University of Bristol.

Author biographies

Dr Rachel Cohen is a qualitative researcher with experience in evaluating care and treatment pathways in mental health care at Bristol Medical School, University of Bristol. Rachel's additional areas of interest and expertise include media representations of mental illness and forensic mental health service delivery for women.

Dr Lucy Biddle is a qualitative social scientist with a long-standing interest in suicide prevention research at Bristol Medical School, University of Bristol. Lucy has conducted several research projects exploring the impact of the internet and social media on suicidal behaviour and help-seeking.

References

Allen, K.A., Ryan, T., Gray, D.L., McInerney, D.M. and Waters, L. (2014) Social media use and social connectedness in adolescents: the positives and the potential pitfalls. *Australian Journal of Educational and Developmental Psychology 31*, 1, 18–31.

Bainbridge, C. and Yates, C. (eds) (2014) *Media and the Inner World: Psycho-Cultural Approaches to Emotion, Media and Popular Culture*. London: Palgrave Macmillan.

Bauman, Z. (2004) *Identity: Conversations with Benedetto Vecchi*. Cambridge: Polity Press.

Belfort, E., Mezzacappa, E. and Ginnis, K. (2012) Similarities and differences among adolescents who communicate suicidality to others via electronic versus other means: a pilot study. *Adolescent Psychiatry 2*, 3, 258–262.

Biddle, L., Derges, J., Goldsmith, C., Donovan, J. and Gunnell, D. (2018) Using the internet for suicide-related purposes: contrasting findings from young people in the community and self-harm patients admitted to hospital. *PLoS One 13*, 5.

Biddle, L., Derges, J., Goldsmith, C., Donovan, J. and Gunnell, D. (2020) Online help for people with suicidal thoughts provided by charities and healthcare organisations: a qualitative study of users' perceptions. *Social Psychiatry and Psychiatric Epidemiology 55*, 1157–1166.

Bould, H., Mars, B., Moran P., Biddle, L. and Gunnell, D. (2019) Rising suicide rates among adolescents in England and Wales. *The Lancet 394*, 10193, 116–117.

Boyd, A., Golding, J., Macleod, J., Lawler, D.A. *et al.* (2013) Cohort profile: the 'children of the 90s' – the index offspring of the Avon longitudinal study of parents and children. *International Journal of Epidemiology 42*, 111–127.

Chan, M., Li, T.M., Wong, P.W., Chau, M. *et al.* (2017) Engagement of vulnerable youths using internet platforms. *PloS One* 12, 12, e0189023.

Cheng, Q., Kwok, C.L., Zhu, T., Guan, L. and Yip, P.S. (2015) Suicide communication on social media and its psychological mechanisms: an examination of Chinese microblog users. *International Journal of Environmental Research and Public Health 12*, 9, 11506–11527.

Cooney, G. and Morris, J. (2009) Time to start taking an internet history? *The British Journal of Psychiatry 194*, 2, 185.

Daine, K., Hawton, K., Singaravelu, V., Stewart, A., Simkin, S. and Montgomery, P. (2013) The power of the Web: a systematic review of studies of the influence of the internet on self-harm and suicide in young people. *PloS One 8*, 10, e77555.

Das, R. (2019) A field in flux: the intriguing past and the promising future of audience analysis. *Television and New Media 20*, 2, 123–129.

Dervin, F. and Abbas, Y. (2009) Introduction. In Y. Abbas and F. Dervin (eds) *Digital Technologies of the Self*. Cambridge: Cambridge Scholars Publishing.

Donnelly, E. and Kuss, D.J. (2016) Depression among users of social networking sites (SNSs): the role of SNS addiction and increased usage. *Journal of Addiction and Preventative Medicine 1*, 2, 107.

Giddens, A. (1991) *Modernity and Self-Identity: Self and Society in the Late Modern Age*. Cambridge: Polity Press.

Hill, H., Hill, C. and Kim, J.W. (2019) Prospective physician awareness of the associations between social media and mental health. *Academic Psychiatry 44*, 1, 78–81.

Hills, M. (2014) Playing and Pathology: Considering Social Media as 'Secondary Transitional Objects'. In C. Bainbridge and C. Yates (eds) *Media and the Inner World: Psycho-Cultural Approaches to Emotion, Media and Popular Culture*. London: Palgrave Macmillan.

Hilty, D.M., Ferrer, D.C., Parish, M.B., Johnston, B., Callahan, E.J. and Yelowlees, P.M. (2013) The effectiveness of telemental health: a 2013 review. *Telemedicine and e-Health 19*, 6, 444–454.

Hong, F.Y., Huang, D.H., Lin, H.Y. and Chiu, S.L. (2014) Analysis of the psychological traits, Facebook usage and Facebook addiction model of Taiwanese university students. *Telematics and Informatics 31*, 4, 597–606.

Jasso-Medrano, J.L. and Lopez-Rosales, F. (2018) Measuring the relationship between social media use and addictive behaviour and depression and suicide ideation among university students. *Computers in Human Behaviour 87*, 183–191.

Lucassen, M., Samra, R., Iacovides, I., Fleming, T. *et al.* (2018) How LGBT+ young people use the internet in relation to their mental health and envisage the use of e-Therapy: exploratory study. *JMIR Serious Games 6*, 4, October–December.

Luxton, D.D., June, J.D. and Fairall, J.M. (2012) Social media and suicide: a public health perspective. *American Journal of Public Health 102*, 52, S195–S200.

Marchant, A., Hawton, K., Stewart, A., Montgomery, P. *et al.* (2017) A systematic review of the relationship between internet use, self-harm and suicidal behaviour in young people: the good, the bad and the unknown. *PloS One 12*, 8, e0181722.

Mars, B., Heron, J., Biddle, L., Donovan, J. *et al.* (2015) Exposure to, and searching for, information about suicide and self-harm on the internet: prevalence and predictors in a population-based cohort of young adults. *Journal of Affective Disorders 185*, 239–245.

Martin, L.H., Gutman, H. and Hutton, P.H. (eds) (1988) *Technologies of the Self: A Seminar with Michel Foucault*. London: Tavistock.

Moreno, M.A., Jelenchick, L.A. and Breland, D.J. (2015) Exploring depression and problematic internet use among college females: a multisite study. *Computers in Human Behaviour* *49*, 601–607.

Odaci, H. and Kalkan, M. (2010) Problematic internet use, loneliness and dating anxiety among young adult university students. *Computers and Education 55*, 3, 1091–1097.

Ofcom (2015) The Communications Market Report. Accessed on 27/07/20 at: www.ofcom.org. uk/__data/assets/pdf_file/0022/20668/cmr_uk_2015.pdf

Orsal, O., Orsal, O., Unsai, A. and Ozalp, S.S. (2013) Evaluation of internet addiction and depression among university students. *Prodecia-Social and Behavioural Sciences 82*, 445–454.

Robinson, J., Bailey, E., Hetrick, S., Paix, S. *et al.* (2017) Developing social media-based suicide prevention messages in partnership with young people: exploratory study. *JMIR Mental Health 4*, 4, e40.

Sedgwick, R., Epstein, S., Dutta, R. and Ougrin, D. (2019) Social media, internet use and suicide attempts in adolescents. *Current Opinion in Psychiatry 32*, 6, 534–541. https://doi. org/10.1097/YCO.0000000000000547

Silverstone, R. (1994) *Television and Everyday Life*. London and New York: Routledge.

Turkle, S. (2008) Always-on/Always-on-You: The Tethered Self. In J.E. Katz (ed.) *Handbook of Mobile Communication Studies*. Cambridge, MA: MIT Press.

CHAPTER 6

From Suicidal Thoughts to Behaviour

Theoretical Perspectives on Student Suicide

KATIE DHINGRA, PETER J. TAYLOR AND E. DAVID KLONSKY

Overview

This chapter:

- outlines three contemporary theories of suicide that advance our understanding of suicide, and are consistent with the ideation-to-action framework

- identifies risk factors and mechanisms that could be targeted in treatment and prevention efforts

- suggests two key directions for future research.

Introduction

A promising, recent development in suicide theory is the ideation-to-action framework. This framework may help advance our knowledge of suicidal behaviour and help prevent student suicide. This framework stipulates that 1) the development of suicidal ideation and 2) the progression from ideation to suicide attempts are distinct phenomena with distinct explanations and predictors. This chapter provides an outline of three theories positioned within this framework, namely the Interpersonal Theory of Suicide (ITS), the Integrated Motivational–Volitional Model (IMV) and the Three-Step Theory (3ST). The ideation-to-action framework provides a lens through which educators and practitioners can understand suicide in a more precise and nuanced manner and may guide prevention and intervention efforts.

Background

Despite over five decades of research aimed at identifying reliable risk factors for suicide, little progress has been made in the field's ability to predict (Franklin *et al.* 2017) or prevent (Zalsman *et al.* 2016) suicidal behaviour. There are many potential explanations for this lack of progress, including the poor specificity of most risk factors, the low base rate of suicidal behaviour, as well as the fact that risk factors are often assessed in isolation and in a static rather than in a dynamic fashion (Franklin *et al.* 2017). However, inadequate knowledge about the transition from suicide ideation to attempts has been suggested as a key factor (Klonsky and May 2014). The attempter–ideator distinction is critical because although many individuals may consider suicide, most will not act on these thoughts (Nock *et al.* 2008). Moreover, research indicates that the majority of established risk factors (including depression and hopelessness) are actually risk factors for suicide ideation in the total population rather than risk factors for suicide attempts among people with suicidal ideation (Klonsky and May 2014; May and Klonsky 2016). This is an important limitation given that most suicide prevention efforts focus on the prevention of attempts among people with suicidal ideation.

Many students may experience suicidal thoughts and feelings during their time in higher education, but only a minority of these will go on to engage in suicidal behaviour. Whilst all those who struggle with suicidal feelings may benefit from support, higher education institutions (HEIs) will also benefit from considering the specific needs of those students at risk of suicidal behaviour. Thus, improved knowledge about the transition from suicide ideation to attempts is crucial for improved suicide prediction and prevention among students. In this chapter, we describe theories of suicide positioned within the ideation-to-action framework, a framework that addresses this knowledge gap and should be used to guide the next generation of suicide theory, research and prevention (Klonsky, Qiu and Saffer 2017).

Theoretical models of suicidal behaviour are important. They provide a basis for predicting which individuals or groups may be most at risk and can help highlight possible avenues for intervention and prevention (Klonsky 2020). A good theoretical model needs to be supported by the research evidence, but it also needs to have practical value. For student cohorts, for example, a useful model will help indicate which students may be more at risk, at which times (e.g. times of stress or transition), and suggest what kind of intervention may best help these individuals.

A useful model should capture the factors and experiences that are key to understanding suicidal behaviour but should not be so convoluted that it is not accessible to health services.

Below, we describe three recent theories of suicide positioned within the ideation-to-action framework, including: main propositions, conceptual similarities and differences with other ideation-to-action theories, and current empirical evidence of particular relevance to students. We use fictional case studies to illustrate these different models and processes. We then outline some more general treatment and intervention approaches consistent with the ideation-to-action framework, before identifying important knowledge gaps and directions for further research.

The Interpersonal Theory of Suicide (ITS)

The Interpersonal Theory of Suicide (ITS; Joiner 2005; Van Orden *et al.* 2010) states that suicidal ideation emerges when individuals simultaneously experience thwarted belongingness (TB; i.e. feelings of alienation or social isolation from family and other valued groups) and perceived burdensomeness (PB; i.e. the belief that one's life is a burden to family, friends and/or society) and are hopeless (i.e. 'this will never change') about the improvement of these cognitive–affective states. The theory further posits that suicidal behaviour occurs only when suicidal ideation is present within the context of acquired capability (AC) for suicide. The construct of AC was introduced because a desire for death by suicide is viewed as necessary but not sufficient for a potentially lethal suicide attempt to occur. Even among individuals high on suicidal desire, evolutionary grounded survival mechanisms of fear of death and physical pain represent significant barriers to suicide. Therefore, to be capable of dying by suicide, or making a suicide attempt, an individual must have developed fearlessness about death and tolerance for physical pain. The ITS thereby provides a theoretical framework that connects multiple risk factors to more precisely understand suicidal thoughts and behaviours.

Capability for suicide is presumed to be the result of repeated exposure and habituation to physically painful and/or fear-inducing experiences (PPEs; Smith and Cukrowicz 2010; Smith *et al.* 2012). Consequently, individuals who have experienced a higher frequency of PPEs, such as childhood maltreatment, previous suicide attempt, self-starvation and other-directed violence, are expected to possess greater AC. Thus, individuals who have high levels of all three constructs (PB, TB and AC) are said to be at greatest risk for lethal suicidal behaviour, as they possess both the desire for and capability to attempt suicide (see Figure 6.1).

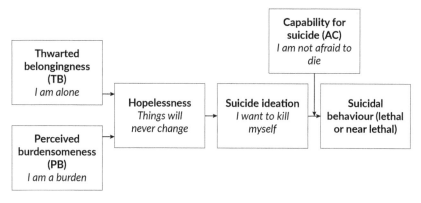

Figure 6.1: Causal pathways to suicidal behaviour from the perspective of the IPT; sample items are presented in italics

The ITS aligns with previous risk factor research (O'Connor and Nock 2014), is relevant to student populations and provides an aetiological perspective that has been largely missing in risk factor research more generally. However, despite considerable empirical support for the key premises underpinning the ITS (for a review, see Chu *et al.* 2017), a systematic review of 66 studies (Ma *et al.* 2016) found limited evidence for the hypothesized three-way interaction between TB, PB and AC for predicting suicide attempts. The authors conclude that there may be other crucial variables that may help to better predict suicide ideation and attempt(s), which are not accounted for in this theory. Therefore, following a case study illustrating the ITS, we describe two additional ideation-to-action theories (Klonsky and May 2014; Klonsky, Saffer and Bryan 2018) that, likewise, portray suicidal desire and capability as independent processes.

CASE STUDY 1

Mark, a first-year sociology student, has been invited to a meeting with his academic advisor after missing several lectures and appearing disengaged in those he had attended. Mark told his advisor how he had been really struggling with the transition to university, feeling he does not really fit in with others on his course, and how he often feels different and isolated. He was also concerned about his initial grades on the programme and feared he would 'mess up' his chance at university. He talked about being a burden on his family who were funding his studies. Mark describes feelings of burdensomeness and thwarted belongingness, which could suggest he is at risk of suicidal thoughts and feelings. It is not clear if Mark has acquired the capability to harm himself, as he has not mentioned any past experiences (e.g. previous self-harm, experiences of violence) that may have led to this capability. Mark's advisor recognizes there is a potential risk here and that Mark is clearly distressed and struggling and so discusses a referral to the student counselling service.

The Integrated Motivational–Volitional Model (IMV)

The IMV, first articulated in 2011 (O'Connor 2011) and refined in 2018 (O'Connor and Kirtley 2018), uses a similar structure to the ITS. First, the motivational phase of the model addresses the development of suicide ideation. Specifically, diverse life events and circumstances can lead to feelings of defeat/humiliation (i.e. a perception of failed struggle and powerlessness resulting from the loss or significant disruption of social status, identity or hierarchical goals), which in the context of certain moderators (e.g. ruminative cognitions, poor problem solving and attribution biases) lead to feelings of entrapment. Entrapment can be internal (i.e. perceptions of being trapped by one's own thoughts or feelings) or external (i.e. perceptions of being trapped by events or experiences in the outside world) in nature. In turn, in the context of other moderators (e.g. TB, PB and impaired positive future thinking), entrapment can lead one to view suicide as a salient solution to life circumstances, and result in suicidal ideation and intent. Second, the volitional phase addresses the transition from thinking about suicide to attempting/dying by suicide. In the context of moderators such as Joiner's concept of AC, impulsivity, planning, exposure to the suicidal acts of others, access to means, past suicidal behaviour and mental imagery about death, suicidal ideation progresses to suicidal behaviour in the form of a suicide attempt.

The IMV is similar to the ITS in three ways: 1) its ideation-to-action structure, 2) the incorporation of TB and PB into the motivational phase, and 3) its incorporation of AC into the volitional phase. At the same time, the IMV diverges from the ITS in at least two key ways: 1) the featured pathways to suicidal ideation are defeat and entrapment, not TB and PB, and 2) the volitional phase of the IMV expands beyond AC to include factors such as impulsivity, access to lethal means, intention/planning and imitation (e.g. social contagion/modelling), thus accounting for a more complex relationship between suicidal ideation and the transition to a suicide attempt.

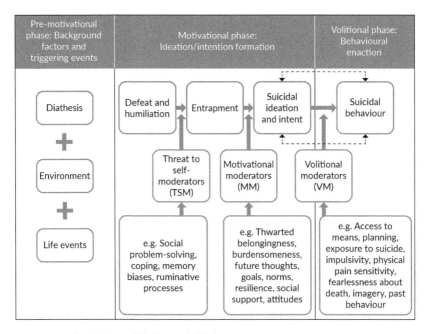

Figure 6.2: The IMV model of suicidal behaviour

Several studies have tested the main facets of the IMV model, providing promising evidence (for a review, see Wetherall *et al.* 2020). Dhingra, Boduszek and O'Connor (2015) found support for the IMV in a large sample of university students. In particular, they found that those who reported suicidal ideation did not differ in motivational phase variables (e.g. TB, PB, depression) from individuals who had attempted suicide in multivariate analyses, but they did differ on volitional phase variables (e.g. self-harm exposure, fearlessness about death, impulsivity), as per the IMV model. Similar results were obtained in a larger sample of UK-based university students, though impulsivity did not predict suicide attempts (Dhingra, Boduszek and O'Connor 2016). Additionally, in a population-based birth cohort of adolescents, exposure to the self-harm of others (alongside psychiatric disorder) was key to differentiating between adolescents who had made a suicide attempt compared to those who had thought about but not attempted suicide (Mars *et al.* 2019). Finally, in a large, nationally representative sample of young people (18–34 years), only volitional phase variables differentiated between those with a history of suicidal ideation and those who had reported a suicide attempt. The suicide attempt group reported higher levels of trait impulsivity (i.e. a tendency to display behaviour characterized by little or no forethought, reflection or consideration of the consequences), AC and mental imagery about death, and they were more likely to have been exposed to the suicide attempt of a friend (Weatherall *et al.* 2018).

In summary, growing empirical evidence is consistent with the IMV's proposition that both defeat and entrapment relate robustly to suicidal ideation, and that a set of volitional variables broader than AC help to distinguish people who make suicide attempts from people with suicidal ideation. However, as is common in suicide research more generally, there is a dearth of longitudinal studies testing the proposed temporal pathway from defeat and humiliation to entrapment, then progressing onwards to suicidal ideation. Consequently, further research is required. The IMV encompasses a large number of variables, recognizing the complexity of suicidal behaviour. This may present a challenge, however, in trying to translate the model into clinical practice. Moreover, whilst the model outlines how suicidal behaviour may initially occur, it provides less clarity about how this risk is maintained over time (e.g. for students who have already attempted suicide).

CASE STUDY 2

Sarah was known to the university counselling service, with whom she had regular contact. Prior to university, she had attempted to end her life, and she had struggled throughout her life with periods of low mood and recurrent suicidal thoughts. During her second year at university, she shared with her counsellor that her history of mental health difficulties left her feeling like she was not as good as her housemates and peers, because she was not able to do the things they found so easy, and that she had 'failed'. Sarah often ruminated over these feelings and had started to feel trapped ('I will always be different or broken'). The counsellor recognized that these feelings of defeat and entrapment could fuel a recurrence of suicidal feelings for Sarah. Given Sarah's prior experiences of suicidal behaviour, the counsellor is concerned that such feelings could lead to further suicidal behaviour. The counsellor focuses on moderators that may help reduce suicidal feelings including focusing on positive future goals, helping Sarah to reappraise her circumstances, and using cognitive techniques to counter the rumination Sarah experiences. They also develop a safety plan around what Sarah can do if feeling suicidal.

The Three-Step Theory (3ST)

The Three-Step Theory (3ST) is the most recently published idea-tion-to-action theory of suicide (Klonsky and May 2015; see Figure 6.3). Step 1 suggests that the combination of pain (whether it be physical or psychological – e.g. interpersonal conflict and loss, chronic medical pain) and hopelessness is what brings about suicidal ideation. The 3ST posits that when life is aversive/painful, one begins to desire to avoid life. However, if one has hope that the pain can be diminished with time and/or effort, one's focus will be on achieving a better future rather than suicide. Therefore, pain and hopelessness in combination are required to develop and sustain suicidal ideation.

Step 2 of the 3ST suggests that suicide ideation escalates from modest/passive (e.g. 'I have no wish to be alive') to strong/active (e.g. 'I would kill myself if I could') when pain exceeds or overwhelms connectedness. Connectedness can refer not only to connections with other people, but also to a valued job, project, role, interest or any sense of perceived purpose or meaning that keeps one invested in living. It is important to note that the 3ST's emphasis on pain, hopelessness and connectedness does not suggest that other traditional risk factors for suicidal ideation are irrelevant. Instead, as Klonsky and May (2015) argue, 'they are relevant in a specific way, through their effects on pain, hopelessness, and/or connectedness' (p.118).

Step 3 suggests that strong/active suicidal ideation progresses to action when one has the capacity to attempt suicide. Capacity, according to the 3ST, comprises acquired, dispositional and practical components. The acquired component mirrors the ITS description of capability. The dispositional component involves innate biological and genetic characteristics (e.g. predisposition to violence, disinhibition, sensation seeking) that enable suicide attempts. In other words, 'capability may not function as an *outcome*...but rather may function as a *vulnerability*...that increase[s] the likelihood of developing or manifesting other risk factors for suicide' (Bryan, Sinclair and Heron 2016, p.383, emphasis in original). This indicates that some individuals may be more inherently capable of suicide than others (Smith *et al.* 2012). Finally, the practical component refers to knowledge of, expertise in and access to lethal means (i.e. the logistical components that facilitate the transition from ideation to action; Klonsky and May 2015). Not only is access to lethal means required for a suicide attempt to occur, but knowledge and expertise can help someone feel less fearful that the attempt would result in unanticipated pain or injury.

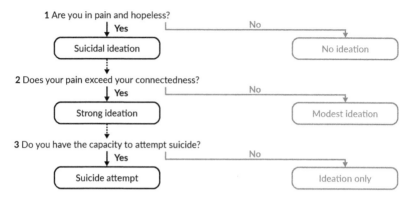

Figure 6.3: The three-step theory of suicide (Klonsky and May 2015)

The 3ST shares two key features with the ITS: 1) a role for connectedness (belongingness in the ITS) in the development of suicidal ideation, and 2) a role for AC in the progression from suicidal thoughts to behaviour. However, the 3ST differs from the ITS in two important ways (at least): 1) the featured pathways to suicidal ideation are pain and hopelessness, not TB and PB, and 2) the 3ST extends the concept of capability for suicide beyond AC to include dispositional and practical contributors. In terms of featured pathways, from the perspective of the 3ST, PB and TB can cause the pain and hopelessness that leads to the emergence of suicidal ideation, but neither is necessary for two reasons: 1) causes of pain and hopelessness exist beyond PB and TB, and 2) PB and TB can be experienced without suicidal ideation developing. Instead, the 3ST emphasizes connectedness for its protective role among those with pain and hopelessness, and emphasizes that diverse forms of pain and hopelessness have similar associations with increased suicidal ideation. In terms of capability, the 3ST is more similar to the IMV, which incorporates factors beyond AC (e.g. access to means) to explain the progression from ideation to action. However, common across each of these theories is an emphasis on the fact that thoughts of suicide are only one component of risk and, on their own, are unlikely to result in a suicide attempt.

Since the 3ST was published in 2015, research has only begun to directly evaluate it. The study introducing the 3ST (Klonsky and May 2015) provided supporting data from a large US-based online adult sample gathered through Amazon's Mechanical Turk (MTurk) online worker programme. Specifically, consistent with step 1, pain and hopelessness interacted to robustly predict suicidal ideation and better so than PB and TB. Consistent with step 2, connectedness, as well as the extent to which connectedness exceeded pain, predicted increased suicidal idea-tion among those high in pain and hopelessness. Finally, and consistent with step 3, dispositional, acquired and practical contributors to suicide capacity each predicted suicide attempt history over and above suicidal ideation. A UK-based study of university students largely replicated these findings (Dhingra, Klonsky and Tapola 2019), as did a large study of Chinese undergraduates, except that only practical capability was linked to suicide attempts (Yang *et al.* 2019).

Other studies of 3ST constructs provide additional empirical support. For example, converging evidence from both adolescent and adult samples have found that pain and hopelessness motivate suicide attempts more than other factors such as TB, PB and help-seeking (May and Klonsky 2013; May, Pachkowski and Klonsky 2020; May *et al.* 2016). Thus, accumulating research supports the 3ST's emphasis on pain and hopelessness rather than other factors in the development of suicidal desire and motivation.

Similar to the ITS, the 3ST has been subject to claims that a parsimo-nious theory is inappropriate for explaining a highly complex and con-textual phenomenon like suicide (Hjelmeland and Knizek 2019; Nock, Ramirez and Rankin 2019). However, as argued by Klonsky (2020), even if parsimonious theories are unable to predict the next suicide death, they can lead us to better consider the potential causes of suicide as well as more effectively informing how we might improve prevention efforts – at both individual and population levels – and save lives (e.g. Anestis *et al.* 2017). In fact, numerous useful theories in psychology (e.g. behaviourism) and other areas of science (e.g. laws of motion) have strong validity and utility, yet struggle with real-world prediction (Klonsky 2020). Moreover, neither the ITS nor the 3ST place constraints on the specific factors that may influence the central theorized processes. Countless and diverse psychosocial, biological, environmental, economic and cultural variables can be relevant – the theory simply postulates the pathways through which they are relevant. As with the other two theories reviewed, lon-gitudinal supporting research is lacking. Consequently, further research is required to test the specific mechanisms implied in the model.

CASE STUDY 3

Marek, a postgraduate student, arrives at a meeting with his advisor in an ex-treme state of distress. Marek explains how his father recently died. Marek is overwhelmed with feelings of loss. He currently lives alone, away from family, and is feeling very isolated, rarely seeing people outside of those he works with. He has also been struggling to focus on or motivate himself to engage in his studies and is starting to feel hopeless about his chances of completing his degree. Marek has a history of self-harm, and his advisor is therefore concerned about Marek and the possibility of further harm. They discuss signposting and referrals that may help provide Marek with support. They also talk about how Marek may be able to feel more connected with others, including groups for postgraduate students that Marek could get involved in.

Conclusions and general practical recommendations

Notions of suicide prediction and risk assessment are problematic, because predicting low base-rate phenomena such as suicide with reliability is not possible (Franklin *et al.* 2017). In other words, because suicide deaths occur so infrequently, a practitioner would actually be correct much more often if they predicted that an individual would not attempt suicide regardless of clinical presentation. Consequently, a more appropriate focus of attention is on recognizing when an individual has entered into a heightened state of risk (i.e. by observing alterations in dynamic factors identified in the reviewed theories) and appropriately responding. Such distress recognition requires an assessment of each individual's specific situation and needs. More precisely, based on the ideation-to-action theories, there are a number of areas that would be useful focuses in clinical assessment. These areas include: an identifiable precipitant or stressors; the presence of hopelessness; a sense of connection waxing and waning; the nature of their suicide ideation (i.e. modest vs strong); and their capability (acquired, practical and dispositional) for suicide.

In terms of treatment, cognitive therapy techniques (e.g. cognitive-behavioural therapy [CBT]) may be used to help individuals identify and restructure maladaptive cognitions that underlie perceptions of isolation or burden, and to build meaningful social connections (e.g. Stangier *et al.* 2011). Alternatively, interpersonal therapy (ITS), which focuses on improving the interpersonal relationship quality, may serve to decrease feelings of TB and PB (e.g. Tang *et al.* 2009). Dialectical behaviour therapy (DBT) also offers a variety of skills for regulating negative emotions, responding to negative thoughts, and improving interpersonal relationships (Miller, Rathus and Linehan 2006). Such therapies could also help students to address the challenges associated with emerging adulthood, such as increased autonomy from parents (e.g. leaving the home), exam/assessment stress, marked shifts in social roles, and relational instability (Sussman and Arnett 2014), all of which may lead to distress.

At an HEI level, academic advisors could be more mindful of whether students seem to feel trapped or defeated, and signpost to relevant support services, if appropriate. It should, however, be noted that the use of constructs drawn from the ideation-to-action theories outlined in this chapter as the *sole* indicators of possible suicidality is not currently supported by empirical data. This is because suicide likely culminates due to the influence of hundreds of risk factors (O'Connor and Nock 2014). However, the reduction of pain, hopelessness and disconnection may reduce desire for suicide, and the reduction of capability (e.g. safety plan, safe storage of firearms and prescription medication) can reduce the likelihood of suicide attempts. For example, practitioners should explicitly address the degree to which individuals are currently experiencing feelings of pain (physical and/or psychological) and hopelessness, as well as the degree to which they feel connected to life (i.e. to family, friends, community, work, hobbies) and have capability (practical, acquired, dispositional) for lethal self-injury. Prevention approaches that address connectedness and contribution (e.g. extra-curricular activities), in particular, should be considered in educational settings (Whitlock, Wyman and Barreira 2012).

Theories positioned within the ideation-to-action framework have meaningfully advanced our understanding of suicide. In particular, accumulating evidence suggests that pain, hopelessness and related variables motivate suicidal desire, whereas capability for suicide helps differentiate attempters from ideators. While there are multiple opportunities for additional advancement, we conclude with two key future directions. First, longitudinal studies over various time frames (minutes, hours, days, weeks, months) are necessary to further evaluate and elaborate ideation-to-action theories of suicide. In particular, research is needed to identify which variables (e.g. TB, PB, defeat, entrapment, pain, hopelessness) from these theories more strongly predict or motivate current suicidal desire. Second, interventionist–causal approaches are needed that could evaluate interventions derived from these models, and in doing so, test out the putative mechanisms believed to contribute to suicidal behaviour.

Author biographies

Dr Katie Dhingra is a Reader in Psychology at Leeds Beckett University, UK. Her research examines why people behave in ways that are harmful to themselves, with an emphasis on suicide and non-suicidal self-injury.

Dr Peter J. Taylor is a senior clinical lecturer in psychology, and clinical psychologist, at the University of Manchester, UK. His research focuses on the psychosocial mechanisms underlying suicide and self-harm.

Dr E. David Klonsky is a professor of psychology at the University of British Columbia, Canada. His research examines suicide, including the pursuit of parsimonious models of suicide and better understanding of suicide motivations and warning signs.

References

Anestis, M., Law, K., Jin, H., Houtsma, C., Khazem, L. and Assavedo, B. (2017) Treating the capability for suicide: a vital and understudied frontier in suicide prevention. *Suicide and Life-Threatening Behavior 47*, 5, 523–537.

Bryan, C., Sinclair, S. and Heron, E. (2016) Do military personnel 'acquire' the capability for suicide from combat? A test of the interpersonal-psychological theory of suicide. *Clinical Psychological Science 4*, 3, 376–385.

Chu, C., Buchmann-Schmitt, J., Stanley, I., Hom, M. *et al.* (2017) The interpersonal theory of suicide: a systematic review and meta-analysis of a decade of cross-national research. *Psychological Bulletin 143*, 12, 1313–1345.

Dhingra, K., Boduszek, D. and O'Connor, R. (2015) Differentiating suicide attempters from suicide ideators using the Integrated Motivational–Volitional model of suicidal behaviour. *Journal of Affective Disorders 186*, 211–218.

Dhingra, K., Boduszek, D. and O'Connor, R. (2016) A structural test of the Integrated Motivational–Volitional model of suicidal behaviour. *Psychiatry Research 239*, 169–178.

Dhingra, K., Klonsky, E. and Tapola, V. (2019) An empirical test of the Three-Step Theory of suicide in UK university students. *Suicide and Life-Threatening Behavior 49*, 2, 478–487.

Franklin, J., Ribeiro, J., Fox, K. and Bentley, K. *et al.* (2017) Risk factors for suicidal thoughts and behaviors: a meta-analysis of 50 years of research. *Psychological Bulletin 143*, 2, 187–232.

Hjelmeland, H. and Knizek, B. (2019) Epistemological differences in the discussion of the interpersonal theory of suicide: a reply to the response. *Death Studies 45*, 2, 163–165.

Joiner, T. (2005) *Why People Die by Suicide*. Cambridge, MA: Harvard University Press.

Klonsky, E. (2020) The role of theory for understanding and preventing suicide (but not predicting it): a commentary on Hjelmeland and Knizek. *Death Studies 44*, 459–462.

Klonsky, E. and May, A. (2014) Differentiating suicide attempters from suicide ideators: a critical frontier for suicidology research. *Suicide and Life-Threatening Behavior 44*, 1, 1–5.

Klonsky, E. and May, A. (2015) The three-step theory (3ST): a new theory of suicide rooted in the 'ideation-to-action' framework. *International Journal of Cognitive Therapy 8*, 2, 114–129.

Klonsky, E., Qiu, T. and Saffer, B. (2017) Recent advances in differentiating suicide attempters from suicide ideators. *Current Opinion in Psychiatry 30*, 1, 15–20.

Klonsky, E., Saffer, B. and Bryan, C. (2018) Ideation-to-action theories of suicide: a conceptual and empirical update. *Current Opinion in Psychology 22*, 38–43.

Ma, J., Batterham, P., Calear, A. and Han, J. (2016) A systematic review of the predictions of the Interpersonal–Psychological Theory of Suicidal Behavior. *Clinical Psychology Review 46*, 34–45.

Mars, B., Heron, J., Klonsky, E.D., Moran, P. *et al.* (2019) What distinguishes adolescents with suicidal thoughts from those who have attempted suicide? A population-based birth cohort study. *Journal of Child Psychology and Psychiatry 60*, 1, 91–99.

May, A. and Klonsky, E. (2013) Assessing motivations for suicide attempts: development and psychometric properties of the inventory of motivations for suicide attempts. *Suicide and Life-Threatening Behavior 43*, 5, 532–546.

May, A. and Klonsky, E. (2016) What distinguishes suicide attempters from suicide ideators? A meta-analysis of potential factors. *Clinical Psychology: Science and Practice 23*, 1, 5–20.

May, A., O'Brien, K., Liu, R. and Klonsky, E. (2016) Descriptive and psychometric properties of the inventory of motivations for suicide attempts (IMSA) in an inpatient adolescent sample. *Archives of Suicide Research 20*, 3, 476–482.

May, A., Pachkowski, M. and Klonsky, E. (2020) Motivations for suicide: converging evidence from clinical and community samples. *Journal of Psychiatric Research 123*, 171–177.

Miller, A., Rathus, J. and Linehan, M. (2006) *Dialectical Behavior Therapy with Suicidal Adolescents*. New York: Guilford Press.

Nock, M., Borges, G., Bromet, E., Alonso, J. *et al.* (2008) Cross-national prevalence and risk factors for suicidal ideation, plans and attempts. *The British Journal of Psychiatry 192*, 2, 98–105.

Nock, M., Ramirez, F. and Rankin, O. (2019) Advancing our understanding of the who, when, and why of suicide risk. *JAMA Psychiatry 76*, 1, 11–12.

O'Connor, R. (2011) Towards an Integrated Motivational–Volitional Model of Suicidal Behaviour. In R.C. O'Connor, S. Platt and J. Gordon (eds) *International Handbook of Suicide Prevention: Research, Policy and Practice*. Chichester: Wiley Blackwell. pp.181–198.

O'Connor, R. and Kirtley, O. (2018) The integrated motivational–volitional model of suicidal behaviour. *Philosophical Transactions of the Royal Society B: Biological Sciences 373*, 1754, 20170268.

O'Connor, R. and Nock, M. (2014) The psychology of suicidal behaviour. *The Lancet Psychiatry 1*, 1, 73–85.

Smith, A., Ribeiro, J., Mikolajewski, A., Taylor, J. *et al.* (2012) An examination of environmental and genetic contributions to the determinants of suicidal behavior among male twins. *Psychiatry Research 197*, 1–2, 60–65.

Smith, P. and Cukrowicz, K. (2010) Capable of suicide: a functional model of the acquired capability component of the interpersonal-psychological theory of suicide. *Suicide and Life-Threatening Behavior 40*, 3, 266–275.

Stangier, U., Schramm, E., Heidenreich, T., Berger, M. and Clark, D. (2011) Cognitive therapy vs. interpersonal psychotherapy in social anxiety disorder: a randomized controlled trial. *Archives of General Psychiatry 68*, 692–700.

Sussman, S. and Arnett, J. (2014) Emerging adulthood: developmental period facilitative of the addictions. *Evaluation & The Health Professions 37*, 2, 147–155.

Tang, T., Jou, S., Ko, C., Huang, S. and Yen, C. (2009) Randomized study of school-based intensive interpersonal psychotherapy for depressed adolescents with suicidal risk and parasuicide behaviors. *Psychiatry and Clinical Neurosciences 63*, 4, 463–470.

Van Orden, K., Witte, T., Cukrowicz, K., Braithwaite, S., Selby, E. and Joiner, T. (2010) The interpersonal theory of suicide. *Psychological Review 117*, 2, 575–600.

Wetherall, K., Cleare, S., Zortea, T. and O'Connor, R. (2020) Status of the Integrated Motivational–Volitional Model of Suicidal Behaviour. In D. De Leo and V. Poštuvan (eds) *Reducing the Toll of Suicide: Resources for Communities, Groups, and Individuals*. Boston, MA: Hogrefe. pp.169–184.

Whitlock, J., Wyman, P. and Barreira, P. (2012) *Connectedness and Suicide Prevention in College Settings: Directions and Implications for Practice*. Ithaca, NY: Brofenbrenner Center for Translational Research, Cornell University.

Yang, L., Liu, X., Chen, W. and Li, L. (2019) A test of the three-step theory of suicide among Chinese people: a study based on the ideation-to-action framework. *Archives of Suicide Research 23*, 4, 648–661.

Zalsman, G., Hawton, K., Wasserman, D., van Heeringen, K. *et al.* (2016) Suicide prevention strategies revisited: 10-year systematic review. *The Lancet Psychiatry 3*, 7, 646–659.

CHAPTER 7

Transitions and Student Suicide

The Role of Higher and Further Education Sectors

KATIE RIGG AND ELLEN MAHONEY

Overview

This chapter explores key research in the areas of transitions and suicide prevention in higher education (HE) and further education (FE), and provides an overview of guidance and available resources. The objectives of this chapter are to help HE and FE professionals to:

- learn how to apply findings from key research to support student transitions

- strengthen transition programmes to better support student wellbeing during periods of change

- develop a whole-institution approach to wellbeing.

Introduction

Transitions and suicide prevention have each emerged as areas of focus for student support services in recent years. Although limited in number, studies that look at the link between these two phenomena provide important insights into how the experiences of transition have served as contexts to some suicides. The ways that schools, higher education institutions (HEIs) and further education institutions (FEIs) support students through transition periods can have a significant impact on student mental health and may help to prevent future suicides.

The research

Transitions

Studying at an HEI or FEI can be a wonderful time for students as they acquire new knowledge, meet new people, learn about themselves and form lasting friendships. It can also be layered with difficulties as students leave one life behind and begin another. This transition is set against the backdrop of transitioning to adulthood, as young people explore their own identities and think about who they want to be as adults (Macaskill 2012). Young people also undergo a series of transitions during their time at their HEI or FEI. These might include transitions into private accommodation, towards financial independence, away from structured learning and working towards the transition into employment (Harris 2019; Macaskill 2012).

Student mental health and suicide

Students are a high-risk group for mental health difficulties based on their age, with 15 to 24 years being the peak period for the onset of mental disorders (Harris 2019; Stanley *et al.* 2009). International research also suggests that the mental health of young people has deteriorated over recent decades, with levels of distress, anxiety and depression on the rise (Collishaw *et al.* 2010; Thorley 2017). Against this backdrop, suicide has become the second leading cause of death for university-aged students (Rosiek *et al.* 2016).

The link between transitions and suicide

Literature on suicide and educational transitions, albeit limited, provides us with important insights. Key research includes a ten-year study of suicides on HEI campuses in the United States (US) and a RaPSS report of 20 students who died by suicide (Silverman *et al.* 1997; Stanley *et al.* 2009). These studies suggest that some risk factors in student suicides mirror those in the general population (Stanley *et al.* 2009). Others, however, take on a specific form in the student population. Transitions are key amongst these and can, if not managed well, increase a young person's risk of experiencing depression, anxiety and suicidal ideation (Zarb 2010).

Studies point out that university is often the first time that students live away from home and are expected to look after their own basic needs, and that alcohol and peer pressure can sometimes make other transition stresses harder to bear (Harris 2019; Macaskill 2012; Student

Minds 2014). They also point to the financial stress and significant pressure that many students are under, to succeed academically while living up to the narrative of university being a time of intense enjoyment.

> you are told that university is the time of your life and these are the friendships you'll hold onto forever... When that doesn't happen, it is very difficult to say actually, 'I've got a problem here' particularly when you are 18. (Young person, Universities UK and PAPYRUS 2018, p.8)

Studies also highlight strong links between extreme fear of failure and suicide:

> His worst thing was failure, he hated failure, and I suppose failing first year at uni[versity] was obviously a massive trigger. (Young person, Stanley *et al.* 2009, p.426)

The RaPSS study showed that the stresses HEI students experienced were clustered in transitional periods in the academic year, with 15 out of the 20 deaths examined occurring either at the beginning or at the end of the academic year. The authors reflected that the sense of being 'in between' may be heightened during these periods, when students might naturally contemplate future demands and pressures more than they would during the year, whilst also being deprived of sources of support (Stanley *et al.* 2009). A parent contemplated her son's suicide before the start of his second year at his HEI:

> I think probably he was coming out of depression and didn't want to go back into the state he'd been in...you know it was obviously bad for him...so it was my guess that it was the confusion and...the rest of it and not being able perhaps to see the way forward. (Parent, Stanley *et al.* 2009, p.427)

These findings are consistent with figures from Japan, where more students die by suicide on 1 September, their first day back to school after the holidays, than any other day of the year (Stega 2017).

How can schools, HEIs and FEIs support students?

Drawing on research findings and the authors' professional experiences, here are six ways that schools, HEIs and FEIs can support students through transition periods.

1. Building students' resilience from an early stage – school practices

> many of them [the students] have been here a very long time and feel very safe and closeted. And suddenly find themselves in a wholly alien environment [in an HEI]. (Teacher, Harris 2019, p.19)

Preparing students well in advance of their move into an HE or FE is important. Schools can do this in a range of ways. In addition to practical issues, it is important for schools to explore social and emotional topics that will help young people to maintain good mental health. These might include, for example, running sessions that explore one's identity and finding a sense of belonging; upholding one's own boundaries against social pressure; identifying and pursuing one's own interests rather than conforming to other people's notions of success; identifying and managing distressing emotions; having realistic expectations about HEs and FEs; managing the losses that can accompany break-ups; learning how to monitor and protect one's own wellbeing; identifying and reporting discrimination and abuse; and seeking help when needed (Stanley *et al.* 2009; Student Minds 2014). Ideally, these sessions should be underpinned by a whole-school approach to wellbeing, which normalizes conversations around mental health and embeds social and emotional literacy and comprehensive sexual education throughout the curriculum (Council of International Schools 2020; Harris 2019).

Studies also look at the critical importance of schools developing students' emotional resilience to perceived failure or adversity and addressing perfectionist tendencies (Wrench, Garrett and King 2013).

> No longer was I thought 'talented' or 'gifted' because I could work for eight hours a day or read an 800-page novel in a day. At [name of HEI] everyone I know could do that. I was no longer special... Inside that bubble, where perfection was the norm, falling short of my own expectations tormented me. (Young person, Macaskill 2012, p.21)

Facilitating opportunities for students to fail safely; working directly with students to overcome struggles, rather than relying on parents to solve issues for their children; and taking students outside their comfort zone and having them experience transitions within the school environment have all been referred to as helpful in building students' resilience to perceived failure (Harris 2019).

the school works with the student directly...that's the resilience building and independence. (Teacher, Harris 2019, p.24)

RESOURCE TIPS

- *Safe Passage* looks at programmes for students moving between international schools, www.dougota.nl/the-book

- **Supporting students in transition from school to university** provides further information and resources, www.cois.org/about-cis/perspectives-blog/blog-post/~board/perspectives-blog/post/student-mental-health-and-well-being-supporting-students-in-transition-from-school-to-university

- The *Know before You Go* toolkit helps students to anticipate, identify and navigate situations they will encounter when entering an HE or FE, www.studentminds.org.uk/knowbeforeyougo.html

2. Implement robust and effective transition programmes and consider how to embed these throughout student life

Student orientation programmes at HEIs and FEIs are critical and commonplace. The existing guidance on how to build these programmes, whilst helpful in supporting students with academic and practical issues, does not always explore in sufficient depth issues related to student mental health. When considering how to strengthen transition programmes, it can be useful to draw on the growing body of evidence on transitions in international schools, which traditionally cater to highly mobile student bodies and have hence built up experience and expertise in this area. This evidence suggests that for transitions support programmes to be successful, they need to be embedded throughout the institution, including in the curriculum, in the admissions process, in pastoral and counselling services, in parent outreach, and in peer support programming and student activities.

Recognizing that responsibility for transitions support cannot lie solely with one person or department, many international schools have developed transitions resource teams consisting of counsellors, tutors, teachers, admissions officers, division leaders, parents and students. It is important that these teams capture the work they are doing so that it can be passed on to new teams when staff move on to other schools. At HEIs and FEIs, this aspect is significant when inviting students to champion this work, as they often will only be able to help for a limited time. The evidence also highlights the need for leaders to be well informed about wellbeing and transition support, so that they can allocate time, training and funding to it. Emphasizing the transitions experience in the hiring process and promoting it in professional learning opportunities are also encouraged. Even though international schools are a valuable resource to learn from, most schools do not evaluate their own programmes. HEIs and FEIs can learn from this by ensuring they design programme evaluation opportunities (Mahoney and Barron 2020).

Orientation programmes that enable students to form social connections and build meaningful relationships are often amongst the most successful and can increase students' sense of belonging (Wrench *et al.* 2013).

> [the course] allowed first year students to make friends which I believe is critical especially for those students who don't know anyone. (Student, Wrench *et al.* 2013, p.736)

Barriers to meaningful connections include large classes, limited access to academic staff, limited time to interact with other students and multiple campuses.

> I have less support and do feel lonely because at school you had everyone every day. (Young person, Macaskill 2012, p.9)

Although the focus of orientation programmes has traditionally been on the first term or the first year, it is important that these programmes also support students through other transitions that they undergo. The transition to second year, for example, can be particularly difficult, with rates of mental ill health at their highest amongst second year students (Macaskill 2012). This transition is when structured support often decreases, students are sometimes required to transition out of halls of residence, student debt may start to become a reality and academic pressures can increase. Orientation programmes should also consider how to ensure availability of support at the beginnings and endings of academic years and, if possible, during holiday periods which, as we have seen, may constitute periods of particular vulnerability (Stanley *et al.* 2009).

RESOURCE TIPS
Guide for Orienting Students to College, https://files.eric.ed.gov/fulltext/ED558878.pdf

Transition into University Guide, www.studentminds.org.uk/transitionintouniversity.html

3. Adopt a whole-university or whole-college approach

Focusing on transition is necessary but not nearly enough, and professionals in this field are increasingly urging institutions to take a whole-institution approach, by which they mean taking a holistic view, involving all members of the community and weaving prevention, identification and response throughout the fabric of the institution (Student Minds 2017). Key to this is creating a culture of care in which students and staff support each other, every person feels able to be their whole selves, and the culture of the institution is such that the experience of working or studying in it enhances people's lives. Education, training and awareness raising are at the core of a whole-institution approach (Universities UK and PAPYRUS 2018).

> Nothing about us without us. (Charlton 2000)

As a first step, HEIs and FEIs should always involve their students in these discussions and co-produce policies and resources with them. This can provide valuable insight into the weaknesses and strengths of an institution's approach and how this can be improved in a way that best meets students' actual needs. Peer support programmes are also seen as increasingly important to support student mental health (Harris 2019).

Adopting a whole-institution approach involves looking at policies related not only to wellbeing but also to issues like leave and mitigating circumstances requests. It requires institutions to look at how they organize tutor systems, what the impact of financial support is on students receiving it, how the curriculum addresses wellbeing, what it does to support staff and volunteers, how its vice-chancellor, principal and trustees lead on issues and how the institution supports social interactions and builds community (Wrench *et al.* 2013). It also requires a review of the academic structure, feedback and requirements. Students consistently highlight the anxiety that can be caused by inconsistencies in requirements across courses, ambiguous marking and feedback, lack of clarity around expectations and lack of opportunities to learn from low marks (Harris 2019; Wrench *et al.* 2013). Students have also highlighted concerns related to study structure and exam timetables (Harris 2019; Student Minds 2014).

A whole-institution approach also requires a commitment to suicide prevention as a critical student safety issue, with institutions reviewing the ways in which they prevent and respond to suicide. Considering how to support a community in the aftermath of a suicide and developing response plans are key and will support ongoing prevention work. It also requires support for staff who support students who are self-harming or suicidal.

RESOURCE TIPS

- **Universities UK's *Stepchange* framework**, www.universitiesuk. ac.uk/policy-and-analysis/reports/Pages/stepchange-mhu.aspx

- **The JED Foundation**, www.jedfoundation.org/what-we-do/ colleges

- **What Works Centre for Wellbeing**, https://whatworkswellbeing. org/category/he-mental-health/#practice

- **Samaritans**, www.samaritans.org/how-we-can-help/schools/ step-step/step-step-resources/creating-response-plan

- ***Co-producing Mental Health Strategies with Students: A Guide for the Higher Education Sector***, www.studentminds.org.uk/ co-productionguide.html

- **Mind** and **Minds@work**, www.mentalhealthatwork.org.uk/ organisation/mind and www.mindsatworkmovement.com

- ***Suicide Safer Universities***, www.universitiesuk.ac.uk/policy-and-analysis/reports/Documents/2018/guidance-for-sector-practitioners-on-preventing-student-suicides.PDF

4. Embed equity, diversity and inclusion throughout your institution

Some groups of students can experience additional mental health challenges throughout their time in education, including during transition periods (Harris 2019). LGBT individuals, for example, are at higher risk of developing mental health disorders, having suicidal ideation and self-harming than their heterosexual peers (Student Minds 2018). We also know that minority groups can be at particular risk of abuse and discrimination, and that students who experience abuse are at higher risk of suicide (Belford 2017; Universities UK and PAPYRUS 2018). Students from cultures in which mental ill health is particularly stigmatized, or which treat authority figures formally, may also be less likely to seek help (Harris 2019).

Within the counselling service, language variables, class and culture-bound values can all inhibit effective cross-cultural counselling. Many students report that having to explain their concerns to counsellors who do not speak their language or who do not understand their life experiences can be draining and a barrier to seeking help (Zarb 2010). This is consistent with research into LGBT students which shows that a major barrier to accessing support at university is feeling misunderstood or judged by support services (Student Minds 2018).

It is only by understanding and welcoming all forms of diversity and adopting the broad lenses of intersectionality, equity, diversity and inclusion that HEIs and FEIs can hope to support their diverse groups of students through transitions. This may require broadening the linguistic and ethnic make-up of staff, practising cultural humility when working with diverse groups, reviewing disciplinary policies that often disproportionately impact black students, and close collaboration and consultation with the groups of students whose voices have traditionally been marginalized (Zarb 2010).

RESOURCE TIPS

- **The MGH Center for Cross-Cultural Student Emotional Wellness** produces publications and articles on how to promote good mental health amongst international students, www.mghstudentwellness.org/resources

- The **Council of International Schools** supports research, produces articles and hosts workshops aimed at promoting whole-institution approaches to mental health and building equity, diversity and inclusion in schools, HEIs and FEIs, www.cois.org

5. Provide opportunities for students to seek help at an early stage and strengthen your systems so that you can identify students in need of support

In a caring and compassionate organisation, you are not only ill once you have filled out a form. (Anonymous, Universities UK 2019)

Many HEIs and FEIs provide excellent support to students who are proactive in seeking help. However, the majority of students with mental health difficulties do not seek help and two out of three students who die by suicide are not previously known to the HEI or FEI mental health services (Macaskill 2012; Universities UK and PAPYRUS 2018). This is particularly important when looking at periods of transition into, throughout and beyond HE and FE, as these can naturally create gaps through which students can fall.

> it's good that [support is] anonymous; if I had a problem I wouldn't want to go to a teacher, because they knew who I am, they would treat me as if I'm special and need help forever. (Student, Harris 2019, p.22)

Stigma is the primary reason for students not accessing support, and fears about being seen as weak, struggling or unsuccessful lead students to hide how they are feeling. Fears about their peers finding out are particularly prevalent amongst first-year students who may not yet have formed a solid friendship group (Harris 2019). Other barriers to seeking help include lack of awareness of the relevant sources of help, difficulty navigating support systems and perceptions of support systems as inaccessible, unresponsive or ineffective (Harris 2019; Stanley *et al.* 2009; Student Minds 2014).

Efforts to address these barriers include building trusting relationships between staff and students, putting in place visible, accessible and culturally relevant support services and helplines, offering multiple avenues for disclosure, using peer support programmes and continuing to work to remove the stigma around mental health (Harris 2019). Strengthening the pastoral role of advisors can also help to improve reporting rates. Students and staff alike have reported that having at least one trusted person to support a student, a single point of call, is needed to make a successful transition (Council of International Schools 2020; Harris 2019; Student Minds 2014).

> not being successful makes me feel low and ready to quit and not having the assurance of any 'teacher like' figure. Everyone expecting something different. (Student, Wrench *et al.* 2013, p.735)

Reviewing the institution's core values and how these are communicated to students and staff is also key. For example, does the institution encourage young people to aspire to perfection, set unrealistic goals and/or imply that an individual's value is wholly linked to their academic and professional achievements? Given the societal context in which we live, it can be easy to promote these messages without realizing it, but these messages can make it harder for young people to seek help and admit that they are struggling (NUS 2017). They can also make it much more difficult for young people to manage disappointment when they do not obtain the goals set for them. On the other hand, organizations that prioritize and place value on individual wellbeing and the quality of relationships can foster protective relationships where students feel comfortable seeking help.

We also need to look at how HEIs and FEIs can identify students who are not able to seek help or refer themselves to student services.

> I don't think the universities are the best at identifying someone who is struggling, because of the nature of what they do – professors are experts in a certain area, rather than the pastoral side. (Teacher, Harris 2019, p.18)

Some students describe feeling worse after telling a staff member about their mental health problems. Other students expressed concerns that their tutors dealt with mental health issues as disciplinary issues (NUS 2017). Training for all student-facing staff on spotting signs of mental ill health across cultures is critical. Staff feel confident identifying students who may be struggling, asking them if they would like support, and referring them to wellbeing and counselling services. Training for academic staff on suicide awareness, handling disclosures of mental ill health and protecting their own wellbeing are also encouraged (Yap 2019).

An institution's policy and practice on information sharing, disclosure and consent are all important. Having in place clear and centralized reporting lines and recording systems that enable concerns to be triangulated and patterns to be spotted at an early stage is key (Universities UK and PAPYRUS 2018). As HEIs and FEIs have to manage large quantities of data, this can be challenging. New developments in learning analytics have the potential to change the way that these institutions record and analyse wellbeing data, and a number of HEIs are working to put in place alert systems to detect patterns of difficulty, such as not engaging with academic work, not paying rent, fees or fines, disciplinary issues, or not engaging with other students or staff (Universities UK and PAPYRUS 2018). Holding meetings with staff from different areas of the institution to talk about students who are struggling is another important way of triangulating information. Student focus groups and wellbeing surveys can also provide valuable insight, as can social events that enable staff to identify students who might be struggling.

RESOURCE TIPS

Peer Support for Student Mental Health, www.studentminds.org.uk/ uploads/3/7/8/4/3784584/peer_support_for_student_mental_health.pdf

Digital Leaders Programme, https://digital-leaders.childnet.com

The Charlie Waller Memorial Trust, https://charliewaller.org/ what-we-do/for-educators

Early Alerts as a Tool for Student Success, www.ellucian.com/assets/en/ white-paper/whitepaper-early-alerts-tool-student-success.pdf

Student Wellbeing and Mental Health: The Opportunities in Learning Analytics, http://repository.jisc.ac.uk/6916/1/student-wellbeing-and-mental-health-the-opportunities-in-learning-analytics.pdf

Self-harm and suicide prevention frameworks, www.hee.nhs.uk/ our-work/mental-health/self-harm-suicide-prevention-frameworks

6. Strengthen connections between schools, HEIs and FEIs

The more that schools, HEIs and FEIs collaborate to address student well-being, the easier the transition will be for students. Discussions around this topic are too frequently limited either to *just* schools or to *just* HEIs or FEIs. Including all groups can build connections, improve understanding of each other, generate new ideas and strengthen information sharing. For example, when a school needs to share information about a vulnerable student with an HEI, they often don't know who at the HEI they should share that information with, or how it will be stored or used.

Greater cooperation between schools, FE and HE will also help schools to prepare students and encourage those with mental health needs to seek help from their HEI or FEI at an early stage. Providing opportunities for FE and HE staff to get to know students before they arrive on campus can also help them to identify mental health challenges early on and can increase the student's sense of belonging. Current disclosure rates are low with only 37 per cent of students in the UK disclosing or intending to disclose mental health conditions to their chosen university (Thorley 2017). Explaining clearly to students what the benefits are of disclosing and how that information is going to be shared will help to increase these rates.

> with our FE students we have an idea of who's coming through the door...we have an idea of their support needs and can get everything in

place before they arrive, but with HE because of the way UCAS works, we don't have an awful amount of information about their mental health needs...it's difficult to get that information unless the student is disclosing it...where can they disclose it confidentially? There isn't really anywhere. (Head of Wellbeing at a college, Harris 2019, p.26)

The UCAS application form allows students to disclose mental health conditions under the disability section, although young people may not self-identify as having a disability and may be cautious to disclose it in this way. UCAS is currently reviewing this question in partnership with young people, with a view to making it easier for students to share mental health concerns or support needs with their chosen university (Harris 2019).

There is also a lack of clarity about whether schools can share information about a student's support needs and safeguarding concerns with HEIs (Heycock 2017). A wellbeing manager, in one study, explained how she wished that schools would share more information with her on their students' needs, including their safeguarding file (where there is one), as this would help her to support the young person, and would prevent the young person from having to repeat any upsetting past experiences (Harris 2019). This is a complex area involving legal issues and more guidance is needed.

RESOURCE TIPS

Freshers: from vulnerable children to adults at risk? What schools and universities need to know about the transfer of safeguarding information between institutions, www.farrer.co.uk/news-and-insights/ freshers-from-vulnerable-children-to-adults-at-risk-what-schools-and-universities-need-to-know-about-the-transfer-of-safeguarding-information-between-institutions

Supporting students through the transition from school to university, www.universitiesuk.ac.uk/blog/Pages/schoolchild-to-student-supporting-transition.aspx

Disclosing a mental health difficulty: your rights, www.ucas.com/connect/blogs/disclosing-mental-health-difficulty-your-rights

The benefits of disclosing a mental health difficulty, www.ucas.com/connect/blogs/benefits-disclosing-mental-health-difficulty

TRANSITIONS SUPPORT CASE STUDY

This case study illustrates what transitions support can look like in practice.

University of Bath

Using the Lizzio and Wilson (2006) 'five senses of success' model for successful university transitions to guide their work, the university has a clear path for transitions support. The model supports students by addressing the academic, personal and social transition process to university, focusing on students' sense of student identity, sense of connection, sense of capability, sense of purpose and sense of resourcefulness. The support begins before students apply and is continued throughout their student experience. Multiple departments work together to deliver this support and communicate with each other to prevent new students from falling through the cracks.

The list of supports is extensive – these services are only a sample:

- *Peer support*: Senior students volunteer to 'buddy up' with new students to mentor them through this transition.

- *Safety and wellbeing support*: Wellbeing professionals in Student Services and Security staff work together to be available for students 24 hours a day.

- *Personal tutors*: Personal tutors are a personalized point of contact for students, supporting their academic and personal development.

- *Advice line*: University staff members can call this line to get advice on how best to support students they are concerned about.

- *Student living ambassadors*: These are students assigned to create a sense of belonging by facilitating the creation of community living agreements and engaging students in shared social activities.

- *Induction*: Induction and welcome at the University of Bath is an extended experience that includes pre-arrival education on support, safety and expected behaviours; ongoing opportunities to explore topics like employability and student involvement; and time for students to meet with peer-supporters and their personal tutor.

Conclusion

We know that living with a mental health condition can be devastating, and that the transitions into, throughout and beyond university or college can increase students' exposure to mental ill health and suicide. We also know that early interventions can change the trajectory of a person's life. By looking more holistically at transitions and at the institution's overall approach to wellbeing, schools, universities and colleges are ideally placed to provide support, build resilience to transition stressors and transform people's lives.

Author biographies

Katie Rigg is head of Safeguarding and Student Well-being at the Council of International Schools. A child protection lawyer by training, Katie helps schools and higher and further education institutions (HEIs and FEIs) to embed safeguarding and wellbeing throughout their organizations.

Ellen Mahoney is the CEO of Sea Change Mentoring and the Circulus Institute. Through training and consultation, she guides schools in improving the wellbeing of students and faculty and strengthening teacher–student relationships.

Katie and Ellen both work internationally, with education institutions whose student and staff populations are culturally diverse and globally mobile.

References

Belford, N. (2017) International students from Melbourne describing their cross-cultural transitions experiences: culture shock, social interaction, and friendship development. *Journal of International Studies 7*, 3, 499–521.

Charlton, J. (2000) *Nothing About Us Without Us*. Berkeley: University of California Press.

Collishaw, S., Maughan, B., Natarajan, L. and Pickles, A. (2010) Trends in adolescent emotional problems in England: a comparison of two national cohorts twenty years apart. *Journal of Child Psychology and Psychiatry 51*, 8, 885–894.

Council of International Schools (2020) *Understanding Student Well-being Needs in the Transition to Higher Education*. Leiden: Council of International Schools.

Harris, A. (2019) *Finding Your Own Way: Mental Health and Moving from School to Further and Higher Education*. London: Centre for Mental Health. Accessed on 20/08/20 at: www.centreformentalhealth.org.uk/sites/default/files/2019-01/CentreforMH_FindingOurOwnWay.pdf

Heycock, K. (2017) *Freshers: From Vulnerable Children to Adults at Risk? What Schools and Universities Need to Know about the Transfer of Safeguarding Information between Institutions*. London: Farrer & Co. Accessed on 20/08/20 at: www.farrer.co.uk/globalassets/news-articles/downloads/freshers---from-vulnerable-children-to-adults-at-risk.pdf

Lizzio, A. and Wilson, K. (2006) Enhancing the effectiveness of self-managed learning groups: understanding students' choices and concerns. *Studies in Higher Education 31*, 6, 689–703.

Macaskill, A. (2012) The mental health of university students in the United Kingdom. *British Journal of Guidance and Counselling 41*, 4, 426–441.

Mahoney, E. and Barron, J. (2020) *Surveying the Landscape: Common Practices, Challenges and Opportunities in International School Transitions-Care*. San Francisco: Sea Change Mentoring. Accessed on 29/10/20 at: https://seachangementoring.com/wp-content/uploads/2020/11/INTERNATIONAL-SCHOOL-TRANSITIONS-CARE-REPORT-2020-1.pdf

National Union of Students (NUS) (2017) *Further Education and Mental Health Report: A Report on the Experiences of Further Education Students and Mental Health in 2017*. Accessed on 25/08/20 at: www.nusconnect.org.uk/resources/further-education-and-mental-health-report

Rosiek, A., Rosiek-Kryszewska, A., Leksowski, Ł. and Leksowski, K. (2016) Chronic stress and suicidal thinking among medical students. *Int J Environ Res Public Health 13*, 2, 212.

Silverman, M.M., Meyer, P.M., Sloane, F., Raffel, M., Pratt, D.M. and Shatkin, J. (1997) The Big Ten Student Suicide Study: a 10-year study of suicides on midwestern university campuses. *Suicide & Life Threatening Behavior 27*, 3, 285–303.

Stanley, N., Mallon, S., Bell, J. and Manthorpe, J. (2009) Trapped in transition: findings from a UK study of student suicide. *British Journal of Guidance & Counselling 37*, 4, 419–433.

Stega, I. (2017) More teenagers commit suicide on this day in Japan than any other day of the year. Quartz, 1 September. Accessed on 30/03/21 at: https://qz.com/1067558/in-japan-more-teenagers-commit-suicide-on-sept-1-than-any-other-day-of-the-year-because-of-anxiety-of-going-back-to-school

Student Minds (2014) *Grand Challenges in Student Mental Health*. Oxford: Student Minds. Accessed on 25/08/20 at: www.studentminds.org.uk/grandchallenges.html

Student Minds (2017) *Student Voices*. Oxford: Student Minds. Accessed on 25/08/20 at: www.studentminds.org.uk/uploads/3/7/8/4/3784584/170901_student_voices_report_final.pdf

Student Minds (2018) *LGBTQ+ Student Mental Health: The Challenges and Needs of Gender, Sexual and Romantic Minorities in Higher Education*. Oxford: Student Minds. Accessed on 25/08/20 at: www.studentminds.org.uk/uploads/3/7/8/4/3784584/180730_lgbtq_report_final.pdf

Thorley, C. (2017) *Not by Degrees: Improving Student Mental Health in the UK's Universities*. London: Institute for Public Policy Research. Accessed on 20/08/20 at: www.ippr.org/research/publications/not-by-degrees

Universities UK (2019) Conference. Mental health: a whole university approach. Accessed on 30/03/21 at: www.universitiesuk.ac.uk/events/Pages/Mental-Health-A-Whole-University-Approach.aspx

Universities UK and PAPYRUS (2018) *Suicide-Safer Universities*. London: Universities UK and PAPYRUS. Accessed on 25/08/20 at: www.universitiesuk.ac.uk/policy-and-analysis/reports/Documents/2018/guidance-for-sector-practitioners-on-preventing-student-suicides.PDF

Wrench, A., Garrett, R. and King, S. (2013) Guessing where the goal posts are: managing health and well-being during the transition to university studies. *Journal of Youth Studies 16*, 6, 730–746.

Yap, J. (2019) *Suicide Prevention in Universities*. Mental Health Foundation blog. Accessed on 30/06/21 at: www.mentalhealth.org.uk/blog/suicide-prevention-universities

Zarb, A. (2010) Suicide risk and ideation with higher education. *Michigan Journal of Social Work and Social Welfare 1*, 57–67.

CHAPTER 8

The Integrated Motivational–Volitional (IMV) Model and Suicide Risk in Students

The Role of Perfectionism

DR SEONAID CLEARE, DAVE SANDFORD, HEATHER MCCLELLAND, TIAGO ZORTEA AND RORY O'CONNOR

Overview

In this chapter, we provide an overview on what perfectionism is, then focus on socially prescribed perfectionism in the context of the IMV model – specifically, how perfectionism might develop and how it might interact with other risk factors contributing to the emergence of suicidal thoughts and behaviours. We use a case study to detail how perfectionism may present in an individual and give an overview of how the IMV model could be used to identify and support potentially vulnerable individuals.

The reader will:

- learn how socially prescribed perfectionism and other psychological vulnerabilities may develop

- learn how these factors may contribute to increased suicide risk

- gain an understanding of risk factors for suicidal ideation and suicidal behaviour.

Introduction

Suicide is the second leading cause of death in young people aged 15–29 years globally (WHO 2018) and the number of people who attempt suicide or engage in non-suicidal self-harm (NSSH) is thought to be around

20 times higher than those who die (WHO 2018). Suicide attempts and NSSH are a significant concern in higher education (Universities UK 2018). Although suicide rates in student populations remain lower than in the general population (age standardized rate 10.1 per 100,000; ONS 2018a), they have been increasing in line with the general population trends and reached 95 deaths (4.7 deaths per 100,000) in 2017 (Gunnell *et al.* 2020; ONS 2018b).

Many motives underpin any act of self-harm with or without suicidal intent. Irrespective of motive, however, self-harm is an indicator of unbearable emotional distress (O'Connor and Nock 2014) and is one of the most consistent predictors of a future suicide attempt or death by suicide (Arensman, Griffin and Corcoran 2016; Chan *et al.* 2016). Given the devastating burden of suicide and self-harm, research has focused on identifying and understanding factors which may increase an individual's vulnerability to suicide (Hawton and van Heeringen 2009; Turecki *et al.* 2019). Although a wide range of biological, psychological and social factors have been identified, in this chapter we are directing our attention on one personality factor: perfectionism. This is timely as research suggests that perfectionism has been increasing in students over the last 30 years (Curran and Hill 2019), and it has been estimated that three in ten young people display perfectionistic characteristics (Flett and Hewitt 2014). A particular type of perfectionism, socially prescribed perfectionism (SPP), is the focus in this chapter because it has repeatedly been linked with a wide range of adverse mental health outcomes including suicide risk (Hewitt, Flett and Turnbull-Donovan 1992; O'Connor 2007; Smith *et al.* 2018).

However, as noted above, suicide is usually the end-product of a complex interplay of factors rather than the result of a single risk factor. Despite this recognition, suicide research has often investigated factors in isolation rather than in the context of theoretical models, thereby rendering it difficult to identify *under what circumstances* individuals within high-risk groups might be especially vulnerable to suicide (Franklin *et al.* 2017; O'Connor 2011b; O'Connor and Kirtley 2018).

One theoretical model which may be well placed to address this dearth in understanding is the Integrated Motivational–Volitional (IMV) model of suicidal behaviour (Figure 8.1; O'Connor 2011a; O'Connor and Kirtley 2018). The IMV model incorporates major components from the psychopathology, suicide research and health psychology literatures to delineate the final common pathway to ideation and enactment of self-harm and suicidal behaviour (O'Connor 2011a; O'Connor and Kirtley 2018).

What is perfectionism?

Although there are many different ways to conceptualize perfectionism, most researchers agree that it is a multidimensional personality trait consisting of intra- and interpersonal dimensions (Flett and Hewitt 2002a; Flett and Hewitt 2002b; Hewitt and Flett 1991). In this chapter, we focus on Hewitt and Flett's conceptualization as it has been applied most widely to understanding suicide risk. Hewitt and Flett (1991) conceptualized three dimensions of perfectionism: 1) self-oriented perfectionism (SOP), which they defined as an intrapersonal construct where the self is required to be perfect across all endeavours and success may be viewed as an all-or-nothing construct, with a focus on one's own flaws and past failures; 2) other-oriented perfectionism (OOP), where others are required to be perfect; and 3) socially prescribed perfectionism (SPP), where the individual believes that others require perfection from them.

Although each dimension has been shown to be differentially related to various indices of psychological distress (Hewitt and Flett 1991), SPP has been repeatedly associated with suicide risk (O'Connor 2007; O'Connor and Kirtley 2018; O'Connor and Nock 2014) and, as a result, is the main focus here. Indeed, models such as the perfectionism social disconnection model (PSDM; see Hewitt *et al.* 2006) show how the burden of SPP may contribute to an individual's suicide risk. According to this model, individuals high in SPP often display behaviours designed to maintain their perfect façade. These include striving to promote a perfect image (perfectionistic self-promotion), and avoiding displaying imperfection through behaviours and verbal interactions, notably non-display of imperfection and non-disclosure of imperfection respectively (Hewitt *et al.* 2003) to maintain perfectionistic self-presentation.

Situations where an individual perceives themselves as constantly failing to meet others' expectations can lead to feelings of not belonging, perceived social isolation and social disconnection through the individual withdrawing from others (Hewitt *et al.* 2006). Perceived social isolation has also been repeatedly associated with suicide risk, and in the context of the IMV model, perceived social isolation and feelings of not belonging increase the likelihood that entrapment develops into suicidal ideation (O'Connor 2011a; Van Orden 2015).

The Integrated Motivational–Volitional (IMV) Model of Suicidal Behaviour

The IMV model (Figure 8.1) is a tripartite (pre-motivational, motivational and volitional phases) diathesis–stress framework which details the final common pathway to suicidal thoughts and behaviours. As seen in Figure 8.1, the motivational phase of the model highlights factors that increase the likelihood that feelings of defeat may become feelings of entrapment (threat to self-moderators – e.g. rumination and problem solving) and then how and when feelings of entrapment may develop into suicidal ideation and intent (motivational moderators – e.g. resilience and social support). The volitional phase details the factors that influence the likelihood that someone makes the transition from suicidal ideation to a suicide attempt (volitional moderators – e.g. having access to means and reduced sensitivity to pain). As it is beyond the scope of this chapter to describe the evidence in support of these pathways, the reader is directed to O'Connor and Kirtley (2018).

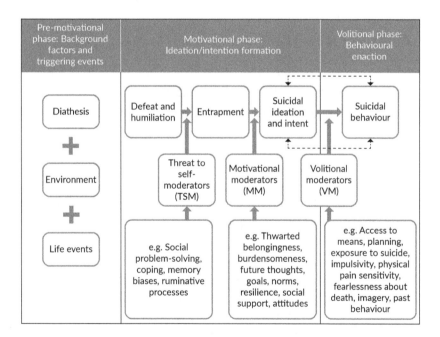

Figure 8.1: The Integrated Motivational–Volitional (IMV) Model of Suicidal Behaviour (O'Connor and Kirtley 2018)

In the context of the IMV model, perfectionism is located within the pre-motivational phase (O'Connor and Kirtley 2018), acting as a stable personality factor that increases an individual's vulnerability to suicidal behaviour. A key premise of the IMV model is the recognition that pre-motivational phase factors influence constructs throughout the motivational and volitional phases (O'Connor 2011a; O'Connor and Kirtley 2018). For instance, in a sample of clinically depressed adolescents (Hewitt *et al.* 2014), SPP interacted with daily hassles and predicted suicide potential. The study found that for adolescents who experienced medium to high levels of daily hassles, higher SPP was associated with higher suicide potential. These findings may indicate that SPP increases suicide potential by lowering an individual's threshold to stress. Similarly, individuals high in SPP may be more sensitive to emotional pain (pre-motivational factor) compared to those low in SPP (Kirtley, O'Carroll and O'Connor 2015). These studies suggest that when faced with acute or chronic life stressors, characteristics such as SPP may increase the likelihood that an individual transitions into the motivational phase of the model (O'Connor 2007; Rasmussen, Elliott and O'Connor 2012).

Perfectionism as a diathesis for suicide risk

To understand how perfectionism may act as a vulnerability factor for suicide risk, it is important to explain the relationship between a *diathesis* (i.e. vulnerability, risk predisposition) and *stress*. A diathesis is generally conceptualized as a predispositional factor (or set of factors) that increases the likelihood that a disordered state emerges (Monroe and Simons 1991). Predispositional influences include *historical factors* and *personality traits* that remain relatively persistent over time or tend to be resistant to change. For instance, factors such as exposure to trauma, past history of parenting/upbringing and history of suicidal thoughts and behaviours are unalterable historical risk factors (although interpretation of such events may change). Whereas difficulties with emotion regulation, perfectionism and insecure attachment, for example, are more trait-like factors that, although modifiable, are generally resistant to change (Bryan and Rudd 2018; O'Connor 2011b).

Alongside historical and personality trait risk factors, the absence of *protective factors* that mitigate suicide risk such as social support, problem-solving skills, healthy coping, psychological flexibility or resilience may increase the deleterious effects of maladaptive perfectionism. An individual's level of vulnerability differs based on one's specific accumulation and combination of risk and protective factors. Highly vulnerable individuals, therefore, are those with many diathesis factors combined with few protective factors, while those with low vulnerability levels possess few diathesis factors combined with many protective factors (Bryan and Rudd 2018). Consequently, when encountering stressful life events or traumatic memories, individuals with higher vulnerability levels are more likely to experience suicidal thoughts and to attempt suicide compared to those with lower vulnerability (Rudd 2006). Indeed, the transition into a university environment, like any other transition, brings new challenges and potential vulnerabilities which may require new skills and behaviours. An increase in vulnerability generally happens if the new environment lacks the provision of protective factors such as social/emotional support (Friedlander *et al.* 2007).

Returning to perfectionism, the relationship between diatheses and stress is complex and dynamic. Stressful situations such as receiving a disappointing exam mark may trigger a perfectionist's core belief (e.g. 'I am not good enough'), which may have developed during childhood and adolescence. Simultaneously, these core beliefs can render the experience of the disappointing mark more intense and distressing. Additionally, negative social feedback has been linked with rumination in individuals with perfectionism (Hewitt *et al.* 2017), therefore maintaining or even increasing the distress of a disappointing mark. According to the IMV model, perfectionism can facilitate the emergence of suicidal thoughts (via defeat and entrapment), by increasing one's sensitivity to stressful events. Moreover, individuals with higher levels of SPP may have increased sensitivity to signals of defeat and humiliation (O'Connor 2007) as they may be hypervigilant to indicators of perceived failure (SPP; Hewitt and Flett 1991).

Perfectionistic traits are thought to have pervasive effects; indeed they are strongly associated with cognitive rigidity (i.e. a resistance to adjust or modify beliefs, attitudes or habits, or the propensity to develop and maintain the use of the same mental or behavioural sets). The cognitive rigidity associated with perfectionism is implicated in suicide risk (Greenberg, Reiner and Meiran 2010; Schultz and Searleman 2002). Not accepting alternative solutions to problems or issues can make the individual especially vulnerable by facilitating the emergence of feelings and self-perceptions of defeat – e.g. 'I am a failure', 'I can't do anything right' – and entrapment – e.g. 'I can't see another alternative', 'There is no solution nor way out.' If the individual lacks social support, resilience and other protective factors (threat-to-self and motivational moderators within the IMV model), suicidal ideation is more likely to emerge (O'Connor and Kirtley 2018).

Emergence of suicidal ideation and perfectionism

Within the motivational phase of the IMV model, perceived defeat and entrapment are the key factors posited to lead to suicidal thinking, bridging the connection between perfectionism, stress and suicidal ideation (O'Connor and Kirtley 2018). In the presence of stress, those with high levels of SPP are at increased risk of developing adverse psychological responses including depression (Hewitt and Flett 1993), suicidal ideation and/or behaviour (O'Connor and Kirtley 2018). According to the perfectionist diathesis–stress model (Flett and Hewitt 2002a), perfectionism can accentuate the effect of everyday life stressors (Hewitt *et al.* 2014). Indeed, a large-scale study of college students (Ross, Niebling and Heckert 1999) found that common daily life stressors included changes in sleeping habits, changes in eating habits, new responsibilities and increased class workload. Given individuals with SPP already experience a great deal of stress (through the real or perceived pressures they put on themselves), these authors argued that in the presence of stress those with perfectionism are brought closer to 'breaking-point' and potential suicidal ideation and/or behaviour. In another study, Blankstein, Lumley and Crawford (2007) identified a gender difference whereby social hassles moderated the relationship between SPP and suicide risk in females, while academic hassles were more likely to be a moderator for males, highlighting that the effects of perfectionism may vary by stressor type and demographic characteristics. The following case example illustrates how perfectionism may develop and present outwardly, as well as highlighting a potential mechanism by which it may impact on psychological wellbeing.

CASE STUDY – PART 1

Alice's parents always expressed pride in their daughter's high academic achievement and placed a strong emphasis on achieving a 'good' education. Alice felt that her parents had high expectations of her to continue this trajectory from school to university. As a result, Alice developed the belief that her self-worth was primarily contingent on her academic achievements. Alice struggled with the transition to university. It took her a while to establish a friendship group; Alice found the atmosphere in seminars to be highly competitive, and believed her cohort were more 'naturally' academic than her. Although Alice successfully completed the year, she was very dismissive of her achievements ('I was lucky with my first-year results', 'the exam questions fell kindly for me'). Being conscious that results now counted towards her final degree, Alice vowed to strive harder in her second year to maintain her identity as a high achiever. She began to focus solely on her work but experienced increasing doubts in the quality of her efforts and ability. To cope with this Alice began to procrastinate, spending excessive time researching and re-formatting her coursework rather than writing. She began to miss deadlines and her grades were penalized accordingly. Alice's anxiety to succeed meant that she struggled to effectively manage her time between course assessments, leading her to fail her mid-year exams and neglect her friends and family both at home and at university. At this time, Alice experienced excessive tiredness, irritability, poor concentration, low mood and began to experience thoughts of suicide.

As illustrated in the case example, SPP can be linked with social isolation and is associated with maladaptive coping styles. Prud'homme *et al.* (2017) found SPP uniquely predicted both avoidant coping methods and daily stress at three years when compared to SOP and OOP. Avoidant coping, for example, defined as distancing oneself from the source of stress, has been identified as a maladaptive coping style which, despite yielding short-term respite, is ultimately unhelpful in the long term (Reid-Quiñones *et al.* 2011). Furthermore, prolonged avoidant coping strategies can make recovery from the stressful situation more challenging and have been associated with suicidal ideation and/or behaviour.

Additionally, according to the PSDM (Hewitt *et al.* 2006), the behavioural responses of the student suffering perfectionism (e.g. 'second-best isn't good enough') may be perceived by others as overly sensitive or even hostile. This can contribute to a perceived sense of detachment from others or actual difficulties with relationships. Relating this back to the IMV model, it is reasonable to posit that this may add to a thwarted sense of belonging and a perceived reduction in social support, key motivational moderators that contribute to the emergence of suicidal ideation and intent.

However, although the stress produced by environmental and life events is associated with suicide risk, it is important to highlight that not all individuals who are exposed to such environments, or who encounter stressful life events, develop suicidal ideation. Similarly, not everyone who thinks about suicide will go on to act on those thoughts (Kessler *et al.* 2005). Indeed, as summarized below, the final phase of the IMV model details factors which aid the transition from suicidal ideation to a suicide attempt.

Volitional factors of the IMV

Figure 8.2 illustrates the eight volitional factors of the IMV model that are posited to be associated with the transition from suicidal ideation to behaviour. When the IMV model was updated in 2018, the authors emphasized that the ideation–enactment relationship is both cyclical and progressive (O'Connor and Kirtley 2018), as indicated by the dotted lines in Figure 8.1. That is, those who engage in suicidal behaviour are statistically likely to re-engage (Kapur *et al.* 2013), and if/when they do it is often with increasing potential lethality (Bostwick *et al.* 2016).

Most of these volitional factors, for example mental imagery, physical pain endurance and sensitivity and planning, act by increasing an individual's capability for suicide behaviour. However, other factors must be considered, including access to means (environmental factor) or having known someone who has either died by suicide or engaged in suicidal behaviour (social factor). These environmental and social volitional factors can be dangerous as they may normalize suicidal behaviour or make it more cognitively accessible to envisage and plan a suicidal act (O'Connor and Kirtley 2018). There is growing support for the volitional factors in differentiating between suicidal ideation and behaviours in young people (Dhingra, Boduszek and O'Connor 2015; O'Connor, Rasmussen and Hawton 2012). For example, O'Connor *et al.* (2012) identified factors such as a friend who harms themself, beliefs about a friend's self-harm and impulsivity as important volitional moderators in young people which distinguished between young people who think about self-harm and those who engage in self-harm.

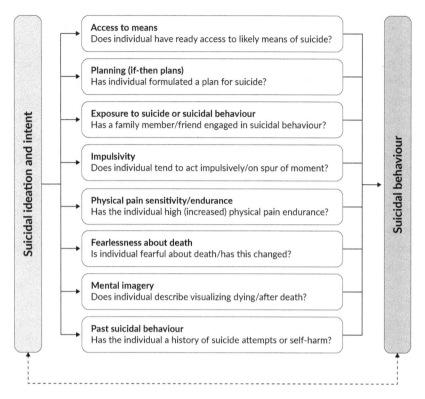

Figure 8.2: The eight volitional factors of the IMV model: the transition from suicidal ideation to suicidal behaviour (O'Connor and Kirtley 2018)

The 'face' of perfectionism

Most studies in the field of perfectionism have focused on clinical presentations within healthcare settings. As such, published perspectives from those in higher and further education regarding student presentations of perfectionism, or the 'face' of perfectionism, are lacking. Notwithstanding the limited evidence, it is recommended that educators are vigilant in identifying behaviours known to be associated with SPP such as submissive behaviour (Flett, Hewitt and Sherry 2016), diminished self-esteem (Chen *et al.* 2019), irrational fears (Blankstein *et al.* 1993) and avoidant coping styles (Mills and Blankstein 2000). In such students, perfectionism may manifest itself in terms of extreme displays of emotion, catastrophic thinking and declining academic performance and/or attendance, as illustrated in the case example of Alice on the following page.

CASE STUDY – PART 2

Alice's tutor had been concerned about her poor and uncharacteristic lack of attendance at seminars. On a rare appearance, the tutor noticed that Alice was quiet, withdrawn and 'not her usual self'. The tutor spoke to Alice following the seminar where Alice appeared tearful and extremely stressed and deflated. The tutor persuaded Alice to refer herself to the university counselling service. After a few counselling sessions, Alice was able to explain that for the past few weeks she had been experiencing increasingly frequent suicidal thoughts and had begun to stockpile medication.

A safety plan was agreed including enlisting the help of Alice's remaining close friend and disposing of the tablets. During counselling, Alice described how she had become fixated on the certainty of failure, she could see no way out of her situation and had flash forwards of having to face her family's disappointment if/when she failed. She had begun to imagine the scene of her own funeral.

Perfectionism is a transdiagnostic factor (Egan, Wade and Shafran 2011) in that it is implicated as a maintenance factor in a number of common mental health problems (OCD, eating disorder, depression) and, as described earlier, it is also one of the moderating factors that may influence the shift from the pre-motivational to motivational stages of the IMV model.

Applying a cognitive model of perfectionism, according to Shafran, Egan and Wade (2010), students who are prone to perfectionism could be faced by a 'triple bind'. If they meet the inflexible standards they perceive others expect of them, they are likely to minimize ('I should have done better'), discount ('I only got that grade because I worked through the night') or ignore their success ('I have the next exam to revise for') and, consequently, reset the required standard to a higher level ('raise the bar'). If they judge that they have failed to meet the expected standard (being awarded a 2:1 grade rather than a first) they are likely to be very self-critical ('I'm such an idiot, I should have known better') and redouble what are often counterproductive efforts (increase checking, strive harder, work longer hours, reduce recreational activity) to 'succeed' in the future. Finally, if they are fearful of not meeting the standard, they may also adopt avoidant behaviours (procrastinating, prevaricating, poor attendance, distraction). Taken together, this cycle of thoughts and behaviours is maladaptive.

The challenge of perfectionism

It can be difficult for students to moderate their perfectionism, particularly as they may view it as functional in achieving the success they have historically enjoyed. In supporting students, it is helpful to identify and acknowledge productive striving that is admirable and functional, as well as developing their ability to accept less than 100 per cent. Whilst it is difficult (and not necessarily desirable) to get a student to give up on high standards, it is better to work alongside them to strengthen behaviours that support productive striving. Such an approach is sustainable and is more likely to result in goals that are realistic and attainable. Similarly, exploring relational expectations and addressing an individual's expectations of perfection from self or others is also helpful. Encouraging thought-challenging, acceptance and a positive attitude towards adversity will further equip the young person to managing stress in future, thereby re-configuring their coping strategies from maladaptive to adaptive.

CASE STUDY – PART 3

During counselling, Alice focused on recognizing and adapting her behaviours (e.g. putting off handing in work, repeated checking) and thinking styles (e.g. 'anything short of my target grade is a failure') that maintained her perfectionism. Initially, this was anxiety provoking for Alice (handing in an essay that was 'good enough' was really difficult) until she reflected on the positive feedback and grades she received as a result of these changes. She worked to reappraise her understanding of how other people viewed her, the basis on which those closest to her valued her, and how she gained the acceptance of people she met. She learned that others placed greater value on her personal characteristics (e.g. kindness and loyalty) than they did on her academic achievements. The process of gathering information (e.g. seeking opinion from friends and family) to support this helped her reconnect with people and be more open about her struggles. Alice practised showing herself greater compassion as an alternative to her more habitual self-criticism. She developed a healthier balance of activity, dedicating more time to socializing and exercising. Alice began to differentiate between problem solving and worry. As she developed a plan to get back on track with her studies and started re-engaging in positive future planning, she was able to develop more flexible and achievable goals.

Conclusions and implications

Perfectionism is a pervasive personality trait thought to develop in early life which has been repeatedly associated with suicide risk. Given the relatively stable nature of perfectionism it is important for clinicians and practitioners to work with an individual to help them manage detrimental perfectionistic behaviours, rather than trying to eradicate them completely. For instance, rather than trying to ameliorate an individual's goal-driven behaviour, it may be more pragmatic to support the individual to recognize and reduce obstructive behaviours (e.g. excessive checking of work, missing deadlines because work isn't deemed to be ready). Alternatively, individuals can be encouraged to channel their goal-driven behaviour into sports and recreation, thereby incentivizing students to connect socially and relieve their frustrations in a healthier way, which can improve their mood and ability to cope.

Educators should be mindful of the detrimental impact that SPP may have on individuals in higher education settings and should be aware of the sensitivity to criticism that may be experienced by those who rate high on socially prescribed perfectionism, especially as a key characteristic is their struggle to acknowledge they need help lest they shatter the perfect image they are driven to portray. As indicated throughout this chapter, individuals who are high in SPP are prone to perfectionistic self-promotion (Hewitt *et al.* 2003). Although it may appear to external observers that students are achieving desirable marks, the student may be experiencing feelings of defeat and humiliation from failing to meet their own high standards. It may be beneficial for anyone working with individuals with perfectionism to recognize this potential discord and work collaboratively with individuals to find an acceptable balance for their expectations – for example, looking for evidence to support the worries they are having, as in most cases there isn't any.

Perfectionism is not sufficient in itself to trigger suicidal thoughts and behaviours. However, perfectionism may increase an individual's vulnerability to stressors, which can in turn increase the likelihood that an individual enters the motivational phase of the IMV model and develops suicidal thoughts via perceptions of defeat and entrapment.

Routinely screening for entrapment during clinical appointments could allow for early identification of the most at-risk individuals. The importance of identifying and working with defeat and entrapment has been recently highlighted in the new *Self-Harm and Suicide Prevention Competence Frameworks* for children and young people, adults and older adults (National Collaborating Centre for Mental Health 2018). These frameworks are aimed at educators and clinicians and, based on research evidence, highlight key skills for any professional supporting people who are suicidal, as well as highlighting competencies at the organizational level to support policy and ethics. They also highlight requirements to support others affected by suicide, including relatives or peers of the individual.

Research has highlighted the need for greater precision in understanding suicide risk in the higher and further education sectors – in particular, extending the focus to include how and under what circumstances these factors contribute to the aetiology and course of psychological distress and suicide risk (Franklin *et al.* 2017). Models such as the IMV model may be well placed to assist in the early identification of when individuals may be at increased risk of suicide.

Author biographies

Dr Seonaid Cleare is a researcher within the Suicidal Behaviour Research Laboratory (SBRL) at the University of Glasgow. Seonaid's research focuses on factors which may provide individuals some protection from emotional distress and self-harm and suicide.

Dave Sandford is a senior psychotherapist in Lancashire and South Cumbria NHS Foundation Trust and is a concurrent PhD student within the SBRL at the University of Glasgow looking at the impact on practitioners of losing a patient to suicide.

Heather McClelland is a researcher within the SBRL at the University of Glasgow investigating subjective loneliness, among other mechanisms, in relation to suicidality. She has a background in suicide prevention and postvention clinical research as well as three years' experience leading a self-help therapy clinic to support mood disorder in children and young adults.

Dr Tiago Zortea is a clinical psychologist and currently postdoctoral researcher within the SBRL, University of Glasgow. He is also a co-chair of the Early Career Group of the International Association for Suicide Prevention and member of the editorial team of netECR, the International Network of Early Career Researchers in Suicide and Self-harm.

Professor Rory O'Connor leads the SBRL at the University of Glasgow.

Rory has been conducting theoretically grounded and innovative research into suicide and self-harm since 1994 and he established the SBRL in 2003.

References

Arensman, E., Griffin, E. and Corcoran, P. (2016) Self-Harm. In R.C. O'Connor and J. Pirkis (eds) *The International Handbook of Suicide Prevention*. Chichester: John Wiley and Sons. pp.61–73.

Blankstein, K.R., Flett, G.L., Hewitt, P.L. and Eng, A. (1993) Dimensions of perfectionism and irrational fears: an examination with the fear survey schedule. *Personality and Individual Differences 15*, 3, 323–328.

Blankstein, K.R., Lumley, C.H. and Crawford, A. (2007) Perfectionism, hopelessness, and suicide ideation: revisions to diathesis-stress and specific vulnerability models. *Journal of Rational-Emotive & Cognitive-Behavior Therapy 25*, 4, 279–319.

Bostwick, J.M., Pabbati, C., Geske, J.R. and McKean, A.J. (2016) Suicide attempt as a risk factor for completed suicide: even more lethal than we knew. *The American Journal of Psychiatry 173*, 11, 1094–1100.

Bryan, C.J. and Rudd, M.D. (2018) *Brief Cognitive-Behavioral Therapy for Suicide Prevention* (1st edn). New York: The Guilford Press.

Chan, M.K.Y., Bhatti, H., Meader, N., Stockton, S. *et al.* (2016) Predicting suicide following self-harm: systematic review of risk factors and risk scales. *The British Journal of Psychiatry: The Journal of Mental Science 209*, 4, 277–283.

Chen, C., Hewitt, P.L., Flett, G.L. and Roxborough, H.M. (2019) Multidimensional perfectionism and borderline personality organization in emerging adults: a two-wave longitudinal study. *Personality and Individual Differences 146*, 143–148.

Curran, T. and Hill, A.P. (2019) Perfectionism is increasing over time: a meta-analysis of birth cohort differences from 1989 to 2016. *Psychological Bulletin 145*, 4, 410–429.

Dhingra, K., Boduszek, D. and O'Connor, R. (2015) Differentiating suicide attempters from suicide ideators using the Integrated Motivational–Volitional model of suicidal behaviour. *Journal of Affective Disorders 186*, 211–218.

Egan, S.J., Wade, T.D. and Shafran, R. (2011) Perfectionism as a transdiagnostic process: a clinical review. *Clinical Psychology Review 31*, 2, 203–212.

Flett, G.L. and Hewitt, P.L. (2002a) Perfectionism and stress processes in psychopathology. In G.L. Flett and P.L. Hewitt (eds) *Perfectionism: Theory, Research, and Treatment*. Washington, DC: American Psychological Association. pp. 255–284.

Flett, G.L. and Hewitt, P.L. (2002b) Perfectionism and Maladjustment: An Overview of Theoretical, Definitional, and Treatment Issues. In G.L. Flett and P.L. Hewitt (eds) *Perfectionism: Theory, Research, and Treatment* (1st edn). Washington, DC: American Psychological Association. pp.5–31.

Flett, G.L. and Hewitt, P.L. (2014) A proposed framework for preventing perfectionism and promoting resilience and mental health among vulnerable children and adolescents. *Psychology in the Schools 51*, 9, 899–912.

Flett, G.L., Hewitt, P.L. and Sherry, S.S. (2016) Deep, Dark, and Dysfunctional: The Destructiveness of Interpersonal Perfectionism. In V. Zeigler-Hill and D.K. Marcus (eds) *The Dark Side of Personality: Science and Practice in Social, Personality, and Clinical Psychology*. Washington, DC: American Psychological Association. pp.211–229.

Franklin, J.C., Ribeiro, J.D., Fox, K.R., Bentley, K.H. *et al.* (2017) Risk factors for suicidal thoughts and behaviors: a meta-analysis of 50 years of research. *Psychological Bulletin 143*, 2, 187–232.

Friedlander, L.J., Reid, G.J., Shupak, N. and Cribbie, R. (2007) Social support, self-esteem, and stress as predictors of adjustment to university among first-year undergraduates. *Journal of College Student Development 48*, 3, 259–274.

Greenberg, J., Reiner, K. and Meiran, N. (2010) 'Mind the trap': mindfulness practice reduces cognitive rigidity. *PLoS One 7*, 5, e36206.

Gunnell, D., Caul, S., Appleby, L., John, A. and Hawton, K. (2020) The incidence of suicide in university students in England and Wales 2000/2001–2016/2017: record linkage study. *Journal of Affective Disorders 261*, 113–120.

Hawton, K. and van Heeringen, K. (2009) Suicide. *Lancet 373*, 9672, 1372–1381.

Hewitt, P.L. and Flett, G.L. (1991) Perfectionism in the self and social contexts: conceptualization, assessment, and association with psychopathology. *Journal of Personality and Social Psychology 60*, 3, 456–470.

Hewitt, P.L. and Flett, G.L. (1993) Dimensions of perfectionism, daily stress, and depression: a test of the specific vulnerability hypothesis. *Journal of Abnormal Psychology 102*, 1, 58–65.

Hewitt, P.L., Caelian, C.F., Chen, C. and Flett, G.L. (2014) Perfectionism, stress, daily hassles, hopelessness, and suicide potential in depressed psychiatric adolescents. *Journal of Psychopathology and Behavioral Assessment 36*, 4, 663–674.

Hewitt, P.L., Flett, G.L. and Mikail, S. (2017) *Perfectionism: A Relational Approach to Conceptualization, Assessment, and Treatment.* London: The Guilford Press.   .

Hewitt, P.L., Flett, G.L., Sherry, S.B. and Caelian, C. (2006) Trait Perfectionism Dimensions and Suicidal Behavior. In T.E. Ellis (ed.) *Cognition and Suicide: Theory, Research, and Therapy.* Washington, DC: American Psychological Association. pp.215–235.

Hewitt, P.L., Flett, G.L., Sherry, S.B., Habke, M. *et al.* (2003) The interpersonal expression of perfection: perfectionistic self-presentation and psychological distress. *Journal of Personality and Social Psychology 84*, 6, 1303–1325.

Hewitt, P.L., Flett, G.L. and Turnbull-Donovan, W. (1992) Perfectionism and suicide potential. *British Journal of Clinical Psychology 31*, 2, 181–190.

Kapur, N., Cooper, J., O'Connor, R.C. and Hawton, K. (2013) Non-suicidal self-injury v. attempted suicide: new diagnosis or false dichotomy? *British Journal of Psychiatry 202*, 5, 326–328.

Kessler, R.C., Berglund, P., Demler, O., Jin, R., Merikangas, K.R. and Walters, E.E. (2005) Lifetime prevalence and age-of-onset distributions of DSM-IV disorders in the National Comorbidity Survey Replication. *Archives of General Psychiatry 62*, 6, 593–602.

Kirtley, O.J., O'Carroll, R.E. and O'Connor, R.C. (2015) Hurting inside and out? Emotional and physical pain in self-harm ideation and enactment. *International Journal of Cognitive Therapy 8*, 2, 156–171.

Mills, J. and Blankstein, K.R. (2000) Perfectionism, intrinsic vs extrinsic motivation, and motivated strategies for learning: a multidimensional analysis of university students. *Personality and Individual Differences 29*, 6, 1191–1204.

Monroe, S.M. and Simons, A.D. (1991) Diathesis-stress theories in the context of life stress research: implications for the depressive disorders. *Psychological Bulletin 110*, 3, 406–425.

National Collaborating Centre for Mental Health (2018) *Self-Harm and Suicide Prevention Competence Framework: Community and Public Health.* Accessed on 28/03/21 at: www.rcpsych.ac.uk/docs/default-source/improving-care/nccmh/self-harm-and-suicide-prevention-competence-framework/nccmh-self-harm-and-suicide-prevention-competence-framework-public-health.pdf?sfvrsn=341fb3cd_6

O'Connor, R.C. (2007) The relations between perfectionism and suicidality: a systematic review. *Suicide and Life-Threatening Behavior 37*, 6, 698–714.

O'Connor, R.C. (2011a) The integrated motivational–volitional model of suicidal behavior. *Crisis 32*, 6, 295–298.

O'Connor, R.C. (2011b) Towards an Integrated Motivational-Volitional Model of Suicidal Behaviour. In R.C. O'Connor, S. Platt and J. Gordon (eds) *International Handbook of Suicide Prevention.* Chichester: John Wiley and Sons. pp.181–198.

O'Connor, R.C. and Kirtley, O.J. (2018) The integrated motivational–volitional model of suicidal behaviour. *Philosophical Transactions of the Royal Society B: Biological Sciences 373*, 1754, 20170268.

O'Connor, R.C. and Nock, M.K. (2014) The psychology of suicidal behaviour. *The Lancet Psychiatry 1*, 1, 73–85.

O'Connor, R.C., Rasmussen, S. and Hawton, K. (2012) Distinguishing adolescents who think about self-harm from those who engage in self-harm. *British Journal of Psychiatry 200*, 4, 330–335.

Office for National Statistics (ONS) (2018a) *Estimating Suicide among Higher Education Students, England and Wales: Experimental Statistics.* London: ONS. Accessed on 28/03/21 at: www.

ons.gov.uk/peoplepopulationandcommunity/birthsdeathsandmarriages/deaths/articles/estimatingsuicideamonghighereducationstudentsenglandandwalesexperimentalstatistics/2018-06-25

Office for National Statistics (ONS) (2018b) *Suicides in the UK: 2017 Registrations*. London: ONS, 1–20.

Prud'homme, J., Dunkley, D.M., Bernier, E., Berg, J.L., Ghelerter, A. and Starrs, C.J. (2017) Specific perfectionism components predicting daily stress, coping, and negative affect six months and three years later. *Personality and Individual Differences 111*, 134–138.

Rasmussen, S.A., Elliott, M.A. and O'Connor, R.C. (2012) Psychological distress and perfectionism in recent suicide attempters: the role of behavioural inhibition and activation. *Personality and Individual Differences 52*, 6, 680–685.

Reid-Quiñones, K., Kliewer, W., Shields, B.J., Goodman, K., Ray, M.H. and Wheat, E. (2011) Cognitive, affective, and behavioral responses to witnessed versus experienced violence. *American Journal of Orthopsychiatry 81*, 1, 51–60.

Ross, S.E., Niebling, B.C. and Heckert, T.M. (1999) Sources of stress among college students. *Social Psychology 61*, 5, 841–846.

Rudd, M.D. (2006) Fluid Vulnerability Theory: A Cognitive Approach to Understanding the Process of Acute and Chronic Suicide Risk. In T.E. Ellis (ed.) *Cognition and Suicide: Theory, Research, and Therapy.* Washington, DC: American Psychological Association. pp.355–368.

Schultz, P.W. and Searleman, A. (2002) Rigidity of thought and behavior: 100 years of research. *Genetic, Social, and General Psychology Monographs 128*, 2, 165–207.

Shafran, R., Egan, S.J. and Wade, T.D. (2010) *Overcoming Perfectionism: A Self-Help Guide Using Cognitive–Behavioural Techniques.* London: Constable and Robinson.

Smith, M.M., Sherry, S.B., Chen, S., Saklofske, D.H. *et al.* (2018) The perniciousness of perfectionism: a meta-analytic review of the perfectionism–suicide relationship. *Journal of Personality 86*, 3, 522–542.

Turecki, G., Brent, D.A., Gunnell, D., O'Connor, R.C. *et al.* (2019) Suicide and suicide risk. *Nature Reviews Disease Primers 5*, 1, 74.

Universities UK (2018) *Minding Our Future: Starting a Conversation about the Support of Student Mental Health.* Accessed on 30/03/21 at: www.universitiesuk.ac.uk/minding-our-future

Van Orden, K.A. (2015) The interpersonal theory of suicide: A useful theory? *Advancing the Science of Suicidal Behavior: Understanding and Intervention 117*, 2, 41–52.

World Health Organization (WHO) (2018) *National Suicide Prevention Strategies: Progress, Examples and Indicators.* Geneva: WHO. Accessed on 30/03/21 at: www.who.int/mental_health/suicide-prevention/national_strategies_2019/en/#.XagybrhRwiY.mendeley

CHAPTER 9

Suicide Clusters and Contagion in the HE and FE Student Population

ANN JOHN

Overview

By the end of this chapter the reader will:

- understand suicide clusters, who is at risk from them and what are the mechanisms that underlie them

- have considered how we can respond to an apparent suicide cluster in a university or FE college, including practical suggestions about how they may be countered in the student population to maximize the effectiveness of the response of the HE institution or FE college

- have explored how HE and FE institutions can develop policies and procedures that can respond to a suicide cluster as it emerges.

Introduction

The impact of a death of a student by suicide in an HE or FE context is deeply felt across the whole community and this is exacerbated if it occurs as part of a suicide cluster. Young people are much more likely to be part of a suicide cluster than older age groups. The mechanisms involved may include direct exposure to the behaviour, media reporting, belief that the behaviour is commonplace, vulnerable individuals sharing social groups, and the influence of social media and the internet. Once a cluster is suspected there should be a carefully coordinated and preferably pre-planned response, ideally by an identified cluster response group. The response should include bereavement support, provision of help for vulnerable individuals, proactive responses to media interest and community approaches to support and prevention. This chapter discusses the evidence in relation to prevention of suicide clusters and develops an understanding of the underlying mechanisms associated with them, including the concepts of contagion and imitation.

What is a suicide cluster?

Suicide clusters, while uncommon, cause a great deal of concern in the communities where they occur. A 'suicide cluster' is defined as a situation in which more suicides than expected occur in terms of time, place or both and usually includes three or more deaths (Hawton *et al.* 2020). There are different types of suicide cluster (see below).

However, two suicides occurring in young people in a single HE or FE setting over a short time period should be taken very seriously in terms of possible links and impacts, even if the deaths are seemingly unconnected. It is important to recognize that there do not have to be clear recognizable connections for multiple deaths by suicide to be contained within a single cluster. Students are well connected online through social media and electronic communications across different HEI and FE colleges, and suicidal behaviour can spread this way (Marchant *et al.* 2017; Robertson *et al.* 2012). As a result, clusters associated with links between students through the online environment may be harder to recognize and would require a level of communication and coordination of response between institutions that may be challenging to achieve.

What are the types of suicide cluster?

- *Point clusters (or tempero-spatial clusters)*: A greater than expected number of suicides in the same specific location within the same time period. This might be in a community or an institution (e.g. HEI or FE college) or at a specific site (e.g. a bridge, cliff or building)
- *Mass clusters (or temporal clusters)*: A greater than expected number of suicides across different geographical locations but within the same time period, e.g. following the death by suicide of a celebrity

---

- *Clusters involving a specific method of suicide*: Sometimes clustering can involve a particular method of suicide. This can occur in both point and mass clusters
- *Echo cluster*: A cluster occurring in the same location as a previous cluster, but sometime later in time.

Mechanisms underlying suicide clusters

There are few studies focusing on point suicide clusters in general, or in HE or FE in particular, that develop our understanding of the mechanisms underlying suicide clusters (Bell *et al.* 2015; Haw *et al.* 2013). Many studies reporting on HEI-based clusters aim to identify specific risk factors associated with suicide (McLaughlin and Gunnell 2020). The evidence base for suicide in adolescents is stronger and so has been drawn on in this chapter. Four distinct mechanisms have been suggested to explain the occurrence of suicide clusters: social transmission, descriptive norms, social integration and regulation, and assortative relating. However, they are not mutually exclusive and may act together in different measures within a suicide cluster within and between individuals in the student population.

Social transmission

Social transmission is often called 'suicide contagion', somewhat unfortunately drawing on infectious disease outbreak terminology. A causal effect, where exposure to a death by suicide can increase suicidal behaviours in others, is still contentious (Joiner 2003). The hypothesis acknowledges that the effect of the exposure is not experienced evenly and that particular characteristics and risk factors of individuals, as well as environmental factors, will affect suicide outcomes. Exposure can occur directly through knowing the person who died by suicide, or indirectly through the media or social media.

There is a growing body of evidence that media portrayal of suicide may instigate or prolong some suicide clusters in young people. In a study comparing 48 communities with youth suicide clusters in the USA, with a matched control group of 95 communities where non-cluster suicides occurred, newspaper coverage of suicide was associated with the initiation of the suicide clusters, particularly where those stories were about the young people who died (Gould *et al.* 2014). Particular characteristics highlighted in the reporting of newspaper stories following the first cluster suicide (i.e. the death by suicide that initiated the cluster) in young people were: more prominent (e.g. front-page placement and included a picture); more explicit (headlines containing the word 'suicide' or highlighting the method used); and more detailed (publicizing names, specific details of method, contents of suicide notes). The finding that only stories about suicidal individuals, as opposed to other types of newspaper stories about suicide, were associated with the occurrence of a subsequent suicide supports the theory that the media effect operates, albeit indirectly, through the mechanism of identification – that is, the story is either about someone similar to the reader or revered by them (e.g. a celebrity). Stories about teen suicides in the study had the strongest effect on subsequent teen suicides and are consistent with this theory of differential identification. Studies of other suicide clusters in young people have also highlighted the role of poor quality and sensationalist reporting (John *et al.* 2016).

Descriptive norms

Descriptive norms are an individual's perception or beliefs about how common a particular behaviour, such as suicidal behaviour, is among peers – for example, thinking that suicide is more widespread among the HE or FE student community than it really is. Perceived social norms surrounding a given behaviour have been evidenced to influence an individual's own engagement in that behaviour (Cialdini, Reno and Lallgren 1990; Rimal and Real 2003). A number of studies in adolescents have found that those who believe suicidal behaviour to be widespread were more likely to consider suicidal behaviour themselves (O'Connor, Rasmussen and Hawton 2012; Reyes-Portillo *et al.* 2019). Descriptive norms may be an under-explored mechanism by which suicide clusters occur in HE and FE students.

Social integration and regulation

Social integration and social cohesion are constructs describing the structure of social relationships surrounding individuals that may regulate their emotional and physical health. While we frequently hear about the protective nature of social integration and cohesion, increasing evidence is emerging that high levels of social integration, such as HE campuses which are relatively closed communities, may also have a negative impact on individuals and may promote the occurrence of point clusters of suicide (Mueller and Abrutyn 2016). The speed at which information is spread in close, tight-knit communities may increase pressure to react in line with cultural expectations. This may create a tense environment for vulnerable young people, and potentially increase the risk of suicide.

Assortative relating

Young people who are vulnerable to considering suicidal behaviour are more likely to be friends with one another – that is, they cluster together and have shared risk factors (Joiner 2003). In contrast to social transmission, the increased risk of suicidal behaviours in those exposed to a death by suicide is not causal but an association – that is, between friends who have shared risk factors and experiences. However, assortative relating suggests that those closest to the deceased would be at the highest risk, whereas current research suggests that it is actually those peers who are friends but not close friends who are at highest risk (Gould *et al.* 2018). Exposure to a peer's suicidal behaviour increased the risk of suicidal behaviour even after controlling for a wide range of variables potentially involved in assortative selection of peers (Randall, Nickel and Colman 2015). These included factors such as physical health, depressive symptoms, impulsivity, fearfulness, anxiety symptoms, parental relationship, relationship with friends, sexual orientation, minority status, self-esteem, attractiveness, parental use of public assistance, intelligence, neighbourhood environment, exercise, counselling, drug and alcohol use and involvement in fights and violence. A study using computer simulation modelling to explore assortative relating as a possible mechanism behind suicide clustering found that assortative relating was less likely than social learning to generate point clusters and unlikely to generate purely temporal clustering of suicides (Mesoudi 2009). Therefore, the effects of assortative relating are relatively unknown.

Who is at risk from suicide clusters?

It is difficult to know the exact extent to which clusters of suicide contribute to overall suicide rates or how many suicides are attributable to clusters, and of those, how many originate in HE populations

(Niedzwiedz *et al.* 2014). Young people have consistently been shown to be at higher risk for suicide clusters (Cox *et al.* 2012; Gould 1990; Haw *et al.* 2013) and HEI and FE colleges hold a large number of young people in a specific geographic location. The relative risk of suicide following exposure to another individual's suicide is two to four times higher among 15- to 19-year-olds than among other age groups (Gould 1990). In Australia, youth suicides have been shown to be approximately twice as likely to occur as part of a cluster than adult suicides – that is, suicide clusters accounted for 5.6 per cent of suicides in young people aged under 25 years, compared to approximately 2.3 per cent of suicide in adults aged 25 years and over (Robinson *et al.* 2016).

With the exception of age and exposure to a suicide death, the risk factors associated with individuals being involved in suicide clusters do not differ greatly from non-cluster suicides (Haw *et al.* 2013; Niedzwiedz *et al.* 2014). Sex is specifically not mentioned here. Some studies have found males are more frequently involved in suicide clusters, with females more commonly involved in clustering of self-harm or suicide attempts (Brent *et al.* 1989; Fowler *et al.* 2013). However, these findings have not been replicated in large-scale, population-based studies (e.g. Cheung *et al.* 2014; Robinson *et al.* 2016; Too *et al.* 2017).

Suicide risk has been found to be lower in postgraduate than undergraduate students and in black students compared to other ethnic groups (Gunnell *et al.* 2019). Gunnell *et al.* found a marked excess of student suicides in January, with 14 per cent of all suicides occurring in this month compared to 9 per cent in the general population of a similar age. They suggested this might relate to exam pressure, as many universities hold exams in January, or the challenges of returning to studies after the Christmas break. A study of a suicide cluster in an HEI in the UK found that students who died by suicide were more likely than other students at their institutions to be male and to be in receipt of a bursary or other financial assistance or have experienced academic difficulties (McLaughlin and Gunnell 2020). Other factors strongly related to risk included suspension of studies, repeating a year and changing course. In addition, factors that appeared to be related to risk, albeit less robustly, were drug or alcohol misuse, personal life difficulties including relationship break-up, bereavement, prior self-harm or suicide attempts and previous or current contacts with secondary care mental health services. As highlighted before, these are all well-recognized risk factors for suicide in the general population. Of note is the fact that few of the students (10.8%) in the McLaughlin and Gunnell (2020) study had disclosed a mental health issue when they registered with the HEI and up to half had no record of contact with health services for mental health issues. Based on a study of mental health in HE students (Farrell *et al.* 2017) Gunnell *et al.* (2019) suggested that around 17 per cent of student suicides occurred in those who had been in current or recent contact with NHS psychiatric services.

How do we respond to an apparent suicide cluster in an HEI or FE college?

Rates of suicide amongst HE students have been found to be considerably lower than those in the general population in the USA and England and Wales (Gunnell *et al.* 2019; Schwartz 2011). However, there is no doubt that as a setting where a large number of young people are living their lives in a close community, an HE setting is amenable to suicide prevention activities. Given the rise in suicide rates in young people over the last decade, this offers a real suicide prevention opportunity (Bould *et al.* 2019). However, the evidence base for interventions in this area is evolving and thus the approaches to responding to suicide clusters described are largely based on good practice derived from experience (Public Health England 2019; Universities UK and PAPYRUS 2018). Such experience indicates that ideally plans should be developed prospectively rather than in the event of an actual cluster, to contain anxiety, anger and blame and instil confidence in the response. This involves a whole university approach.

Suicide prevention strategy

Suicide prevention, interventions and postvention (i.e. supporting those bereaved) should be outlined in a specific co-produced strategy, distinct from student death policies. Co-production should include students, staff, carers/parents, HE and FE leads for wellbeing, third sector organizations and academics with expertise (where available). The strategy should be compatible with and sit alongside broader mental health and wellbeing strategies in the HEI or FE college. Ideally, the HEI or FE college should also link with a local suicide prevention group (where it exists). It should include a multi-stakeholder group across health, social care, third sector, police, etc. and develop its strategy alongside local initiatives. The strategy should have visible and strong support from the HE or FE senior executive team and clear governance and reporting structures should be explicitly included. A named lead on the senior executive team whose portfolio includes suicide prevention is an effective way to achieve this. A senior member of the HEI or FE college should be responsible for ongoing monitoring of student deaths, including suspected suicides. Implementation should be supported by a multiagency action plan taking a public health approach.

The HE and FE environment provides an important opportunity to promote healthy behaviours and life skills (e.g. problem solving, coping) that will help students respond to life's challenges as well as make a successful transition into employment. Less than 20 per cent of students who died by suicide used their school's counselling service as a resource (Gallagher Taylor 2014). According to one study on help-seeking and access to mental health care in an HE student population, 49 per cent of students said that they would know where to go for mental health care while enrolled and 59 per cent of students were aware of free counselling services on campus (Eisenberg, Golberstein and Gollust 2007). However, only 36 per cent of students who screened positive for major depression received either medication or therapy in the past year. This suggests that HEI and FE colleges need to make students more aware of available re-sources and services available within their institutions but also accessible outside through a range of formats – face-to-face, webchat, telephone, etc. They should tackle the stigma, culture and attitudes around the topics of suicide and mental health, acknowledging that the stigma associated with them is different, but ensuring that more students feel comfortable and empowered to seek help when in distress.

Immediate response to a suicide cluster

Where concerns arise about a possible suicide cluster in an HEI or FE college, there should be an immediate communication with the local public health suicide prevention lead and close collaboration in the development of a response plan. If a possible cluster is identified or suspected a meeting should be organized immediately. At this stage it is usually helpful to keep the meeting to a relatively small group of people. Membership might include:

- senior members of the HEI or FE college responsible for wellbeing (e.g. pro-vice-chancellor for students and the director of student services in an HEI or the principal and safeguarding/health and safety lead in an FE college or their equivalent)

- senior member of the communications/media department of the HEI/comms lead for the FE college

- public health suicide prevention lead (usually local authority or NHS based)

- staff member leading response to individual student deaths

- head of HEI or FE counselling service (or equivalent)

- local police

- at an early stage, a senior student union representative, such as the president or one of the executive officers.

The primary task of this group is to assess the situation and agree the right balance of response. This can be challenging at a time when emotions are running high and there is a lot of uncertainty regarding possible links between any students who have died. The aim is for responses that are reflective and proactive rather than reactive, maintaining oversight of the situation without increasing institutional anxiety. The initial objective is to decide the level of concern and appropriate interventions. In the early stages, it is important that these meetings occur frequently, even daily, to ensure new information is captured as circumstances evolve and, if necessary, plans are revised. A clear plan to liaise with the parents should be made as soon as possible, agreeing who the point of contact should be. Where a student has had difficulties with their studies or behaviours this will need to be handled sensitively.

The initial meeting of the group is particularly important in terms of deciding leadership and planning of the response. Experience of suicide clusters at HEIs has shown that levels of anxiety will be considerable and rumours will be rife. There may be confusion of roles and leadership, together with uncertainty about what should be done. It is important to remember that for some members of the group this may be the first time they have had to respond to a situation where grief, confusion, panic and distress are being experienced across the institution. It is important to acknowledge and recognize that a suicide in any community will affect a large number of people, and when it is in a young person the aftermath can be profoundly distressing (Pitman *et al.* 2014). This can cause uncoordinated interventions to be introduced that can do more harm than good.

It is vitally important to decide leadership of the response group at the outset. Close collaboration between the HEI or FE college and local public health is essential (joint leadership is likely to be the most effective). The local public health lead can provide wider community intelligence and vital links with the police and local coroner and potentially may have experience of managing suicide deaths in other community settings such as schools or prisons; the HE or FE lead can offer contextual information about individual deaths and the HE or FE community. Records will need to be kept of discussions, decisions and continued surveillance of suicide deaths but also self-harm and suicidal behaviours. Appropriate confidentiality and information sharing protocols must be in place.

Following identification of a cluster

A key responsibility of response groups is identifying people who are bereaved, affected and vulnerable, by supporting those who were closest to the individual (bereavement support), improving access to general mental health support across communities, and improving media coverage. This should cover both staff and students.

Media coverage and information sharing

Media coverage is more likely following the suicide of a young person (Marzano *et al.* 2018), so a death in an HE or FE student is likely to draw media attention. Experience from other clusters in young people highlights the importance of a named communications lead from one organization who is the single point of media contact and spokesperson, working closely with other organizations likely to be contacted and staff and student representatives.

Managing the media response is an important aspect of suicide prevention. It requires coordination and sensitivity. We know irresponsible reporting can promote suicidal behaviours and that reporting that promotes the importance of support, raising awareness of sources of help and focusing on stories of hope and recovery can be protective against subsequent suicides (Niederkrotenthaler *et al.* 2010). Guidance for media reporting is readily available from Samaritans (2019).

Information sharing with staff and students needs to weigh the desires and sensitivities of the family of the student who has died by suicide. It often needs to be done at speed. One of the challenges of safe communication after a suicide and during a cluster of suicides in particular is to balance the amount of information shared. Too little sharing may make students feel that the HEI/FE is hiding things and raise anxiety and rumours. Too much information may raise the risk of identification and distress. As a guiding principle, it is essential to convey a sense of empathy but also to reassure students and the community and help contain anxiety and distress.

Pastoral care and bereavement support

A key role of the response group is to identify those who are vulnerable to suicidal behaviours through the mechanisms described above. Those immediately bereaved, such as friends and staff on the same course or household, are often known within HEI networks. It can be harder to find less obviously connected individuals who may identify with the deceased individual or have a previous history of self-harm or suicidal behaviour and be at potential risk themselves. This is where the roles of members of the response group, such as the director of wellbeing, and their contacts with staff members who are working directly with students can triangulate information relating to those who are already seeking help for mental health issues or have a history of suicidal behaviours.

The Circles of Vulnerability model (Public Health England 2019) is often recommended as an approach that can help identify those who are vulnerable, and some FE colleges and HEIs have found it useful as a way to start thinking about and approching those potentially at risk. This model identifies three factors that can act in isolation or in combination to increase the potential for future risk following exposure to a suicide death (or other unexpected death). These include: 1) geographical proximity to the death – that is, the physical distance individuals are from the suicide, including those who may have witnessed or discovered the death; 2) social proximity, which refers to the relationships individuals have with the deceased – for example, friends, peers or others who are part of the same social circle, including online social networks; and 3) psychological proximity, which refers to the extent to which an individual can relate to the deceased. While each factor may contribute to elevated risk, individuals most at risk are likely to be those who fall into the overlapping portions of the model, and who already display some underlying vulnerabilities or risk factors for suicide, such as past suicide-related behaviour, bereavement or mental health difficulties. Where vulnerable individuals and groups can be identified it is possible to target supportive interventions both for mental health and bereavement.

A student suicide is likely to result in significantly increased demand for student wellbeing services. Anecdotally, at one HEI there was a 60 per cent increase in referrals to the student counselling service. It can sometimes be challenging for HEI services to meet this extra demand, but any curtailing of access can further fuel community anxiety, anger and mistrust. Drawing on plans for extra demand for these services during exams may be useful. It will be important for HEI and FE colleges to have plans in advance for where they will draw on additional counselling and bereavement support resources, which could include local mental health and voluntary services. Local voluntary agencies providing such support (e.g. Samaritans, PAPYRUS, Cruse) do not necessarily or generally need to be part of the response group, although they should be informed of the situation. HEI and FE colleges may experience residual impact of the loss of a student for months or years, with particular times of increased vulnerability (e.g. inquest and potential further media reporting, anniversaries, exams or graduations), particularly in students or staff still at the institution.

Online environment

It is important to remain alert to harmful internet and social media coverage. In the immediate aftermath, some people may feel angry and focus blame on certain people, in turn creating further vulnerabilities. A study from a high school in the USA (there is currently little evidence in HE students) showed that young people used social media to memorialize the deceased, reminisce about shared experiences and as a place for receiving and providing support (Heffel et al. 2015). However, some students reported feeling that this impeded their recovery following the suicide, with unexpected reminders of the deceased or negative comments interfering with the grieving process. The public nature of social media also appeared to highlight social pressures and uncertainty about who was entitled to grieve. Young people who were close to the deceased reported feeling angry at other students for constantly posting on the deceased's social media page and attributed these behaviours to attention-seeking. Other young people described feeling obligated to be sad at school and were uncertain whether or not it was acceptable to laugh or when mourning about the death would end.

It may be useful for staff who work with students to monitor online news articles and memorial sites and report offensive content. Social media can be used proactively to promote a sense of social connection and mutual support, which may be protective. It can be effectively used to disseminate information about the grieving process, as well as advice on how to intervene or who to contact if students or staff are aware of, or concerned about, messages they see online in the aftermath of a suicide. HEI and FE suicide prevention strategies should potentially incorporate a digital media policy that aims to counter the potential spread of rumour and misinformation following the death of a young person in the community, focusing instead on sources of support and help.

How do you know when it's over?

It can be difficult to know when to step down from a cluster response. Some individuals may require ongoing support and an institution's responses need to remain mindful of certain periods of vulnerability such as anniversaries and graduation. It is worth the named lead continuing with the monitoring of suicide, building on pre-existing plans with lessons learned from the responses to the recent cluster and sharing knowledge across institutions about what worked and what proved less useful. This learning is an essential but often forgotten aspect of suicide prevention – to understand what could be done differently next time and share good practice.

Conclusion

Young people are much more likely to be part of a suicide cluster than older age groups and this applies to HE and FE students. The mechanisms involved may include direct exposure to the behaviour, media reporting, belief that the behaviour is commonplace, vulnerable individuals sharing social groups, and influence of social media and the internet. Once a cluster is suspected there should be a carefully coordinated and preferably pre-planned response, ideally by an identified cluster response group. The response should include bereavement support, provision of help for vulnerable individuals, proactive responding to media interest, and community approaches to support and prevention. Social media can provide a powerful means for dissemination of information and help.

Author biography

Ann John is a clinical professor of public health and psychiatry at Swansea University Medical School. Her research focuses on suicide and self-harm prevention and the mental health of children and young people. She chairs the Welsh Government's National Advisory Group on Suicide and Self Harm Prevention.

References

Bell, J., Stanley, N., Mallon, S. and Manthorpe, J. (2015) Insights into the processes of suicide contagion: narratives from young people bereaved by suicide. *Suicidology Online 6*, 1, 43–52.

Bould, H., Moran, P., Mars, B., Biddle, L. and Gunnell, D. (2019) Rising rates of suicide in adolescents. *Lancet 394*, 116–117.

Brent, D.A., Kerr, M.M., Goldstein, C., Bozigar, J., Wartella, M. and Allan, M.J. (1989) An outbreak of suicide and suicidal behavior in a high school. *J Am Acad Child Adolesc Psychiatry 28*, 6, 918–924.

Cheung, Y.T.D., Spittal, M.J., Williamson, M.K., Tung, S.J. and Pirkis, J. (2014) Predictors of suicides occurring within suicide clusters in Australia, 2004–2008. *Soc Sci Med. 118*, 135–142.

Cialdini, R.B., Reno, R.R. and Kallgren, C.A. (1990) A focus theory of normative conduct: recycling the concept of norms to reduce littering in public places. *J Pers Soc Psychol. 58*, 6, 1015–1026.

Cox, G.R., Robinson, J., Williamson, M., Lockley, A., Cheung, Y.T.D. and Pirkis, J. (2012) Suicide clusters in young people. *Crisis 33*, 4, 208–214.

Eisenberg, D., Golberstein, E. and Gollust, S.E. (2007) Help-seeking and access to mental health care in a university student population. *Med Care 45*, 7, 594–601.

Farrell, S., Kapur, N., While, D., Appleby, L. and Windfuhr, K. (2017) Suicide in a national student mental health patient population 1997–2012. *Crisis 38*, 82–88.

Fowler, K.A., Crosby, A.E., Parks, S.E., Ivey, A.Z. and Silverman, P.R. (2013) Epidemiological investigation of a youth suicide cluster: Delaware 2012. *Del Med J. 85*, 1, 15–19.

Gallagher, R.P. and Taylor, R. (2014) *National Survey of College Counseling Centers*. The International Association of Counseling Services. Accessed on 28/04/21 at: https://d-scholarship.pitt.edu/28178/1/survey_2014.pdf

Gould, M.S. (1990) Suicide Clusters and Media Exposure. In S.J. Blumenthal and D.J. Kupfer (eds) *Suicide over the Life Cycle: Risk Factors, Assessment, and Treatment of Suicidal Patients*. Washington, DC: American Psychiatric Press. pp.517–532.

Gould, M.S., Kleinman, M.H., Lake, A.M., Forman, J. and Midle, J.B. (2014) Newspaper coverage of suicide and initiation of suicide clusters in teenagers in the USA, 1988–96: a retrospective, population-based, case-control study. *Lancet Psychiatry 1*, 1, 34–43.

Gould, M.S., Lake, A.M., Kleinman, M., Galfalvy, H., Chowdhury, S. and Madnick, A. (2018) Exposure to suicide in high schools: impact on serious suicidal ideation/behavior, depression, maladaptive coping strategies, and attitudes toward help-seeking. *Int J Environ Res Public Health 15*, 3, 455.

Gunnell, D., Caul, S., Appleby, L., John, A. and Hawton, K. (2019) The incidence of suicide in university students in England and Wales 2000/2001–2016/2017: record linkage study. *Journal of Affective Disorders 261*, 113–120.

Haw, C., Hawton, K., Niedzwiedz, C. and Platt, S. (2013) Suicide clusters: a review of risk factors and mechanisms. *Suicide and Life-Threatening Behavior 43*, 1, 97–108.

Hawton, K., Hill, N., Gould, M., John, A., Lascelles, K. and Robinson, J. (2020) Clustering of suicides in children and adolescents. *The Lancet Child & Adolescent Health 4*, 1, 58–67.

John, A., Hawton, K., Gunnell, D., Lloyd, K. *et al.* (2016) Newspaper reporting on a cluster of suicides in the UK: a study of article characteristics using PRINTQUAL. *Crisis 38*, 17–25.

Joiner, T.E. (2003) Contagion of suicidal symptoms as a function of assortative relating and shared relationship stress in college roommates. *Journal of Adolescence 26*, 4, 495–504.

Heffel, C.J., Riggs, S.A., Ruiz, J.M. and Ruggles, M. (2015) The aftermath of a suicide cluster in the age of online social networking: a qualitative analysis of adolescent grief reactions. *Contemporary School Psychology 19*, 4, 286–299.

Marchant, A., Hawton, K., Stewart, A., Montgomery, P. *et al.* (2017) A systematic review of the relationship between internet use, self-harm and suicidal behaviour in young people: the good, the bad and the unknown. *PLoS One 13*, 3, e0193937.

Marzano, L., Fraser, L., Scally, M., Farley, S. and Hawton, K. (2018) News coverage of suicidal behavior in the United Kingdom and the Republic of Ireland. *Crisis 39*, 5, 386–396.

McLaughlin, J.C. and Gunnell, D.J. (2020) Suicide deaths in university students in a UK city 2010–2018: case series. *Crisis*, https://doi.org/10.1027/0227- 5910/a000704

Mesoudi, A. (2009) The cultural dynamics of copycat suicide. *PLoS One 4*, 9, e7252.

Mueller, A.S. and Abrutyn, S. (2016) Adolescents under pressure: a new Durkheimian framework for understanding adolescent suicide in a cohesive community. *Am Sociol Rev. 81*, 5, 877–899.

Niederkrotenthaler, T., Voracek, M., Herberth, A., Till, B. *et al.* (2010) Role of media reports in completed and prevented suicide: Werther v. Papageno effects. *Br J Psychiatry 197*, 3, 234–243.

Niedzwiedz, C., Haw, C., Hawton, K. and Platt, S. (2014) The definition and epidemiology of clusters of suicidal behavior: a systematic review. *Suicide Life Threat Behav. 44*, 5, 569–581.

O'Connor, R.C., Rasmussen, S. and Hawton, K. (2012) Distinguishing adolescents who think about self-harm from those who engage in self-harm. *Br J Psychiatry 200*, 4, 330–335.

Pitman, A., Osborn, D., King, M. and Erlangsen, A. (2014) Effects of suicide bereavement on mental health and suicide risk. *Lancet Psychiatry 1*, 1, 86–94.

Public Health England (2019) *Identifying and Responding to Suicide Cluster: A Practice Resource.* London: Public Health England.

Randall, J.R., Nickel, N.C. and Colman, I. (2015) Contagion from peer suicidal behavior in a representative sample of American adolescents. *J Affect Disord. 186*, 219–225.

Reyes-Portillo, J.A., Lake, A.M., Kleinman, M. and Gould, M.S. (2019) The relation between descriptive norms, suicide ideation, and suicide attempts among adolescents. *Suicide Life Threat Behav. 49*, 2, 535–546.

Rimal, R.N. and Real, K. (2003) Understanding the influence of perceived norms on behaviors. *Communication Theory 13*, 2, 184–203.

Robertson, L., Skegg, K., Poore, M., Williams, S. and Taylor, B. (2012) An adolescent suicide cluster and the possible role of electronic communication technology. *Crisis 33*, 4, 239–245.

Robinson, J., Too, L.S., Pirkis, J. and Spittal, M.J. (2016) Spatial suicide clusters in Australia between 2010 and 2012: a comparison of cluster and non-cluster among young people and adults. *BMC Psychiatry 16*, 417–426.

Samaritans (2019) *Media Guidelines for Reporting Suicide.* London: Samaritans.

Schwartz, A.J. (2011) Rate, relative risk, and method of suicide by students at 4-year colleges and universities in the United States, 2004–2005 through 2008–2009. *Suicide Life Threat Behav. 41*, 353–371.

Too, L.S., Pirkis, J., Milner, A. and Spittal, M.J. (2017) Clusters of suicides and suicide attempts: detection, proximity and correlates. *Epidemiol Psych Sci. 26*, 5, 491–500.

Universities UK and PAPYRUS (2018) *Suicide-Safer Universities.* Universities UK. Accessed on 04/04/21 at: www.universitiesuk.ac.uk/policy-and-analysis/reports/Pages/guidance-for-universities-on-preventing-student-suicides.aspx

Responses to Risk

CHAPTER 10

A Model for Student Suicide Prevention in Higher Education

TREASA FOX AND JO SMITH

Overview

This chapter:

- examines international research evidence in relation to student suicide prevention

- outlines a model for further education (FE) and higher education (HE) student suicide prevention

- provides an HE institution (HEI) case study example where student suicide prevention strategies have been embedded into practice.

Introduction

Currently, there are wide variations in suicide prevention policy and provision across UK universities. In 2017, in the UK, universities were encouraged to embrace the Universities UK (2017) *Stepchange: Mental Health in Higher Education Framework* and take a holistic approach to student support. The objective was to encourage a more consistent culture wherever a student goes to university, including suicide prevention training and support programmes based on evidence from what works in reducing adult suicide. Every part of the university environment, including teaching culture, estates planning, social media policy, training, campaigning and awareness-raising to facilitate early identification and access to appropriate support, can play a part in effective student suicide prevention.

In September 2018, Universities UK with PAPYRUS published a *Suicide-Safer Universities* toolkit providing guidance for universities specifically in relation to student suicide prevention and postvention. Several countries, notably the USA, Ireland, Australia and Canada, have focused attention on student mental health and suicide prevention. These contexts offer international perspectives on these issues and key common elements that may be usefully applied in a UK FE and HEI context. This chapter also considers key common features of successful suicide prevention programmes which have been positively evaluated in other non-educational settings. This includes the international Zero Suicide movement which, although primarily concerned with suicide prevention in healthcare settings, may offer useful shared learning for educational settings in the drive to reduce student suicide. Finally, the chapter concludes by outlining a model for HE student suicide prevention in the UK and provides an HEI case study example where student suicide prevention strategies have been successfully implemented and embedded into routine practice.

Features of successful suicide prevention programmes

As far as we are aware, there is no published research evaluating the implementation of student suicide prevention strategies in HEIs in the UK or internationally. This gap is particularly notable given that there is evidence from successful suicide prevention programmes positively evaluated in other contexts, including work places (WHO 2006), community (Hegerl *et al.* 2013), health settings (While *et al.* 2012) and the US air force (Knox *et al.* 2003). All of these programmes emphasize the importance of a strategic, documented approach to suicide prevention which employs multiple strategies and specific interventions which target whole communities, with the aim of increasing protective factors and reducing risk factors.

Section learning points
- Develop a strategic, documented approach to suicide prevention.
- Employ multiple strategies and specific interventions.
- Target whole communities to increase protective factors and reduce risk factors.

Zero Suicide

Zero Suicide (Brodsky *et al.* 2018) is a suicide prevention model focused on clinical healthcare systems guided by the aspirational goal of eliminating suicide in institutional settings. It involves a systematic, leadership-driven, continuous quality improvement approach to suicide reduction, emphasizing the importance of institution-wide training, access to evidence-based treatments and clear care support pathways. Key elements for successful suicide prevention include:

- leadership centred on a safety-driven culture informed by evidence and lived expertise

- a teamwork approach when engaging those who are suicidal

- active involvement of the person who is suicidal, health professionals and family members/carers in safety planning and transition to aftercare

- a data-driven quality improvement approach to inform system changes to improve outcomes and better care for those at risk.

The Zero Suicide approach has been adopted widely in the USA and is gaining traction internationally as an evidence-based suicide prevention model (Covington and Hogan 2019).

Some HEIs in the USA have adopted Zero Suicide prevention programmes. For example, Georgia Tech have introduced Tech Ends Suicide Together (Georgia Tech 2019) based on the Zero Suicide initiative. The Zero Suicide model, however, would need to be adapted to be 'fit for purpose' for FE and HE settings in the UK and requires a hearts and minds shift from anxieties about reputation, recruitment, duty of care and corporate responsibility to an overt focus on student suicide prevention and data-driven quality improvement.

Section learning points
- Importance of leadership, a safety-driven culture, institution training, teamwork and an approach informed by evidence and lived experience
- Key to successful suicide prevention is the recording/monitoring of serious self-harm and suicide combined with a data-driven quality improvement approach to inform system changes.

International practice in relation to student suicide prevention

In recent years, several countries have specifically focused on the area of student mental health and creating suicide-safer student environments. The key details of these will be explored in this section.

USA

The mental health needs of university students have received national focus in the USA (Prince 2015), although there is currently no nation-wide strategy to address the issue. At the turn of the century, the USA's National Strategy for Suicide Prevention recognized young people as a group vulnerable to suicide and highlighted the suicide prevention needs of adolescents and, specifically, students on campuses (US Department of Health and Human Services 2001). In 2004, the US Congress passed the Garrett Lee Smith Memorial Act that provided federal funding to states and colleges across the USA to implement community- and college-based youth and young adult suicide prevention programmes.

The Jed Foundation, a non-profit organization which aims to reduce student suicide, has been instrumental in supporting student mental health in the USA. Their primary mission is to promote emotional health and prevent suicide among college and university students through promoting awareness that 'mental illness is treatable, and that suicide is preventable' (Prince 2015, p.8). They provide action plans for campus mental health and protocols for responding to suicidal students (SPRC/JED 2011). It is a whole system approach that supports emotional health and reduces the risks of substance abuse and suicide (JED 2019a). Their model is designed to offer an evidence-based 'comprehensive approach' to student suicide prevention on university campuses (SPRC and JED 2019). It draws on evidence from the US Air Force Suicide Prevention Program, a population-based strategy to reduce risk factors and enhance protective factors for suicide based on the Zero Suicide approach (Knox *et al.* 2003, 2004, 2010). The programme succeeded in reducing the suicide rate among Air Force personnel by 33 per cent during its first five years (JED 2006, 2011; Knox *et al.* 2003, 2010). The framework developed by The Jed Foundation aims to guide universities in formulating and implementing a strategic comprehensive mental health promotion and suicide prevention programme to become a 'Jed Campus' (JED 2006, 2011, 2016b, 2019b).

The original 2006 Jed Campus framework consisted of nine domains.

Strategic planning served as the foundation that supported eight other domains and was seen as a crucial aspect in developing, implementing, monitoring and evaluating a comprehensive approach. It was emphasized that a strategic plan should be fully documented in a suicide prevention policy. The other eight domains included educational training for staff and students as well as screening and questionnaires to identify students at risk, social marketing to increase help-seeking behaviour, promoting mental health services, following crisis management procedures, restricting access to potentially lethal means, developing life skills (money management, distress tolerance, study skills) and promoting social connectedness (supportive social relationships and feeling connected to campus life).

In the 2011 version (JED 2011), these nine domains were refined to eight where educational training and screening were combined into 'identify students at risk' and social marketing was renamed 'increase help-seeking behaviour' (see Figure 10.1).

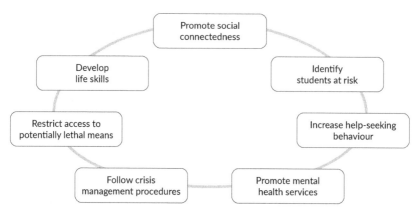

Figure 10.1: JED comprehensive approach
(*Original source: JED 2019b*)

There are over 200 US universities recognized by The Jed Foundation as 'Jed Campuses' (JED 2018). Currently, there is no data evaluating the model's effectiveness, although a longitudinal evaluation is planned. Although a number of US researchers (Drum *et al.* 2009; Westefeld *et al.* 2006) have advocated a community approach to student suicide prevention on campuses and described possible approaches, none have articulated or developed a framework as comprehensive as The Jed Foundation framework or included additional novel strategies.

Section learning points

- Strategic planning as the underpinning foundation and a plan which is documented in a suicide prevention policy
- Training for staff and students to identify students at risk
- Screening to identify students at risk
- Campaigning and awareness-raising to increase help-seeking behaviour
- Promotion of mental health services
- Following crisis management policy and procedures
- Restricting access to potentially lethal means
- Developing student life skills (money management, distress tolerance, study skills)
- Promoting social connectedness.

Ireland

In 2018, the Higher Education Authority (HEA) convened a working group of student mental health and suicide prevention experts to address identified actions under strategic goals in *Connecting for Life: Ireland's National Strategy to Reduce Suicide 2015–2020* (Department of Health and Children 2015). A priority action was identified:

> Work with the HSE to develop national guidance for higher education institutions in relation to suicide risk and critical incident response, to address any gaps which may exist in the prevention of suicide in higher education.

Simultaneously, a research team led by one of the authors (TF) secured research funding to scope suicide prevention activities across all HEIs in Ireland, to identify gaps and challenges, to review international guidance and identify best practice and evidence-based interventions. When the synergies between both were identified, the research team agreed to develop a suicide prevention framework on behalf of the HEA Connecting for Life Working Group. In developing the framework, it became clear that suicide prevention could not be addressed in isolation from student mental health, as 'upstream' mental health interventions such as awareness and education, promotion of help-seeking for mental health difficulties and provision of on-campus mental health services are part of the early intervention bedrock of suicide prevention. Education and awareness, identifying students vulnerable to mental ill health and suicide risk and targeting interventions to these groups, as well as improving access to services within and outside the institution, are some of the features that are common to all international guidance for HE.

Ireland's *National Student Mental Health and Suicide Prevention Framework* (Higher Education Authority 2020) adopts the same comprehensive whole system approach present in guidance described throughout this chapter. It identifies nine themes to guide policy, planning and implementation at the national sectoral level and within institutions (see Figure 10.2). Throughout the framework, and in the accompanying *Implementation Guide*, the authors signpost relevant resources under each theme to facilitate implementation in universities and colleges. It is understood that time and resources to effect change advocated under the framework are often in short supply on campuses, so providing links to resources, materials and other guides to facilitate this change was considered as important as the framework itself.

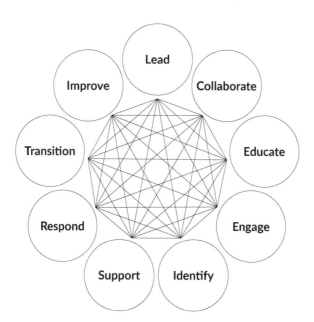

Figure 10.2: The nine themes in Ireland's *National Student Mental Health and Suicide Prevention Framework* (Higher Education Authority 2020)

One theme, Collaborate, describes how institutions should develop relationships at a local and national level with health and NGO (non-governmental organization) services. An early output under this theme was a partnership between psychological counsellors in Higher Education Ireland (PCHEI), the representative body for student counselling services, and the crisis text service 50808 which, without this impetus, would have otherwise taken much longer to achieve. Students use the keyword of their institution to begin a text conversation with a trained volunteer in the 50808 service, an anonymous text service 'providing everything from a calming chat to immediate support for people going through a mental health or emotional crisis – big or small'.

Section learning points

- Develop a whole sector and whole institution approach.
- Leadership, a 'champion' for student mental health both at sector and institution levels, is crucial.
- Identify and develop positive collaborations between the HEIs and local and national health services and NGOs.
- Implementation of a new framework is more likely to be successful if relevant tools and resources are included.

Canada

Post-Secondary Student Mental Health: Guide to a Systemic Approach (2013) was developed by the Canadian Association of College and University Student Services (CACUSS) and the Canadian Mental Health Association (CMHA) and aims to support the creation of third-level campus communities that are 'conducive to transformative learning and mental wellbeing'. It is designed as a resource to develop a whole institution systemic approach to student mental health and supports campus self-assessment, strategic goal setting and the identification of options for change that can be used to inform planning and evaluation. Post-secondary institutions across Canada have independently developed policies and programmes using this guide to respond to student mental health issues. DiPlacito-DeRango (2016) suggested that despite improvements, student mental health remains a problem in Canadian HE settings. A new national standard championed by the Mental Health Commission of Canada (MHCC) to guide policies, procedures and practices that promote positive student mental health and wellbeing, developed for use by post-secondary institutions, was launched in October 2020. The standard is designed to enhance and expand strategies already put in place by Canada's universities, colleges, institutes, CEGEPs (general and vocational colleges) and polytechnics to promote and support student mental health. The standard is based on a socio-ecological model and the planned framework includes clear leadership and expectations of a campus culture that, although not specifically mentioning student suicide prevention, 'promotes and supports student psychological health and safety and supports student success' (Mental Health Commission of Canada 2019).

Section learning points

- A whole institution systemic approach to student mental health, including student suicide prevention
- Self-assessment, strategic goal setting and the identification of options for change to inform planning and evaluation
- Clear leadership
- A campus culture that promotes and supports student mental health and safety.

Australia

HEIs across Australia have independently developed policies and programmes to respond to student mental health and wellbeing on campus (Orygen 2017). In 2017, Orygen, the National Centre for Excellence in Youth Mental Health, published *Under the Radar: The Mental Health of Australian University Students*. The report identified that youth mental health policies, services and programmes should engage with and provide support to HEIs. This includes extending government funded school-based mental health programmes beyond secondary school into tertiary education settings (Orygen 2017). The report aimed to improve data collection on student mental health, identify reasonable expectations of HEIs in responding to student mental health issues, describe opportunities for partnerships with community mental health services and promote use of evidence-based, appropriate and acceptable programmes and interventions (Orygen 2017). Orygen was subsequently awarded funding to develop a National University Mental Health Framework, which was published at the end of October 2020.

Section learning points

- Improve data collection on student mental health and student suicide.
- Identify reasonable expectations of universities in responding to student mental health issues.
- Develop a partnership between universities and community mental health services.
- Use evidence-based, appropriate and acceptable programmes and interventions.

UK

In 2017, Universities UK (UUK) launched the *Stepchange* framework, encouraging HEI leaders to adopt a strategic approach to the mental health of their populations. The primary aim of the framework was to offer guidance to HEIs on suicide prevention. Universities UK have also worked in partnership with the Department of Health, Public Health England and the Office for National Statistics (ONS) to improve the national HE student suicide dataset (ONS 2018). In 2018, *Suicide-Safer Universities* guidelines were published to help HEIs specifically prevent student suicide (UUK and PAPYRUS 2018).

The UK Institute of Public Policy Research (IPPR) suggested that HEIs needed to make student mental health a strategic priority and adopt a whole university approach based on promotion, prevention, intervention and postvention as well as established referral pathways to specialist care. 'There is currently too much variation in the extent to which universities are equipped to meet this challenge' (Thorley 2017, p.3). A sector-led approach needs to be accompanied by strengthened health service provision and government-level initiatives. It is in this context, informed by the IPPR findings, that the Stepchange framework was introduced.

The Stepchange approach is being piloted at the Universities of West England (Bristol), Cardiff and York with support from the student mental health charity Student Minds. The pilots are being funded by the Higher Education Funding Council for England. Dissemination of the framework continues with adoption by multiple HEIs.

The Stepchange framework set out eight domains (Figure 10.3) and recommended a continuous improvement process driven by a sustained leadership focus as well as engagement with students and staff. This whole university approach aims to embed mental health across the whole university and into all aspects of student and staff experience. Through collaboration between Universities UK, Student Minds and various stakeholders, the Stepchange framework has been remodelled to become the *UUK Mentally Healthy Universities* model (UUK 2020).

Figure 10.3: Stepchange framework (UUK 2017)

In December 2019, Student Minds UK launched *The Universities Mental Health Charter* (Hughes and Spanner 2019). The vision of the Charter is for all HEIs in the UK to adopt a whole university approach to mental health and become places where mental health and wellbeing are promoted for students and all members of the university community. The Charter's view of a whole university approach is one that has adequately resourced, effective and accessible mental health services and proactive interventions. It should provide an environment and culture that not only reduces poor mental health but supports good mental health.

There are two main aims:

- To create an evidence-informed Charter that can provide a reference point for HEIs to adopt a whole system approach to mental health and inform ongoing enquiry and debate.

- To develop a Charter Award Scheme, which will assess HEIs against the Charter and recognize providers that demonstrate excellent practice, providing further structure and building an evidence base which can inform ongoing improvement.

The Charter Award Scheme was piloted in 2020 to determine the feasibility, validity and reliability of the assessment methods and refine the process and methodology. The final scheme is due to be launched more widely in 2021.

In 2018, UUK and PAPYRUS, a national charity dedicated to the prevention of young suicide, published guidance aimed at university leaders and practitioners to prevent student suicide. The guidance provides a framework, with real HEI case study examples, to understand student suicide, mitigate risk, intervene when students get into difficulties and respond to a student death by suicide. It includes a useful checklist, summarizing key actions for university leaders to make their communities suicide safer, including identifying, training and publicizing suicide intervention and postvention teams and providing suicide awareness training for all student-facing staff. It also provides advice on the development of a suicide prevention, intervention and postvention strategy, which should be distinct from a student death policy, and an overarching institutional mental health strategy.

The strategy should be agreed by and have visible support from the senior leadership team and be owned by a member of the executive team. It should set out a clear ambition and objectives and an action plan that is created in partnership with student support staff (including personal tutors and staff groups in student-facing roles), students and external stakeholders. The strategy and suicide-safer related policies and procedures should be reviewed on a regular basis and refined based on lessons learned. The importance of creating strong links with local and national partners from the health sector, voluntary sector and local authority, and actively contributing to local suicide prevention partnerships, is encouraged. Similarly, the importance of working with local schools, colleges and other universities to ensure smooth transitions between educational settings is also emphasized.

Section learning points

- Develop a suicide prevention, intervention and postvention strategy as a specific component of an overarching institutional mental health strategy.
- Identify and train suicide intervention and postvention teams.
- Provide suicide awareness training for all student-facing staff.
- Create strong links with local and national community partners and actively contribute to local suicide prevention planning.
- Work with local schools, colleges and other HEIs to ensure smooth transitions between educational settings.

Student suicide prevention in UK HEIs

The Association of Managers of Student Services in Higher Education (AMOSSHE 2001), National Union of Students (NUS Disabled Students 2016), PAPYRUS (Stanley *et al.* 2007) and UUK (UUK and PAPYRUS 2018) have all highlighted the need for UK HEIs to implement student suicide prevention and postvention strategies. These should include staff training, policies and procedures for student suicide prevention, collaboration with external agencies, on-call campus provision, postvention responses and social support and integration for students.

A key gap in our current knowledge is a lack of available information about what is actually happening in UK HEIs in relation to student suicide prevention. In response to this, a current PhD study at the University of Worcester, UK (Vinyard *et al.* 2019), has surveyed publicly funded HEIs (n=167) to explore how many had suicide prevention strategies and which specific prevention strategies are typically employed. This involved a 25-item online survey sent directly to vice-chancellors asking whether they had a student suicide prevention policy, the availability of specific suicide prevention training and activities, the monitoring and recording of student suicide and whether the institution had experienced a student suicide in the previous three years and, specifically, in the previous year. Survey responses showed the lack of a strategic approach to student suicide prevention in the majority of HEIs that provided survey responses and wide variation in strategy implementation, with many key activities (information and training provision, monitoring and recording procedures, restricting access to lethal means) under-utilized except for the promotion of suicide helpline information promoted by all HEI survey respondents. Interestingly, institutions that had experienced a student suicide in the previous three years were more likely to have a suicide prevention policy and those that had not had a suicide had all restricted access to means. There was also an association found between having a student suicide prevention policy and providing suicide prevention information and training (Vinyard *et al.* 2019). A second study involved a multiple case study approach, and involved interviewing staff from four HEIs to explore factors influencing provision of student suicide prevention strategies. This identified the importance of an institutional culture that proactively engaged with a student suicide prevention agenda and the importance of leadership and staff in key roles driving policy and provision. Barriers identified included staff capacity, training costs and lack of priority given to specific student suicide prevention or it being seen as an issue requiring a specific strategy and action plan (Vinyard *et al.* 2019).

Some UK HEIs are implementing whole campus suicide prevention strategies including the University of Worcester Suicide-Safer project (NUS Disabled Students 2016; PHE 2020; Smith 2016; Student Minds 2017; Thorley 2017), the University of Cumbria's Compassionate Campus project (Thorley 2017) and the University of Wolverhampton's 3 minutes to save a life project (Pearce 2019), which all have student suicide prevention as an explicit aim. Many more HEIs have instituted strategies which promote student mental health including peer support initiatives, resilience building, life skills training, promotion of counselling services, support to students at higher risk and integration of wellbeing activities into course curricula (Thorley 2017), which are all helpful interventions for student suicide prevention.

A model for student suicide prevention

All UK and international guidance for suicide prevention in HE point to the need for a whole institution systemic approach, a socio-ecological model, with all component parts connecting with each other to create an institutional culture that promotes and supports student mental health *and* safety. This whole system approach can only be effected if there is strong leadership at a senior level and somebody identified as a champion for student mental health and suicide prevention within the institution. Senior leadership is key to ensuring strategic prioritization and planning, supporting policy development, reducing access to lethal means, adequately resourcing student mental health needs and ensuring that all at the institution are engaged to fully participate while also addressing obstacles to change.

Much of the international guidance reviewed emphasizes the importance of having a strategic documented plan to address student mental health which includes suicide prevention as a specifically identified component of a broader institutional mental health strategy. The process needs to start with self-assessment building on identified current strengths and assets to identify options for change to inform strategic goal setting. A strategy should include ongoing review and evaluation processes (including routine ongoing serious self-harm and suicide recording, monitoring and review) to create an iterative data-driven quality improvement feedback loop to inform further system change.

Interventions should be evidence based and informed by lived student and staff experience to ensure they are appropriate, acceptable and fit for purpose. Successful suicide prevention programmes have been shown to employ multiple strategies including specific targeted interventions for at-risk groups as well as broad-based, institution-wide interventions such as developing student life skills, embedding mental health and well-being within the student curricula and promoting social connectedness. The most successful universal suicide prevention intervention to date has been the restriction of access to potentially lethal means (JED 2016a; SPRC 2019). This should be included in the brief of any institution safety or safeguarding lead or committee, as well as ensuring review processes are in place following incidents of serious self-harm, suicide attempts or student death by suicide on campus to ensure organizational learning and improve future safety planning and intervention. Campaigning and awareness raising should promote help-seeking and early intervention, including self-help, online and non-specialist interventions as well as availability of, and access to, more specialist counselling, mental health and crisis intervention support. Implementation is likely to be more successful if relevant tools and resources are made available and actively promoted to students and staff.

Common across all the guidance is the need to promote and provide education and awareness-raising training for all members of the campus community, including security and facilities staff, as well as all student-facing staff. This can help to reduce stigma, improve identification of students who are in distress and are at risk for suicide or self-harm, and improve help-seeking and accessing of services. Such education should also include specialist suicide prevention, intervention and postvention training for student support and counselling staff and any staff group that may be directly involved in crisis intervention or postvention, including campus security, chaplaincy and residential accommodation staff.

One final message from much of the guidance reviewed is the importance of institutions identifying and forging positive collaborations and links with local and national health and community partners, including NGOs, while also actively contributing to and learning from local suicide prevention planning and initiatives. One key partnership identified in UK guidance is that undertaken with local schools, colleges and other HEIs to ensure smooth transitions for students between educational settings. This is particularly relevant to suicide prevention as transition has been specifically identified as a key risk factor potentially contributing to poor student mental health and suicide (see Chapter 7).

HEI CASE STUDY EXAMPLE OF STUDENT SUICIDE PREVENTION IN PRACTICE
University of Worcester (UK) Suicide-Safer project

In 2014, the University of Worcester established a multiagency Suicide-Safer project inviting university staff, county council public health, NHS trust and third sector organizations to develop a multi-faceted suicide prevention model to contribute to a suicide-safer university and, in a phased plan, to a suicide-safer city and county as an active partner in the local authority mental wellbeing and suicide prevention plan. The project had a specific student suicide prevention strategy, including an updated annual action plan, and employed a dedicated part-time Suicide-Safer project lead. Included here are the core details to illustrate how such a project may be undertaken.

The project comprised four key strands:

1. *Campaigning* to raise awareness about student suicide, tackle stigma and signpost to available support. This included suicide prevention and support awareness campaigns across the university academic year.

2. *Education/training* to improve staff and student mental health and suicide prevention literacy and skills and embed mental health and suicide prevention training into student and staff teaching curricula. This included specific training in mental health first aid (Morgan, Ross and Reavley

2018) for domestic staff and ASIST[1] suicide prevention training (Rodgers 2010) for security staff who play a key role in out-of-hours and weekend crisis support on campus. Online mental health (CWMT 2018) and suicide prevention training (HEE 2018; Zero Suicide Alliance 2017) modules for HE staff were trialled with a range of staff groups and embedded into staff induction and staff training curriculum modules.

3. *Student and staff support* to improve awareness of and access to mental health and suicide prevention/postvention resources and support for students and staff. These support options ranged from self-help, peer support and first line interventions to more specialist support/onward referral. The University Counselling and Mental Health Service offered daily triage appointments providing crisis assessment and immediate support for students and concerned staff members. Specific guidance was produced for staff on supporting and signposting students who were struggling, and a dedicated 24/7 crisis texting service #TALKWORC was established, linked to and run by the national SHOUT crisis text line service.

4. *Research* whereby the university proactively contributed to UK student suicide research by establishing two funded PhD studentships exploring aspects of HE student suicide prevention and postvention practice and involvement in other national student mental health research projects.

The project had buy-in and support from its inception from senior leadership at the university. The university's vice-chancellor initiated the multiagency project and the pro-vice-chancellor chaired the multiagency Suicide-Safer project group meetings. The project made a wider local and national contribution to student suicide prevention through contributions to the local authority county suicide prevention plan development and activities including a national Public Health England HE suicide prevention master class. Project staff supported other universities to develop their own student suicide prevention plans and were involved in several UUK national task groups on student mental health and suicide prevention. The work was identified as a best practice example in several national guidance documents and student and sector publications (NUS Disabled Students 2016; PHE 2020; Smith 2016; Student Minds 2017; Thorley 2017), and was a finalist for the *Times Higher Education* 2018 Outstanding Support for Students Award. The project was also featured extensively as a positive practice example in local and national media reports on student suicide prevention.

---

1   Applied Suicide Intervention Skills Training

Conclusion

This chapter has outlined a model for FE and HE student suicide prevention drawing on a synthesis of existing research evidence, published international HEI frameworks and practice guidance. A whole system approach can only be effected if there is strong leadership at a senior level within institutions prioritizing and adequately resourcing student mental health and suicide prevention. A UK HEI survey carried out in 2018 (Vinyard *et al.* 2019) revealed the lack of a strategic approach to student suicide prevention in HEIs and wide variation in strategy implementation, with many key interventions under-utilized. Sadly, it appears that reactive institutional responses to student suicide prevention are currently more likely to be mobilized following the experience of a student death (or series of deaths) by suicide and associated media publicity. This reactive model is likely to continue unless student mental health is given a sustained, priority place in the FE and HE agenda at a sector and governmental level, with expectations on FE and HE institutions to respond proactively to student mental health and safety issues. Interestingly, in the current climate of competition for scarce resources, falling student numbers and continuing impact of Covid-19, the impetus to change may also start to come internally from institutions themselves. Institutions, now needing to ensure sustained income and growth, may realize that an institutional culture that proactively and overtly promotes student mental health and wellbeing and engages with a student suicide prevention agenda may well be becoming an increasingly important factor influencing consumer (prospective student and parents) FE and HE institution choices.

Resources to support suicide prevention strategy development in FE and HE

- PAPYRUS (2018) *Building Suicide-Safer Schools and Colleges: A Guide for Teachers and Staff*, www.papyrus-uk.org/wp-content/uploads/2018/08/toolkitfinal.pdf

- UUK and PAPYRUS (2018) *Suicide-Safer Universities* **toolkit**, https://universitiesuk.ac.uk/policy-and-analysis/reports/Documents/2018/guidance-for-universities-on-preventing-student-suicides.pdf

Author biographies

Treasa Fox was Project Lead of the research team that drafted the *National Student Mental Health and Suicide Prevention Framework* for Ireland's Higher Education Authority (HEA 2020). Treasa has over 25 years' experience as Head of Student Counselling in Athlone Institute of Technology, Ireland.

Professor Jo Smith was Project Lead for the University of Worcester 'Suicide-Safer' student suicide prevention initiative (2014–2020) and co-author of an 'International Declaration on Zero Suicide in Healthcare' (2015). She was on national working groups which produced UUK (2017) *#Stepchange: Mental Health in Higher Education*, UUK (2018) *Minding Our Future* and UUK and PAPYRUS (2018) *Suicide-Safer Universities*.

References

Association of Managers of Student Services in Higher Education (AMOSSHE) (2001) *Responding to Student Mental Health Issues: 'Duty of Care' Responsibilities for Student Services in Higher Education*. Winchester: AMOSSHE.

Brodsky, B.S., Spruch-Feiner, A. and Stanley, B. (2018) The Zero Suicide Model: applying evidence-based suicide prevention practices to clinical care. *Frontiers in Psychiatry 9*, 33.

Canadian Association of College and University Student Services (CACUSS) (2013) *Post-Secondary Student Mental Health: Guide to a Systemic Approach*. Vancouver, BC: CACUSS.

Charlie Waller Memorial Trust (CWMT) (2018) Higher Education and Further Education e-Learning Sessions, https://learning.cwmt.org.uk/e-learning

Covington, D. and Hogan, M. (2019) Zero suicide: the dogged pursuit of perfection in health care. *Psychiatric Times 36*, 1, 16–17.

Department of Health and Children (2015) *Connecting for Life: Ireland's National Strategy to Reduce Suicide 2015–2020*. Dublin: Department of Health.

DiPlacito-DeRango, M. (2016) Acknowledge the barriers to better the practices: support for student mental health in higher education. *The Canadian Journal for the Scholarship of Teaching and Learning 7*, 2, 2.

Drum, D.J., Brownson, C., Burton Denmark, A. and Smith, S.E. (2009) New data on the nature of suicidal crises in college students: shifting the paradigm. *Professional Psychology: Research and Practice 40*, 3, 213.

Georgia Tech (2019) End Suicide: QPR Training, https://endsuicide.gatech.edu/content/qpr-training-0

Health Education England (HEE) (2018) *We Need to Talk about Suicide*. e-Learning suicide prevention module, www.e-lfh.org.uk/programmes/suicide-prevention

Hegerl, U., Rummel-Klugea, C., Värnik, A., Arensmanc, E. and Koburger, N. (2013) Alliances against depression – a community based approach to target depression and to prevent suicidal behaviour. *Neuroscience & Biobehavioral Reviews 37*, 10 (1), 2404–2409.

Higher Education Authority (HEE) (2020) *National Student Mental Health and Suicide Prevention Framework*. Accessed on 28/10/20 at: https://hea.ie/assets/uploads/2020/10/HEA-NSMHS-Framework.pdf

Hughes, G. and Spanner, L. (2019) *The University Mental Health Charter*. Leeds: Student Minds.

JED (2006) *Framework for Developing Institutional Protocols for the Acutely Distressed or Suicidal College Student*. New York: The Jed Foundation.

JED (2011) *ULifeline Online Resource for College Mental Health*. New York: The Jed Foundation.

JED (2016a) *Means Restriction Saves Lives*. New York: The Jed Foundation.

JED (2016b) *Framework for Developing Institutional Protocols for the Acutely Distressed or Suicidal College Student*. New York: The Jed Foundation.

JED (2018) JED announces 2 million student milestone for JED campus initiative, www.jedfoundation.org/jed-announces-2-million-student-milestone-jed-campus-initiative

JED (2019a) *Comprehensive Approach, What We Do*. New York: The Jed Foundation.

JED (2019b) *The Crisis in College and University Mental Health*. New York: The Jed Foundation.

Knox, K.L., Conwell, Y. and Caine, E.D. (2004) If suicide is a public health problem, what are we doing to prevent it? *American Journal of Public Health 94*, 1, 37–45.

Knox, K.L., Litts, D.A., Talcott, W., Feig, J.C. and Caine, E.D. (2003) Risk of suicide and related adverse outcomes after exposure to a suicide prevention programme in the US Air Force: cohort study. *British Medical Journal 327*, 7428, 1376.

Knox, K.L., Pflanz, S., Talcott, G.W., Campise, R.L. *et al.* (2010) The US Air Force Suicide Prevention Program: implications for public health policy. *American Journal of Public Health 100*, 12, 2457–2463.

Mental Health Commission of Canada (2019) *Post-Secondary Student Standard*. Ottawa: Mental Health Commission of Canada.

Morgan, A., Ross, A. and Reavley, N. (2018) Systematic review and meta-analysis of mental health first aid training: effects on knowledge, stigma, and helping behaviour. *PloS One 13*, 5, e0197102.

NUS Disabled Students (2016) *Mental Health and Suicide Prevention Guide: An In-Depth Guide for Students' Unions and Student Activists*. London: NUS.

Office for National Statistics (ONS) (2018) *Estimating Suicide among Higher Education Students, England and Wales: Experimental Statistics*. London: ONS.

Orygen (2017) *Under the Radar: The Mental Health of Australian University Students*. Melbourne: Orygen.

Orygen (2020) *Policy: University Mental Health Framework*. Melbourne: Orygen.

PAPYRUS (2018) *Building Suicide-Safer Schools and Colleges: A Guide for Teachers and Staff*. Preston: PAPYRUS.

Pearce, L. (2019) 3 minutes to save a life: the course designed to raise suicide awareness. *Nursing Standard 34*, 3, 26–27.

Prince, J. (2015) University student counseling and mental health in the United States: trends and challenges. *Mental Health and Prevention 3*, 1–2, 5–10.

Public Health England (PHE) (2020) *Local Suicide Prevention Planning: A Practice Resource*. London: PHE.

Rodgers, P. (2010) *Review of the Applied Suicide Intervention Skills Training Program (ASIST): Rationale, Evaluation Results, and Directions for Future Research*. Calgary: Living Works Education Incorporated.

Smith, J. (2016) Student mental health: a new model for universities. *The Guardian Higher Education Network*, 3 March 2016.

Stanley, N., Mallon, S., Bell, J., Hilton, S. and Manthorpe, J. (2007) *Responses and Prevention in Student Suicide (RaPSS)*. Preston: PAPYRUS.

Student Minds (2017) *Student Living: Collaborating to Support Mental Health in University Accommodation*. Leeds: Student Minds.

Suicide Prevention Resource Centre (SPRC) (2019) *Restricting Access to Lethal Means at Colleges and Universities*. Waltham, MA: SPRC.

Suicide Prevention Resource Centre (SPRC) and JED (2011) *Guide to Campus Mental Health Action Planning*. Waltham, MA: SPRC.

Suicide Prevention Resource Centre (SPRC) and JED (2019) *Comprehensive Approach to Mental Health Promotion and Suicide Prevention for Colleges and Universities*. Waltham, MA: SPRC.

Thorley, C. (2017) *Not by Degrees: Improving Student Mental Health in the UK's Universities*. London: Institute for Public Policy Research.

Universities UK (UUK) (2017) *Stepchange: Mental Health in Higher Education Framework*. London: UUK.

Universities UK (UUK) (2018) *Minding our Future: Starting a Conversation about Support for Student Mental Health*. London: UUK.

Universities UK (UUK) (2020) *Stepchange: Mentally Healthy Universities*. London: UUK.

Universities UK (UUK) and PAPYRUS (2018) *Suicide-Safer Universities*. London: UUK.

US Department of Health and Human Services (2001) *National Strategy for Suicide Prevention: Goals and Objectives for Action*. Rockville, MD: Dept HHS.

Vinyard, C., Jones, L., Mitchell, T., Mahoney, B. and Smith, J. (2019) Provision and nature of student suicide prevention strategies in UK HEIs and factors influencing implementation. Conference paper, 30th World Congress of the International Association for Suicide Prevention (IASP): Breaking Down Walls, Building Bridges, Derry-Londonderry, 17–21 September 2019.

Westefeld, J.S., Button, C., Haley, J.T., Kettmann, J.J. *et al.* (2006) College student suicide: a call to action. *Death Studies 30*, 10, 931–956.

While, D., Bickley, H., Roscoe, A., Windfuhr, K. *et al.* (2012) Implementation of mental health service recommendations in England and Wales and suicide rates, 1997–2006: a cross-sectional and before-and-after observational study. *Lancet 379*, 1005– 1012.

World Health Organization (WHO) (2006) *Preventing Suicide: A Resource at Work*. Geneva: WHO.

Zero Suicide Alliance (2017) Suicide awareness e-training, https://zerosuicidealliance.com

CHAPTER 11

How Can We Support Staff to Talk Safely about Suicide?

CLARE DICKENS AND STUART GUY

Overview

This chapter will offer a space for readers to:

- critically reflect on their support role within a higher education (HE) context, and their contribution to a democratized and inclusive suicide prevention strategy

- consider a higher education institution (HEI) case study where training is offered to all front-facing staff to support safe and appropriate responses

- explore key tenets and hopes of the training strategy and offer practical tips in how staff can respond to distress at the most basic of levels.

Introduction

A core aim of this chapter is to offer a space for critical reflection, where preconceived or rigid ways of hearing and talking about suicide prevention within an HE context can be challenged. The reader will be presented with an HEI case study describing how training has been embedded within the organizational development offered to staff in all student-facing roles. The reader will then be invited to critically explore key aims and considerations of this approach, and consider their role in suicide prevention and barriers that may exist in their own thinking that could prevent them from feeling they can offer any meaningful help. Discussions in this chapter are framed by what current research evidence suggests supports suicide prevention – that is, appropriate and timely help seeking (Gould *et al.* 2004; Ko, Frey and Harrington 2019). It will consider aspects of successful help-seeking as well as potential barriers. A case will be presented for how we can talk about suicide prevention in a safe and considered way.

The chapter will conclude with practical tips for those identified in the literature as 'emergent' gatekeepers. Gatekeepers are posited as naturally occurring helpers, who have face-to-face contact with large numbers of community members as part of their usual role, and who therefore may come into contact with those who might be at risk and potentially in a position to observe warning signs and make referrals to help (Osteen, Frey and Ko 2014).

How we should begin thinking about suicide prevention in an HE context

Much of the current mental health promotion narrative is targeted firmly at the individual, telling them to talk to someone, with the promise that this will help. It is also aligned to wider public health initiatives in the UK, which encourage the promotion and development of individual resilience. This chapter encourages the reader to consider how talking to others can help and reflect upon how they can better connect with and respond to those seeking help by meaningfully listening to the sources of their distress.

Questions for reflection

- What mental health awareness have you experienced in your HEI?
- What suicide prevention training have you received in your HEI?
- How beneficial have you found this beyond the training?
- How did the training make you feel?

CASE STUDY: UNIVERSITY OF WOLVERHAMPTON

Between 2014 and 2015, based on increasing need, staff members who had been first responders to disclosures from students were increasingly 'scared that they would say the wrong thing'. In these circumstances, staff often adopted an emergency-level response to any suicidal ideation or self-harming behaviour disclosed by students. This could present in the form of calling a designated mental health professional, or referral to external formal mental health services, in the hope of an immediate response or intervention. While this approach was commendable and designed to ensure the safety of students in crisis, it potentially had the capacity to increase risk, particularly if a consistent and immediate response from external services was not offered. In addition, students can fall between gaps, fail to attend appointments with university-based mental health services and there can often be a delay between referral and any subsequent specialist assessment. This type of approach was acknowledged by the university as potentially delaying and amplifying the real, dangerous and imminent risk without ameliorating possible causes of distress, which in many cases arose from difficulties students were experiencing in their studies and social lives. An alternative approach would be to support these types of difficulty at that initial disclosure.

A strategy embracing this type of whole systems approach to mental health and wellbeing, where all staff are equipped to offer a response, could identify that only a small proportion of students at any one time would be deemed as experiencing high levels of distress where situational factors may increase their risk of dying by suicide. Instead, many more students may be experiencing much less overt levels of distress, or may be experiencing thoughts that their life is not worth living, but not be known to be in distress or not have an established risk profile. In these cases, there is the potential for their difficulties to be minimized if they are not considered to be part of a traditional 'at risk' group in the absence of traditional demographic risk factors or suicidal thoughts escalate because of a lack of disclosure potentially due to stigma (Cole-King and Platt 2017). Any number of reasons may contribute to an inability to connect with a source of help or find a solution to their distress triggers. This can be further compounded by a lack of compassionate responses from university staff members in a front-facing role, driven by myth and misunderstanding about what suicidal thoughts mean and what they may be communicating; and low confidence and self-belief in intervening successfully to prevent a suicide.

In order to respond to this, staff groups are offered the Connecting with People training from 4 Mental Health. This is delivered in the course of a one-day programme, using a combination of bite-size modules. These act as building blocks to shift delegates beyond fear of talking about what can be difficult topics, to a position where they feel more confident to offer a response to those in distress. The building blocks are modules on:

- *Suicide awareness* – aimed at reducing stigma by uncovering and demystifying common assumptions, judgements, fears about suicide and barriers to disclosure in a safe environment. It introduces a common language and approach to help delegates understand how distress develops and how people can be best supported. It mirrors and explores the concept that suicidal thoughts are on a continuum (Cole-King *et al.* 2013; Waters and Cole-King 2017). This continuum considers that suicidal thoughts can present as more 'passive' (such as having no plans or desire to die, but you consider life difficult and possibly not worth living) through to distressing, persistent suicidal thoughts with a well-formed plan for suicide coupled with access to means, where a crisis 999 response is required. It also gives delegates the confidence and the skills practice of talking to someone in distress, shares a compassionate approach for demanding and time-pressured environments, and offers consistency in response as well as basic safety planning access for all.

- *Self-harm awareness* – aimed at reducing stigma, dispelling myths and common assumptions about self-harm, as well as understanding barriers to disclosure. It explores some of the functions of self-harm, the need to assess and focus on solutions for underlying distress, and the interrelationship between self-harm and suicide risk.

- *Emotional resilience* – focuses on staff wellbeing, resilience and resourcefulness, and safety planning. It aims to enhance emotional literacy, challenges stigma around emotional distress and tackles barriers to help-seeking. It explores different levels of distress and shares effective self-help strategies suitable for different levels of distress. It aims to prepare staff to be receptive and responsive to others' distress by equipping delegates with positive ways to cope with their own stress or emotional distress and develop a personal plan to build their wellbeing.

Deconstructing how we think about suicidal thoughts

One of the most powerful models that shapes our mental health literacy has been the biomedical model, which characteristically emphasizes individual incapacities, implying that the impairment is that which limits and defines the whole person (Evans 1999). Herein, the focus is on the failure of the individual and on them being the sole source of their distress. In an HE context, this fails to acknowledge the possible tension points and triggers that may arise from what students experience during the course of their studies. This can range from modules pedagogically designed with limited regard for mental health and inclusivity, to experiences that by default of their student status or course of study have to be endured. For example, a paramedic science student may have to spend part of their week in university, the other part engaging in 12-hour shifts where they are exposed to traumatic incidents in the context of lives which may involve managing relationships with peers and family, childcare demands, maintaining a sleep routine and all while navigating assessment deadlines.

Suicide prevention and mental health promotion remain heavily aligned to governmental and biomedical discourses and ways of viewing origins of distress. This can lead to exclusion and pose a barrier to students within HE where their cultural identity or understandings of their difficulties do not align with the dominant way of viewing distress – for example, with international students. Laing (2016) argues that society can psychologically nudge people to view difficult feelings, including suicidal thoughts, as being consequences of a personal chemical imbalance, causing illness that requires treatment to homogenize and deaden such feelings. However, there is an acceptance that you do not necessarily have to experience mental ill health to experience a thought that your life is not worth living (Burgess and Hawton 1998). This is a welcome shift towards an understanding of suicidal thoughts and their transdiagnostic span, uncoupling them from individual mental disorders (Glenn *et al.* 2017). Since 1999, the World Health Organization (WHO) has steadfastly highlighted suicide as a complex problem for which no single cause or reason exists, instead suggesting it results from a complex interaction of biological, psychological, social, cultural and environmental factors (WHO 1999). Therefore, it is important to recognize that someone's distress triggers may be varied and that it may be disadvantageous to consider that something is 'wrong' with them, but instead move towards an acceptance that a lot is happening to them.

Therefore, we need to better understand what suicidal thoughts actually mean and where they appear on a continuum of distress. This embraces a holistic view of mental health comprising both illness and wellbeing, and where suicidal thoughts can occur anywhere along this continuum. If we do not, we may inadvertently be failing to consider the diversity of the student population. According to Meyer (1995) it may add to the stress of groups within a minority, and one of their subsequent distress triggers may be the experience of having to assimilate to a dominant way of understanding. This places us at risk of getting tangled up in the wrong kind of debates in our HE contexts, trying to offer something before asking what is actually needed (Dickens 2020).

What kind of mental health literacy are we talking about?

Higher education literature has identified a need for improvement in mental health literacy in emergent gatekeepers (King, Strader and Vidourek 2008; Lee *et al.* 2013). This is a key element of the Stepchange model (UUK 2017), which determines that such steps are necessary to identify students who fit 'high-risk' criteria and refer them on to mental health services for specialist support. From the perspective of the gatekeeper this may include an understanding that 'high risk' means that an individual presents, describes and otherwise expresses their distress in a particular way. There is a risk that if the 'help-seeker's' presentation does not align with the gatekeeper's literal understanding of what suicidal distress is or means, it may result in a lack of empathy, understanding and hope. Instead, a space needs to be created that allows staff to listen and explore the triggers of the student's distress with the aim of understanding and supporting. Although onward referral may be required to keep that person safe or for them to access further support, we should resist the urge to 'pass on' by default immediately as this may communicate to that person that they are a potential burden. It may also miss an opportunity to offer a possible solution and hope in response to a distress trigger which is within the power and remit of staff to solve, and to offer 'something' that may immediately help to tip the balance back to safety. Examples might include offering practical advice on how to apply for extenuating circumstances, navigate the university web pages or apply for a hardship fund; supporting them to understand and offering reassurance related to recent academic feedback; or supporting them in resubmitting their academic work.

Therefore, the default widespread reductionist suicide prevention and mental health response, shaped and constructed through a dominant biomedical discourse, risks leaving some students behind, because it views suicide prevention as the preserve of mental health professionals and distress as a result of mental ill health difficulties alone. Some students may fear being labelled, others may worry about being offered a response or support they do not want or fear their disclosure may automatically be attributed to a crisis need. Therefore, training offered to HE staff must seriously consider offering a more inclusive response that may be more appropriate at this community level. Or to put it another way, students require compassion, not medicalization (Seldon and Martin 2017).

The tension between high risk and low risk

In 2018, an Office for National Statistics (ONS) report compared the incidence of student suicides with those of their non-student peers across the same age demographic between 2016 and 2017 (ONS 2018). It has been interpreted that as numbers were lower in the student group, students are in a 'lower-risk' category, and hints have been posited that higher education may even be protective, reducing rather than increasing suicide risk. However, it should be noted that in the year on which the report focused, 95 students died by suicide, equating to a student death every four days.

The term 'high risk' in relation to studies conducted in an HE context (Anderson *et al.* 2014a; Anderson *et al.* 2014b; Garlow *et al.* 2008; Gask *et al.* 2017; Mueller and Waas 2002) was established well before the ONS (2018) report. In order for the concept of risk to be useful, we should consider that although someone may not meet any demographic high-risk factors, or be overtly presenting as at high risk, they may still be very distressed and at risk of dying by suicide. Worryingly, the judgement of risk is often very subjective, may differ from person to person and across time, creating a space for inconsistent and inequitable responses.

Questions for reflection

- If a score of 10 represents the highest risk and 0 represents no risk at all, at which number would you place someone who says that their life is not worth living? At what number would you score them to be considered 'high risk'?
- If you had to support a referral to any formal services, do you think their understanding of 'high risk' would be the same as yours?
- Imagine being someone who is in distress. Reflect on how you would feel not being taken seriously because someone perceived your level of risk to be 'low'.

The identification of risk and the tolerance of and response to another individual's distress can be subject to complex interactions, such as the time of day the disclosure is made and the amount of experience and distress tolerance the person receiving the disclosure has (Bajaj *et al.* 2008; Michail and Tait 2016). Furthermore, the level of accuracy in assessing risk can be very low, which can leave some clinicians resigned to feeling helpless in their ability to offer meaningful support that will ensure safety (Cole-King *et al.* 2013; NCISH 2018).

Consequently, at a community level, it is prudent and simpler to take seriously on every occasion all expressions of hopelessness, reduction in worth, or expressed desire and/or plans to end it all, even if this is not the first time you have heard this from the individual (Cole-King *et al.* 2013). In this way, we mitigate the risk placed not merely within the individual, but indeed within a system of gatekeepers, who may all speak a similar language, but whose distress tolerance and levels of understanding may differ from person to person, and day to day.

What makes it difficult to listen?

Question for reflection

– As an emergent or identified gatekeeper, what may prevent you from wanting to hear the distress of someone else?

Barriers to listening may include worrying about saying the wrong thing, making matters worse, or increasing a person's risk. Others may reflect that they do not have the time to respond to every expression of distress, nor do they know that this investment of time will actually be successful in pulling that person back to a safe space. For some, the burden of responsibility that comes with such a disclosure may make them feel responsible for that person's life. This, and all of the above, are valid and understandable.

Compassionate boundaries and the need for self-care

These reflections lead us to consider the need for self-care within this community of support. A study by the National Association of Disability Practitioners (NADP) proposed that the health and wellbeing of staff are not only important in their own right but can be directly related to the health and wellbeing of students. In short, members of staff who are struggling with their own mental health will, consequently, struggle to support students (Wilson *et al.* 2020).

Burnout is often defined as a response to prolonged exposure to demanding interpersonal situations and is characterized by emotional exhaustion, depersonalization and reduced personal accomplishment (Maslach, Schaufeli and Leiter 2001). This supports the case for creating a wider web of gatekeepers who are positioned to offer help as part of a whole community approach. This negates the need and risk that responding to those in distress falls to those identified as 'single points of contact' or 'mental health champions' within their place of work or study. Additionally, it is vital that those who identify and respond to a student in distress have the skills, confidence and self-care practices to do this effectively whilst also maintaining their own wellbeing and ability to self-regulate their own emotional response.

As well as a call for providing a more considered and social model of assessment and response to students, Wilson *et al.* (2020) challenge HEIs to conceive their psychological contract with staff by providing a safe and wellbeing conscious environment in which staff can work. Their study highlighted that staff benefit from more informal peer-to-peer support and an opportunity to debrief with colleagues. A possible benefit of training all staff in emotional literacy and a compassionate response is that it may not only be for the benefit of the student body but also for peer-to-peer support for colleagues and themselves, and self-help.

Stigma

Stigma is often cited as a barrier to timely help-seeking. Those who perpetuate suicidal stigma engage in behaviours that include *stereotyping*, *distrust*, *shunning* and *avoidance* towards those affected (Cvinar 2005). The non-thinking and non-critical adoption of commonly held ideas or truths about suicide can perpetuate this cycle. For example, the Zero Suicide Alliance promotes a message that we should challenge the inevitability of suicide. When we pick this statement apart, it taps into a commonly expressed understanding that if someone wants to 'do it' there is little we can do to stop them, or if someone wanted to 'do it' they would have done so by now. Many of us have lost count of the number of times we have heard these statements in both professional and personal life contexts, and these were/are possibly sentiments we once held or still do hold in relation to this topic. However, affording ourselves a time, space and place to challenge this collective attribution, we can conceive how it may tap into our own perceptions of helplessness. Instead, it may be more constructive to believe that suicide is not inevitable and is therefore preventable (Cole-King and Platt 2017; Cole-King *et al.* 2013; WHO 1999) and gain this truth by listening to suicide survivors' stories and reflect on the principles and actions that supported them back to a point of safety (Hines, Cole-King and Blaustein 2013).

Joiner (2007) posits that suicidal thoughts occur when someone's prolonged self-perception of burdensomeness, sense of low belongingness and social isolation drives their desire for escape. Williams (1997) offers justification for a proposed shift from suicidal thoughts and attempts as representing a 'cry for help' (which over the years has been replaced and misunderstood to being a 'mere' cry for help, and not serious enough to warrant support) to a 'cry of pain' where disclosures are seen as a communication and expression of pain that may be invisible to those external to the person experiencing it. Combining these two principles, we need to move to a position in our thinking such that when people disclose their difficulties they are communicating internal pain, seeking our connection and potential problem solving ability to aid its remedy.

How to respond at a basic human level

If a student or colleague discloses that they are experiencing increased emotional distress, feeling that their life is not worth living, or expressing a desire and/or plan to end it all, take this seriously but try to remain calm. Configure this as a request for help or connection-seeking. Remember, this may be their first step in gaining the support they need. However, if risk is imminent and the person is in immediate danger, which may present as disorientation to place and time, an inability to engage in a conversation due to their distress levels and depletion of hope, or they have already harmed themselves, this needs to be recognized as a medical emergency where a 999 crisis response is required.

If this is not the case, listen first to try to understand what is happening and driving that distress. Try not to judge their distress against your own personal threshold or experiences. Judging ourselves against others can lead us into a trap of feeling more hopeless for them, or less sympathetic, whichever way the pendulum sways. Therefore, try to avoid saying 'it cannot be that bad'. Instead, validate their distress. Resist an urge to collapse the complexity of that person's distress into one single aspect, and instead try to explore some of those underpinning distress triggers, with a commitment to help and problem solve if you can.

Try to support the individual to identify what is happening, and create a list of distress triggers, worries or factors they find playing on their mind or that they feel trapped by. If you can help to write them down, this can communicate that you are listening and you are committed to helping them try to find some solution. Engaging in a process of problem solving may be useful, as it has been identified that suicidal and self-harming thoughts can commence from a difficulty or inability to problem solve (Townsend *et al.* 2001). It may be helpful to start with problems that are pertinent to their HE context. A student may be struggling to meet their impending assessment demands, may have trouble accessing their personal tutor, and may be experiencing difficulties in university accommodation, money problems, struggling to make friendships or, more likely, a combination of these factors. A colleague may be finding their work or home or social life difficult. You may not be able to solve or support every issue that is presented but consider the need and benefit of assisting with at least one immediate issue, and offering signposting to appropriate support to address others.

Language around suicide

How we talk of suicide is important, and we should try to use language that does not stigmatize or criminalize (Nielsen 2016). We do not believe that people 'commit' suicide, nor does anyone 'successfully' die by suicide and nor are suicide attempts 'failed'. However, we have not presented a list or dichotomy of words to use and words to avoid. There is a risk that policing people's language may serve to detract from the thinking space we need to create and gain a more comfortable relationship with talking about the topic. However, this chapter has not adopted terms that are often used when discussing suicide. One way to reduce the use of potentially unhelpful terms may be by not continually debating their use.

Conclusions

It is hoped that anyone engaging with this chapter will have gained something from doing so. We do not, however, underestimate how difficult it can be to reflect on our own role and beliefs about an issue that has so many layers of complexity, fear and history wrapped around it. Yet we all form a part of a point in time and a developing history, understanding and relationship with this topic. The direction in which suicide prevention in HE travels is in part within our power, and as fellow human beings we are challenged to consider our own relationship as helpers in this democratized vision. We hope this chapter adds to this story and offers a springboard for readers to consider the need to engage in face-to-face training, which a book chapter can never replicate. Here a physical time and a safe place and permission to discuss a topic usually silenced can be offered and shared with others. Here a compassionate community that connects multiple forms of resource, insight and experience can hopefully emerge.

Key practice implications

- All university staff should be equipped with the skills to offer support and mitigate suicide risk should they find themselves in the role of first responder or gatekeeper.

- Training offered must be safe and move participants beyond suicide awareness to an appropriate level of competence to respond at community levels.

- Self-harm and suicidal thoughts need to be met with understanding and taken seriously on every occasion.

- People experiencing suicidal ideation are ambivalent; their help-seeking can be the first step back to a tipping point of safety (Dickens and Guy 2019).

Author biographies

Clare Dickens is a registered mental health nurse, senior lecturer and academic lead for mental health and wellbeing at the University of Wolverhampton. Clare is currently studying for a professional doctorate focusing on professional bereavement by suicide. Clare also chairs Wolverhampton's suicide prevention stakeholders' forum.

Stuart Guy is a registered mental health nurse and senior lecturer within the School of Nursing at the University of Gloucester.

References

Anderson, D., Bapat, M., Bernier, J., Cimini, D. *et al.* (2014a) Implementing early intervention for residential students who present with suicide risk: a case study. *Journal of American College Health 62*, 4, 285–291.

Anderson, D., Bernier, J., Cimini, M., Murray, A. *et al.* (2014b) Implementing an audience specific small-group gatekeeper training programme to respond to suicide risk among college students: a case study. *Journal of American College Health 62*, 2, 99–100.

Bajaj, P., Borreani, E., Ghosh, P., Methuen, C., Patel, M. and Joseph, M. (2008) Screening for suicidal thoughts in primary care: the views of patients and general practitioners. *Mental Health in Family Medicine 5*, 4, 229–235.

Burgess, S. and Hawton, K. (1998) Suicide, euthanasia, and the psychiatrist. *Philosophy, Psychiatry, & Psychology 5*, 113–126.

Cole-King, A. and Platt, S. (2017) Suicide prevention for physicians: identification, intervention and mitigation of risk. *Medicine 45*, 3, 131–134.

Cole-King, A., Green, G., Gask, L., Hines, K. and Platt, S. (2013) Suicide mitigation: a compassionate approach to suicide prevention. *Advances in Psychiatric Treatment 19*, 276–283.

Cvinar, J.G. (2005) Do suicide survivors suffer social stigma? A review of the literature. *Perspectives in Psychiatric Care 41*, 1, 14–21.

Dickens, C. (2020) Mental Health and Wellbeing in Higher Education. In B. Bartram (ed.) *Understanding Contemporary Issues in Higher Education.* London: Routledge.

Dickens, C. and Guy, S. (2019) 'Three minutes to save a life': addressing emotional distress in students to mitigate the risk of suicide. Mental Health Practice. DOI: 10.7748/mhp.2019. e1290

Evans, J. (1999) Feeble Monsters Making up Disabled People. In J. Evans and S. Hall (eds) *Visual Culture: A Reader.* London: Sage.

Garlow, S., Haas, A., Hendin, H., Koestner, B. *et al.* (2008) An interactive web-based method of outreach to college students at risk for suicide. *Journal of American College Health 57*, 1, 15–22.

Gask, L., Coupe, N., Green, G. and McElvenny, D. (2017) Pilot study evaluation of suicide prevention gatekeeper training utilising STORM in a British university setting. *British Journal of Guidance and Counselling 45*, 5, 593–605.

Glenn, J.J., Werntz, A.J., Slama, S.J.K., Steinman, S.A., Teachman, B.A. and Nock, M.K. (2017) Suicide and self-injury-related implicit cognition: a large-scale examination and replication. *J. Abnorm. Psychol. 126*, 199–211.

Gould, M., Velting, D., Kleinman, M., Lucas, C., Thomas, J. and Chung M. (2004) Teenagers' attitudes about coping strategies and help-seeking behavior for suicidality. *J Am Acad Child Adolescent Psychiatry 43*, 9, 1124–1133.

Hines, K., Cole-King, A. and Blaustein, M. (2013) Hey kid, are you OK? A story of suicide survived. *Advances in Psychiatric Treatment 19*, 292–294.

Joiner, T.E. (2007) *Why People Die by Suicide.* Cambridge, MA: Harvard University Press.

King, K., Strader, J. and Vidourek, R. (2008) University students' perceived self-efficacy in identifying suicidal warning signs and helping suicidal friends find campus intervention resources. *Suicide and Life-Threatening Behavior 38*, 5, 608–617.

Ko, J., Frey, J.J. and Harrington, D. (2019) Preventing suicide among working-age adults: the correlates of help-seeking behavior. *Inquiry 56*, 46958019850979. DOI: 10.1177/0046958019850979

Laing, O. (2016) *The Lonely City: The Art of Being Alone.* London: Canongate Books.

Lee, J., Miles, N., Prieto-Welch, S.L., Servaty-Seib, H.L. *et al.* (2013) The impact of gatekeeper training for suicide prevention on university residential assistants. *Journal of College Counselling 16*, 1, 64–78.

Maslach, C., Schaufeli, W.B. and Leiter, M.P. (2001) Job burnout. *Annual Review of Psychology 52*, 379–422.

Meyer, I. (1995) Minority stress and mental health in gay men. *Journal of Health and Social Behavior 36*, 38–56.

Michail, M. and Tait, L. (2016) Exploring general practitioners' views and experiences on suicide risk assessment and management of young people in primary care: a qualitative study in the UK. *BMJ Open 6*, e009654.

Mueller, M. and Waas, G. (2002) College students' perceptions of suicide: the role of empathy on attitudes, evaluation, and responsiveness. *Death Studies 26*, 4, 325–341.

National Confidential Inquiry into Suicide and Safety in Mental Health (NCISH) (2018) *The Assessment of Clinical Risk in Mental Health Services*. Manchester: The University of Manchester.

Nielsen, E. (2016) Mind your 'C's and 'S's: the language of self-harm and suicide (and why it matters). Institute of Mental Health (IMH) blog. Accessed on 01/07/20 at: https://imhblog. wordpress.com/2016/01/22/emma-nielsen-mind-your-cs-and-ss-the-language-of-self-harm-and-suicide-and-why-it-matters

Office for National Statistics (ONS) (2018) *Estimating Suicide among Higher Education Students, England and Wales: Experimental Statistics*. London: ONS.

Osteen, P.J., Frey, J.J. and Ko, J. (2014) Advancing training to identify, intervene, and follow up with individuals at risk for suicide through research. *American Journal of Preventive Medicine 47*, 3, S216–S221.

Seldon, A. and Martin, A. (2017) *The Positive and Mindful University*. Oxford: HEPI.

Townsend, E., Hawton, K., Altman, D.G., Arensman, E. *et al.* (2001) The efficacy of problem-solving treatments after deliberate self-harm: meta-analysis of randomized controlled trials with respect to depression, hopelessness and improvement in problems. *Psychological Medicine 31*, 6, 979–988.

Universities UK (UUK) (2017) New framework for universities to help improve student mental health. Accessed on 06/05/20 at: www.universitiesuk.ac.uk/news/Pages/New-framework-for-universities-to-help-improve-student-mental-health.aspx

Waters, K. and Cole-King, A. (2017) Assessing Risk of Suicide and Self-Harm. In M. Chambers (ed.) *Psychiatric and Mental Health Nursing: The Craft of Caring* (3rd edn). Abingdon: Routledge.

Williams, J.M.G. (1997) *Cry of Pain: Understanding Suicide and Self-Harm*. London: Penguin.

Wilson, L., Martin, N., Conway, J. and Turner, P. (2020) *The Wellbeing of Disability Professional in the Further and Higher Education Institution Workplace*. Report by the National Association of Disability Practitioners (NADP). Aylesbury: NADP.

World Health Organization (WHO) (1999) *Figures and Facts about Suicide*. Geneva: WHO. Accessed on 30/04/21 at: https://apps.who.int/iris/handle/10665/66097

CHAPTER 12

Supporting Student Mental Health and Wellbeing in Higher Education

MARK AMES

Overview

This chapter:

- illustrates how the University Mental Health Charter uses an extensive evidence base to inform a framework for universities, allowing them to adopt a whole institution approach to supporting mental health and wellbeing

- provides examples from the University of Bristol to illustrate the kind of approaches being taken to support mental health and wellbeing

- shows how the principles of good practice recommended by the Charter can be used to inform the development of support.

Introduction

Support for student mental health and wellbeing in universities in the UK has been undergoing a transformation over recent years. Previously, academic personal tutors and hall wardens, or their equivalent, had been the main sources of pastoral support for students. Student health services, counselling services, disability services and chaplaincy teams supplemented this support. Over the last decade or so, as the student population has grown and become more diverse, there has been a significant increase in the number of students with emerging and existing mental health conditions. Mental health advisers have been introduced by many universities to help students navigate and make the most of their studies and the wider student experience, as well as assisting with access to the specialist mental health care needed from the NHS. There has also been a significant increase in the proportion of students seeking support for their general mental health and wellbeing. The role of wellbeing adviser has emerged in many institutions to respond to this need and alleviate some of the pressures on academic and other professional services staff.

Alongside the general increase in staff primarily concerned with supporting student mental health and wellbeing, work has been underway across the sector to develop whole university approaches to support the mental health and wellbeing of students and staff. The latest of these, the University Mental Health Charter (Hughes and Spanner 2019), provides an excellent evidence- and consultation-informed framework for adopting a whole university approach to supporting mental health and wellbeing. The authors of the Charter acknowledge that improvements to our understanding and practice across this dynamic, complex and multi-faceted area will continue to depend on the contributions we can all make as researchers, practitioners and students. In this spirit, some of the latest thinking and practice relating to supporting student mental health and wellbeing through adopting a whole university approach will be explored in this chapter. The needs of staff should be considered as part of any whole university approach, and this will be covered separately in Chapter 20.

This chapter will outline some of the key evidence and features of the Charter framework and use examples of recent developments at the University of Bristol to illustrate the kind of approaches being developed at many universities. It will also highlight how the principles of good practice recommended by the Charter can be used to sense-check and inform the development of good practice at individual institutions. Given the limits to how many aspects of a whole university approach can be included in a chapter of this length, the examples used will focus on three specific areas: supporting the wellbeing of all students, providing additional support for the mental health and wellbeing of some students through a range of integrated services, and the role of leadership in developing and delivering a whole university approach.

Charter evidence and framework

The introduction to the Charter (Hughes and Spanner 2019) notes an increasing concern about the mental health of students and staff in higher education, including a doubling of the number of students declaring a pre-existing mental illness since 2014/15, and similar increases in the number of students seeking support. It highlights the evidence that this is impacting adversely on student learning, performance, persistence and health. In addition, there is increasing awareness of poor mental health being experienced by postgraduate research students associated with elements of their university life such as supervision, identity, preparation and belonging. Finally, it draws attention to a deterioration in the mental health and wellbeing of an increasing number of staff working in higher education as a growing area of concern which also has the potential to impact adversely on students.

In addition to the focus on mental health and mental illness, universities are increasingly considering how they can support the general wellbeing of all students and staff, as this can have a direct impact on how we feel and our ability to function. The introduction to the Charter (Hughes and Spanner 2019, p.7) notes that 'most models of wellbeing agree that engagement with meaningful activity, learning, being connected to a community and achievement can have a positive effect on wellbeing'. Therefore, all universities have the potential to be conducive environments within which to promote the mental health and wellbeing of all members of their community.

The Charter framework draws together evidence from the literature and consultation with staff and students across higher education to set out those areas of university activity that appear to be most important to mental health and wellbeing. This framework is also reflected in the *Stepchange: Mentally Healthy Universities* (Universities UK 2020) guidance for leadership. It is composed of 13 interrelated themes, which are mapped against the four domains of Learn, Support, Work and Live (see Table 12.1) and five enabling themes which are:

- leadership, strategy and policy
- student voice and participation
- cohesiveness of support across the provider
- inclusivity and intersectional mental health
- research, innovation and dissemination.

Within each of the themes, the Charter sets out what it covers, the evidence supporting why it matters and what is important and principles of good practice. These principles will form the basis of a Charter Award Scheme which recognizes the need to be context appropriate given the differing scale and nature of universities.

Table 12.1: Map of domains against themes

Domain	Theme
Learn	Transition into university Learning, teaching and assessment Progression
Support	Support services
	Risk
	External partnerships and pathways
	Information sharing
Work	Staff wellbeing
	Staff development
Live	Proactive interventions and a mentally healthy environment Residential accommodation Social integration and belonging Physical environment

Recent developments at the University of Bristol

1. Context

The University of Bristol is a research-intensive institution of 26,000 students and 7000 staff with the strategic ambition to have its education and student experience recognized as being of a similar quality to that of its world-leading research. The University of Bristol launched its new Vision and Strategy in 2016 in which it committed to review and enhance the ways in which student pastoral support was provided to ensure the wellbeing of all students. An additional recurrent commitment of £1 million per annum was made to fund a new Student Wellbeing Service embedded in academic schools with a clear focus on proactively supporting the wellbeing of all students, as well as identifying and ensuring access to more specialist support for those with additional needs. In parallel, a review was launched of the pastoral support in residences with a view to ensuring a similar level of proactive support for residential life, student wellbeing and early access to additional support.

During 2016/17, the University of Bristol experienced a highly publicized cluster of student deaths by suicide which served to reinforce the need for existing plans to enhance support for the wellbeing of all students, as well as increase the capacity of specialist counselling and mental health provision. It was also the catalyst for a review and the development of a suicide prevention and response plan (University of Bristol 2018c). Another cluster of student deaths by suicide occurred during 2017/18. Meanwhile, the new Residential Life and Student Wellbeing services were being prepared to launch, and the specialist therapeutic and mental health services which were under considerable strain were being strengthened. In September 2018, the new services were launched, and the whole institution student and staff mental health and wellbeing strategies (2018a, 2018b) were published, based on the *#Stepchange: Mental Health in Higher Education* (Universities UK 2017) framework. Further changes were introduced in September 2019 to help students find the right support more easily. They also enabled the assessment, allocation and coordination of that support more effectively across different teams, as well as reduced significantly the waiting times for student counselling.

2. Supporting the wellbeing of all students

Under the transition theme of the 'Learn' domain, the Charter (Hughes and Spanner 2019) notes that for some decades 'there has been evidence demonstrating that the transition into university and the first-year experience are hugely significant for student success, confidence, belonging and wellbeing' (p.24). It goes on to state, 'How students are supported during the first days and weeks of term and the strategies, tools and assistance which the university provides to enable success and belonging can have significant impacts' (p.25). Under the learning, teaching and assessment theme, the Charter (Hughes and Spanner 2019) notes, 'students may also benefit when relevant, good quality psycho-education and meta-learning is included in the curriculum, supporting them to develop their ability to manage their own wellbeing and learning' (p.27). However, it advises that 'thought should be given to ensuring that psycho-education is delivered by appropriate staff. It should not be assumed that untrained academics can automatically provide this safely and effectively' (p.27).

It was this focus on equipping first-year undergraduate students with the understanding and skills to manage their own wellbeing which prompted the development of The Science of Happiness by Professor Bruce Hood (2020). He describes the course as:

a radically different 1st year open unit course that brings together a wide variety of topics from diverse academic fields of research in the field of human mental well-being in a format that is suitable for students without any previous background knowledge. The course has no graded examination and credits are awarded on the basis of engagement. Uniquely, there is no default provision of lecture recordings and digital devices are not allowed (unless there are extenuating circumstances) in order to maximize student attention on the content.

Throughout the course, students explore the latest results from research in psychological science about how to be happier, how to feel less stressed and how to flourish. It promotes critical thinking and drills down into both the strengths and weaknesses in the field. It begins with a look at student mental well-being and goes on to explore some of the misconceptions about happiness and what generates happiness. The course explores some of the common flaws in the human mind when reasoning, using examples from perception and cognitive psychology to demonstrate how the human mind is infested with cognitive biases which can impede healthy mental well-being.

Students are also provided with opportunities to put strategies into practice to build some of the habits that will allow them to live a more fulfilling life through the support of the 'happiness hubs' for which they gain engagement credit. These small group (up to 8 students) weekly meetings are facilitated by trained senior and post-graduate students who act as mentors and keep a register of attendance and engagement. Students are also expected to journal their experiences weekly and complete repeated self-report standard assessments of mental well-being online.

Although the Science of Happiness introduces students to scientifically validated strategies for living a more satisfying life, it is not intended as therapy or an alternative form of treatment for those with mental health problems. Mentors on the course are expected to signpost the University of Bristol well-being services for any student who needs help. It is first and foremost an educational course but one that includes a practical and reflective component which may or may not improve mental well-being depending on the level of individual student engagement.

So far 150 students have taken the course in the first semester with an anticipated 240 taking the course in second semester. Preliminary feedback and analyses are very encouraging. In addition, there is evidence that levels of student mental well-being are significantly raised over the duration of the course in comparison to those students awaiting to take the unit in the second term. Future analysis will seek to establish how long the benefits are maintained after the unit has been completed.

The Science of Happiness has been a well-received and effective example of providing first-year undergraduate students with access to psycho-education in the form of an accredited open unit as part of their first-year student experience. The themes of wellbeing and happiness are clearly of interest to many students, as evidenced during the pilot year in 2018/19 when over 800 students signed up for the course even though it carried no academic credit. During 2019/20, the number of students opting to take this course reduced due to the challenge of communicating the option effectively in a crowded curriculum to the wider university community. This highlights the importance of making space for such options and ensuring staff recognize the benefits which they then communicate to their students. Developing approaches that engage all students with proactively thinking about and learning how to manage their wellbeing is complex. There is also a need to consider how such learning opportunities can be delivered at scale to thousands of students who will have a whole range of competing priorities and interests. The Science of Happiness clearly benefits from Professor Hood being a charismatic and engaging lecturer, as well as a leading expert in his field. However, the strength he brings as an individual may ultimately limit the potential to increase the reach and sustainability of this approach.

One option would be to offer this kind of course online as a combination of video and written content, as well as moderated group learning. Hassed and Chambers (2020) from Monash University lead a good example of how such a course can be delivered online with their *Mindfulness for Wellbeing and Peak Performance*. More scalable approaches being developed at Bristol and other universities include embedding elements of psycho-education designed to underpin a student's ability to learn into the curriculum and/or pedagogy, so they reach all students. For example, using the evidence-based *Five Ways to Wellbeing* – Connect, Be active, Take notice, Keep learning, Give – developed by Aked *et al.* (2008) at the New Economics Foundation to provide a thematic approach to introducing a wellbeing perspective across the curriculum and pedagogy. Another example is Fika (Bennett and Fryer 2020), which is working with universities to map and embed their five-minute emotional workout app across the curriculum. Bitesize pieces of evidence-based psycho-education can be delivered in an integrated, consistent and interactive way into mainstream learning and teaching without depending on the expertise and capabilities of individual academic staff.

Engaging the majority of students with learning how to actively manage their wellbeing can be challenging, as many will be disinclined to do so until experiencing some of the difficulties associated with poor wellbeing. Embedding elements of psycho-education into mainstream learning activities and the wider student experience can help increase initial levels of engagement. However, other approaches are likely to be needed to encourage and support a more sustained and impactful level of engagement. These might include the use of online resources, supported discussions, academic credit, and the expectation that student wellbeing will be actively considered in the running of other activities such as student clubs and societies. Any such approaches also need to be sustainable, as there are too many examples of resource-hungry initiatives that do not stand the test of time.

3. Integrated student support services

The Charter (Hughes and Spanner 2019, p.32) notes that 'support services have long been at the forefront of responding to student mental health and remain a key element in a whole-university approach'. At the University of Bristol, the long-established support services include a Students' Health Service, Student Counselling Service, Student Funding Service, Disability Service and Multifaith Chaplaincy. More recently, a Mental Health Advice Team was established, and a Student Inclusion Service which focuses on the additional needs of UK students from non-traditional backgrounds, as well as international students. These services tend to be primarily reactive in nature, responding to individual students seeking support for their mental health and wellbeing, as well as a broader range of issues that may impact on their wellbeing, such as funding, disability and faith. In addition, the Student Inclusion Service is focused on ensuring the mainstream provision of learning, teaching and support is more effectively meeting the needs of all students.

The Charter (Hughes and Spanner 2019) identifies some key principles to meet student need; they must be safe, effective, accessible to all, appropriately resourced, relevant to local context and well governed. At the University of Bristol, the safety of services is ensured through the appropriate recruitment, management and clinical supervision of trained and experienced staff with clear expectations of the nature and limits to support provided by each role. There are also clear routes of escalation to more senior and/or specialist colleagues, including services outside the university such as the NHS. Aside from the Students' Health Service, which provides NHS Primary Healthcare, the other university student services are intended to support students to make the most of their studies and wider student experience through short-term interventions. Therefore, while still measuring clinical change as a means of ensuring the safety and efficacy of services, there is also a focus on student perceptions of ease of access and helpfulness of support.

The Charter (Hughes and Spanner 2019) identifies long waiting times for services as an accessibility issue, and this had become a problem for the Student Counselling Service at Bristol, especially in the context of increased anxiety about student deaths by suicide. The decision to invest in new Residential Life and Student Wellbeing services rather than simply to grow existing services was intended to give the capacity to provide all students in their residences and academic schools with more proactive, non-clinical support for their wellbeing. This included support for transitions, inclusive community building, wellbeing skills development, and the early identification and access to individual support. It was also designed to relieve pressure on academic staff, professional services colleagues and senior students in their roles as personal tutor, school administrator, hall warden and senior resident respectively. They were finding their time increasingly dominated by responding to the growing volume of student requests for support, some of which were increasingly complex, high risk and often beyond their ability and level of training and experience to manage safely.

At the same time as launching the new services, the Student Counselling Service started to introduce Single-Session 'One-at-a-Time' Therapy, as developed by Dryden (2019). This approach frames each session as a complete entity with the potential to book another appointment once there has been an opportunity to reflect on the impact of each session. A key benefit of this approach, now it has been fully implemented, is a significant reduction in waiting time targets, from six to two weeks, with more urgent cases being seen sooner. Students report that speed of access is very important to them. They also respond positively when asked about the helpfulness of this approach. This is a good illustration of how universities are innovating to meet the increase in demand and changing expectations of students, as well as investing in more staff capacity.

The Charter (Hughes and Spanner 2019) identifies the cohesiveness of support across the provider as an enabling theme. In particular, the principles of good practice include ensuring cohesion and appropriate collaboration among professional services and with academic teams, underpinned by appropriate information sharing to support individual students, and effective signposting and triaging across the university. At the University of Bristol, collaboration with academic teams is primarily coordinated through briefings and regular case management meetings between the Residential Life and Student Wellbeing services staff, senior tutors and professional administrative colleagues in schools. This has helped to improve mutual understanding and trust, as well as ensure individual students are more consistently identified and supported in a coordinated manner. However, despite these efforts to work closely with colleagues in academic schools, it became increasingly apparent that while generally positive about the quality of support available, students and the staff supporting them were often struggling to identify which service to approach in the first instance. A significant number of students were also referring themselves or being referred to the Student Counselling Service and were then disappointed that they were being referred to other services for support that were assessed as being more appropriate to their current needs.

One of the learnings from this first year of operation was that the headline message about how to seek support needed to be simple and unambiguous. Students should ideally have a single point of access, and it should be up to the university to manage the complexities associated with assessing need and allocating and coordinating support. During the first year of operation, it also became clear that despite the physical presence of student wellbeing advisers in academic schools, 79 per cent of students were choosing to make their initial contact with the service via phone or email. Although the Residential Life and Student Wellbeing Services were intended to manage student casework in a consistent and coordinated manner, they were starting to develop different approaches which were only partly due to the differing nature of the contexts in which they were working.

In preparation for the second year of operation, Wellbeing Access

(Slater 2019) was launched to offer 24/7 telephone and email support, staffed by a combination of Residential Life and Student Wellbeing advisers working alongside each other to undertake an initial assessment of needs and allocation of support based on information captured by an online request for support form. There had been concerns that this online form might put some students off seeking support, but in practice it seems that most students find this a helpful and accessible means of articulating support needs in their own words. The sharing of the information in this document via an electronic case management system means that all staff are working with the same information and students do not need to repeat their story multiple times, which had been a source of frustration for many. Wellbeing Access also became the only route into therapeutic support from the Student Counselling Service, as well as an additional route into support from Disability Services. From the student's perspective, they need only submit their request for support, and the next member of staff to contact them will be the person best placed to provide them with the support they need.

During the first year of operation, the Residential Life and Student Wellbeing services had provided individual support to over 5000 students. Wellbeing Access was launched at the beginning of their second year of operation, and during the first four months of that year the two services supported over 6000 students. The Student Counselling Service continued to support as many students as it did in the previous year, but they are no longer 'disappointing' students asking for counselling who were offered an alternative form of support. Meanwhile, Disability Services has experienced a significant increase in the number of students seeking support compared with the same period in the previous year. This is likely to be a combination of more students who might benefit from such support being identified at an earlier stage by Wellbeing Access, as well as an overall increase in the number of students seeking disability-related support.

The joint working of advisers to assess and allocate support for students has enhanced relationships between the two teams and helped with progress towards more consistent ways of working using a new integrated case management framework (Golden-Wright 2019). This framework uses behaviour across various domains including academic progress, physical health, mental health, social isolation and behaviour to assess levels of potential risk, allocate support and/or escalate to more senior staff for consideration. Those students whose support needs cannot be met by an adviser-led approach are escalated to daily case allocation meetings which include senior colleagues from the Residential Life, Student Wellbeing, Student Counselling and Disability services. They determine the appropriate support for each individual student and who will contact the student to offer support. Students who are regarded as being at more immediate medium- to high-level risk, or with particularly complex support needs, will be escalated to a group of senior staff who decide how best to support them and manage any associated risk. They also monitor and adjust that support until such time as the student is no longer considered to be a risk to themselves or others.

The Charter (Hughes and Spanner 2019, p.40) notes there has been 'significant debate within the sector and the media, as to whether universities should share information with families, or other relevant people in the lives of students, when there are concerns about an individual student's mental health'. The University of Bristol was a catalyst for much of this debate when it decided to amend its Student Emergency Contact Procedure (Ames 2019) so students could give their consent at registration for the university to use their nominated emergency contact in the event that there were serious concerns about their wellbeing. Over 90 per cent of students opted in during the first year of operation and this level of participation continued into the second year. This perhaps illustrates a generational shift in how more students now expect those close to them to be involved in their support. It also represents a significant shift in professional practice for staff as there is now a greater onus on accounting for why they did not use the emergency contact when they had serious concerns about a student's wellbeing, rather than why they did.

Under the enabling theme of inclusivity and intersectional mental health, the Charter (Hughes and Spanner 2019, p.72) identifies as a principle of good practice that universities should 'ensure support services work to improve their cultural competence and are able to respond to different student backgrounds, characteristics and experiences'. This certainly reflects concerns raised by students at the University of Bristol. In response, recruitment to the new Residential Life and Student Wellbeing services focused on reaching out to local communities that might not ordinarily consider applying to work at the university and had some significant success in diversifying the staff profile. It has proven a greater challenge to attract a more diverse profile of student counsellors, though some aspects of their actual diversity may not be immediately visible.

Staff undertake regular awareness-raising training to understand the likely needs and perspectives of different groups of students. External organizations, such as Nilaari (2000) which provides culturally appropriate counselling and Big White Wall (2007) – now called Togetherall – which offers a wide choice of therapists from around the world via webcam therapy, are commissioned by the university to diversify the available support. Inclusivity remains an increasingly complex, challenging and important issue to address.

Providing an integrated, stepped and culturally competent range of student support services is a complex and challenging undertaking. It requires a clear differentiation between the types and levels of support being offered, as well as the ability to assess student needs and allocate appropriate support in a timely and efficient manner. Access to support should not require students, or the staff supporting them, to be able to navigate their way to the most appropriate support. Instead, students need a clear and unambiguous single point of access which allows them to articulate their support needs either online and/or in person. Skilled and informed staff then need to make the necessary assessment of how best to meet the student's support needs. An electronic case management system and regular case meetings are essential to monitoring and coordinating the support required by individual students, including the management of any risk. It is generally helpful to consider with students how they might draw on support from family or friends, as well as to agree under what circumstances the university may initiate contact with the emergency contact of a student about whom they have serious concerns.

4. Leadership, strategy and policy

The Charter (Hughes and Spanner 2019, p.62) highlights that 'university leaders play a significant role in helping to establish a shared culture, structure and environment that supports change and individual well-being'. They can ensure 'their university takes a strategic approach to mental health, that it is identified as a priority and appropriate resources are allocated... They can also influence the value the community places on wellbeing through public modelling.' This was very much the case at the University of Bristol where the vice-chancellor and other senior colleagues identified student and staff mental health and wellbeing as key institutional strategic priorities and personally led aspects of this work.

This included establishing a VC's Taskforce on Mental Health and Wellbeing which oversaw the development and implementation of the student and staff mental health and wellbeing strategies (2018a, 2018b), including the approval of additional resource when needed and the introduction of annual reports for the Board of Trustees. These senior staff also provided the personal support needed to progress some important but controversial changes – engaging directly with staff, students and third parties, including the media. They also led on challenging the stigma and discrimination associated with mental ill health through leading the Time to Change Pledge (2011) signing ceremony, as well as conferring an honorary degree on award-winning mental health campaigners Jonny Benjamin and Neil Laybourne (2018). More recently, a new pro-vice-chancellor Student Experience role was created to provide additional senior academic leadership in student mental health and wellbeing, student inclusion and student engagement.

However, as the Charter notes, it can be difficult to effect and sustain change without the engagement of leaders in faculties and schools given that universities such as Bristol have a distributed power structure. Local autonomy is relatively high and enhancing support for mental health and wellbeing is just one of many competing priorities and pressures on these leaders. Embedding mental health and wellbeing considerations into mainstream policies and activities can help ensure good practice at the local level. For example, staff and students have been asked to reflect on and use the school-level data from the annual Student Mental Health and Wellbeing Survey to consider the local actions that might help address some of the issues raised. These are then included in their Education Action Plans which are formally reported on during the academic year and updated annually.

Conclusion and recommendations

This chapter has described how the University Mental Health Charter (Hughes and Spanner 2019) uses an extensive evidence base to inform a framework of good practice principles for universities adopting a whole institution approach to supporting mental health and wellbeing. It is not possible in a chapter of this length to provide a comprehensive account of such a holistic approach, and the examples from the University of Bristol are intended for illustrative purposes only rather than being recommended as exemplars for the sector to adopt. Instead, universities need to develop whole institution approaches relevant to their local context which meet the changing and increasing expectations and needs of their students and staff.

I recommend all universities consider using the new Charter framework as the basis for reviewing their current institutional arrangements for supporting mental health and wellbeing. This will enable each university to identify and build on existing good practice, as well as develop an enhancement action plan for those areas requiring further development. Progress with agreeing and implementing a whole university approach will require senior leadership support and oversight. Success in this important area will enable more students to make the most of their academic and wider student experience, as well as prepare them to lead more satisfying and productive lives.

Author biography

Mark Ames has worked in further and higher education for over 35 years with an interest in supporting the broader personal development of students alongside their intellectual development. As Director of Student Services at the University of Bristol from 2014 to 2020, he was responsible for the development and implementation of a whole university approach to supporting student mental health and wellbeing, as well as the associated professional services. He is now an independent consultant and executive coach in higher education.

References

Aked, J., Marks, N., Cordon, C. and Thompson, S. (2008) *Five Ways to Wellbeing*. New Economics Foundation. Accessed on 31/03/21 at: https://neweconomics.org/uploads/files/8984c5089d5c2285ee_t4m6bhqq5.pdf

Ames, M. (2019) *Student Emergency Contact Procedure*. University of Bristol. Accessed on 31/03/21 at: www.bristol.ac.uk/media-library/sites/university/documents/governance/policies/student-emergency-contact-procedure.pdf

Benjamin, J. and Laybourne, N. (2018) Honorary degrees for award-winning mental health campaigners. Press release, 17 July. University of Bristol. Accessed on 31/03/21 at: www.bristol.ac.uk/news/2018/july/neil-jonny-degree.html

Bennett, N. and Fryer, G. (2020) *Mental Fitness Courses for Education, Workplace and Healthcare*. Fika. Accessed on 31/03/21 at: www.fika.community

Big White Wall (2007) Live Therapy, London. (Big White Wall is now Togetherall, https://togetherall.com/en-gb)

Dryden, W. (2019) *Single-Session 'One-at-a-Time' Therapy: A Rational Emotive Behaviour Therapy Approach*. Abingdon: Routledge Focus.

Golden-Wright, A. (2019) *Integrated Case Management Framework*. University of Bristol.

Hassed, C. and Chambers, R. (2020) *Mindfulness for Wellbeing and Peak Performance*. Future Learn. Accessed on 31/03/21 at: www.futurelearn.com/courses/mindfulness-wellbeing-performance

Hood, B. (2020) *The Science of Happiness*. University of Bristol.

Hughes, G. and Spanner, L. (2019) *The University Mental Health Charter*. Leeds: Student Minds. Accessed on 31/03/21 at: www.studentminds.org.uk/charter

Nilaari (2000) Culturally Appropriate Counselling, Bristol. Accessed on 31/03/21 at: www.nilaari.co.uk

Slater, C. (2019) *Wellbeing Access*. University of Bristol.

Time to Change Pledge (2011) London: Time to Change. Accessed on 31/03/21 at: www.time-to-change.org.uk/get-involved/get-your-workplace-involved/employer-pledge

Universities UK (2017) *#Stepchange: Mental Health in Higher Education*. Universities UK.

Universities UK (2020) *Stepchange: Mentally Healthy Universities*. Universities UK. Accessed on 31/03/21 at: www.universitiesuk.ac.uk/policy-and-analysis/reports/Pages/stepchange-mhu.aspx

University of Bristol (2016) *Vision and Strategy*. Accessed on 31/03/21 at: www.bristol.ac.uk/university/strategy

University of Bristol (2018a) *Mental Health and Wellbeing: Our Staff Strategy*. Accessed on 31/03/21 at: www.bristol.ac.uk/university/media/strategies/staff-mental-health-wellbeing-strategy.pdf

University of Bristol (2018b) *Mental Health and Wellbeing: Our Student Strategy*. Accessed on 31/03/21 at: www.bristol.ac.uk/university/media/strategies/student-mental-health-wellbeing-strategy.pdf

University of Bristol (2018c) *Suicide Prevention and Response Plan*. Accessed on 31/03/21 at: www.bristol.ac.uk/university/media/strategies/suicide-prevention-response-plan.pdf

CHAPTER 13

How Can We Talk Safely about Suicide with Students?

KATIE STAFFORD AND JO SMITH

Overview

This chapter aims to help staff, peers and family members:

- talk to someone who may be at risk of suicide
- dispel common myths and anxieties that can inhibit us from intervening
- identify useful questions to ask
- identify helpful interventions, useful training and resources.

Introduction

Young people can be reluctant to consult health practitioners when experiencing mental distress (Biddle, Gunnell and Sharp 2004). The majority of young people who take their own lives are not under the care of student services (NCISH 2017) or a mental health team, and many have not had recent contact with mental health services (McLaughlin and Gunnell 2020). In the 2017 National Confidential Inquiry into suicides in children and young people (NCISH 2017), 34 per cent of the suicides were by students but only 12 per cent of these students were reported to be seeing student counselling services. More recently, McLaughlin and Gunnell (2020), in a case series review of 37 student suicide deaths, found 51 per cent were already known to the NHS regarding their mental health difficulties, and 40.5 per cent had been known to secondary mental health services at some point in their lives. Thirty-five per cent had made initial contact with student support services (some many months before their death) and then either failed to complete registration, respond to initial contact or attend one or more appointments, and 29.7 per cent had sought help from academic or administrative staff in their university school or department. Significant concerns about the students who died by suicide had been identified by their peers in at least 13.5 per cent of the cases, but peers had felt uncertain about how to help.

These findings pose challenges for student suicide prevention, when the majority of distressed students are not linked into student counselling or specialist mental health service provision. Instead, recognition of and immediate response to a suicidal crisis in many cases relies on the awareness of, and confident interventions by, peers, family and staff in contact with the student. This may include keeping them safe until such time as they decide to seek help for themselves or can be persuaded to seek more specialist support.

For most people expressing suicidal ideation or behaviours, suicide is not inevitable and up to the point of death is potentially reversible. Many express ambivalence about ending their lives and suicide can be an impulsive response to acute stressors. Ordinary people have the potential, without formal mental health training, to play a key role in suicide prevention (Owens, Derges and Abraham 2019). Public health campaigns, published guidance and suicide 'first aid' training are all predicated on a simple 'spot, say, signpost' message or its equivalent. There has only been limited research to understand obstacles and barriers that need to be overcome or what may be needed to intervene effectively (Owens and Charles 2017; Owens et al. 2011, 2019).

This chapter considers the role that untrained peers, family and staff can play in student suicide prevention within an FE or HE community and evidence for its impact in encouraging help-seeking and preventing harm. Untrained individuals, including student peers, need to feel confident about intervening (McLaughlin and Gunnell 2020). It may involve dispelling common myths that surround talking openly about suicide. It requires them to overcome a number of barriers including accurately identifying signals of suicidal distress, appreciating the significance of events as well as overcoming concerns that may inhibit them from intervening or sharing concerns with others outside of their immediate social network (Owens and Charles 2017). Intervening requires courage and confidence as well as skills in how to start a conversation, what to say, when to say it, as well as what to do (Owens and Charles 2017; Owens et al. 2019). These various issues and dilemmas will be considered and addressed in this chapter.

Does enquiring about suicidal intent help or harm?

Research shows that asking about suicidal intent does help. A review by Dazzi *et al.* (2014) found no evidence for increases in suicidal ideation when people were specifically asked about suicidal thoughts. Instead, they found that acknowledging and talking about suicide reduced rather than increased suicidal ideation of individuals who were seeking help. A further meta-analysis of 18 studies (Blades *et al.* 2018) also found no evidence that asking about suicide increases the risk or likelihood of a person engaging in suicidal behaviour. Instead, it was associated with small reductions in suicidal ideation, particularly for adolescents, and less likelihood of engaging in suicidal behaviour.

Can interventions by family and friends make a difference?

Yes, interventions by family and peers can make a difference! One study (Heinsch *et al.* 2020) found that individuals experiencing a suicidal crisis were more likely to seek support from family and friends initially and that they played a crucial role linking them with support services. Suicidal individuals who were encouraged to access services through interventions from friends and family were more likely to seek help again when facing future suicidal crises. Individuals who had experienced positive responses within their circle of support identified that this had a crucial impact on their decision not to attempt suicide in the future.

What may be helpful to say or do?

Your outward behaviour in terms of your facial expression, how you talk and appear, and your attitude are important. Jordan *et al.* (2012) interviewed young men (aged 16–34) to elicit their experiences of being suicidal and views on what constituted meaningful caring and specific caring processes that might make a difference. They identified that a person's demeanour and attitude were crucial to their engagement with them. What was identified as most important in countering suicidal ideation and perspectives was 'a sense that they mattered, that someone else was concerned about and interested in them' (Jordan *et al.* 2012, p.9).

Recognizing that someone is suicidal and taking action are also key to a successful intervention, but this can be problematic. Owens *et al.* (2011) interviewed relatives and friends of people who had died by suicide to understand the difficulties they faced in doing this. They found that there were few clear warning signs, and signals given by the suicidal person were often ambiguous, contradictory and open to interpretation. When friends and family recognized that something was wrong, fear often rendered them unable to say or do anything to prevent the subsequent tragedy. The findings highlighted a need to acknowledge and address the emotional needs of interveners as well as providing practical advice in public education resources. This informed the development of the 'It's Safe to Talk about Suicide' leaflet for families and friends (Owens and Charles 2017), which provides simple information about warning signs and encourages supporters to trust gut instincts and act on their concerns. The leaflet title and content challenges a popular myth that mentioning suicide (they call this using the 'S' word) may put the idea into someone's head and advocates instead asking someone directly whether they are having thoughts of suicide as the best way to keep them safe and ensure they access help (see 'Useful resources' below).

How you make the suicidal person feel appears to be much more important than what you say or do. Unique research by Owens and colleagues (2019) interviewed suicide survivors (people who had been prevented by a stranger from taking their own life) and interveners (people who had intervened to prevent a stranger from taking their own life) to identify core components of effective interventions by a member of the general public. They found that suicidal people typically displayed no visible distress and described themselves as being dissociated as if 'in a bubble'. Interveners were just ordinary people who were socially aware and prepared to act. Successful intervention comprised three main tasks:

- *Bursting the bubble*: reconnecting the suicidal person with self, others and the everyday world

- *Moving to a safer location*: using direct appeal ('Please come away from that edge'), indirect appeal ('Let's go for a coffee') or restraint (grabbing the person to remove them from a place of imminent danger)

- *Summoning help.*

The findings suggested that people do not need an intervention script and should not be afraid of saying 'the wrong thing'. Authenticity, calmness and compassion of the intervener were important. What interveners said or did appeared to be much less important than whether the suicidal person experienced feeling safe, connected and validated from an intervener conveying a very clear message that 'you matter'.

That said, recognizing and reaching out to those who may be at risk of suicide was not always experienced by interveners as straightforward, particularly when trying to keep the person safe while also summoning help or trying to extricate themselves from the situation. The study also identified that following such an intense encounter, interveners were often left disturbed by what had taken place, thinking about the person and their continued safety, and had found it difficult to return to normal activities. This highlights the crucial importance of self-care by the intervener and the need to seek support and an opportunity to debrief following an intense encounter of this nature (see the section later in the chapter on self-care interventions).

Guidance to support online intervention to posts about suicide

International #chatsafe guidance is available to support online intervention when responding to someone who might be suicidal or to deal with harmful online content. An Australian #chatsafe project (Robinson *et al.* 2018a, 2018b), based on a Delphi study with young people, developed and published evidence-informed guidelines to support safe communication about suicide online as a resource for young people, teachers, parents and health professionals. This includes guidance on safe posting, responding to someone who might be suicidal and dealing with harmful content. The original Australian #chatsafe guidelines[1] are available for use internationally (see 'Useful resources' below).

Dispelling myths and anxieties that can hold us back from intervening

For HE staff (or friends or family members) who do not have experience of working with suicide risk, a number of anxieties and uncertainties may arise if you are worried about someone having thoughts of suicide which can ultimately prevent or hinder effective intervention:

- *If I ask a student about suicide, it will put the idea in their head.* It is a commonly held belief that directly asking a person if they are thinking of suicide or of ending their life or even mentioning the word 'suicide' will lead a vulnerable person to begin to think

---

[1]   Available at www.orygen.org.au/chatsafe

about suicide or encourage them to act on thoughts. There is no evidence that this is the case (Blades *et al.* 2018). Without asking directly about suicidal thoughts we cannot accurately assess the risk of suicide. Without asking directly, we miss the opportunity to intervene to support that student.

- *Suicide is rare and only happens in people with serious mental health conditions.* Completed suicide remains a rare occurrence (ONS 2020), although thoughts of suicide are common and can happen to anyone, with or without a mental health condition. Certain characteristics and 'risk' factors may increase the likelihood of death by suicide (MHFAA 2016), no-one is immune to being at risk and it can happen to anyone. There is always value in asking someone if we have concerns even if we believe there is no chance they would die by suicide.

- *It will be obvious if a student is really at risk of suicide.* There can be signs that someone is at risk of suicide such as social withdrawal, changes in sleeping and eating patterns, increased alcohol/drug use, expressing a lack of hope or talking about death (MHFAA 2016). Equally, there can be no signs at all, and a student may show no outward indications that they are thinking about suicide. It is never safe to assume that a student is not thinking about suicide based on how they are behaving alone. We can only be sure if we ask directly.

- *If I find out a student is suicidal, I won't be able to help because I'm not a mental health professional.* A student who is suicidal will be in a dark and distressing place and likely to be feeling cut off from those around them. Contact with someone who demonstrates to the student that they are available and open to listening is an important first step in that student beginning to feel 'heard' and safe. There are numerous interventions that require only the ability to be present, listen and be supportive. Indeed, evidence suggests that just the act of someone else (a lay person, not a professional) intervening at a critical point connects the suicidal person with the present and the outside world and just the presence of that person helps to reduce risk (Owens *et al.* 2019).

- *If I intervene, it will be upsetting and anxiety provoking for me and I won't be able to cope.* Undoubtedly, intervening to help someone who is suicidal is a challenging and emotionally charged experience for the rescuer both during and after. Prior to intervening, it is important to check in with yourself as to how you are feeling, whether you feel able to intervene and where you can get further support for the person and for yourself after the event. If you don't feel emotionally able or equipped to intervene, it is important to find someone else you can inform about the person at risk. After you have intervened to help a student who is expressing suicidal thoughts, it may be helpful to seek support for yourself and to talk about what has just happened with a trusted friend or colleague.

Useful questions to ask

If you find yourself in a situation in which you are concerned that a student may be at risk of suicide, it can be helpful to know in advance some questions to ask and how to ask them. People are often concerned that they may say the wrong thing or something unhelpful. A useful guide to keep in mind would be to listen attentively, ask open-ended questions, not express judgment or opinion, and clarify information that you are not clear on – in a gentle manner (MHFAA 2016). There is no perfect or 'right' thing to say. Asking is better than not saying anything at all.

If someone's behaviour leads you to consider that they may be thinking about suicide, you could ask directly:

Are you thinking of suicide?

Do you feel suicidal?

Are you thinking of ending your life?

This can feel a difficult or uncomfortable way to talk with someone but is necessary. We can also say something along the lines of:

Sometimes when people say [comment about feeling hopeless, like they can't go on, etc.] they might be having thoughts about suicide, I wondered if that was true for you?

I saw that you posted [something concerning on social media] and it made me worry that you might be thinking of ending your life. Is that the case? (PAPYRUS 2018)

If a student lets you know that they are feeling suicidal or having thoughts of suicide, it would be helpful to let them know that you appreciate that they have told you, validate their experience and let them know you are there to help:

> I'm sorry that you feel like that, and I would like to help you. What can I do to help?

It is important to establish if the student is at immediate risk of harming themselves by asking:

> Have you made a plan to act on your thoughts of suicide?

> Do you feel able to keep yourself safe currently?

> Have you told anyone else how you are feeling?

If you are concerned that the student is at immediate risk of acting on suicidal thoughts (they have a specific suicide plan, the means to carry out the plan, a time set for doing it, and an intention to do it), try to work collaboratively with them to ensure their safety. They need to be encouraged to access emergency services or you may need to do that for them. It is important to remain with them until such a time that the care can be handed over to an emergency practitioner. Remind them that suicidal thoughts need not be acted on and there are solutions to problems and ways of dealing with them other than suicide (MHFAA 2016).

If the student has let you know that they are not at immediate risk of acting on suicidal thoughts, it is still important to remain with them. Some further questions that you could ask might include:

> How long have you been feeling like this?

> Have you had these thoughts before?

> What have you found helpful in the past when you've had these thoughts?

> Do you have anyone that you feel able to talk to?

> Would you like to talk to me?

> How would you like me to support you?

It is important to strike a balance between finding out more information whilst not being in 'interrogation' mode. Be directed by how the person responds to your questions. Be patient and not pushy.

Helpful interventions

There are a number of helpful things you can do to help a student who is expressing suicidal intent to keep them safe in the short term until support arrives to take them to a place of safety or the suicidal crisis has passed.

- *Social connection.* You can help to connect the student back into the social world by taking the time to talk to them, remaining with them and showing interest in and validating their experiences. Remind them of friends and family members in their life who may well be protective factors and emphasize that they are important and have a role in the world. Sitting and having a cup of tea, going for a walk or having a conversation with them about their lives and their interests will serve to increase feelings of being connected. It may also help to move their focus away from their suicidal thoughts towards reasons for living.

- *Distraction.* Suicidal thoughts can be accompanied by rumination on negative or difficult thoughts which can maintain suicidal thinking. Distracting the student from their thoughts for a while can be useful to reduce their risk in the short term. You might encourage them to listen to music, watch a TV show, play a game, do a crossword or 'shoot some hoops' with them. This could be especially helpful for a student who finds it difficult to talk.

- *Safety plan.* The student may already have a safety plan that they use when in crisis (see Chapter 16). You could check this out with them and, if they do, support them to enact their safety plan – this might involve making contact with specific people (often friends, family members or a mental health professional they are working with) or engaging in certain activities that distract or soothe them.

- *Accessing support.* It can be helpful to provide phone numbers of mental health support lines, crisis lines or other support services the student can access when in crisis. You might offer to call a support line on behalf of the student or stay with them whilst they call or support them to go to a safe place to access support.

Self-care interventions

Exposure to someone expressing suicidal thoughts can impact upon your own wellbeing and trigger personal negative thoughts and feelings. It is normal to feel upset or troubled by an intense emotional experience like this and what the person may have shared with you. If you are feeling upset or overwhelmed, you could try talking to someone you trust about what happened and how you are feeling. It is sometimes hard to immediately return to everyday tasks and home or work demands. It may be helpful instead to take a break and engage in some form of self-care. This might include a walk or gentle exercise, taking a warm bath or engaging in a mindful or calming activity. If you are struggling, it is important that you let someone know and seek out support for yourself to debrief and process what has happened.

Suicide awareness training

There are several online suicide awareness training resources and face-to-face 'suicide first aid' training courses. Training covers basic skills in opening up a conversation about suicide and signposting to appropriate help and resources:

- **Zero Suicide Alliance's suicide awareness training** provides an understanding of signs to look out for and skills required to approach someone who is struggling with suicidal thoughts, www.zerosuicidealliance.com

- **Health Education England and Public Health England's *We Need to Talk about Suicide*** is a free e-learning suicide prevention course (60–90 minutes) for non-mental health practitioners, www.nwyhelearning.nhs.uk/elearning/HEE/SuicidePrevention

- **MindEd Suicide and Self-Harm Prevention has three separate modules on suicide and self-harm prevention** including 'Skills for Schools', 'Young People' (young-people-related content) and 'Skills for Adults' (adult-related content) to help teachers and others working with young people and adults, www.minded.org.uk

- **Suicide first aid training courses** range from 90 minutes to six hours. They include:

  - 'Living Works', www.livingworks.net

- 'Safe Talk', www.livingworks.net/safetalk

- Samaritans 'Managing Suicidal Conversations' workplace training, www.samaritans.org

- SFA 'Suicide First Aid' course, www.suicidefirstaid.uk

- PAPYRUS 'SP-ARK' (awareness), 'SP-OT' (suicide prevention overview), 'SP-EAK' (skills building) training series, www.papyrus-uk.org

Useful resources

- *#chatsafe A Young Person's Guide for Communicating Safely Online about Suicide* (Robinson *et al.* 2018b), www.orygen.org.au/chatsafe

- **'It's Safe to Talk about Suicide'**: A leaflet developed at the University of Exeter Medical School in collaboration with The Alliance of Suicide Prevention Charities (TASC) and produced by Devon County Council, www.devon.gov.uk/care-and-health/factsheet/suicide-prevention

- **PAPYRUS 'Conversation Starters'**: Examples of conversation starters if you are worried about someone, www.papyrus-uk.org/wp-content/uploads/2018/09/papyrus_conversation_starters.pdf

- **Mental Health First Aid Guidelines, *Suicidal Thoughts and Behaviours***: Practical advice for non-professionals on what kind of questions to ask, how to keep someone safe and how to link them in with professional help, https://mhfa.com.au/sites/default/files/MHFA_suicide_guidelinesA4%202014%20Revised.pdf

- **PAPYRUS HOPELINEUK:** If you are worried about someone who is suicidal or you are a young person having thoughts of suicide contact HOPELINEUK. Call: 0800 068 4141, Text: 07860 039 967, Email: pat@papyrus-uk.org, Website: www.papyrus-uk.org/hopelineuk

- **Shout Crisis Text Line:** If you do not want to talk to someone over the phone, the SHOUT crisis text line is open 24 hours every day for anyone. Text 'SHOUT' to 85258

Conclusion

Peers, family and staff can play a critical early role in the detection of students at risk of suicide and in rapidly signposting students to more appropriate healthcare and crisis support. To do this successfully, they require knowledge about what support and resources may be available and possess the confidence and skills to intervene. Decisions to intervene or not by peers, family and the general public are not without associated costs and consequences. Debriefing opportunities and self-care are important for interveners and need to be recognized and appropriately supported.

Author biographies

Katie Stafford is a mental health nurse who has spent her career working with children and adolescents in both inpatient and community settings. She currently works in a CAMHS team for the Manchester University NHS Foundation Trust in which she supports and helps young people with suicidal thoughts and self-harm behaviours on a daily basis.

Professor Jo Smith was Project Lead for the University of Worcester 'Suicide-Safer' student suicide prevention initiative (2014–2020) and co-author of an 'International Declaration on Zero Suicide in Healthcare' (2015). She was on national working groups which produced UUK (2017) *#Stepchange: Mental Health in Higher Education*, UUK (2018) *Minding Our Future* and UUK and PAPYRUS (2018) *Suicide-Safer Universities*.

References

Biddle, L., Gunnell, D. and Sharp, D. (2004) Factors influencing help seeking in mentally distressed young adults: a cross-sectional survey. *British Journal of General Practice 54*, 248–253.

Blades, C.A., Stritzke, W.G.K., Page, A.C. and Brown, J.D. (2018) The benefits and risks of asking research participants about suicide: a meta-analysis of the impact of exposure to suicide-related content. *Clinical Psychology Review 64*, 1–12.

Dazzi, T., Gribble, R., Wessely, S. and Fear, N.T. (2014) Does asking about suicide and related behaviours induce suicidal ideation? What is the evidence? *Psychol Med 44*, 16, 3361–3363.

Heinsch, M., Sampson, D., Huens, V., Handley, T. *et al.* (2020) Understanding ambivalence in help-seeking for suicidal people with comorbid depression and alcohol misuse. *PLoS One 15*, 4, e0231647.

Jordan, J., McKenna, H., Keeney, S. and Cutcliffe, J. (2012) *Providing Meaningful Care: Using the Experiences of Young Suicidal Men to Inform Mental Health Care Services*. Short Report. Ulster: Health & Social Care Research and Development Division, Public Health Agency, Northern Ireland.

McLaughlin, J.C. and Gunnell, D.J. (2020) Suicide deaths in university students in a UK city 2010–2018: case series. *Crisis: Journal of Crisis Intervention and Suicide Prevention*, https://doi.org/10.1027/0227-5910/a000704

Mental Health First Aid Australia (MHFAA) (revised 2016) *Suicidal Thoughts and Behaviours: First Aid Guidelines*. Melbourne: Mental Health First Aid Australia.

National Confidential Inquiry into Suicide and Homicide by People with Mental Illness (NCISH) (2017) *Suicide by Children and Young People*. Manchester: University of Manchester.

Office for National Statistics (ONS) (2020) Suicides in England and Wales: 2019 registrations. Newport: ONS.

Owens, C. and Charles, N. (2017) Development and evaluation of a leaflet for concerned family members and friends: 'It's safe to talk about suicide'. *Health Education Journal 76*, 5, 582–594.

Owens, C., Derges, J. and Abraham, C. (2019) Intervening to prevent a suicide in a public place: a qualitative study of effective interventions by lay people. *BMJ Open 9*, e032319.

Owens, C., Owen, G., Belam, J., Lloyd, K. *et al.* (2011) Recognising and responding to suicidal crisis within family and social networks: qualitative study. *BMJ 343*, d5801.

PAPYRUS (2018) Conversation Starters. Preston: PAPYRUS. www.papyrus-uk.org/wp-content/uploads/2018/09/papyrus_conversation_starters.pdf

Robinson, J., Hill, N.T.M., Thorn, P., Battersby, R. *et al.* (2018a) The #chatsafe project. Developing guidelines to help young people communicate safely about suicide on social media: a Delphi study. *PLoS One 13*, 11, e0206584.

Robinson, J., Hill, N., Thorn, P., Teh, Z., Battersby, R. and Reavley, N. (2018b) #chatsafe. A young person's guide for communicating safely online about suicide. Melbourne: Orygen.

CHAPTER 14

Supporting Students

The Role of the NHS

CLARE DICKENS

Overview

This chapter will offer a space for readers to:

- reflect on a student case study illustrating a crisis point, when individual and higher education (HE) distress triggers have combined

- consider the national and local landscapes in which suicide prevention sits within the UK, and the complexity that the span of such strategies poses to staff

- explore how higher education institutions (HEIs) can work in partnership with other agencies to enable navigation and access to external services.

Introduction

This chapter will use a case study to discuss the needs that can present in an HE student with a range of mental and social health needs. This case study exists within the context of success and crisis presented by Thorley (2017), whereby a mismatch of provision and need is possibly created by the reduction in stigma and the success of public-facing campaigns such as 'Time to Change'. This, in turn, may make students more confident to come forward to disclose their difficulties with the expectation that this will be met with an offer of appropriate and timely support. This chapter will focus on the role of universities, which sit alongside public health, primary care and specialist mental health services, and also have a role in working directly with student support services in providing joined-up care for vulnerable and at-risk students.

CASE STUDY: LUKA

Luka is approaching the end of his third year at university. He is studying on an undergraduate civil engineering degree course and has progressed well in his first two years. He is approaching the end of semester two and his results have come in; he will need to resit a module assessment because he didn't meet all of the learning outcomes. Luka is a first-generation university student at a post-1992 university. He opted to live away from his home with his parents and siblings, approximately 25 miles away, in order to embrace the full package that the university experience can offer. He does part-time work at a local bar to support himself, increasing the number of shifts when his finances get tight. He lives with other civil engineering students in a university-run flat, and has made some good friends. Luka was known to Child and Adolescent Mental Health Services (CAMHS) prior to arriving at university. His discharge was planned and the commencement of his university course was seen as a positive sign of progress in his recovery journey.

Making his way to the library, Luka is spotted by Ray, one of the hall's caretakers, who he sees at least every other day. They are on friendly speaking terms. Ray notices that Luka is not his usual self: he is withdrawn, is avoiding eye contact, and the puffiness of his eyes shows he has clearly been upset recently. Ray asks Luka a simple question, 'Are you OK?' Luka says, 'Not really,' and following a short conversation unexpectedly discloses that he self-harmed last night for the first time in years, and now feels that he has let himself down.

- Put yourself in Ray's shoes – what would your initial response to this disclosure be?
- What questions would you ask Luka?
- Within your current FE, HE and community context, what signposting opportunities would exist for a hall caretaker or a similar support staff member like Ray?
- What barriers might Luka have navigated in order to reveal his recent self-harm?

The scale of the mental health problem in HE

Luka's story sits within an HE landscape where mental health difficulties can manifest. A United Kingdom (UK) study by the IPPR think tank (Thorley 2017) claims to have revealed a 'mental health crisis' in universities. The study notes a fivefold rise in students reporting a mental health issue in their first year of study over the last ten years. The narrative of 'crisis' can, however, be challenged when we consider campaigns such as 'Time to Change' whose aim is to reduce the stigma associated with mental health issues. Such campaigns and others like it call for us to talk, and by default can lead to increased disclosure. The central tenet of the crisis possibly lies in the fact that behind each of these disclosures is an individual, with individual needs, and there may be a lack of awareness about how such disclosures should be responded to. Furthermore, there may be insufficient capacity in professional support services to respond to these disclosures in a timely and safe manner.

Stepchange is a campaign from a Universities UK (UUK) national working group that is chaired by Professor Steve West. It includes a call for action, identifying that one of the four reasons why mental health should be a strategic priority is an increasing number of students dying by suicide. It further highlights the duty of care HEIs have to their students (UUK 2017). There is a push within the model to adopt a whole population approach to student mental health, asking HEIs to reconfigure themselves as health-promoting and supportive environments. It sets out a number of recommendations, one of which is that HEIs should develop regular high-level links with NHS commissioners and services, local authorities and the third sector to encourage an integrated approach between HE support services and local primary care and mental health services, ensuring signposting, and enhance support for students during transition periods (UUK 2017).

Suicide prevention in a wider UK context

In order to embrace this call for HEIs to consider how they should interact with NHS organizations, we need to first consider the wider societal contexts in which such care sits. At the time of writing this chapter, the UK along with other countries worldwide have navigated over a decade of politically imposed austerity. Inequalities have become entrenched, with 49 per cent funding cuts to local authorities (Maguire and Chakelian 2018), and the NHS, which was already prone to pressures from population-based ill health and structural crisis, has been left with a chronic gap between needs and resources (Hopkins 2019). These societal-level factors trickle down to the individual which can, in turn, perpetuate social disadvantage (Batty *et al.* 2018), social disconnection and limited social support (O'Connor and Nock 2014), including loneliness (Bennardi *et al.* 2017), all of which feature in the interpersonal theory of suicide (Van Ordern *et al.* 2010). Wilkinson and Picket (2018) found that in every country where inequality has widened there has been an associated rise in the number of people reporting increased distress. The Royal College of Psychiatrists (RCP) also reports a correlation between inequality and worse mental health outcomes (RCP 2010). Thus, regardless of how we frame this distress, the evidence shows that inequality causes suffering.

With this wider context in mind, we can gain some insight into Luka's response from Gilbert, Prince and Allan (1995) who show how an environment in which inequalities exist may nurture unfavourable social comparison, which may, in turn, tap in to distress and exacerbate vulnerability. This is possibly further compounded by contemporary movements that see competition as a defining characteristic of human relationships, with indicators of personal success being cast as dependent on ability and effort alone. Luka lives with other students studying on the same course, and understandably their daily discussions feature heavily in course assessments, their progress and hopes for the future. It would be difficult for him not to pitch or compare himself against his peers. This current period of distress has been preceded by many previous experiences which have often left him feeling inadequate and lonely. These are feelings he does not confide to anyone. None of Luka's family are civil engineers, he doesn't even know any beyond the course academic staff, while his peers either have family members who are engineers or have associated connections. This worries Luka deeply when he considers his future employment prospects beyond HE, which has been compounded by his recent failure of a module, which his peers passed.

- Do FE and HE miss some of these hidden social and cultural capital factors when designing courses with a focus on employability?
- Why might a focus on Luka being the sole source of his distress prove unhelpful?

Where does HE sit in a wider context of strategic suicide prevention?

In 2012, a cross-government National Suicide Prevention Strategy for England charged local government with the coordination of local partnerships, and a planning role to prevent suicides (DH 2012). Most local authority areas now have established suicide prevention plans and multiagency partnerships to deliver them (DH 2012). This strategy was updated in 2017 to broaden the original focus so that it covered another five key areas. These included self-harm prevention and better targeting of those considered to be within high-risk groups, such as men and LGBTQ members of our community (DH 2017). The national strategy was further underpinned by recommendations from the government-commissioned Independent Mental Health (MH) Taskforce setting out NHS England's Five Year Forward View for MH, which mandated NHS services to contribute to a 10 per cent reduction in local suicide rates through local system partnerships (Farmer and Dyer 2016). Notably, there was little guidance on how to do so while working with scant resources.

It should be highlighted that in the UK in 2019, only 28 per cent of recorded suicides were linked to individuals who had been under the care of Mental Health Services (NCISH 2019). Clearly, the majority of deaths by suicide occur in the wider population, and less than one third of suicidal individuals seek help or make use of secondary mental health services. There are further considerations within primary care and where consultation remains the main barrier to suicide prevention. It is suggested that the higher rate of suicide among men may be partly attributed to the lower rate of consultation among this group (Biddle *et al.* 2004). It is estimated that suicide risk is increased by 67 per cent in those who are non-consulters with their GP (NCISH 2014). By inference, we have to consider that there are additional barriers for suicidal individuals to overcome, such as low perceived need, shame, a preference for self-management and availability of suitable services (Andrade *et al.* 2014; Bruffaerts *et al.* 2011), and within this, a focus on exploring the intricacies and barriers to help-seeking based on gender requires much deeper exploration (Mallon *et al.* 2016). There is a challenge for FE colleges and HEIs to ensure they form wider collaborative partnerships with health and public health partners, in a much broader health and suicide prevention strategy. The best way to achieve the starting point required is to gain a seat at the table where local suicide prevention strategies are deliberated and created.

Principles for how to achieve this are set out within the Stepchange model (UUK 2017). They include the need to establish and sustain strategic links between HE and health leadership, to consider joint needs assessments, integrated services and improved data sharing. HEIs and FE colleges have the challenge of ensuring that their student and staff population needs are considered in order to better understand commissioning priorities. If they are achieved, HEIs and FE colleges have the opportunity to voice what support they can offer, and equally, what the limits are on this. In some of these negotiations, HEIs and FE colleges can also consider hosting some of the services on campus, bringing services to students and staff, whilst enhancing accessibility and reach. These principles are not limited to secondary services but should also embrace the third sector and primary care (UUK 2017).

- What strategic and provision-based relationships does your HEI or FE college have with some of the bodies and services featured above?
- Do you have a means of feeding into the agenda and plans of local NHS, public health and third sector services, to offer HE and FE insights, experiences and needs?

The role of primary care

One of the key priorities for any student should be to ensure they are registered with a local general practitioner (GP), who can often be the gatekeeper to a range of services for any health or wellbeing need. Therefore, HEIs and FE colleges do have to weave in to their communication with students the importance of registering locally with a GP. This should be done at varying and repeated points within the academic calendar to ensure the message is picked up, particularly when students have to navigate so many other tasks and systems. The role of primary care can also be a significant feature within the suicide prevention support map for any individual. In May 2019, Samaritans and the University of Exeter published an independent report on local suicide prevention planning in England (Chadwick, Owens and Morrissey 2019). The report had a number of high-level recommendations and suggested that in order to achieve greater impact, local authorities should consider developing regional priorities through a sector-led improvement (SLI) framework.

In addition, the planning and delivery of national strategy area actions at a local level should include reducing risk in men, bereavement support, improving acute mental health care, reducing suicides at high-frequency locations and, pertinently, improving depression pathways within primary care.

A Centre for Mental Health report entitled *Strengthening the Front Line* focuses on primary care for effective suicide prevention and outlines five areas of focused need. These include effective and ongoing training for GPs, increasing capacity to enable longer consultation, emotional support for GPs, establishing health and social care pathways for those who are considering that their life is not worth living and making it easier to refer and receive support (Centre for Mental Health 2019). There are some emerging areas of good practice within primary care, such as in Derbyshire where they have embraced and implemented many of the principles set out above. For example, they have placed emphasis on compassionate care, creating parity of esteem with physical health, suicidal thoughts representing emotional pain and on everyone having access to safety planning. They have also emphasized means reduction, safer prescribing and 'safe for now' principles, and individualized assessment and referral (Cole-King and Platt 2017). However, not every student's experience of accessing primary care may be prompt, seamless or easy. Therefore, HEI and FE colleges can play a role by making a commitment to aid students beyond merely encouraging them to register with a GP, and by helping them to navigate and gain support from primary care if necessary.

Referral routes

One referral route within primary care, and, in some areas, via self-referral, is to Improving Access to Psychological Therapies (IAPT) introduced in 2008. It has been posited as the NHS's answer to improving outcomes in the 'treatment' of common and 'low-level' mental health difficulties. Within this model, cognitive behavioural therapy (CBT) comprises one of the service offerings that can see someone receive intervention within a stepped model of care, from low to high intensity. A systematic review of evidence conducted by Hawton *et al.* (2016) found that CBT-based psychotherapy (comprising cognitive-behavioural and problem-solving therapy) has been associated with fewer participants repeating self-harm at six months. There were also significant improvements in the secondary outcomes of depression, hopelessness, suicidal ideation and problem solving. Within this model and other therapeutic interventions, there are services on offer that can support students to explore their thinking, core beliefs and patterns of coping, as well as their problem-solving ability.

It would be wrong, however, not to critically explore barriers to successfully accessing the IAPT model, if we perceive this as part of a student's support mapping. Difficulty locating and accessing the service, shortage of therapy sessions and having to fight to gain additional sessions may all comprise a student's difficulties within the referral pathway. In 2018–2019, IAPT services received 1.6 million GP and self-referrals. If any of those 1.6 million referrals were students, they may have spent a considerable chunk of their semester on a waiting list, as waiting times for access to therapy could take anything between 6 and 18 weeks, depending on what part of the country the individual is in (DH 2015). The head of policy for the British Association for Counselling and Psychology (BACP), Suki Kaur, has offered a response, noting that it is not good enough that currently people in need are subject to a postcode lottery in relation to service provision (BACP 2019). This concern is shared by the University of York in their *Student Mental Health and Wellbeing Strategy 2017–2020* (University of York 2017). There are a number of things that HE and FE can do in order to meet this challenge, and the University of Bristol note in their health and wellbeing student strategy (University of Bristol 2018) that they will continue to advocate for further government investment in services in their community and lobby for increased investment in local mental health services and local charities that provide vital services for students, all of which are currently over-subscribed or have long waiting lists.

Whilst universities should continue to advocate for and work with external partners to improve pathways between them and local mental health services, which will enable navigation and access, offering support within the HEI or FE college context may also serve a helpful purpose for students. For Luka in our case study, in the interim, while waiting for any onward referral to come to fruition, a conversation to consider some of his immediate and practical problems may be of benefit. For example, following his encounter with Ray, he was signposted to the wellbeing service within the university, which responded within a day via a phone call, and co-explored the issues and the desired solution. This approach has been adopted by many universities, such as the University of Worcester in their STAR (Support, Triage, Advice, Referral) model

(University of Worcester 2021). For Luka, accessing the university's hardship fund and emergency loan provision (though they do not exist in every university) might enable him to take on fewer shifts at work in order to focus on his re-sit module. Given that he lives in halls and his agreement may not cover the re-sit period, support to extend it by a few weeks may aid him; the further upheaval of moving out in the midst of focusing on his re-submission might put extra strain on his ability to do so successfully. He would also possibly benefit from gaining study skills support in order to prepare for his exam re-submission, and gain advice and reassurance from his personal tutor about his personal perception that he is an academic failure.

Crisis support

Any suicide prevention strategy within any HEI or FE college should not neglect to consider the need to promote clear and unambiguous advice about how to access support when in a crisis, where an emergency and possible medical intervention is required, in order to keep students safe. This advice should promote what the HEI or FE college can offer and at what time, and where to gain such support in the event a crisis occurs at a time when staff are not available to support. Here, an HE or FE security team can play a vital role; as such a response should really be requested via them so that they can support emergency services to locate the student in distress and/or danger if they are on campus. Such intricacies are outlined in the University of York student mental health and wellbeing strategy, and the University of Wolverhampton web page under the banner of 'If you need help now' where they promote the local Black Country NHS crisis service and how to access them given the vast majority of their students commute to university.

The role of HE and FE staff recognizing, referring, holding and amplifying student need

In studies within an HE context, Lee *et al.* (2013), Anderson *et al.* (2014) and Gask *et al.* (2017) have evaluated the effectiveness of gatekeeper training and reported marked improvements in confidence and ability to spot signs of suicide risk in the participants' post-training test measures. All studies define 'designated' gatekeepers as people who already work as helping professionals. By contrast, 'emergent' gatekeepers are community members, who may not have been formally trained to intervene with someone at risk of suicide but emerge as potential gatekeepers when approached for support by someone at risk and are in a position to make referrals to help. In our case study, the caretaker who Luka passed in the corridor of his hall is a gatekeeper of some sort, but he can also be a source of support and solution in the context of Luka's distress in that immediate moment of disclosure, in part to help him recognize and consider accepting the support and help that is available.

There has, however, been growing unease for many years about whether it is the role of counselling services within HE and FE to compensate for what seem to be shortfalls in NHS provision (Cowley 2007). Given increasing demand and complexity from student referrals, counsellors and mental health advisors also have to support students to access, and in many cases wait for, NHS provision. Indeed, Gask *et al.* (2017) articulate a concern that HE and FE staff trained and identified as 'gatekeepers' experience a high degree of frustration when mental health services are not receptive to the referrals they make.

We should, however, be reminded that at the centre of the case study within this chapter is a human being who wants help, and there is a further challenge to HE and FE, and indeed to NHS and non-statutory services. This is not to ask students 'What is the matter with you?' but instead to consider asking 'What matters to you?', embracing principles of students as motivated partners within the HE and FE experience (Brovill 2014) and not submissive and silent recipients of their experience (Haggis 2006). We should ask students what experiences are happening to them and how these are making them feel if we are to move students' thinking away from what is to 'What if?' – what future do they want for themselves and what support and opportunity do they need to get there? This can be helpful in the immediate moment (Hopkins 2019). If we ask these questions of every student who is experiencing heightened distress, at any point in their student journey, we may find that there are some common threads of similarity, and in some cases differences that are unique to individual students. This taps in to the stark point made by Hockings (2010) that students do not want to stand out as different, but they do want to be recognized as individuals and instead to consider the individual nature of the origins of their distress and their preferences and needs for support.

There is a concern that if we get tangled up in debates about funding, whose responsibility student mental health is, and provision versus need, we start off with an assumption that we know what it is students are going through and what support they need in order to survive and thrive within an HE or FE context and beyond. There is no doubt that NHS and third sector services have a role to play in the support landscape we plot out for students as a group, and some of our role within HE and FE should be to navigate and advocate a student's needs in order that they do not find themselves acting as their own care coordinator.

However, the NHS cannot be seen as the default response or source of resolution for all students experiencing heightened distress, times when they may feel their life is not worth living or in response to self-harming behaviour. Gaining meaningful and proportionate help that may be required for students can often sit within their HE or FE community, whether it is the caretaker along the corridor in the case of Luka, or their personal tutor, or a mental health advisor. This can often start with the most commonplace questions, enquiring 'Are you OK?' on the back of an observation or gut feeling that the student does not appear to be OK. If, as in the case of Luka, the response indicates that the student is not OK, these gatekeepers should not be concerned that exploring the nature of the student's distress, particularly when the student may be considering that their life is not worth living or has made plans to harm themselves, will introduce that idea into their thinking. A review of evidence by Dazzi *et al.* (2014) found that this was not the case. Indeed, this question may be the key to understanding what level of response is needed in that immediate moment and can create an opportunity to explore the distress triggers that are driving the student's feelings of hopelessness. This can then inform and guide signposting to appropriate support to help keep the student safe, offer hope and facilitate a resolution of their difficulties.

Conclusions

The drivers of distress that underpin someone considering that their life is not worth living, or that lead to them feeling increased emotional intensity, can come about as a consequence of numerous and complex internal and external factors. Part of the role of FE and HE, and in the task of navigating and cementing relationships with community partners, is to acknowledge the complexity that leads to suicidal thoughts and actions in the first instance and the need for sustained partnership working thereafter. The case study in this chapter saw a young man navigating the tail end of his studies at a time that would place him between commonly understood transition points, and where his pattern of success within his studies received a blow when he failed one of his year three semester two modules. However, this epoch for Luka had deeper and longer-term entrenched fears about his place and role in society, which this event unearthed as a result of conversations with those in a position to offer support. This would lead us to consider that with an immediate route to help-seeking, those challenges can be turned into opportunities. In the midst of this, the NHS, public health and the third sector may have a role to play, but the student and their needs should always take centre stage in being directors in identifying their support needs and their support journey that then plays out.

Author biography

Clare Dickens is a registered mental health nurse, senior lecturer and academic lead for mental health and wellbeing at the University of Wolverhampton. Clare is currently studying for a professional doctorate focusing on professional bereavement by suicide. Clare also chairs Wolverhampton's suicide prevention stakeholder's forum.

References

Anderson, D., Bernier, J., Cimini, M., Murray, A. *et al.* (2014) Implementing an audience specific small-group gatekeeper training programme to respond to suicide risk among college students: a case study. *Journal of American College Health 62*, 2, 99–100.

Andrade, L.H., Alonso, J., Mneimneh, Z., Wells, J.E. *et al.* (2014) Barriers to mental health treatment: results from the WHO World Mental Health surveys. *Psychol Med 44*, 6, 1303–1317.

BACP (2019) Long waiting times for IAPT 'unacceptable'. Accessed on 01/04/21 at: www.bacp.co.uk/news/news-from-bacp/2019/5-december-long-waiting-times-for-iapt-unacceptable

Batty, G.D., Kivimaki, M., Bell, S., Gale, C.R. *et al.* (2018) Psychosocial characteristics as potential predictors of suicide in adults: an overview of the evidence with new results from prospective cohort studies. *Transl Psychiatry 8*, 22.

Bennardi, M., Caballero, F.F., Miret, M., Ayuso-Mateos, J.L. *et al.* (2017) Longitudinal relationships between positive affect, loneliness, and suicide ideation: age-specific factors in a general population. *Suicide Life Threat Behav. 49*, 1, 90–103.

Biddle, L., Gunnell, D., Sharp, D. and Donovan, J.L. (2004) Factors influencing help seeking in mentally distressed young adults: a cross-sectional survey. *The British Journal of General Practice 54*, 248–253.

Brovill, C. (2014) An investigation of co-created curricula within higher education in the UK, Ireland and the USA. *Innovations in Education and Teaching International 51*, 1, 15–25.

Bruffaerts, R., Demyttenaere, K., Hwang, I., Chui, W. *et al.* (2011) Treatment of suicidal people around the world. *British Journal of Psychiatry 199*, 1, 64–70.

Centre for Mental Health (2019) Strengthening the frontline: investing in primary care for effective suicide prevention. Accessed on 01/04/21 at: www.centreformentalhealth.org.uk/publications/strengthening-frontline

Chadwick, T., Owens, C. and Morrissey, J. (2019) Local suicide prevention planning in England. Accessed on 30/06/21 at: https://www.samaritans.org/news/samaritans-and-university-exeter-publish-first-state-nation-report-local-suicide-prevention

Cole-King, A. and Platt, S. (2017) Suicide prevention for physicians: identification, intervention and mitigation of risk. *Medicine 45*, 3, 131–134.

Cowley, J. (2007) Stepped care: the Cardiff Model. *AUCC Journal*, 2–5.

Dazzi, T., Gribble, R., Wessely, S. and Fear, N.T. (2014) Does asking about suicide and related behaviours induce suicidal ideation? What is the evidence? *Psychological Medicine 44*, 16, 3361–3363.

Department of Health (DH) (2012) *Preventing Suicide in England: A Cross-Government Outcomes Strategy to Save Lives.* London: HM Government. Accessed on 10/11/20 at: https://assets.publishing.service.gov.uk/government/uploads/system/uploads/attachment_data/file/430720/Preventing-Suicide-.pdf

Department of Health (DH) (2015) *The Mandate: A Mandate from the Government to NHS England: April 2015 to March 2016.* London: DH. Accessed on 01/04/21 at: www.gov.uk/government/uploads/system/uploads/attachment_data/file/386221/NHS_England_Mandate.pdf

Department of Health (DH) (2017) *Preventing Suicide in England: Third Progress Report of the Cross-Government Outcomes Strategy to Save Lives.* London: HM Government. Accessed on 10/11/20 at: https://assets.publishing.service.gov.uk/government/uploads/system/uploads/attachment_data/file/582117/Suicide_report_2016_A.pdf

Farmer, P. and Dyer, J. (2016) *The Five Year Forward View for Mental Health: A Report from the Independent Mental Health Taskforce to the NHS in England.* London: NHS England.

Gask, L., Coupe, N., Green, G. and McElvenny, D. (2017) Pilot study evaluation of suicide prevention gatekeeper training utilising STORM in a British university setting. *British Journal of Guidance and Counselling 45*, 5, 593–605.

Gilbert, P., Prince, J. and Allan, S. (1995) Social comparison, social attractiveness and evolution: how might they be related? *New Ideas in Psychology 13*, 2, 149–165.

Haggis, T. (2006) Pedagogies for diversity: retaining critical challenge amidst fears of 'dumbing down'. *Studies in Higher Education 31*, 521–535.

Hawton, K., Witt, K.G., Salisbury, T., Arensman, E. *et al.* (2016) Psychosocial interventions following self-harm in adults: a systematic review and meta-analysis. *Lancet Psychiatry 3*, 8, 740–750.

Hockings, C. (2010) Towards Inclusive Learning and Teaching – Principles into Practice, The Higher Education Academy – 2010 workshop presentation at the Research Conference: Promoting Equity in Higher Education, 27–28 January 2010.

Hopkins, R. (2019) *From What Is to What If: Unleashing the Power of Imagination to Create the Future We Want.* London: Chelsea Green Publishing.

Lee, J., Miles, N., Prieto-Welch, S.L., Servaty-Seib, H.L. *et al.* (2013) The impact of gatekeeper training for suicide prevention on university residential assistants. *Journal of College Counselling 16*, 1, 64–78.

Maguire, P. and Chakelian, A. (2018) The deepest cuts: austerity measured. *New Statesman*, 10 October.

Mallon, S., Galway, K., Hughes, L., Rondón-Sulbarán, J. and Leavey, G. (2016) An exploration of integrated data on the social dynamics of suicide among women. *Sociology of Health and Illness 38*, 662–675.

National Confidential Inquiry into Suicide and Homicide by People with Mental Illness (NCISH) (2014) *Suicide in Primary Care in England.* Manchester: University of Manchester.

National Confidential Inquiry into Suicide and Safety in Mental Health (2019) *Annual Report: England, Northern Ireland, Scotland and Wales 2019.* Manchester: University of Manchester.

O'Connor, R.C. and Nock, M.K. (2014) The psychology of suicidal behaviour. *Lancet Psychiatry 1*, 73–85.

Royal College of Psychiatrists (RCP) (2010) *No Health without Public Mental Health: The Case for Action.* Position statement. London: RCP. Accessed on 01/04/21 at: www.rcpsych.ac.uk/pdf/PS04_2010.pdf

Thorley, C. (2017) *Not by Degrees: Improving Student Mental Health in the UK's Universities.* London: IPPR.

Universities UK (UUK) (2017) New framework for universities to help improve student mental health. Press release. Accessed on 01/10/20 at: www.universitiesuk.ac.uk/news/Pages/New-framework-for-universities-to-help-improve-student-mental-health.aspx

University of Bristol (2018) *Mental Health and Wellbeing: Our Student Strategy.* University of Bristol.

University of Worcester (2021) Welcome to the Counselling & Mental Health Service. Accessed on 01/04/21 at: www2.worc.ac.uk/counselling

University of York (2017) *Student Mental Health and Wellbeing Strategy 2017–2020.* University of York.

Van Orden, K.A., Witte, T.K., Cukrowicz, K.C., Braithwaite, S.R. *et al.* (2010) The interpersonal theory of suicide. *Psychol. Rev. 117*, 575–600.

Wilkinson, R. and Picket, K. (2018) *The Inner Level: How More Equal Societies Reduce Stress, Restore Sanity and Improve Everyone's Wellbeing.* London: Allen Lane.

CHAPTER 15

Supporting Students

The Parents' Perspective

NATALIE DAY

When we lost [David] in those early years we were grappling with a
lot. Since then we've learned so much through PAPYRUS and our
contacts with other parents. We have a clearer picture; when we look
back now with this perspective we can see how it all panned out. Our
thinking is that it shouldn't be left to that student to ask for help, it
can't just stay with tutors on the course. There needs to be contact,
follow-ups, there need to be conversations and training. It's something
every university needs. (Sarah, mother of David)

Overview

This chapter will explore parents' experiences of losing a child to suicide
whilst they were studying at university. The chapter will discuss and
advise on issues and policy regarding:

- the responsibilities and roles of universities and their staff in
  the management of at-risk students, and issues around support
  availability and communication of concerns regarding students'
  mental health or potential suicide risk

- confidentiality policies within universities concerning suicidal
  thoughts or attempts – and the impact of this within universities,
  for parents and for students

- the importance of an effective postvention strategy in universities
  for the prevention of further suicides.

Introduction

On average, 95 university students end their lives by suicide each year (ONS 2018). The number of students who die by suicide each year is a statistic that sees some fluctuation but generally remains fairly consistent with each passing year. An accompanying phenomenon that is not captured by this statistic is the number of university students who attempt to end their lives or experience thoughts of suicide, which is predicted to be much higher than the number of deaths per year. Research has demonstrated that adolescents and young adults are at a higher risk of suicide due to their unique situational, individual and socio-cultural factors (WHO 2012) – factors which are interwoven through their educational environment and experience. Suicide bereavement impacts on families, communities within educational organizations and within wider communities. It is estimated that 60 people are bereaved or personally affected by each death by suicide, with the greatest impact being on the close or immediate circle of the person who ends their life (Cerel *et al.* 2016; Spillane *et al.* 2018).

PAPYRUS Prevention of Young Suicide, a suicide prevention organization operating a national helpline service based in Warrington, was founded by parents who were bereaved by suicide. Many of the children were within the education system at the time of their deaths. Suicide is the leading cause of death for young people under the age of 35 (ONS 2019), an age group that makes up the vast majority of the UK student population (Higher Education Statistics Agency 2019). PAPYRUS receives calls on a daily basis to their helpline, HOPELINEUK, from university students across the UK contemplating suicide based on situational or emotional struggles in their lives. The ethos of PAPYRUS is grounded within evidence that shows awareness raising and effective training in person-centred interventions that focus on facilitating safety from suicide throughout universities could prevent many young deaths by suicide (WHO 2014). Within the UK, most suicide bereavement or prevention services are provided by charitable organizations with very little input from psychiatric or mental health services (Pitman *et al.* 2014). The work of the charities and their connection to real-life experiences of those struggling with suicidal thoughts, and to those who have been bereft by suicide, therefore offers a wealth of insight into these issues, which will be explored within this chapter.

The chapter examines the role and experiences of parents who have lost a child through suicide during their time as a student in university-level education. It has been informed by parents with a personal connection to PAPYRUS who have shared their experiences which will be quoted throughout the chapter, although the names have been changed to protect the identity of the families and their children. The chapter explores parents' experiences of university involvement in supporting their children and discusses the provision of suicide prevention strategies within higher education. Examining intimate experiences of student suicide and parental bereavement is a poignant task, yet one of significant importance. The objective of such discussions is to learn from these lived experiences with the aim of informing future policy and practice, as well as, crucially, preventing suicides under similar circumstances in universities.

The chapter also discusses and critiques emerging models that seek to ensure that parents are consulted about students at risk, including those that facilitate new ways of managing the issue of confidentiality. Parents' experiences and their own suggestions for changes to policy and practice will be discussed in relation to the aspect of student confidentiality and universities' duty of care to the student body. Universities are also encouraged to consider their student population as typically young, 'emerging adults' who are often partially or significantly dependent on parents for multiple aspects of their wellbeing (Arnett 2000). Discussions with parents impacted by student suicides reveal common themes within their experiences, which will be explored within the chapter.

Issues that are experienced by bereaved parents will be discussed throughout this text. Recommendations for policy changes will be given to encourage universities and education providers to consider the role of parents, who often are excluded from such discussions, in supporting students who are struggling with thoughts about ending their lives. Evidence-based practical guidance and further support will be identified and discussed within each area.

Communication and care pathways within universities

A common theme and concern for parents who have lost a child at university to suicide is the issue of responsibilities and information sharing within universities regarding concerns for a student's welfare or safety. Tragically, hindsight and inquests following a death by suicide often reveal missed opportunities for signposting and suicide prevention support. Michael and Sarah lost their 23-year-old son David to suicide in

2009 and have been involved in raising awareness of suicide prevention ever since. David was a postgraduate student and a high achiever studying medicine. He had begun to struggle with his mental health whilst on his course. David's parents understand that he had contacted multiple course tutors for support in the months prior to his death.

In response to David's contact with the department regarding his mental health and difficulties on the programme, he was encouraged to partner up with other students to support him in his studies and was also given the option of deferring his course for a year. Both of these supports are common practice in universities for students who encounter difficulties on their programme. However, research indicates that an increase in responsibility or high-pressured situations, like career decision making, at a time of psychological distress can exacerbate symptoms of poor mental health (Paulus and Yu 2012; Rottinghaus, Jenkins and Jantzer 2009). Conversely, mental health issues are also known to impact on decision making skills (Murphy et al. 2001), leaving a student, given an ultimatum in regard to their studies, on the back foot from the outset.

Despite the existence of such data, it is unclear whether research such as this is made available across the sector to university staff who make decisions about students' futures and wellbeing. Many students therefore continue to find themselves faced with difficult decisions regarding their education and future when mental health issues impact upon their university work. The importance of effective discussion and communication around a student's options in the face of mental health difficulties is therefore critical, so that the course of action selected is truly in the best interest of the individual student's needs. Training for staff in this area, and appropriate protocols for them to follow when a student begins to struggle with their university work in connection to their mental health, are of equal importance. David's parents have described the apparent pitfalls in the system of support that their son received from staff at his university:

> I don't think they had any specific training, I think that's the problem. There is no one person, they don't have that in-house professional that staff can go to when they have a young man or a young woman who needs help, or when the tutor needs to liaise with that professional and say 'I've got this young student in front of me, will you take a look or can I book an appointment?' It needs to go further, not just to the tutors on the course.

Sadly, in more recent times, similarities in support falling short have been demonstrated in cases where students have ended their lives whilst at university. Helen and Richard lost their daughter Molly to suicide in 2018 during her second year of university where she was studying for a four-year Master of Science. Molly struggled with social anxiety, which significantly impacted on her during her time in higher education where vivas and oral presentation were compulsory elements of her course. The inquest into Molly's death heard that the university were aware of Molly's struggles with her mental health, and that alternative assessment options to alleviate the anxiety she had faced had been discussed within the staff team. However, her parents say it is unclear exactly what information was communicated to Molly, how such adjustments would have been implemented, and whether or not such changes were appropriate or sufficient given the nature of her condition. None of the adjustments which were discussed by staff were made for Molly prior to her death.

At the inquest, Molly's parents heard that she had received some support from an administrative staff member who on one occasion had escorted Molly to her GP appointment. However, numerous opportunities to share key information with the vulnerable-student support service had been missed by those responsible for her wellbeing. The coroner concluded that Molly had been let down by local mental health services. The adequacy of support provided by student services was not considered at the inquest. Multiple professionals in Molly's life became aware of her suicidal thoughts and actions in the months leading up to her death; however, the communication about this within and between departments and services was found to be ineffective. Helen and Richard have called for a more proficient system in which students are supported and concerns about mental health and suicide are handled proactively and more effectively:

> Communication needs to be on all counts. Communication with the students is really important. In [Molly]'s case it was even more important to have communication with other people because [Molly] found it so difficult to talk about her problems. We need communication within the department, within the wider university, and in some cases maybe even with other agencies. Collectively the information about [Molly] was there, it just wasn't shared, it needed bringing together.

Cases like Molly's demonstrate the need for proactive strategies in suicide prevention – rather than reactive support that often comes too late or allows people to slip through the system. In taking what could be described as a 'hands-off' approach to suicide prevention or mental health support in general, the responsibility of care and support for students at risk may fall to individual staff members who lack the training or capacity to support a suicidal person. Alternatively, the onus may fall upon the peers or immediate social circle of the student at risk. Experiences such as this are not uncommon within universities. In a survey commissioned by PAPYRUS, only 53 per cent of teaching staff reported feeling confident in supporting a student with suicidal thoughts (PAPYRUS 2018). Widening the scope of responsibility with a clearer procedure of care when a student indicates that they are contemplating ending their life, or if a member of staff feels concerned about a student's welfare, ensures that no individual is left feeling helpless when faced with the task of safeguarding against suicide. Helen and Richard say that communication underpins an effective strategy for preventing suicides on a university-wide level:

> We've talked about communication, and that's at every level. We've talked about access to services. We also want to have details about who is responsible, because, you know, the idea that the person who is told about the suicide then becomes responsible for all sorts of things, just because they're the one that happened to be told, is not good. So, I'm thinking of a suicide prevention strategy plan that talks about a whole university approach. We have to be really careful that that doesn't equate to lack of accountability. An individual staff member cannot step back and leave everything to somebody else. No one can say that it is someone else's responsibility. We're all responsible, both individually and collectively.

It is imperative that staff within universities are clear in regard to the support they offer within their roles – and to what extent they must deliver this support. Bereaved parents make a clear call for a change to the systems of suicide prevention within universities, which calls into question how this can be achieved on a national scale. Crucially, better guidelines and clearer communication pathways are needed in universities to safeguard both students and staff members who are concerned about students at risk of suicide. Without an accessible pathway of support for staff members, responsibilities of individual staff members have been shown to become blurred. Students are then at an increased risk of becoming lost within the disjointed systems of support that exist in some universities. Improving communication within university departments themselves, but also between departments and beyond – including students, parents and third-sector organizations involved in supporting students – is essential. Key enablers of an effective suicide prevention strategy include:

- *Training.* In developing and implementing a strategy within universities to ensure greater levels of safety from suicide, training for staff should be considered a key factor. Effective training programmes should be implemented, following advice from health authorities in effective suicide prevention techniques. Public Health England (2012) and the World Health Organization (WHO 2018) both recommend a range of suicide prevention training, including ASIST, safeTALK and Connecting with People, as well as suicide prevention training sessions offered by PAPYRUS. Training in suicide awareness and prevention skills is also provided by the Zero Suicide Alliance.

- *A clear organizational pathway and proactive support.* All staff members should have a readily available and comprehensive guide on who to contact with concerns about a student at risk of suicide. Liaising with GPs, mental health services and support services (both internal and external to the university) can save lives and must be built into an effective communication strategy regarding risk to life. After key members of staff have been trained in ASIST, the names and university contact details of these staff members should then be presented on an organizational chart which should be available to all staff members, students and parents. Should a concern arise, anyone with connection to the university has direct access to a staff member who can offer these potentially life-saving interventions of support. To ensure best practice in this area, universities are encouraged to treat staff members trained in suicide prevention in the same way as first-aiders – identifiable and accessible as soon as possible.

  Universities are encouraged to acknowledge the difficulties for individuals who are struggling with their mental health in accessing support for themselves. Often students are away from their caregivers for the first time in their lives. Many may have recently left various child or adolescent services which provide proactive support and safeguarding measures. If a student indicates that they are struggling they should receive sufficient support and be signposted to available resources and support, and there should always be an arrangement in place for a follow-up or check-in. Staff members should be encouraged to check in with students who may not necessarily have identified themselves as a person in need but have come to the attention of staff due to concerns for their wellbeing. Technology may also play a significant role here. Efficient record keeping through case management systems may shine a light on students' attendance or their levels contact with student support services. This could help to identify students at risk to university staff and open up avenues for support and encourage conversations with students about their wellbeing that may otherwise not occur.

Awareness raising for staff throughout universities, but also for the student body, to destigmatize suicide throughout educational communities is essential. Steps taken to reduce stigma around suicide and raise awareness of these issues both further enable and encourage students to access pathways for support in their educational environment. It is important to acknowledge that often students' preliminary sources of support come from friends and family. Where appropriate, encouraging students to involve parents, carers, guardians or other trusted contacts can strengthen the circle of support around that individual. Training and support opportunities are also available for those supporting students. PAPYRUS' helpline, HOPELINEUK, provides guidance and advice to concerned others on how to support a young person at risk of suicide. Universities can signpost to national services such as these as well as to local options for support when a concerned family or friend gets into contact. Annual freshers' and re-freshers' events are a fantastic opportunity to acquaint students with support pathways both inside and outside the university. Contact with local and national services that can provide stalls, talks and training opportunities to ensure awareness raising takes place at events for students and staff is also a useful step for universities.

- *Developing and maintaining relationships with local and national mental health and suicide prevention organizations.* Connection with external organizations that deliver support ensures advice and guidance is available for anyone who is concerned about suicide – whether it's a young person at risk or a staff member requiring professional support. Public Health England published their Suicide Prevention Atlas, which provides data on suicide, risk factors and available services of support within local authorities across England (Public Health England 2018). Universities UK has published a guidance report, *Minding Our Future* (UUK 2018a), which provides guidance for universities at departmental, organizational and stakeholder level for building connections with local NHS trusts. The aim is to ensure that students have direct pathways between their educational and healthcare systems if they require mental health support. Where the conversation is needed, there is support to help it to begin.

It is essential to co-produce an effective suicide prevention strategy with students, parents and carers, staff and expert third-sector organizations who can offer expert insight and practical advice in these issues. PAPYRUS have developed their *Building Suicide-Safer Schools and Colleges* guide (PAPYRUS 2018) for suicide prevention, intervention and postvention guidance in educational settings, which can be downloaded for free. The *Suicide-Safer Universities* toolkit (UUK and PAPYRUS 2018) offers a structure for a prevention strategy within the context of higher education. It is also particularly important to work closely with local authority suicide prevention partnerships for local and national impact and to benefit from their shared experience, evidence and quality frameworks for effective communication regarding suicide risk.

The key point for learning is a pressing need for effective communication at every level. In the two cases discussed so far, both student suicides coincided with poor or inadequate communication with them regarding their situations, and between staff members and departments responsible for their wellbeing. Training for staff is of upmost importance – suicide first aid should be as accessible and available as a qualified physical health first-aider in every department or building. There should be a clear and concise route of support for students at risk of suicide and for staff in contact with students at risk. This includes support within the university itself, as well as external supports, including national organizations providing advice on suicide prevention policies and guidance via helplines, and local services providing mental health support.

Confidentiality regarding suicide risk in university settings

A much-discussed area in connection to suicides within universities is confidentiality, both internally and externally, and the extent to which a confidentiality policy plays its role in protecting students or isolating them from potential parental support interventions. In a number of cases of suicides in universities, confidentiality policies have been discussed as significant factors that may have prevented opportunities for parents to become involved in supporting their children when mental health issues have arisen for them. David's parents, Michael and Sarah, have shared their thoughts on confidentiality within universities:

> It needs to be changed. It's why so many parents are kept in total ignorance of what has been going on and are not able to help where they otherwise could. When [students] are struggling there should be steps taken to involve the parents and make sure they know 'your child is here and is struggling'. After all, they're young men and women. There's no warning signs shared from any conversations they have with [students], everything was kept private from us, all for the sake of confidentiality which seems to have been more important than safety. Even if we had gone to them they wouldn't have had a discussion with us because he was an adult.

Understandably, there are hesitations and concerns about changes regarding confidentiality policies, particularly with the tightening in the law regarding General Data Protection Regulation (GDPR) guidelines. However, these concerns should be weighed against the consequences of 'risk to life' where critical information is not being shared with appropriate supports. Constraints of confidentiality pose a risk, as staff members may be left with knowledge or a disclosure of suicidal thoughts but may have no obligation to share this information with potential supports, or indeed have a clear pathway of support to follow. This is of particular concern if the staff members who receive these types of disclosures have not received training in suicide prevention skills or mental health first aid. Managing a disclosure of suicidal thoughts effectively, and sharing this information with the appropriate bodies, can be the difference between life and death for a student at risk of suicide. In the event of suicidal thoughts or even attempts, universities, hospitals and mental health services do not always share this information with a next of kin. Where this information is known to universities, they must weigh up the duty of confidentiality against their duty of care. If it is known to any extent that a student may be at risk of suicide, the recommendation – based on evidence discussed within this chapter – is to discuss the support pathway options with the student. Gaining the student's consent to share information at this point of need is ideal, but ultimately sharing the disclosure of suicidal thoughts with the appropriate individuals to support the student of concern, based on their consent at registration, is entirely necessary. This should apply to any student, regardless of where the attempt has taken place or whether the student is accommodated in university-owned halls of residence.

Some universities in the UK have begun to implement changes. It should be stressed that proposed changes do not suggest removing confidentiality for students but adapting policies to ensure that safety of students is the overriding priority. The student should be put at the centre of decision making regarding their wellbeing, and changes to confidentiality should be developed with this in mind. Discussions continue regarding student confidentiality and the potential use of 'opt in' and 'opt out' policies for information sharing with parents when a student is at risk. However, these two options may be limited. Not all families offer a haven of safety and support. Rates of young people who experience difficult family lives across the UK are difficult to quantify. However, difficult relationships with parents or families have been demonstrated to be a significant factor in predicting mental health issues in adulthood (Weich et al. 2009) as well as suicide (Alm, Låftman and Bohman 2019). Clearly, having an opt in or out policy for contacting parents does not protect every student who comes to study at university, and in some cases such an action could worsen issues for students.

Allowing for flexibility, rather than an 'opt in or out' policy, allows students to specify who their notifiable contact may be, and eliminates the issue of a situation being worsened by university contact. Consent for sharing of concerns and specification of a nominated contact at registration with the university is a proactive method of ensuring links to support for each student potentially at a time before any difficulties have arisen for them. This also ensures that if staff become concerned about a student's welfare they already have consent to share their concerns. This may be particularly important if the student becomes difficult to engage with or contact, which is common during mental health difficulties (Bell-Dolan, Reaven and Peterson 1993).

A criticism of the suggested changes to confidentiality policies to ensure that parents or nominated contacts are informed about concerns is that students may be dissuaded from seeking support in university if they are aware that this information could be shared. Each year the Higher Education Policy Institute conducts its Student Academic Experience Survey (HEPI 2019). In 2019, 14,072 undergraduate students across the UK responded and were asked about their thoughts on confidentiality. It showed that 66 per cent of students would want their parents to be contacted by the university 'in the event of extreme circumstances', with a further 15 per cent agreeing to their parents being contacted in any circumstance that aroused concern. Scrutinizing this data by age group showed that only one in four mature students (above the age of 26) disagreed with their parents being contacted under any circumstances. This is an understandable figure, due to the age of this group and the potential differences in dependency needs compared to the rest of the student body under this age. However, this demonstrates the necessity of choice and options for students regarding nominated contacts and in what circumstances information about their welfare should be shared. Such policies and opt-in schemes have already been implemented at the Universities of Bristol, Northumbria, Worcester and Brunel.

Informing parents and guardians about wellbeing concerns is also seen to lower the threshold for vital interests measures – the grounds for which personal information can be shared based on the need to protect life and prevent death. This partially distinguishes proactive from reactive support. Emergency contacts are of course necessary for immediate life or death situations. However, changes to confidentiality policies allow nominated contacts to be utilized before the situation worsens to the point of risk to life. Taking proactive measures with concerns for welfare takes a further step towards a suicide-safer university environment. Training to spot the signs, signposting a student through a robust care pathway and ensuring safety from suicide prevents the need for reactive support. A university-wide approach should train multiple staff members in how to approach conversations around suicide. It should encourage disclosure from students and provide a source of hope to an individual who may be feeling hopeless.

Further guidance on the redevelopment of a confidentiality policy is available through Universities UK's Stepchange campaign (UUK 2020), which has been designed to demonstrate why mental health should be a strategic priority for universities. The framework focuses on four aspects of change within universities – risk, regulation, success and policy – to facilitate a whole-university approach to engage staff and students in wellbeing promotion and to increase the availability of support. The Department of Health produced a Consensus Statement (DH 2014) in consultation with other leading health organizations and bodies in a response to bereaved families' concerns regarding information sharing. It provides guidance for staff in managing suicide risk, and encourages practitioners to make confidentiality decisions with the best interests of the individual at the core of any actions taken. In 2021, Universities UK plan to release guidance regarding information sharing within the whole university, including topics of disclosure and consent in the event of welfare concerns or disclosure of suicidal ideation (UUK 2018b). The hope is that nationally available guidance such as this will encourage a blanket policy on student disclosures of suicide in the UK, but individual universities can begin by implementing these changes themselves.

Key points to take away from this discussion include the importance of considerations about the balance between confidentiality and risk to life. Universities are urged to consider their policy guidelines on confidentiality and whether they present potential barriers to support for the students in their establishments. Allowing students choices and involvement in these discussions develops the best course of action for each individual and empowers students to consider and develop their own circles of support. Informing students' named contacts of their nomination and the circumstances in which they may be contacted may also streamline and add clarity to this process. Confidentiality is an area that can seem intimidating to professionals, but overcoming this and ensuring that pathways for support are clear ensures safer outcomes. Guidance for the development of these areas has been provided and universities are encouraged to utilize these resources.

Postvention

Equally important to prevention and intervention is an effective post-vention strategy. Efficient and transparent record keeping ensures that struggling students have a paper trail and do not vanish into the bustling university system. Also, in the event that a student does end their life, an audit of events and responsibility can be undertaken. Universities have been criticized for avoiding the latter in connection with some student deaths, which has led to incredibly painful and unnecessarily painstaking information gathering processes for bereaved families such as Molly's:

> There didn't seem to be any note of contact with the wellbeing service, they don't keep sufficient records. Important emails and phone calls were not recorded. There's no way you can actually unravel what happened inside the university. So when you get a situation where it all goes horribly wrong there's no way of finding out what happened. We had terrible difficulty finding out who had been involved with [Molly] because they didn't keep any central records. It was often a case of how much could be remembered.

If universities do not develop the necessary auditable procedures that are necessary to examine in detail what has happened in the time before a university suicide, we risk being unable to learn and develop future strategies to address problems and failures in support. A policy for sector-wide post-incident review procedures could ensure that appropriate steps are taken to learn from the past following a suicide. Currently, on a national level, there are no standardized procedures for monitoring or tracking communication with at-risk students, which calls into question the clarity and efficacy of duties of care throughout university establishments. The pressure for changes in post-incident review procedures in this area comes mostly from parents who have been bereaved. Parents like those of young people like David and Molly have expressed their hopes for government ministers to discuss sector-wide changes at government level. However, until this occurs, the responsibilities for change in proceedings fall upon universities themselves.

Aside from effective communication and record keeping, an effective postvention strategy can help prevent further suicides through supporting those impacted by suicide death. Those who are bereaved by suicide are known to be at higher risk of suicide themselves (Pitman, Osborn and Rantell 2016). Therefore proactive support for other students, peers and family members is crucially important. Identifying, training and publicizing a postvention team ensures that such support exists and is readily accessible should an incident of student suicide arise. Senior university staff members should be identified within the policy as responsible for welfare and internal communications following a suicide. It is important that staff responsible for wider internal and external university communications are trained in postvention support and signposting, as well as staff members responsible for pastoral support throughout the organization. Defining responsibilities ahead of such an event eases the process. Family liaison, student support and communication with external and local services are necessary steps to be taken to ensure that no one is left unsupported. The *Suicide-Safer Universities* guide (UUK and PAPYRUS 2018) includes guidance for postvention strategies in universities, and Samaritans' *Step by Step* (2010) guide provides advice and resources for staff in schools and colleges to prepare responses to a suicide.

Key points for development of a postvention strategy echo those of previous sections. Effective communication, including evidence and a paper trail of contact with students at risk, increases the probability of providing effective support for students in a variety of contexts. In the event of a student suicide, it also provides examples of shortfalls, areas for improvement and answers for families who might otherwise be left with unanswered questions. Postvention should be considered equally important to future prevention as other components of this chapter. Without learning from incidents that have occurred, we are likely to see further incidents in similar contexts. Resources and national services which provide guidance on postvention should be utilized in order to develop effective strategies in this area.

Conclusions

Regardless of context or environment, open lines of communication regarding suicide saves lives. Strengthening a nationwide approach to university suicide prevention policy is essential in preventing further suicides. Discussions with bereaved families offer insight into the current system and the impact suicide has on individuals and their circles, and offer a platform of learning to inform future policy. Parents and families can potentially offer a wealth of support to students who may be struggling but feel unable to access help. Universities are encouraged not to overlook these avenues of support for their students, and to put the interests of their students at the very core of welfare-based decisions. Effective postvention support and investigation can shine a light on the issues in current policy, and so by addressing these issues universities can help to prevent further student suicides. Resources and recommendations for policy revisions have been given. Universities are encouraged to revisit their policies, procedures and pathways, with a focus on the prospect that no more parents should experience the loss of a child through suicide.

There's an expectation for students to access services even when they find them difficult to access. If people know [a student] has a problem, then someone's got to come and help them. We need an established pathway, national standards. We need some sort of clarity in what society expects from universities and what they're going to deliver. My hope is that ministers will pick this up and made recommendations sector-wide, that universities do some sort of investigation when there's been a serious incident. And, if someone is in need of help, universities should take a step forward, not a step back. (Richard, father of Molly)

Useful resources
Training

- **ASIST** (Applied Suicide Intervention Skills Training), www.livingworks.net/asist
- **safeTALK**, www.livingworks.net/safetalk
- **Connecting with People**, www.4mentalhealth.com
- **PAPYRUS**, www.papyrus-uk.org/training
- **Zero Suicide Alliance**, www.zerosuicidealliance.com/training

Support, guidance and advice

- **HOPELINEUK**, www.papyrus-uk.org/hopelineuk
- *Suicide-Safer Universities* **guide**, www.papyrus-uk.org/suicide-safer-universities
- **Samaritans Step by Step**, www.samaritans.org/how-we-can-help/schools/step-step

Author biography
Natalie Day is an experienced suicide prevention advisor and trainer at PAPYRUS, the national charity dedicated to the prevention of young suicide. In her work on the helpline HOPELINEUK Natalie supports young people experiencing thoughts about suicide, as well as anyone concerned about a young person who may be thinking about suicide. She is a qualified counsellor and doctoral student of counselling psychology at the University of Manchester.

References

Alm, S., Låftman, S. and Bohman, H. (2019) Poor family relationships in adolescence and the risk of premature death: findings from the Stockholm Birth Cohort Study. *International Journal of Environmental Research and Public Health 16*, 10, 16–90.

Arnett, J. (2000) Emerging adulthood: a theory of development from the late teens through the twenties. *American Psychologist 55*, 469–480.

Bell-Dolan, D., Reaven, N. and Peterson, L. (1993) Depression and social functioning: a multi-dimensional study of the linkages. *Journal of Clinical Child Psychology 22*, 3, 306–315.

Cerel, J., Maple, M., Van de Venne, J., Moore, M., Flaherty, C. and Brown, M. (2016) Exposure to suicide in the community: prevalence and correlates in one US state. *Public Health Reports 131*, 1, 100–107.

Department of Health (DH) (2014) *Information Sharing and Suicide Prevention: Consensus Statement.*

Higher Education Policy Institute (HEPI) (2019) Making Parents Aware. In *Student Academic Experience Survey 2019*. Oxford: HEPI.

Higher Education Statistics Agency (2019) Higher Education Student Statistics: UK, 2017/2018 – Student numbers and characteristics. Accessed on 01/04/21 at: www.hesa.ac.uk/news/17-01-2019/sb252-higher-education-student-statistics/numbers

Murphy, F., Rubinsztein, J., Michael, A., Rogers, R. *et al.* (2001) Decision-making cognition in mania and depression. *Psychological Medicine 31*, 4, 679–693.

Office for National Statistics (ONS) (2018) *Estimating Suicide among Higher Education Students, England and Wales: Experimental Statistics.* London: ONS.

Office for National Statistics (ONS) (2019) *Suicides in the UK: 2018 Registrations. Suicide Patterns by Age.* London: ONS.

PAPYRUS (2018) *Building Suicide Safer Schools and Colleges: A Guide for Teachers and Staff.* Warrington: PAPYRUS.

Paulus, M. and Yu, A. (2012) Emotion and decision-making: affect-driven belief systems in anxiety and depression. *Trends in Cognitive Sciences 16*, 9, 476–483.

Pitman, A., Osborn, D., King, M. and Erlangsen, A. (2014) Effects of suicide bereavement on mental health and suicide risk. *Lancet Psychiatry 1*, 1, 86–94.

Pitman, A., Osborn, D. and Rantell, K. (2016) Bereavement by suicide as a risk factor for suicide attempt: a cross-sectional national UK-wide study of 3432 young bereaved adults. *BMJ Open 6*, 1.

Public Health England (PHE) (2012) *Preventing Suicide in England: A Cross-Government Outcomes Strategy to Save Lives.* London: Department of Health.

Public Health England (PHE) (2018) Atlas of Variation. Accessed on 30/04/21 at: https://fingertips.phe.org.uk/profile/atlas-of-variation

Rottinghaus, P., Jenkins, N. and Jantzer, A. (2009) Relation of depression and affectivity to career decision status and self-efficacy in college students. *Journal of Career Assessment 17*, 3, 271–285.

Samaritans (2010) *Help When We Need It Most: Step by Step.* Ewell: Samaritans.

Spillane, A., Matvienko-Sikar, K., Larkin, C., Corcoran, P. and Arensman, E. (2018) What are the physical and psychological health effects of suicide bereavement on family members? An observational and interview mixed-methods study in Ireland. *BMJ Open 8*, 1, 1–11.

Universities UK (UUK) (2018a) *Minding Our Future: Starting a Conversation about the Support of Student Mental Health.* Accessed on 01/04/21 at: www.universitiesuk.ac.uk/policy-and-analysis/reports/Pages/minding-our-future-starting-a-conversation-support-student-mental-health.aspx

Universities UK (UUK) (2018b) New data published on student suicide rates. Accessed on 01/04/21 at: www.universitiesuk.ac.uk/news/Pages/New-data-published-on-student-suicide-rates.aspx

Universities UK (UUK) (2020) *Stepchange: Mentally Healthy Universities.* Accessed on 30/04/21 at: www.universitiesuk.ac.uk/policy-and-analysis/reports/Pages/stepchange-mhu.aspx

Universities UK (UUK) and PAPYRUS (2018) *Suicide-Safer Universities.* Accessed on 01/04/21 at: www.universitiesuk.ac.uk/policy-and-analysis/reports/Pages/guidance-for-universities-on-preventing-student-suicides.aspx

Weich, S., Patterson, J., Shaw, R. and Stewart-Brown, S. (2009) Family relationships in childhood and common psychiatric disorders in later life: systematic review of prospective studies. *British Journal of Psychiatry 194*, 5, 392–398.

World Health Organization (WHO) (2012) *Public Health Action for the Prevention of Suicide: A Framework*. Geneva: WHO.

World Health Organization (WHO) (2014) *Preventing Suicide: A Global Imperative*. Geneva: WHO.

World Health Organization (WHO) (2018) *National Suicide Prevention Strategies: Progress, Examples and Indicators*. Geneva: WHO.

CHAPTER 16

Suicide Safety Planning with Students

CARMEN BETTERIDGE AND ALYS COLE-KING

Overview

This chapter will:

- introduce safety planning as a way for students to navigate suicidal thoughts with greater safety

- provide a summary of the evidence underpinning safety planning

- show how a safety plan can be co-produced and identify useful resources.

Introduction

Historically, our understanding of suicidal thoughts, suicide and the potential for intervention may have been hampered by the belief that they are a symptom of a mental illness. Recent research challenges this view, finding that approximately 50 per cent of people who died by suicide did not have clinically significant signs of mental or psychological disorder at the time of their death (Leske, Crompton and Kolves 2019). This finding is important to how we recognize and respond to students who might be suicidal. This chapter reviews a potential way to engage with and respond effectively to such students, offering hope alongside proportionate and effective intervention. Safety Plans do not replace the need for additional professional support via a GP or mental health services, and 'treatment as usual' occurs in parallel. However, having a safety plan can empower a student in distress, bolster their own resources and coping strategies, and facilitate them in maximizing support.

Background: risk factors and challenges of risk prediction

Suicide risk factors are elements that may occur more commonly for people experiencing suicidal thoughts, who attempt suicide or die by suicide (Rudd *et al.* 2006). While risk factors can provide us with important information in terms of population-level vulnerabilities across the lifespan, they are ineffective at accurately predicting which individuals will die by suicide or attempt suicide at a specific time point. A focus on risk factors has proved to be ineffective at preventing suicide attempt and death (Pokorny 1983). Instead of focusing on suicide risk, and ineffective attempts to accurately predict suicide, the emphasis could be on identifying individual risk factors, needs and strengths, instilling hope and empowering individuals to seek and accept support.

Suicide is preventable and we need a new narrative moving away from 'characterizing, quantifying and managing risk' towards a greater focus on compassion, safeguarding and safety planning (Cole-King and Platt 2021; Cole-King *et al.* 2013). The current approach to suicide risk assessment, using terms such as 'low risk' or 'high risk', and responding only to individuals identified as 'high risk', is unreliable, open to misinterpretation and unsafe (Cole-King and Platt 2021). Suicidal thoughts reflect a range of states of being, from wondering if life is worth living, to death wishes to suicidal actions. They may be short lived and situation specific, which makes them amenable to intervention and support. Using a compassionate and personalized approach is of critical importance to understanding the psychosocial needs of a person experiencing suicidal distress (Cole-King *et al.* 2013; Cole-King and Platt 2021; Hawgood and De Leo 2016). This approach can empower the person's existing strengths and resources, while also connecting them with treatment and support (RCP 2020). One way of doing this is to develop a personal safety plan.

What is safety planning?

A safety plan is a personalized set of actions, strategies and ways to interrupt or dispel suicidal thoughts, reduce or remove suicidal intent and reduce access to suicide means. It typically includes a list of people and/or organizations to contact for support, if someone is concerned about engaging in self-harm or becoming suicidal, or their suicidal thoughts get worse. A safety plan can be made alone or with support from another person. It is typically produced as part of what has become known as 'safety planning'. This can be a brief intervention that can be completed during a single encounter between a student and a helper (Stewart *et al.* 2019). The core principles behind suicide safety planning is to support the student to interrupt and resist suicidal thoughts and/or seek help, when they recognize they are distressed or experiencing warning signs of suicide. They may then implement effective coping strategies that prevent suicidal behaviour (Stanley and Brown 2012).

Safety planning has been demonstrated as promising and effective when undertaken by non-clinicians and in non-clinical contexts (McCabe *et al.* 2018; Vijayakumar *et al.* 2017). Safety plans can be tailored to different ages, personal circumstances, cultural backgrounds and comprehension levels. Their use is of course not limited to students, but in the context of this book we are focusing on how they might be used in an FE/HE context.

The therapeutically validated components of safety planning (Bryan *et al.* 2017; Stanley and Brown 2012), based on research evidence, include:

- identifying/understanding that a person is experiencing suicidality

- compassionate engagement and supportive listening

- identification of warning signs for suicidal crisis

- personalized coping strategies.

More details on these are given later in the chapter.

Safety plans are individualized and brief therapeutic interventions, reflecting person-centred strategies that can support a student in times of crisis. Crucially, safety plans use a stepped or cascading approach. Enacting a safety plan may start with actions or strategies which rely on independently applied personal cognitive, psychological or coping skills (including focusing on positives in their life, strategies to deal with distress, listening to music, exercising, reading, gardening or practising mindfulness). The next level would be social interaction, which may be passive (e.g. shopping) or active (e.g. talking to a friend or relative by phone, or meeting others face to face in a home, social, hospitality or recreational setting). Then there are professional interventions and finally emergency-level interventions. The use of strategies that become progressively more directive reflects the increasing urgency of interrupting a suicidal crisis if it continues to escalate. Over time, with practice and reflection, it is hoped that the implementation of strategies before the suicidal thoughts escalate will prevent the need for the student to engage the more directive strategies.

Warning signs and protective factors

While the development of a safety plan is straightforward, an understanding of risk factors, warning signs and protective factors can be helpful in developing the student's insight and identifying actions towards self-preservation. Here, we explore suicide risk factors and warning signs further before moving to consider the development of a safety plan.

Identifying the warning signs of an emerging suicidal crisis can be important indicators to a student and those around them that they may not be coping, or entering a time of crisis. Although warning signs may be poor indicators of crisis by themselves, they are often better understood in the context of other signs of crisis or distress (Rudd *et al.* 2006). For example, although a person may have a long-standing risk factor of having a depressive illness, the warning sign is the proximal change in the depressive illness to include a marked worsening of hopelessness and insomnia.

Identifying a person's warning signs for suicide can sound challenging, but it may be as simple as hearing that a person is experiencing suicidality and asking them whether they notice their distress in how they think, feel, behave and in their body. By remaining non-judgemental and taking the time to understand how their distress or suicidal behaviour emerged, it may be possible to observe in the student increasing agitation, disclosure of feelings of entrapment and aggressive interactions. All of these are important warning signs that affect how you should respond.

Protective factors are also important areas of consideration in the prevention of suicide in students. There is evidence that enhancing connectedness contributes to suicide prevention. Students can be encouraged to bolster their personal resources and support from confidants. Examples of protective factors relevant to young adults include confidence in problem solving, an internal locus of control and social connectedness (Donald *et al.* 2006). Listening for, observing and eliciting reflections upon a person's protective factors may require some conscious effort, particularly when a person's story is one of despair. However, actively listening and reflecting back protective factors can be as simple as pointing out that they had courage to share their story with you. Protective factors that can be readily deployed as resources, and coping skills, offer the greatest potential contribution to safety planning.

Development of a safety plan

In this section, we will describe various aspects of safety planning in an HE/FE student context.

1. Identify the person's own warning signs for suicide and psychological crisis

The first step in developing a safety plan is often to identify the person's warning signs. If you are proactively making a safety plan with someone before they have experienced suicidal thoughts, then this step will not be completed first. As described above, warning signs are signals experienced by a person that indicate that they are entering a time of crisis or suicidality. Various media campaigns (Beyond Blue 2020; National Institute of Mental Health 2020) have highlighted common warning signs such as social withdrawal, sourcing access to lethal means and disclosing thoughts of suicide. Common warning signs for students include sleep disturbance, while triggering events include conflict with significant others (Berman 2020). Warning signs, when recognized and consciously used to motivate a person to self-manage a potential escalation in suicidal thinking, are one of the essential components of safety plans. When a person is able to recognize their own personal warning signs for crisis, they can implement personally relevant coping strategies that interrupt or distract themselves from a worsening possible crisis.

As a student becomes more familiar with their internal process and experience, they can identify more sensitive warning signs and implement coping strategies earlier in their trajectory. If the student is not able to link warning signs to coping strategies, they may find it harder to interrupt a pattern of crisis that has advanced beyond their own coping resources.

2. Creating a safe environment and removing access to lethal means

Removing or reducing access to means for self-harm or suicide is critically important. It literally involves the removal of any means by which the student might undertake a suicide attempt. Having a specific and compassionate conversation about removing lethal means is known as 'means safety counselling'. Basic means safety is a skill that can be undertaken by anyone prepared to compassionately engage with a person in crisis. The process of engaging in a discussion regarding access to means for suicide will elicit essential information required to locate the potential mechanism or mechanisms for self-harm or suicide. If the student has a well-formed plan and the means for suicide, it is recommended that others become involved in their care at this point. Means removal may need to be performed by police, ambulance or trusted others.

3. Identify personally relevant coping strategies that a person can undertake independently

The third step is to work with the student to identify relevant coping strategies. Work with a student to initiate ideas on coping strategies that are personally relevant and self-initiated (e.g. listening to music or going for a walk). Indeed, often asking someone about the range of coping strategies that they may use across a range of negative circumstances, from mild setbacks through to difficult insults or injury, can shed light on a student's strengths both in that moment, and those that can be utilized within a safety plan. Safety plans that are collaboratively developed with a student with coping strategies that are personally relevant are likely to be the most effective in decreasing the emergence of suicide-related behaviours (Green *et al.* 2018).

Coping strategies that can be independently harnessed during difficult times support the person to practise autonomy and self-management in times of crisis. Ideally, it is useful to include a range of strategies or activities to lift and calm their mood. Although it is unlikely that these personal skills will work every time, over time, they will form an essential foundation to early intervention in a suicidal crisis or escalation period.

4. Employing social distraction to disengage from suicidality

The fourth step is to consider how social distraction can be used to disengage the student from suicidality. Social distractions can include a student consciously and deliberately challenging thought processes that have contributed to social isolation and disengagement. By reversing how the student thinks and responds to the voice of despair, it is possible to nominate key people as supports, or places or distracting activities that can break the rumination cycle.

Social distraction does not necessarily require that the student discusses their mental health, coping or suicidality with those identified as being resources. Rather, these options are simply listed as people, places or activities they can reach out to. Where a social distraction strategy involves speaking to others, it may be helpful to nominate conversational topics about their studies, common interests or activities to assist in a more natural conversation, while also initiating disengagement from ruminative thinking or unhelpful behaviours.

5. Using trusted others to consciously work to resolve the suicidality

The fifth step is for the student to work with trusted individuals to resolve their suicidality. Although it is possible for a person to subvert suicidal thoughts or behaviours prior to this stage, it should not be assumed that all strategies will be effective on all occasions. Therefore, when discussing safety planning with a student, acknowledge that a safety plan is 'work in progress' and that they will be practising some of these skills over time.

If earlier strategies have not been effective and a person's crisis continues, the intensity and directive nature of the safety plan interventions must respond accordingly. This stage in the safety plan should entail the student engaging with trusted people that are known to them to work together to resolve or mitigate the stressors that have fuelled the crisis. A student should ask for help and be commended for having done so. Selecting champions that acknowledge the student's strength in disclosing fear, despair or self-hatred can be difficult. Although the conversation can be initiated by a helper, it will be closely directed by the student's knowledge of the best people to be trusted to work collaboratively with them on this issue.

The trusted other(s) should be engaged to meet an identified function that has been predetermined with the student prior to the suicidal crisis and included in the safety plan. Agreements regarding expectations and anticipated actions should be established to ensure the student remains empowered in the decision-making process and ultimately signs off on decisions which, in a time of crisis, may feel overwhelming or not in their best interests. Further, it can give trusted others permission to value compassionate stances over feeling as though they need to 'rescue' or protect the student concerned. The exact plan for what is expected in safety planning at this point in the intervention is best discussed between all parties, including what happens if someone is not available when needed.

6. Engaging with health professionals, including through first responders, the emergency department/A&E and mental health services

To reach this level of intervention, a student will have exhausted options for coping independently or with social support. At this point, the crisis has become significant and alarming. Consulting with health professionals is a critical next step, for which again the student should be commended and not seen as a failure. Instead, through engaging health professionals across available health services, it should be suggested to the student that they should access formal support at a level which is proportionate to the nature and degree of the crisis they are experiencing. At this point, you should urgently investigate the mental health services available on campus, or available to educational settings. This will allow you to know the key details that can support access or referral of the student to community mental health or emergency departments.

Traditionally, people experiencing any type of suicidal crisis have been urged to immediately engage mental health professionals, bypassing their own resources and capabilities. Being sent immediately to emergency hospital services is often unhelpful when other less intense strategies may be equally effective. We would recommend that HEIs and FEs have robust governance arrangements and training is available to ensure relevant staff and counsellors have the confidence and skills to compassionately engage with a student at risk of suicide and respond in a timely and proportionate way. Often, referral to emergency departments/A&E may reflect the anxiety of the helper rather than being the next safe and appropriate step in a person's management of a suicidal crisis. While emergency department/A&E referral may certainly be necessary in some contexts, it might also risk undermining a person's own resilience and potential for self-directed management and recovery. Referral to emergency services is critical when the student does not believe they can interrupt their thoughts or behaviours, or that they can maintain their own safety.

Safety planning with the student population

When disentangling the factors contributing to a person's distress, we are drawn to consider their individual strengths, available resources and psychosocial needs. If we acknowledge the value and opportunity this provides for developing a safety plan, we can work towards a truly personalized strategy. In the young adult population, there are unique stressors, contexts and considerations that impact upon their experience of psychological distress and suicidal crises. Indeed, it is during FE and HE that young adults often explore opportunities for independence in living, sexuality and gender expression as well as substance use (Berman 2020). Engaging a young person in a compassionate conversation regarding their experience of hardship elicits the opportunity to enquire more deeply into what that experience is like, the resources they have available to them and whether or not they are coping. A safety plan clearly does not prevent the student from experiencing hardship, cure their psychological symptoms or resolve academic demands. Rather it is intended to help a student to ride out psychological, physical and behavioural urges and remain safe or find a place of safety. Safety plans are not stand-alone interventions and best integrated within other therapeutic interventions.

Enquiring with a student about whether they have had thoughts of suicide for some helpers may feel difficult. However, it may provide the first real opportunity for a student to connect with meaningful support and hope for change. While you can provide links for the student to access other supports, co-producing a safety plan in the moment that a student reveals suicidal ideation provides an immediate opportunity to support them in a proportionate way and normalize periods of difficulty. It can also reinforce their capacity for independence through engaging existing coping skills and resources, while identifying points of access to new avenues for coping and adjustment. You do not have to be a mental health expert to support a student to make their safety plan and this can be done by 'anyone' as part of routine contact or 'check-ins', rather than creating additional points of contact for a student and opening the door to ambivalence preventing them from taking the next step (McCabe *et al.* 2018). The steps and inclusions should be familiar, simple to use and cause no additional stress or pressure (Stanley and Brown 2012).

Timing of safety planning

Unfortunately, safety plans are often promoted for use only after a person has entered a situation of crisis or following self-harm. It is more helpful to develop a safety plan prior to a crisis emerging, as this is when a person is potentially more capable of exploring their resources and coping skills and recognizing their warning signs (Melvin, Gresham and Beaton 2016). In crisis, a person's capacity to problem solve and think clearly is often reduced or impaired. Having access to a pre-prepared safety plan significantly reduces the challenge of identifying potent distractions or coping behaviours (Kayman *et al.* 2016). Having a safety plan can be seen as the emotional health equivalent of securing a car seatbelt on when getting into a car. It is an advance preparation for a known risk that may not eventuate.

Ideally, a safety plan is developed in times of relative calm (Cole-King *et al.* 2013); sometimes, safety plans may need to be constructed during times of heightened stress. This may complicate how a student perceives their personal capability to cope, and resources they may access to disrupt an evolving crisis. In these cases, a helper will need to reflect upon their responses, becoming more directive and explicit in stressing the importance of help seeking, using coping strategies that have previously been effective and taking action to engage treatment providers if the crisis becomes life threatening. It is also during a crisis that a student is more likely to express ambivalence or hopelessness towards *any* strategy intended to help them, including a safety plan. It is not uncommon for a person experiencing a crisis to struggle to identify coping skills, resources or people they trust. The relative absence of capability and resources to continue managing the pressures of their life may be due to estrangement from family, conflict with people of importance to them and other factors that reflect personal support absence. Should these scenarios be communicated to you, there may be a sense of despair and hopelessness that aligns with feelings expressed by the student. Although this can be a healthy (temporary) response which will allow you to communicate empathetically and compassionately with the student, it should prompt you to suggest that support strategies need to escalate to the next stage, engaging professional supports including crisis lines.

Safety plans should be evolving works that students may commence with anyone. As their circumstances change and their ability to understand their own needs evolves, the safety plan will likely require revision and reflection with a professional. It should be noted that safety plans are not the end of a suicide prevention intervention, but a crucial start to supporting a person to access essential support. This may include when there are emerging mental health needs, recent traumas or other complex stressors impacting a person's ongoing capacity to cope.

Introducing the safety plan to the student

The role you are in and the immediate resources you have available will influence the preparations you can take in developing a safety plan with a student. One critical consideration is for the helper to believe and expect that they can support a person to transition through the crisis.

Students may have an existing safety plan developed with their treatment providers, so it is often helpful to ask whether they are familiar with safety or crisis response plans. If they confirm that they have one already, engage with them at their level of knowledge and understanding, which may include simply following through with them each stage of their plan to revisit coping strategies and support options.

If they have limited or no knowledge of safety planning, it is helpful to start gently and explain that this is recommended for people who find it hard to cope at times, and especially helpful for those experiencing suicidality. Normalize the use of safety plans, explaining that they have helped many people face difficult times in the past.

Here are some examples of ways to introduce safety planning which you could use or adapt:

> I'm sorry to hear that things have been so hard… What have you done in the past when you were in situations like this?…I'm wondering whether you have ever heard of safety planning?

> Safety planning is like a toolbox of skills to manage how you are feeling, with strategies you might have tried before and know are helpful to you… This might include working to distract yourself from distressing thoughts with the goal to prevent you from coming to harm… How does that sound?

The preparation phase is often supported through having a deep understanding of the concerns impacting the person, their resources and coping strategies. It can take between 15 minutes and an hour to create a safety plan (Kayman *et al.* 2016), depending on a range of factors. Students may experience fear, shame and anxiety about disclosing their difficulties to others (Stanley and Brown 2012). Having access to prepared paper copies of a safety plan template or an anonymized example or being able to refer to a safety planning app, such as the BeyondNow safety planning app (Melvin *et al.* 2019), can help normalize the process of safety planning, in addition to expediting it.

Depending on the template or app used, there may be a domain 'reasons for living' or similar to improve treatment engagement (Bryan *et al.* 2018). In the context of developing a safety plan with a student, this element can support a comfortable 'wrap up' of the interaction by focusing on considerations that are more positive and supportive. This is even when the student is experiencing a suicidal crisis and you are waiting on an emergency response. If a person describes having no reasons to live, this would be a significant indicator that an emergency response is needed.

Resources to support the development of a safety plan

There are some critical components to safety plans that offer therapeutic potency when administered in a person-centred, compassionate way.

Without these components, safety plans, while 'feeling good', have not been evidenced to prevent suicidal behaviour or de-escalate suicidal distress. For this reason, various resources have been developed to support those who wish to utilize safety plans. The following websites contain more information and detailed examples:

- **Staying Safe from suicidal thoughts**, co-funded by NHS England, features short videos on how to make a safety plan, detailed instructions on how to access additional support and a blank safety plan for download or an online option with pre-populated suggestions which can be stored online or printed, www.StayingSafe.net

- **Suicide safety plan leaflet**, https://papyrus-uk.org/wp-content/uploads/2018/09/Suicide-Safety-Plan-Leaflet.pdf

- **My safety plan**, www.studentsagainstdepression.org/wp-content/uploads/2018/09/my_safety_plan.pdf

Below is a case study illustrating how you might approach an individual and a sample safety plan (see Figure 16.1).

SAFETY PLAN FOR OLIVIA[1]

You are the personal tutor for Olivia who is a 20-year-old third-year psychology student. She has been struggling with course work, has missed several lectures and is very worried about her January exams. During your conversation she starts crying, says she's going to quit the course and you notice that she has scars on her right forearm from what appear to be healed cuts indicative of self-harm.

Current situation

Olivia lives in a shared house with three other students and has a small network of friends on her course. Three evenings a week she works in a local bar. Money is very tight; her student debt is mounting, and her family are unable to help her financially. University records show above average grades which have recently deteriorated. You have received two separate emails of concern from other lecturers. Olivia opens up and tells you that she has just split up with her girlfriend of 18 months, has started drinking in her room, that she is distanced from the rest of her housemates and can't be bothered to do anything and especially not study. She is very upset when telling you about her relationship break-up, and as she wipes her tears you notice fresh cuts on her other arm.

---

1   Reproduced with kind permission of 4 Mental Health.

Relevant background information

Olivia begins to open up to you. She tells you that when she was 14 years old she started to self-harm when she was being severely bullied at school and her grandmother died and then whenever she was upset. Over the years she has used self-harm (initially scratching and then cutting) to deal with her distress. When you ask her who she has to support her, Olivia says that although her parents are divorced she remains close to them both and to her two older siblings. Olivia's older sister lives an hour away and they are very close. Olivia says she is especially close to her 12-year-old nephew and 14-year-old niece.

Your response

You have a conversation with Olivia and explain that she can be helped and supported, and that there are things that Olivia can do to help this, things like confide in her parents, sister or another family member and housemates or friends for support, see her GP, seek financial and debt advice from the students' union and plan a strategy to get back on top of her academic work. You reassure her that all is not lost and she has options before she needs to think about quitting her studies. Olivia is very relieved, and you say that you'd like to help her find a way to deal with her distress in a less harmful way than drinking and cutting herself. You tell her about making a safety plan, saying, 'It's the mental health equivalent of putting on a car seat belt, it can help keep you safe when you are feeling very distressed.'

Introducing Olivia to StayingSafe.net

You describe a website called StayingSafe.net and show her all the various parts of the site. You explain that it was made by an organization called 4 Mental Health that wants to help people learn how to deal with their distress. The website was designed by people who have also been through tough times, working with those that have helped to support them, including professionals and other students. Olivia explains that her mum is not well and she doesn't want to burden her, but you reassure Olivia that family members would rather know than not know. You explain to her that it's always best if you can tell people how you're feeling as they can then support you. Olivia agrees that you can help her make a basic safety plan and that she will call her GP tonight to make an appointment. She agrees to a quick call with you tomorrow to check in with how she's feeling and to see how the call home to confide in her mum went.

Safety planning and issues of confidentiality

There are a range of challenges when supporting a student within an educational setting, not least in relation to students who may be minors where it may be difficult to negotiate potential disclosures of suicidality to care providers or parents. Even trained clinicians struggle to come to consensus over what constitutes an appropriate breach of confidence (Duncan, Williams and Knowles 2012). Therefore, those new to providing a suicide intervention response such as safety planning may also find this challenging. In educational settings it is anticipated that policies guiding such disclosures should be in place to ease any potential difficulty. However, for students who may be on the cusp of adulthood, the ethical considerations and potential to preserve life during a suicidal crisis will weigh more heavily than the legal considerations of breaking confidentiality.

The Consensus Statement (DH *et al.* 2014), although written primarily for health professionals, is useful for all disciplines. It clearly states that although we may not have consent to share information, consent is not required to receive information. Additionally, 'if the purpose of the disclosure is to prevent a person who lacks capacity from serious harm, there is an expectation that practitioners will disclose relevant confidential information, if it is considered to be in the person's best interest to do so'. Additionally, the process of asking about giving consent may be undertaken in different ways. A warm and positive style of questioning and discussion which promotes the usefulness of including someone they trust in their care and support because it helps achieve better outcomes is more likely to result in an agreement to share information rather than a simple 'Do I have your consent to tell someone?'.

From a legal perspective, there are multiple factors that will determine liability, as determined by the helper's professional training and experience, whether their response aligned with their employer's policy and procedures (was there a duty of care?) and whether their actions were 'reasonable' (Obegi 2017; Sher 2015). Those with clinical mental health training are likely to be held under greater scrutiny than those without such training, due to the expectation that they can elicit greater insights into the risk profiles and the necessary interventions to reasonably prevent harm (Sher 2015). As a guiding principle, in determining 'reasonable actions', it can be helpful to seek support and guidance from people with experience in responding to students in at-risk situations. Implementing formal (and informal) relationships with student counselling services or external crisis response services, where reflection upon the safety planning intervention can occur, can be valuable.

Useful resources on information sharing

- **New South Wales Department of Education**, https://education.nsw.gov.au/about-us/rights-and-accountability/legal-issues-bulletins/school-counsellors-and-confidentiality

- **Victoria Department of Education**, www.education.vic.gov.au/school/teachers/health/childprotection/Pages/infosharing.aspx#link71

- **South Australia Department of Education**, www.education.sa.gov.au/department/policies-and-legislation/information-sharing-guidelines-and-procedure

- **Department for Education, England**, www.gov.uk/government/publications/safeguarding-practitioners-information-sharing-advice

Conclusions

Suicide safety planning has been in practice for well over a decade, with research evidence continuing to emerge supporting the value of safety plans in supporting people through suicidal crises. Safety plans are not a panacea and should be part of – not the totality of – an initial crisis response plan for a student and incorporated into longer-term management strategies. They should be seen as one aspect of a comprehensive suicide-safer strategy recommended by Universities UK and PAPYRUS (2018).

The importance of taking time to compassionately understand a student's needs, enquiring whether they have thoughts of suicide, while maintaining a hopeful attitude, are foundational steps towards developing a safety plan that can be potent in alleviating a suicidal crisis. With the identification of warning signs for crisis, and collaboratively identifying coping strategies to be implemented commensurate with those signs, a student's suicidal crisis may be averted. Although there are gaps in our knowledge and understanding of suicide safety planning, there is sufficient known about its value to advocate for its integration into our support systems for students in educational systems.

My safety plan

Getting through right now

Look at my holiday photos in Tenerife

Look at Center Parcs photo with Lisa and kids

Listen to my favourite 'happy' playlist

Watch my favourite videos

Message Mum and Lisa

Tell myself to focus on getting through a couple of minutes at a time. Remind myself that I can get through this and that Mum says darkest hour comes just before the dawn.

Making your situation safer

Remove anything I could use to hurt myself

Remove any alcohol from sight

Have a nightlight so I don't feel alone on a bad day

Avoid places I find triggering

Things to lift or calm your mood

Message or text someone

Send a group chat message

Listen to my chill playlist

Watch my favourite comedy series or 'go to' movie

Watch YouTube videos

Things to distract you

French Duolingo (10 minutes)

Watch YouTube videos (30 minutes)

Play guitar (20 minutes)

Watch my favourite online streamed shows

List who you can talk to if you are distressed or thinking about self-harm or suicide

Mum: (24/7; she loves me and it's OK to contact anytime)

Lisa: (24/7; she loves me and it's OK to contact anytime)

PAPYRUS: 0800 068 4141 (weekdays 10am–10pm, weekends 2pm–10pm, Bank Holidays 2pm–5pm)

Samaritans: 116 123 (24/7), www.samaritans.org

Young Minds: (24/7; text the YoungMinds Crisis Messenger, text YM to 85258)

Nightline: Find my local one and jot down number/opening hours, etc.

People to support you

Message Mum (or phone at night): (24/7; she loves me and it's OK to contact anytime)

Lisa (sister): (24/7; she loves me and it's OK to contact anytime)

Message Dad: (7am–7pm)

Family group chat: (7am–9pm; remember the kids are on this too!)

House group chat: (24/7)

Aunty Jen: (9am–9pm)

Emergency professional support

My GP (family doctor): NHS Helpline England: 111

Figure 16.1: My safety plan. Reproduced with kind permission of 4 Mental Health.

Author biographies

Carmen Betterridge is a psychologist, suicidologist and Director of Suicide Risk Assessment Australia, delivering online and face-to-face training, supervision and consultation services to clinical and non-clinical staff and to workplaces with the focus of preventing suicide.

Dr Alys Cole-King is a consultant liaison psychiatrist and clinical director at 4 Mental Health, delivering Connecting with People training, including suicide and self-harm mitigation modules.

References

Berman, A. (2020) Risk factors observed in the last 30 days of life among student suicides: distinguishing characteristics of college and university student suicides. *Journal of American College Health*, https://doi.org/10.1080/07448481.2020.1791884

Beyond Blue (2020) Suicidal warning signs. Accessed on 01/04/21 at: www.beyondblue.org.au/the-facts/suicide-prevention/feeling-suicidal/suicidal-warning-signs

Bryan, C., Mintz, J., Clemans, T., Burch, S. *et al.* (2018) Effect of crisis response planning on patient mood and clinical decision making: a clinical trial with suicidal U.S. soldiers. *Psychiatric Services 69*, 1, 108–111.

Bryan, C., Mintz, J., Clemans, T., Leeson, B. *et al.* (2017) Effect of crisis response planning vs. contracts for safety on suicide risk in U.S. Army soldiers: a randomized clinical trial. *Journal of Affective Disorders 212*, https://dx.doi.org/10.1016/j.jad.2017.01.028

Cole-King, A. and Platt, S. (2021) Suicide prevention for physicians: identification, intervention and mitigation of risk. *Medicine 49*, 3, 126–130.

Cole-King, A., Green, G., Gask, L., Hines, K. and Platt, S. (2013) Suicide mitigation: a compassionate approach to suicide prevention. *Advances in Psychiatric Treatment 19*, 4, 276–283.

Department of Health (DH), Royal College of Psychiatrists, Royal College of General Practitioners, Royal College of Nursing *et al.* (2014) Information Sharing and Suicide Prevention; Consensus Statement. Accessed on 01/05/21 at: https://assets.publishing.service.gov.uk/government/uploads/system/uploads/attachment_data/file/271792/Consensus_statement_on_information_sharing.pdf

Donald, M., Dower, J., Correa-Velez, I. and Jones, M. (2006) Risk and protective factors for medically serious suicide attempts: a comparison of hospital-based with population-based samples of young adults. *Australian and New Zealand Journal of Psychiatry 40*, 87–96.

Duncan, R., Williams, B. and Knowles, A. (2012) Adolescents, risk behaviour and confidentiality: when would Australian psychologists breach confidentiality to disclose information to parents? *Australian Psychologist 48*, 6, 408–419.

Green, J., Kearns, J., Rosen, R., Keane, T. and Marx, B. (2018) Evaluating the effectiveness of safety plans for military veterans: do safety plans tailored to veteran characteristics decrease suicide risk? *Behaviour Therapy 49*, 931–938.

Hawgood, J. and De Leo, D. (2016) Suicide prediction – a shift in paradigm is needed. *Crisis 37*, 4, 251–255.

Kayman, D., Goldstein, M., Wilsnack, J. and Goodman, M. (2016) Safety planning for suicide prevention. *Current Treatment Options in Psychiatry 3*, 411–420.

Leske, S., Crompton, D. and Kolves, K. (2019) *Suicide in Queensland: 2019 Annual Report*. Brisbane, QLD: Australian Institute for Suicide Research and Prevention, Griffith University.

McCabe, R., Garside, R., Backhouse, A. and Xanthopoulou, P. (2018) Effectiveness of brief psychological presentations for suicidal presentations: a systematic review. *BMC Psychiatry 18*, 120.

Melvin, G., Gresham, D. and Beaton, S. (2016) Safety first – not last! Suicide safety planning intervention (SPI). *InPsych 38*, 1.

Melvin, G., Gresham, D., Beaton, S., Coles, J. *et al.* (2019) Evaluating the feasibility and effectiveness of an Australian safety planning smartphone application: a pilot study within a tertiary mental health service. *Suicide and Life-Threatening Behavior 49*, 3, 846–858.

National Institute of Mental Health (2020) Warning signs of suicide. Accessed on 01/04/21 at: www.nimh.nih.gov/health/publications/warning-signs-of-suicide/index.shtml

Obegi, J. (2017) Probable standards of care for suicide risk assessment. *The Journal of American Academy of Psychiatry and the Law 45*, 452–459.

Pokorny, A. (1983) Prediction of suicide in psychiatric patients: report of a prospective study. *Archives of General Psychiatry 40*, 249–257.

Royal College of Psychiatrists (RCP) (2020) *Self-Harm and Suicide in Adults: Final Report of the Patient Safety Group* (College Report CG229). London: RCP.

Rudd, D., Berman, A., Joiner, T., Nock, M. *et al.* (2006) Warning signs for suicide: theory, research and clinical applications. *Suicide and Life-Threatening Behavior 36*, 3, 255–262.

Sher, L. (2015) Suicide medical malpractice: an educational overview. *International Journal of Adolescent Medical Health 27*, 2, 203–206.

Stanley, B. and Brown, G. (2012) Safety Planning Intervention: a brief intervention to mitigate suicide risk. *Cognitive and Behavioural Practice 19*, 256–264.

Stewart, K., Darling, E., Yen, S., Stanley, B., Brown, G. and Weinstock, L. (2019) Dissemination of the Safety Planning Intervention (SPI) to university counselling centre clinicians to reduce suicide risk among college students. *Archives of Suicide Research 24* (supp. 1), 75–85.

Universities UK (UUK) and PAPYRUS (2018) *Suicide-Safer Universities*. Accessed on 01/04/21 at: www.universitiesuk.ac.uk/policy-and-analysis/reports/Pages/guidance-for-universities-on-preventing-student-suicides.aspx

Vijayakumar, L., Mohanraj, R., Kumar, S., Jeyaseelan, V., Sriram, S. and Shanmugam, M. (2017) CASP – an intervention by community volunteers to reduce suicidal behaviour among refugees. *International Journal of Social Psychiatry 63*, 7, 589–597.

PART 2

Responding to Student Death by Suicide

CHAPTER 17

Responding to Student Suicide

A Student Services Perspective

NIC STREATFIELD

Overview

This chapter will cover:

- a case study of a student services response to a suspected suicide

- the importance of a pre-planned response

- establishing vulnerability by proximity

- the importance of good communication.

Introduction

The role of student services in coordinating the response to a student suicide is multivariate and challenging. In this practical chapter, we follow a head of student services as she leads her teams in response to a suspected student suicide. Interspersed between the parts of the case study are questions for the reader to use to reflect on how well prepared their institution is for managing a suspected student suicide. This chapter does not purport to offer a prescribed 'correct' response. Instead, it offers guidance based on a fictitious case study based on the author's significant experiential learning from responding to student suicides at different higher education institutions (HEIs).

It is written with the acknowledgement that no two HEIs are the same, and the team names, role titles and levels of responsibility will differ across the sector. No two student deaths are the same, and while it is vital that staff follow written processes relevant to their role, it is also the case that student support staff must be agile enough to adapt to the unique circumstances of a particular student death.

NOTIFICATION

As soon as the accommodation manager entered her office, the head of student services knew a serious incident had occurred. 'One of our students has been found dead in halls.' The head of student services reached for her notebook and took down the details of what was known. Security had been alerted that morning by a student concerned about a worrying text message he had read when he woke up that had been sent by his flatmate in the early hours. Security went to check on the student and had to force their way into the room. It appears that the student died by hanging himself from the fire door mechanism. Security followed their escalation process and alerted both the emergency services and the accommodation manager.

While the head of student services was experienced in responding to a student death, this did not prevent her heart rate increasing. Making decisions in a crisis when emotions are heightened is unlikely to ensure appropriate, efficient actions are taken. Fortunately, the planning for this eventuality had taken place previously when heads were calm and rational. The head of student services had written a series of response plans for how her teams would respond to major incidents, and she reached for this folder now. This instructional document contained a checklist as to what each team was required to do in this event. Referring to this checklist, the head of student services and accommodation manager were able to agree their next steps and the student support response began.

Each institution should have a clear and accessible notification procedure to inform first responders and senior staff as to who should be notified of the sudden death. The head of student services knew the HEI's business continuity plan, which outlined procedures the institution would follow in the face of crisis, was too high-level for her needs and so had written an operational checklist for a response to a sudden student death. While these plans were also online, she knew the value of having a tangible set of instructions in her hand. Previously having a hard copy of the checklist had proved to be containing for staff, providing them with a clear structure and tasks. The checklist also helps managers to allocate specific tasks without all staff becoming involved in managing the incident and unnecessarily restricting the important 'business as usual' student support.

The immediate aftermath of a suspected suicide can be stressful, confusing, and highly emotive. Having a plan in place, agreed templates for communications and a nominated lead ensures an effective, appropriate and timely response. (UUK and PAPYRUS 2018, p.22)

It is best practice for an HEI to have a suicide prevention strategy which includes a postvention plan (UUK and PAPYRUS 2018) that provides a structure for staff to follow when managing the impact of a suspected student suicide.

Points to consider

- Do you know what the notification protocol is in your institution and particularly who will inform you?
- Does your institution have a suicide response and postvention plan?
- Do you have an operational checklist for your teams clearly detailing their tasks? Is this checklist easily accessible to all who need it?

INITIAL INFORMATION

The head of student services provided the deceased student's name, ID number and date of birth to her team managers, briefed them on the situation and asked them to have their copy of the checklist on their desks to follow. Relevant information on the deceased student was extracted from the HEI student record systems including course, year and any previous contact with student support services, as well as next of kin and the names and contact details of the other students in the deceased student's flat.

Within 15 minutes of the notification of death, contact was made with the security staff on site and information about police activity was ascertained. Two student support staff were allocated to go to the site to speak to the flatmates of the deceased student and ensure cooperation with the emergency services. The checklist states that staff attending an incident cannot go alone, that they must have their ID cards, business cards, paper, pen and mobile telephone so that communication channels remain open.

When the above information was available, the head of student services informed her line manager, as well as the chief operating officer, giving an overview of the situation and ongoing actions. Knowing that the notification policy was not always followed correctly, she alerted chaplaincy, reception and the student's school administration team. They were all reminded that anyone asking questions about the death be referred to the communications team.

Providing accurate facts to staff is vital. Particularly in the age of social media, misinformation can circulate very quickly. Being able to provide the full details of the student, their next of kin, their course, their next scheduled academic session, their attendance and their friends and flat-mates are all important to help the senior team make informed decisions. The immediate response to a suspected student suicide involves gathering different information from lots of different sources. Information will be derived from the various HEI systems, but it will also come from people close to the student. Hence the importance of having emotionally intelligent staff attend the scene.

Points to consider

- Do you know what information you will need to gather to help inform the institutional response? Are your teams able to access all this information?
- This case study is taking place on a weekday morning. Had it happened on a weekend or out of hours there is an extra layer of complexity around collecting information (can your systems be accessed remotely?) and communicating expeditiously (do you have staff contact numbers?).
- Do you know how you would manage the situation out of hours with reduced staff on campus? (Who will come onto campus?)

AT THE SCENE

When the student support staff arrived at the halls of residence, they made themselves known to the emergency service, security and accommodation staff already there. They established a link with the lead police officer to ensure the HEI had the correct police contact details and explained that their primary task was to support the students. The police had secured the whole flat and were currently interviewing the other flatmates in the kitchen. The student support staff garnered the names of the students being spoken to and relayed these to the head of student services, who cross-referenced the names with the list of flatmates provided to her by accommodation. It transpired that there was one person in the flat who was not on the accommodation list. The student support staff were tasked with finding out who this additional person was.

Working with the accommodation team the student support staff established a temporary safe space to talk to students in a nearby domestic's office. When the students had finished answering the police's questions they were brought into this neutral space. The student support staff role is to reduce distress, assist with current needs and find out who else the deceased was close to. They sought to contain and normalize the emotions of the students and to offer practical help to them. Tea and biscuits were sourced, and blankets were brought in for the students, as the team knew shock can make people feel colder. Staff spoke calmly to the students while asking them questions about what help they most needed now and let them know about the support available to them from the HEI. The student support staff made a written note of all the students' questions and requests and, given most of their concerns were about their work, promised to let the relevant academic staff know about their mitigating situation.

Most students had already called home and spoken to their parents. Sensitively, the student support staff made it clear to the students that they should *not* be discussing the incident on social media, nor should they be speculating as to the cause of death with their friends or family. The students were told that the police need to tell the next of kin before anyone else and explained how traumatic it would be for the family if the information about the death emerged on social media.

People will experience a range of emotions and behaviours when in shock. Ensuring that students *feel* supported by their HEI is vital at this early stage. Sending staff who are skilled at sensitively listening to students and in eliciting information about the deceased and their social networks is key. The student support staff at the scene need to provide compassionate human support, practical options and elicit information that will be essential to an effective response. Many senior leaders believe counsellors are best placed to respond in this initial phase. While counsellors may have the necessary skills to carry out this delicate role, the students are experiencing normal distress following exposure to abnormal events and it is not helpful to pathologize their response at this time. It may be that students need to access psychological professional support at a later date and this option should be communicated to them.

Points to consider
- Are staff and students made aware of the importance of a social media silence while the police notify the family?
- Have your first responders been trained in how to respond to a sudden student death?

WHO WILL BE AFFECTED?

Most of the flatmates who contacted their family were now waiting for them to come and take them home. Two wanted to go home but could not get a lift. The head of student services agreed that the HEI would pay for a taxi for their journey. One student did not want to go home but did not want to return to the flat where the death had taken place, so alternative accommodation in halls was sourced for him.

The student support staff remained on site to help other staff from accommodation and security keep the area clear while undertakers removed the body. Seeing a coffin leave campus would be a distressing sight for many, so walkways, paths and buildings were temporarily blocked to minimize the number of students who might be witness to the removal of the body.

By now the head of student services had been informed that the unknown person in the flat was the girlfriend of one of the flatmates. She was a student at another HEI in the city. The head of student services also received the names of three other students who the flatmates said the deceased was good friends with, and that he had been a member of the hockey team and in the Real Ale Society. The Student Information team were delegated the task of getting contact details for these students. This team had already been in touch with the academic school to establish which students were in his cohort and whether he shared teaching sessions with other courses or other year groups.

The head of student services knew the importance of identifying those who may be most at risk after a suspected suicide. Family and close friends could be considered as 'suicide bereaved long term', friends, flatmates and peers as 'suicide bereaved short term', those geographically close to the death, first responders, classmates and teachers as 'suicide affected' and the wider community as 'suicide exposed' (see Figure 17.1).

The head of student services knew finding the swathe of already vulnerable individuals across each group was vital so appropriate, targeted support could be provided. She met with her managers to consider the proximity information they already had using Public Health England's vulnerability matrix (PHE 2019,

Appendix 6, p.79). This concentric circle model considered 'geographic proximity', 'psychological proximity' and 'social proximity'. This discussion enabled the team to spot a group who had been missed. Each hall has a residential assistant in it, usually a postgraduate student, and it was felt that this student may require additional support. The teams were reminded that they were still in the detective stage of establishing who was in the deceased student's proximities (geographic, psychological and social) and, as they were reaching out to those individuals they already knew about, this offered an opportunity to find out about others who may need to be added to the vulnerability matrix.

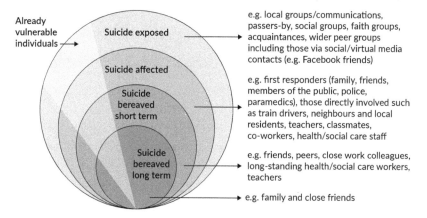

Figure 17.1: The range of individuals who may be affected by suicide (modified with permission)

Source: PHE 2019, Figure 1, p.19, https://assets.publishing.service.gov.uk/government/uploads/system/uploads/attachment_data/file/839621/PHE_Suicide_Cluster_Guide.pdf

It is the responsibility of the emergency services to remove a body and the police will contact the undertaker. It is also the responsibility of the police to notify the next of kin.

There is quite a bit of detective work the support teams need to engage in to ascertain who will fit into the vulnerability matrix and need targeted support. The PHE model the teams use is extremely helpful because it focuses minds on the different types of proximity. 'A vulnerability matrix approach based on the Circles of Vulnerability is a practical approach that can be used to identify and prioritize at-risk individuals and groups and identify appropriate interventions and support' (PHE 2019, p.34). So far, in this case study, only students with a geographical proximity have been supported and the teams need to ensure they reach all those who may be 'bereaved short term' and those who may be 'suicide affected'. There is still work required to capture those in 'social' and 'psychological' proximity. Finding out who is in the deceased student's circle of influence is particularly important in the case of a suspected suicide due to the risk of contagion (PHE 2019).

> **Points to consider**
> - Are you aware of the Public Health England resources on responding to suicide? Is a vulnerability matrix embedded into your student suicide response processes?
> - Is it clear who will take on the detective work and collate the contact details of those within geographic, psychological and/ or social proximity?

FIRST MAJOR INCIDENT TEAM MEETING

With only one hour's notice, the head of student services was invited to attend a major incident team meeting. This was chaired by the chief operating officer who had invoked the HEI's 'Major Incident Response' protocol. Around the table were the deputy dean of the student's academic school (the dean was not available), the director of communications, the student union president, the university secretary, the accommodation manager, and the head of student services. The chief operating officer asked for all the information staff had about the student and what was known about the cause of death. The chief operating officer wanted to know if the deceased student had been known to student support teams and what their academic record and attendance profile looked like. The head of student services confirmed the student was not known to the wellbeing service, but she was still waiting to hear back from the local doctors' surgery. The deputy dean did not know the student personally and did not have attendance or progression details to hand.

Much of this first meeting discussed the notification procedure and how the death would be sensitively communicated to students and staff. The head of student services was asked to write a paragraph detailing the support available to students to send to the director of communications within the hour. As she already had a 'support after a sudden student death' template email, she was able to hand out a printed copy to the group. This led to a conversation about whether to include links to suicide-specific support resources. Senior staff were uncomfortable about any specialist suicide support resources being provided at this early stage. The communications plan was threefold. The director of communications was to write a communication piece to students in the deceased student's halls of residence to say that sadly a student had died, that there was no reason for others to be concerned for their safety and that support was available. The head of student services agreed to email the Public Health England sample letter to students (PHE 2019, Appendix 9, p.86) to the director of communications.

The second communication piece was for the deputy dean and the head of student services to work together to plan on co-delivering the sad news to the deceased student's academic cohort. The next class the deceased was scheduled to attend was in two days' time. The deputy dean agreed to inform relevant staff in the department and the head of student services agreed to ask the chaplain for help with delivering the news.

The third notification strand would be more personal. Students who were close to the deceased student were to be contacted by student support staff on an individual basis. The head of student services was able to provide the information she had so far on those students closest to the deceased.

Referring to her checklist, the head of student services reminded colleagues of the need to update the student's central record, so no communications such as library fines and attendance absence notifications were inadvertently sent to the deceased student.

The head of student services was tasked to find out when the family had been notified by the police and to reach out to his parents and be the link person for the HEI. Her teams were also asked to set up a drop-in support session within the deceased student's halls of residence.

This first meeting focused on ascertaining facts about the incident, finding out what the HEI knew about the student, making sure a sensitive communications strategy is implemented and planning notification and support for the community. The tone and content of communications that the HEI provides are critical. Part of the discussion at this major incident team meeting was about whether to include suicide-specific support resources in the communications. Only a coroner can decide the cause of death, but as the death had taken place in halls and a fellow student had already been sent a text suggesting that this had been a death by suicide, there was concern that not acknowledging this as a suspected suicide could be interpreted as the HEI trying to protect its reputation. Some institutions, such as University College London (UCL 2020), have overcome this dilemma by producing a booklet for 'students affected by a sudden death'. This provides a variety of information and resources, some of which are suicide specific. In this case, the senior staff decided to leave out any reference to suicide-support resources.

> **Points to consider**
> - Would the head of student services be invited to this initial major incident team meeting? If not, why not?
> - Are you aware of the types of questions you may be asked at this first meeting? If not, is there any preparation that could be done now?
> - Does your communications team have a 'sudden student death' communications template? While every incident will be different, having some pre-prepared copy written will help ensure a consistent response.
> - Has your organization decided if it would provide suicide-specific support resources when the death has not been confirmed as suicide?

THE MEDIA

Having established that the police had informed the parents, the head of student services returned to her office and composed herself to call the student's next of kin. The father of the deceased student answered and said that the family had received a 'sorry and goodbye' text message in the early hours of the morning from their son and so believed he had taken his own life. The head of student services responded compassionately and explained that she would be the link with the family, and they exchanged contact details. She asked if the family were religious and found out they were non-practising Christians. Although understandably distraught, the father was appreciative of this supportive phone call from his son's HEI.

The chaplain was the next call and they arranged to meet to discuss how the chaplaincy could support the grief process. The next phone call was to her counterpart at the other HEI in the city to let them know of the suspected suicide and to provide the name of the girlfriend who had been staying overnight in the flat. Following the ethos of proximity increasing vulnerability, it was important the other HEI knew that at least one of their students was affected. Her final phone call was to the local authority lead on the multiagency suicide prevention group. The local authority used a real-time surveillance system for suspected suicide, and they needed to be informed in case other deaths occurred that could suggest a cluster. As the head of student services was about to leave her desk to update her team, she saw the proposed official communications piece. It felt too corporate, so she made some amendments and emailed it back to the director of communications. The phone rang again, and it was the chief operating officer summoning her to another major incident team meeting immediately. At this meeting, she was joined by the director of communications. It transpired that a local newspaper had picked up the story. They did not have the name of the student but the online report on the newspaper website reported that the student had hanged themself in their student room. The head of student services updated the group about the family believing their son had died by suicide and she suggested that the HEI contact the local authority's press team to ask them to remind the newspaper of responsible reporting guidelines (IPSO 2020; NUJ 2015; Samaritans 2020). The director of communications took on this task and 22 minutes later the online newspaper report was amended.

Communications are vital in cases like this, and the prevalence of social media makes it difficult to control the flow of information. Student support teams will not lead on the messages that universities deliver but they should be having an input into and influencing them. Suicide is a public health issue and usually it is the local authority public health team that leads on suicide prevention and postvention in the area. HEIs are part of a wider community; engaging local resources is therefore helpful, particularly in ensuring that all relevant authorities have accurate information so that suicide clusters can be spotted swiftly.

Points to consider

- Is your communications team familiar with the guidelines on responsible media reporting of suicide?
- Do you have good links with public health in your local authority to be able to access support?
- Is the chaplain's role in providing support after a suspected suicide clear?

SUPPORTING THE TEAM

Belatedly, the head of student services was able to meet with her managers to provide an update. The team now had information about who had been close to the student and, because the next of kin had been informed, were able to phone these students to offer them support. So far, all the students spoken to had heard on the grapevine that their friend had died. Each student was invited to come in for a support session, was informed that a student services presence would be in the halls of residence from the following day and was asked who they were currently with and what their immediate plans were. The students were encouraged to engage with others in their support network and given out-of-hours support numbers. They were also asked who else the deceased was close to.

The head of student services thanked her team for all their hard work during the day. She reminded them that it had been a busy and emotional day which may trigger an emotional response in them. It was, she said, important that they looked after themselves, as well as each other.

> **Points to consider**
> - Are your staff trained in suicide postvention? Are they aware of the risk factors to look out for when speaking to bereaved students?
> - Does your checklist have a 'making sure your staff are okay' action point?

DAY TWO MAJOR INCIDENT TEAM MEETING

This early morning meeting saw the head of student services update the group about the students her team had reached out to and the plans to provide a support presence in the halls of residence that day. Her staff would be addressing the men's and women's hockey teams after their training sessions the following day and she would be meeting the student union vice-president for welfare who had concerns about a student in the Real Ale Society. A member of the wellbeing service was meeting with the student union officers to provide them with support, given the likelihood that students would share their grief with them. The wellbeing service were contacting clients whose suicidal ideation may make them more vulnerable to yesterday's death. Now that the newspapers were reporting a suspected suicide and this was the view of the family, the group agreed that more suicide-specific support resources such as *Help is at Hand* (PHE and NSPA 2015) and a link to the PAPYRUS website[1] could be provided.

The head of student services raised the worries of some of the students

---

[1] www.papyrus-uk.org

who had been contacted about their upcoming academic deadlines and the dean took responsibility for ensuring that the students' academic tutors would be in touch to reassure them. While it was clear that the news of the death had spread quickly, it was still felt important that his academic cohort were informed in person at the start of the following day's class. The head of student services asked about what support was being put in place for academic staff.

Because her teams responded so effectively the previous day in gathering proximity information, the head of student services was able to detail how she was deploying her limited resources in a targeted way that ensured the support was visible to the community. Aside from information stands promoting self-help resources, students were being offered individual support as well as group-based support.

As grief is complicated and people respond differently, and at different times, it is vital that a range of support is made available to students and to staff. As more students were informed of the death, there might be more students requiring a supportive intervention from HEI professionals. Students who did not know the deceased might be particularly affected because of a resonance to events in their own lives. Ensuring support is visible and accessible is key after a student death and particularly after a suspected student suicide.

Often, one of the roles senior student support staff undertake is providing informal support to academic staff who are impacted by a student's death. Universities may have an employee assistance programme (EAP) in place which can offer telephone counselling and have occupational therapy provision. However, rarely does it offer critical incident debriefing or face-to-face support for staff struggling to support students at a time of crisis. Samaritans offer a postvention service for HEIs and, in this case, the local authority had a crisis response team which staff or students could access. Encouraging staff to take up that support is needed as often there is a reticence to admit vulnerability or personal need. As Causer et al. (2019, p.20) say, 'Practitioners can experience traumatic and adverse emotional responses to a suicide and that targeted postvention is needed to support practitioners in processing the impact and in developing narratives that enable continued safe practice.' The support the HEI provides for staff should be consistent. In this case study, two of the deceased student's academic lecturers were given time off work, yet this recuperation opportunity was not offered to the professional support staff involved.

Points to consider

- Are you aware of suicide-specific support resources available?
- Are you able to call on additional external postvention expertise and support?
- Does your HEI make adequate provision for supporting staff
  after a critical incident? Which department takes the lead on
  that?

FUNERAL

At the last major incident team meeting of the week, the head of student services updated the senior team by providing the numbers of students who had accessed support. She also reported back on her continued liaison with the deceased student's family, which primarily had been about practical issues such as collecting his belongings, being sent his academic work and Student Finance England liaison. The head of student services had provided the family with suicide-specific support materials, specifically the *Help is at Hand* booklet, and had found a couple of support groups local to the family from Facing the Future and Survivors of Bereavement of Suicide. The head of student services had explained to the family the role of the coroner's office and had asked if the family were happy if staff and students could pay their respects to their son at the funeral. They had agreed to this. The head of student services informed the group that once the funeral date was known she would arrange a coach to take students and staff to the funeral, ensure support was available on the day and suggested the chaplain and the dean of school formally represent the HEI at the funeral. The meeting agreed with her suggestions.

Rituals after death are important in all cultures and the HEI needs to be respectful of the family's wishes, which is why maintaining a single line of good communication is vital. A compassionate, listening approach, coupled with an organized pragmatic response, is likely to best help both the family and the HEI. Funerals are an important part of the grieving process and it is imperative that the HEI supports those who wish to pay their respects. Organizing transportation, flowers, donations, etc. may not fall to a student services department, but whoever takes on this responsibility, and the budget to pay for them, should be made clear in the response plan. While it is likely that students will celebrate their friend's life in their social groups on return to campus, this is potentially a time of increased vulnerability for some, so support must be visible and available immediately after the funeral.

Points to consider
- Who in your institution would arrange funeral attendance logistics?

LONGER-TERM ACTIONS

The wellbeing service had seen an increase in suicidal ideation and distress amongst some of their existing clients after the student's death. The team continued to support those who wanted to talk but not all students on their vulnerability matrix had engaged with support. When focus on the death has reduced and normality is expected to resume, the post-funeral aftermath can be much harder for some. Aware of this, the head of student services asked her team to reach out again to those students who had not accessed support to let them know it was always available for them to take up at any point. She also put the date of the student's death in her diary so that support would be offered on the first-year anniversary of the death.

While the head of student services was pleased with her team's response, she knew that learning never stops. She asked her line manager to lead a debrief of the incident to see what further lessons could be learned.

The first few days after a death are very busy for support services but, particularly after the funeral has taken place, the visibility of the death on campus reduces. This does not mean the impact of the student suicide has dissipated. Ensuring those deemed to be vulnerable are offered ongoing support is key to preventing a suicide cluster emerging. Part of this suicide postvention work should be to always review the HEI's response to the death. This helpful step should be enshrined in policy so that it is not missed. It is beneficial for this reflective exercise to be led by a senior leader who can ensure a cross-institutional perspective. For student services leaders this review is an important opportunity to frame the impact of the suicide as ongoing and emphasize the importance of continued postvention support as suicide prevention.

Points to consider

- Is a review embedded in policy?
- Who would carry out a debrief at your institution?
- Does your institution see this death by suicide as a distinct crisis (i.e. case closed) or as an ongoing issue the institution will continue to address?

Conclusion

As we have seen, the role of student support services in responding to a student suicide is challenging and involves leading on multiple different tasks. The teams are first responders who normalize the anguish of grief; they provide practical support and guidance, engage in detective work to establish those who will be most affected and target appropriate support to help people manage emotionally. They are required to be compassionate communicators ensuring all relevant actors have accurate information and be the focal point for the bereaved family. They also need to look after themselves and each other because responding to a student suicide is difficult and emotionally impactful for everyone.

Useful resources

- Business in the Community (2017) *Crisis Management in the Event of a Suicide: A Postvention Toolkit for Employers*, www.bitc.org.uk/wp-content/uploads/2019/10/bitc-wellbeing-toolkit-suicide-postventioncrisismanagement-mar2017.pdf

- **Facing the Futures** groups, www.facingthefuturegroups.org, provides support for people bereaved by suicide

- **PAPYRUS: Prevention of young suicide**, www.papyrus-uk.org

- Public Health England (2020) *A Guide to Coroner Services for Bereaved People* www.gov.uk/government/publications/guide-to-coroner-services-and-coroner-investigations-a-short-guide

- Public Health England (2016) *Support after a Suicide: A Guide to Providing Local Resources*, https://assets.publishing.service.gov.uk/government/uploads/system/uploads/attachment_data/file/590838/support_after_a_suicide.pdf

- Public Health England (2015) **Help is at Hand**. A comprehensive booklet providing information to those who have been bereaved by a suicide. It contains both practical and support information, www.gov.uk/government/news/you-are-not-alone-help-is-at-hand-for-anyone-bereaved-by-suicide

- Samaritans' **Step by Step** support and guidance for universities, www.samaritans.org/how-we-can-help/schools/universities

- Stanley, N., Bell, J., Hilton, S. and Manthorpe, J. (2007) **Responses and Prevention in Student Suicide**. Preston: University of Central Lancashire.

- **Support After Suicide Partnership** (SASP) is a collaborative partnership and a brilliant compendium of support and information for those who have been bereaved or affected by suicide and those who are developing local support services, https://supportaftersuicide.org.uk

- **Survivors of Bereavement by Suicide** provides support for adults bereaved by suicide, https://uksobs.org

- Universities UK (UUK) and PAPYRUS (2018) **Suicide-Safer Universities**, a guidance document for senior university leaders to help prevent and respond to student suicide, www.universitiesuk.ac.uk/policy-and-analysis/reports/Documents/2018/guidance-for-sector-practitioners-on-preventing-student-suicides.PDF

Author biography

Nic Streatfield is Head of Student Support and Wellbeing at the University of East London and is the AMOSSHE Student Services Organisation Vice Chair for Professional Development.

References

Causer, H., Muse, K., Smith, J. and Bradley, E. (2019) What is the experience of practitioners in health, education or social care roles following a death by suicide? A qualitative research synthesis. *Int J Environ Res Public Health 16*, 18, 3293.

Independent Press Standards Organisation (IPSO) (2020) *Guidance on Reporting Suicide*. Accessed on 04/06/20 at: www.ipso.co.uk/media/1725/suicide-journo-v7-online-crazes.pdf

National Union of Journalists (NUJ) (2015) *Responsible Reporting on Mental Health, Mental Illness and Death by Suicide. A Practical Guide for Journalists by the National Union of Journalists.* Accessed on 20/05/20 at: www.nuj.org.uk/resource/nuj-guidelines-for-reporting-mental-health-and-death-by-suicide.html

Public Health England (PHE) (2019) *Identifying and Responding to Suicide Clusters. A Practical Resource.* Accessed on 20/05/20 at: https://assets.publishing.service.gov.uk/government/uploads/system/uploads/attachment_data/file/839621/PHE_Suicide_Cluster_Guide.pdf

Public Health England (PHE) and National Suicide Prevention Alliance (NSPA) (2015) *Help Is at Hand.* Accessed on 20/05/20 at: https://supportaftersuicide.org.uk/resource/help-is-at-hand

Samaritans (2020) *Media Guidelines for Reporting Suicide.* Accessed on 21/05/20 at: www.samaritans.org/about-samaritans/media-guidelines

Universities UK (UUK) and PAPYRUS (2018) *Suicide-Safer Universities.* Accessed on 20/05/20 at: www.universitiesuk.ac.uk/policy-and-analysis/reports/Documents/2018/guidance-for-sector-practitioners-on-preventing-student-suicides.PDF

University College London (UCL) (2020) *Guide for Students Affected by the Sudden Death of a Peer.* Accessed on 21/05/20 at: www.ucl.ac.uk/students/support-and-wellbeing/look-after-yourself/coping-bereavement/guide-students-affected-sudden-death

CHAPTER 18

Responding to Family Needs after a Student Suicide

DAVID MOSSE

Overview

This chapter will explore the needs of families who have lost a young person to suicide and how the higher education institutions where they studied and lived can provide relevant and meaningful support. The chapter will combine research evidence with a personal narrative of suicide loss. It begins with a short review of salient research to understand what is distinctive about suicide loss for families. It then focuses on the key needs of families around making sense of the suicide and finding social support. I will then turn to a personal account of suicide loss, family needs and the response of the university in question. Finally, the chapter links what is understood about family needs and the lessons from lived experience to suggest some broad areas for action that need attention to support families after the tragedy of a student death by suicide.

Suicide loss and its effects

A student has died by their own hand. This is a tragedy that disturbs all those who personally knew the individual, as well as many who did not: teachers, tutors, counsellors, fellow students, administrative and service staff in academic departments or halls of residence. The effects of this death on a higher education institution community ripple out, touching many, some profoundly, and, in a few instances, connects to existing pain and vulnerability in ways that can have a serious impact on their wellbeing.

The impact of a suicide on close family is often of a different order. The loss of a child, sibling, spouse or partner to suicide is understood to be different from other bereavements in its effects (Jordan 2001; Pitman *et al.* 2018), and these effects are thought to vary with the relationship of the family member and the person who has died (parent, sibling, partner), and with the cultural context of these relationships (Cammarata 2012; Miers, Abbott and Springer 2012; Sugrue, McGilloway and Keegan 2014). The nature of these effects and, therefore, the kind of support that families need in a given context is still poorly understood. Our knowledge about these matters is also shaped by the methods of inquiry, in-depth qualitative studies revealing more of the distinctive experience of suicide loss than larger-scale quantitative surveys. The stories of their own journey with grief told by parents, siblings or partners provide the deepest insight into the pain of suicide loss.

Some of the distinctive characteristics of bereavement by suicide, especially marked in the case of the death of a child or adolescent, and which recur in personal narratives and varied studies are the following. First, and this hardly need be said, such a death is experienced as profoundly life changing. It is a rupture in biographical narratives: the 'end of the world as I know it' (Bell *et al.* 2012; Sugrue *et al.* 2014, p.120). Second, family grief from suicide is characterized by a relentless search for sense-making and meaning which is partly what makes such bereavement complicated (Bell *et al.* 2012; Jordan 2001). This involves self-questioning of a particular kind. There is the insistent question: why? Suicide can involve the experience of what's been called 'agent-regret', in which people take responsibility for something over which they had no control (Kuan 2017). Of the many spinning wheels that come to be aligned to produce a tragic death by suicide (or the long causal chain), we home in on the ethically relevant segment that shouts, 'I could have done something...' This points to the centrality of guilt following suicide; and feelings of moral responsibility. This first-person sense of responsibility, these narratives suggest, is not determined by external (social or circumstantial) factors but by *relational* closeness, and there can be little doubt that the tragic death by suicide of an adolescent, perhaps newly living separate from the family home, triggers a heavy load of such responsibility on parents, and siblings too.

Third, attention turns to the social context of suicide bereavement. Suicide loss disrupts people's way of being in the world; it produces social ellipsis, silences, avoidances, concealments, withdrawals. Unlike most other sudden deaths, suicide cannot be 'absorbed into everyday life' (Das 2015, p.113). The effects that, in surveys, distinguish bereavement by suicide from other sudden deaths are its impact on 'social functioning' – crushing awkwardness, isolation, poor help-seeking, the inability to talk about grief, with consequences such as a high likelihood of dropping out of jobs/college, and increased suicide attempts (Pitman *et al.* 2018). The poor social comprehension of suicide loss leads some to describe such grief as 'disenfranchised' (Bell *et al.* 2012; Doka 1999), meaning that family members are not accorded the social status of the bereaved as in other deaths. This links to the question of whether survivors of suicide loss experience stigma or shame (Cammarata 2012; Cvinar 2005; Hanschmidt *et al.* 2016; Pitman *et al.* 2018).

There is evidence that suicide grief is associated with higher scores on measures of perceived stigma and shame, responsibility and guilt (Pitman *et al.* 2018). In some social/cultural contexts social stigma and shame is real and forceful, and surveys of suicide bereavement reveal social disapproval, shunning, and associated social withdrawal, isolation and grief difficulties (Cammarata 2012, p.14; Feigelman, Gorman and Jordan 2009). One study found that 'twice as many friends terminate relationships as maintain their relations with survivors' (Cammarata 2012, p.49, referencing Dunn and Morrish-Vidners 1995). In other cases, self-stigma and the projection of feelings of guilt may be central. Certainly, as Cammarata notes, 'the constructs of shame and guilt are interwoven and it is difficult to extrapolate where the shame ends and the guilt begins' (2012, p.30). Even where they are not subject to blame and recrimination, family members may be avoided or set apart as 'awkward', 'hard to read'; they carry an emotional burden that alters the rules of social interaction. And for these suicide survivors carrying a fearsome affective load, the social world is harder to navigate, strewn with (hidden) judgement, self-censoring, concealment or anxiety about disclosure. There may be fear of social judgement, stereotyping or pre-emptive explanations of the suicide that is grieved.

Family members will not all be affected to the same degree. Cammarata not only found mothers experienced stigma more than fathers – no doubt a function of socially defined roles – but also that children in the family experienced higher levels of stigma and associated complicated grief effects (2012, pp.84–86). The impact of a suicide on social relationships is also varied. Some relationships become closer after the suicide, and others more distant; new connections are made and others fade. This is true of relationships within families. The dynamics of guilt and blame have their effect on family systems bringing closeness and rupture, conflict, communication problems or avoidance of mentioning the person as family members' different grieving processes align or misalign.

The characteristics of suicide bereavement experienced by families suggest particular needs, two of which are worth highlighting: the need to find a narrative or story, that is, a way of talking about the death, and the need for social support. I will comment on each of these before turning to the specific implications for meeting family needs after a student death by suicide.

Narrating suicide loss

The life-changing nature of a young death by suicide and the search for meaning combine to give particular importance to finding a narrative for the loss, a story that allows not so much 'recovery' but a way of living with such terrible loss. Suicide is not just loss, it is ethical injury. Almost universally, suicide is shaming and staining of the moral identities of those who died and those who survive (Owens *et al.* 2008). It is destructive of the morally self-defining role of parent, or of sibling, or son/daughter, wife/husband or partner. The biographical disintegration that led to their sons' suicides in Owens *et al.*'s study is narrated in the context of the parents' own disrupted biography. It is not just a question of why did this happen to him, but why is this happening to me (Owens *et al.* 2008)? As such, life after suicide requires an account of the death that can rebuild ruptured biographies, social roles and identities. Loss to suicide requires ethical self-*remaking*. We need stories as survival tools, making sense of the past so as to allow investment in a future and to find renewed purpose in living (Owens *et al.* 2008). The greater stigma and complicated grief experienced by children (often following the suicide of a parent) may be related to their particular difficulty in making sense of the death since lacking the cognitive ability or maturity to frame and explain a suicide (Cain 2002; Cammarata 2012, p.86).

As family members ask impossible questions of themselves – why did my child choose to die, was my love not enough? – a wider field of actors becomes implicated. If giving agency to the child or sibling for his death is intolerable (making the family utterly powerless) responsibility must lie elsewhere beyond my child and his reason in agents acting upon him: his depression, the serotonin metabolism in his brain, impulsivity, perfectionism, academic pressure, social media. And close on the heels is the other question, 'Why was he not stopped from killing himself?'

Beyond the almost unscalable mount of parental responsibility lies a field of institutional responsibility, in the failures of knowledge or action of clinicians and counsellors, teachers and anyone having a duty of care. Of course, blame in its various forms, located outside the family, serves the psychological function of displacing anger and guilt (Owens *et al.* 2008). From this point of view, suicide brings a need for the preservation of self from the anxiety of self-blame, and the preservation of the one who has died and our relationship with them, by exteriorizing agency. And this suicide bequeaths circulating culpability that makes relationships within families, and between them and others involved, difficult since however caring and sincere, everyone on the path to the person's self-destruction is part of the story.

I return to what these processes of family meaning-making in the days, weeks, months and years following a suicide entail for professionals and institutions (including the healthcare and education institutions) that had a role in the care of a student who died by suicide. But first, I will turn to disruptions to families' systems of social support.

Social support

> Unfortunately, the components that create the environment for healing, such as social support, increased communication, and empathy, are the very same ones that research has shown to be elusive to the suicide survivors. (Cammarata 2012, p.30)

This is the dilemma for families grieving a loss by suicide. What is most needed is scarcest. A recent review of the evidence confirms that informal social support has a positive effect on post-bereavement well-being, especially in the case of suicide loss (Scott *et al.* 2020). But the bi-directional nature of the relationship (i.e. suicide loss has a negative effect on social supports) means that where families' social networks are altered or weakened after a suicide, this contributes to complicated grief, distress and psychological ill-being. Following a death by suicide, family members turn immediately to those within reach for practical and emotional support, for comfort, consolation and to deal with emotionally laden tasks such as organizing the funeral.

Social support is, of course, found in different places: among friends, colleagues and in the family. Where these sets of relationships within existing social networks are also among those made more difficult by the suicide, family members may seek out new spaces, including peer support groups such as (in the UK) Survivors of Bereavement by Suicide or Compassionate Friends. Indeed, peer-support programmes are found to have positive effects for survivors of sudden death or loss, and especially for survivors of suicide loss, perhaps because of the stigma within friend and family networks (Bartone *et al.* 2019). As a source of new connection, friendships and belonging, such groups can play a crucial role. Bereavement support groups can help in the reframing and understanding that form part of coping with suicide loss (Cammarata 2012, p.28), and in the moral recovery that the guilt, stigma and shame of suicide makes necessary.

In general, this ethical work of living with loss to suicide is not carried out alone; it is interactive and social, whether through families, friends, counselling or peer support groups. Re-casting an individual tragedy as a collective one, making social connections born of the kinship of grief, is necessary and de-isolating. Peer-support groups for survivors of suicide loss are paradoxical. I know myself from having heard hundreds of testimonies over ten years of monthly meetings that a circle of 15 or 25 people living with the most terrible loss and grief is a liberating space. It allows mutual recognition, sharing experiences, co-creating a language for suicide bereavement, work that makes possible the social competences needed to live in the world changed by suicide.

But of course, such groups are not for everyone. They may benefit most those with strong communication abilities, and their gender, age, class and ethnic composition will (and by impression do) create some barriers to access of this particular kind of social support for some individuals and families.

Family needs and HEIs

This overview of the likely needs of a family of a student who has died by suicide has implications for how higher education institutions can respond and support families after a suicide. It is difficult to be prescriptive and 'good practice' is only partly about systems and procedures, and, more significantly, about attitudes, empathy and sensitivity. This is the point at which my explanation of what family needs are, and what helps or does not, is best done through a personal account. I know the terrible grief that suicide brings because a number of years ago, my loving and much loved 23-year-old son, Jake, took his own life. I don't know whether the death of this talented young man with everything to live for (still in his adolescence despite being classified as adult), and with no known history of mental ill-health, could ultimately have been prevented; and, like all bereaved parents, I have faced indescribable guilt surrounding a death, the grief of which hunts like a wolf for blame and responsibility.

Jake was a postgraduate student at university. He faced all the pressures and uncertainties, the self-doubt and competition, that line that increasingly difficult path from childhood to adulthood, and which, today, make higher education institutions places of anxiety and depression (which were reported by a third of students in a survey by Pereira *et al.* 2019). Jake was strong, capable, a perfectionist and high achiever, and a determined party-goer. But behind this determined intelligence was a potential vulnerability, its extent unknown, I suspect, even to himself. At the end of his first year of university, his mother – to whom he was extraordinarily close – died after a six-year struggle with cancer. Of all the members of our family, Jake held himself up, saying at the time that the life of his remarkable mother showed him how valuable life was, not a moment of it was to be wasted. He was not going to allow himself to be ordinary. He had acquired a destiny, and with it something dangerous. Jake was dyslexic but drove himself to a first class degree in Politics, Philosophy and Economics, in the least bookish, most gregarious way, surrounding himself with bright, ambitious and rivalrous friends. Anything seemed possible; success was imperative.

He returned to university as a postgraduate. Within a month, he began to suffer from a depression that would deepen over the next three months. Like a soldier returning from the front line, he no longer had the close embrace of his combat unit. He became isolated; he isolated himself while maintaining an outward front of work and sociability. None of his friends, his brother, nor I, his father, could see the intense self-criticism, the rumination and guilt that was ravaging him inside. Nor would we in the least understand his growing conviction that he had irreparably damaged and permanently destroyed his potential life. Or if we heard these things, we couldn't make sense of them, nor of the black-and-white/all-or-nothing thinking that had overwhelmed his mind. And we certainly couldn't imagine the shame, the humiliation, the social defeat and suicidal worthlessness and hopelessness that was taking hold of this charming young man. Nothing is more haunting than the later realization that the person we so loved had already disengaged from the world of the living.

The help that Jake sought, the role of university counselling, primary care or mental health services, diagnosis, treatment and monitoring, the missed opportunities, the signs that did not warn, the communicative failures between services and with the family are subjects for a different discussion. Here I am reflecting on the family needs after suicide, specifically on what a university can do to support families such as mine.

Jake died close to where he lived in the university town. The news of his death came to us in the most awful manner. The police first contacted his younger brother, a first-year student in the same town, and from his student room he called me at home. The officer then departed, leaving my 20-year-old son unsupported until I arrived. The four-hour journey I made to that student room, the utter disbelief, confusion and emotional turmoil in which we gathered with my younger son's hall of residence flatmates, still resides in my mind and body. That night, I lay in police-arranged hotel accommodation wondering who could help us get through the next few days. The following day, my sister and brother-in-law joined us, accompanied by the police. We identified my son's body at the hospital, my legs and heart threatening to give way at any moment. I was handed an NHS booklet *Help is at Hand: A Resource for People Bereaved by Suicide and Other Sudden, Traumatic Death*,[1] but I wanted a person, perhaps a blue-light emergency rescue team that would save us from this traumatic calamity. But, in truth, we were on our own; there was no proactive contact from police, healthcare or the university, no family liaison. When my study window was broken by a would-be burglar, victim support contacted the family within 48 hours as mandated. After my son killed himself, there was nothing.[2]

In the days and weeks that followed, *Help is at Hand* proved to be an invaluable source of information and contacts as we put together our self-help survival kit. I tried to connect with those who had been in contact with Jake. His university counsellor (with whom I had spoken before)

---

1   A substantially revised 2021 version of this 2008 resource is now available as a Public Health England, National Suicide Prevention Alliance and Support After Suicide Partnership publication (PHE, NSPA and SASP 2021).

2   By 2019 in the UK, recognition of this anomaly and pressure for support for families bereaved by suicide, commensurate with the priority this had as an area of action in England's suicide prevention strategy (Department of Health 2012), had led to a commitment in the NHS *Long Term Plan* (2019) to roll out suicide bereavement services in all regions of the country. Proactive services providing immediate practical and emotional support to families are now being developed, funded by NHS England, supported by the lived-experience-led Support After Suicide Partnership (SASP) and implemented by local public health departments.

was too traumatized to be able to speak to me. The head of counselling stood in to represent her and explained the nature of the contact with Jake, the assessments of low risk, fear of his disengaging if contact with him was too proactive. My traumatized ears heard the GP's account of a muddled referral to a secondary services crisis support team and self-referral to a Priory Centre. A confused image of fragmented and incomplete nets of safety emerged, while discontinued prescriptions and a student Nightline card on his desk signalled help he could not reach.

I also wrote to academics at Jake's university who had known him as an undergraduate, informing them of his tragic death and the planned funeral. I wanted to have contact with those who knew him: teachers who had written shining references, saw his talent and recognized the unspeakable loss of his early death. I was deeply moved by the letters I received in response, telling me about their classroom and supervision encounters with Jake, and their affection for him. The recognizable images of my son, his 'vitality and spirit' in his classes, his 'indomitable energy' that these letters conveyed still bring tears to my eyes. That he was known, cared about and appreciated as 'one of the most eager and enthusiastic students I have ever taught', as one lecturer put it, mattered a great deal in those weeks following his death. Later, I received letters from Jake's undergraduate head of department and the university, but it was these warm personal messages from his teachers that meant the most.

It was two weeks before news reached his master's programme, and unclear lines of communication meant I never had meaningful contact with his most recent teachers or classmates (although I recall a phone call from the Centre director), that is, from those who were in contact with him during the period of his suicidal crisis, aspects of which Jake articulated in terms of his relationship to the course. I never received an account of missed tutorials, the character of supervisions, the concerns of his personal adviser (if he had one) or any sense of his diminished sense of connection or belonging within the course. I had sought contact with the master's programme, via student services, who told me that the convenors had been informed but 'it may be that they are unsure of the appropriateness of contacting you directly'. This is telling of the obstacles to communication between families and professionals I discuss below. More generally, the university responded to my queries, but was not proactive in its engagement with our family. The information that emerged did so ultimately via the coroner's inquest, where the student counsellor gave her witness testimony and heard mine, a deeply sad and distant encounter mediated by the coroner. My impression was of individual responses but an institution that was unprepared and unable to respond to family needs. That was a decade ago, and much has changed since.

In all of this, I was, of course, worried about my younger son who had suspended his studies at a different nearby university and returned home. Contact with his university counselling service to support him at distance and prepare for his return to study was important and helpful to him and me. I cannot honestly remember if anyone from Jake's university made the journey to his funeral, to gather with his many student friends and family. I know that if they had, and had found and spoken to me, I would have appreciated it and found it a comfort.

In the weeks to come at the university, it was Jake's fellow students and the student union that took the lead in responding to his suicide, and all that it meant, all the unanswered questions. In the midst of his grief and pain, Jake's younger brother began to organize student mental health awareness events honouring Jake in the ways that connected to his spirit. They set up an online organization with special mental health themed club nights and other events with posters, branded sweatshirts, took over space in student festivals to talk about depression and suicide, exhibited Jake's photographs and raised money for CALM (Campaign Against Living Miserably). These students reached out to our family, embraced us, carried the spirit of my son in a way that was healing; they merged with the family in a Facebook memorialization. In the months and years that followed, my son's university friends have joined, extended and strengthened our family network, enabling us to live with this loss, and supporting each other.

Family needs and university responses

So, what does our family experience suggest in terms of needs and how universities can meet them while remembering, of course, that this is just one case? Families grieving a suicide are thrown into painful confusion. Self-navigating through this is difficult, so immediate offers of practical and emotional support are important. This is not just the responsibility of the university, since the police and healthcare services are also involved, but the proactive contact from someone at the university in a family liaison role would be important. This might be the head of student counselling but could be others. The role would ensure lines of communication with families from student services and counselling, programme and course leads and student groups as appropriate to individual cases. There might be need for practical support in relation to student finance, handling accommodation and belongings, dealing with the press, or signposting to support for family members themselves (e.g. linking them to local suicide liaison services). This might include, for example, the needs of siblings who may be students in other universities (as in the case of my younger son) by facilitating contact with student services or academic departments. Beyond practical support, there is need for contact with those who knew and can speak about the young person as they were known and encountered. This is a necessary part of the immediate sense-making in relation to the tragic death.

Communication between universities and families may, however, be difficult for both parties, for reasons related to the character of loss from suicide. Families may have an urgent need to contact student services and staff to try to explain what happened, to gain information from those who were witness to the unfolding crisis or to hold people to account for not preventing this tragedy. University staff, taking on their own burden of responsibility – their own 'agent-regret' – and their own 'could-I-have-done-anything?' self-questioning, may understandably be terrified of contact from the family. Following a suicide, it is not just parents who experience guilt and self-blame, or who face the urgent need to preserve the self in face of the terror of culpability. After suicide, everybody has a propensity to feel responsible, thus to try to place themselves and their actions 'beyond reproach' in relation to the fate of the dead with whom their identities are entwined as family, friends, classmates, counsellors or tutors (Fincham *et al.* 2011; Langer, Scourfield and Fincham 2008). This may mean self-distancing from knowledge of the deceased ('we had no idea'; 'he seemed fine'; 'this could not have been foreseen'; 'must have been impulsive…'), or 'transfer[ring] the reasons for the suicide into a sphere outside their area of responsibility and control' (Langer *et al.* 2008, p.303). The difficulty can be that families and professionals may find themselves with different, even incommensurate, projects of moral recovery, and feel judged or blamed, even where no such sentiments exist.

There is another side to this. Everyone who knew and cared for my son is not just part of the narrative of why he killed himself or was not stopped, but also part of the recovery of his identity and memory from this calamity. As I have explained, the validation of my son's character, his talent, his sensitivity and intelligence by university staff and student friends was of great importance to me and my family, immediately and in the longer term. This recognition of the person of my son by the university is also recognition of the true tragedy that his death represents, and a sign of solidarity with our pain and suffering.

This is by no means so in all cases, but many families find in their loss an impulse to act for those who face the peril of suicide. There is a faithfulness to the tragic event (Kuan 2017) as families engage in fundraising, actions and campaigns on suicide prevention as a way to give meaning to a loss that threatens to be unbearable. There will be many opportunities for HEIs to engage families of students who have died in shaping their suicide prevention strategies and action plans, giving recognition to the too-often overlooked contribution and insight of lived experience of those bereaved by suicide. In my case, the impulse to do something was shared with my younger son's student friends. They and the student union took the lead, linking to national campaigns and charities in ways that could have had more engagement from the university staff. This is particularly important to ensure that the gains from awareness of suicide and promotion of support for students in crisis are maximized, while being aware of the risks associated with memorialization that might romanticize or normalize suicide. Unfortunately, I have never been contacted to discuss what happened to my son, what lessons could be learned or to contribute to the university's suicide prevention or postvention strategy.

Conclusion

This chapter has combined evidence on family needs following suicide and lived experience, to highlight ways in which higher education institutions can support families following the death of a student by suicide. These needs and support focus on immediate practical support, liaison to facilitate communication between families and HEI staff who knew their loved one, and support for individual family members, including siblings in other institutions. The chapter explores why such communication is sometimes difficult, but emphasizes the importance to families of both understanding the circumstances in which the person they grieve took their own life and of having their character and qualities recognized and articulated. Families may find engagement with student friends of the person they have lost and student bodies, such as the student union, helpful. Moves by the university to positively engage with families of students who have died by suicide in learning lessons and developing suicide prevention strategies may be appreciated and should be considered.

Author biography

David Mosse is Professor of Social Anthropology, SOAS University of London. He has published extensively on the anthropology of religion, environment and development. He is a Fellow of the British Academy. His current research and public engagement work focuses on mental health, crisis and suicide prevention in the UK and across the world.

References

Bartone, P.T., Bartone, J.V., Violanti, J.M. and Gileno, Z.M. (2019) Peer support services for bereaved survivors: a systematic review. *OMEGA – Journal of Death and Dying 80*, 1, 137–166.

Bell, J., Stanley, N., Mallon, S. and Manthorpe, J. (2012) Life will never be the same again: examining grief in survivors bereaved by young suicide. *Illness, Crisis & Loss 20*, 1, 49–68.

Cain, A.C. (2002) Children of suicide: the telling and the knowing. *Psychiatry: Interpersonal and Biological Processes 65*, 2, 124–136.

Cammarata, R.A. (2012) Stigma, Shame, and Guilt: Familial Relationship and Gender Differences in Suicide Survivors. Ph.D., Fielding Graduate University, California, United States.

Cvinar, J.G. (2005) Do suicide survivors suffer social stigma? A review of the literature. *Perspectives in Psychiatric Care 41*, 1, 14–21.

Das, V. (2015) *Affliction: Health, Disease, Poverty.* New York: Fordham University Press.

Department of Health (2012) *Preventing Suicide in England: A Cross-Government Outcomes Strategy to Save Lives.* London: HM Government, UK. Accessed on 01/07/20 at: www.gov. uk/government/publications/suicide-prevention-strategy-for-england

Doka, K. (1999) Disenfranchised grief. *Bereavement Care 18*, 3, 37–39.

Dunn, R.G. and Morrish-Vidners, D. (1995) The psychological and social experience of suicide survivors. *OMEGA – Journal of Death and Dying 18*, 3, 175–215.

Feigelman, W., Gorman, B.S. and Jordan, J.R. (2009) Stigmatization and suicide bereavement. *Death Studies 33*, 7, 591–608.

Fincham, B., Langer, S., Scourfield, J. and Shiner, M. (2011) *Understanding Suicide: A Sociological Autopsy.* London: Palgrave Macmillan UK.

Hanschmidt, F., Lehnig, F., Riedel-Heller, S.G. and Kersting, A. (2016) The stigma of suicide survivorship and related consequences – a systematic review. *PLoS One 11*, 9, e0162688.

Jordan, J.R. (2001) Is suicide bereavement different? A reassessment of the literature. *Suicide & Life-Threatening Behavior 31*, 1, 91–102.

Kuan, T. (2017) The problem of moral luck, anthropologically speaking. *Anthropological Theory 17*, 1, 30–59.

Langer, S., Scourfield, J. and Fincham, B. (2008) Documenting the quick and the dead: a study of suicide case files in a coroner's office. *The Sociological Review 56*, 2, 293–308.

Miers, D., Abbott, D. and Springer, P.R. (2012) A phenomenological study of family needs following the suicide of a teenager. *Death Studies 36*, 2, 118–133.

NHS (2019) *The NHS Long Term Plan.* Accessed on 13/04/21 at: www.longtermplan.nhs.uk/wp-content/uploads/2019/08/nhs-long-term-plan-version-1.2.pdf

Owens, C., Lambert, H., Lloyd, K. and Donovan, J. (2008) Tales of biographical disintegration: how parents make sense of their sons' suicides. *Sociology of Health & Illness 30*, 2, 237–254.

Pereira, S. Reay, K., Bottell, J., Walker, L. *et al.* (2019) *University Student Mental Health Survey 2018.* London: The Insight Network. Accessed on 01/07/20 at: www.theinsightnetwork.co.uk/uncategorized/university-student-mental-health-survey-2018

PHE, NSPA and SASP (2021) *Help is at hand: support after someone may have died by suicide.* Public Health England, National Suicide Prevention Alliance and Support After Suicide Partnership (March 2021 edition). Accessed on 03/07/21 at: https://supportaftersuicide.org.uk/wp-content/uploads/2020/04/HIAH_Booklet_2021_V5-1-2.pdf

Pitman, A.L., Stevenson, F., Osborn, D.P.J. and King, M.B. (2018) The stigma associated with bereavement by suicide and other sudden deaths: a qualitative interview study. *Social Science & Medicine 198*, 121–129.

Scott, H.R., Pitman, A., Kozhuharova, P. and Lloyd-Evans, B. (2020) A systematic review of studies describing the influence of informal social support on psychological wellbeing in people bereaved by sudden or violent causes of death. *BMC Psychiatry 20*, 1, 265.

Sugrue, J.L., McGilloway, S. and Keegan, O. (2014) The experiences of mothers bereaved by suicide: an exploratory study. *Death Studies 38*, 2, 118–124.

CHAPTER 19

Student Suicide

Responding to the Needs of Bereaved Students

DEIRDRE FLYNN

Overview

The chapter will focus on the needs of students and the university response to student suicide. It is divided into two sections:

1. *Student needs.* This section identifies which individuals or groups of students in the university are potentially impacted by a student death and explores their differing needs.

2. *University response.* This section outlines key factors to be considered in the higher education context, sets out the objectives of a death response plan (DRP) and suggests ways of supporting students in the immediate aftermath and beyond.

Introduction

A student's death by suicide irrevocably changes many lives. The impact on the university community is considerable and can be long lasting, and the way the university responds to student death may have a profound impact on the recovery of affected students (Norton and Harper 2007). The only in-depth UK study on student suicide to date showed that students, parents and staff experienced university responses which ranged from 'excellent' to 'woefully inadequate', with few students reporting positive experiences (Stanley *et al.* 2007). Many HEIs have death response plans (DRPs) (Callahan and Fox 2008), but critically, not all are informed by an understanding of the varying impacts and the needs of students after a suicide. Drawing on relevant research literature and clinical experience, this chapter seeks to address this gap.

Throughout the text, key points are illustrated and reinforced with vignettes representing many of the common themes and experiences encountered by myself and colleagues in clinical practice with students impacted by suicide. In the first section, the needs of bereaved students will be explored. The chapter will then focus on key factors institutions might consider in their response.

1. Bereaved student needs

Student bereavement has been labelled the 'silent epidemic' (Neimeyer *et al.* 2008), with students described as 'the forgotten grievers' (LaGrand 1985). The number of students on campus experiencing bereavement (in the previous 12 months) has been estimated at between 22 and 30 per cent (Balk 2008). Despite this high incidence, and its considerable impact on their personal, academic and social lives (Balk 2008), student bereavement is under-studied, with little research exploring how university students experience grief or what types of interventions are effective (Servaty-Seib and Taub 2010). Specifically, there is scant literature on student bereavement following the death of a fellow student (Owens and Garlough 2007), whether from suicide or other causes. This dearth of research suggests student bereavement may be 'disenfranchised', meaning the loss of the griever is not recognized.

> My mother won't let me even talk about it... She never liked her...she says suicide is wrong...I mean, wrong?

> He wasn't even my boyfriend...just one of the gang...but I miss him so much...I need to talk about him.

University can be a time of close and important relationships when students, especially those living on campus, build deep emotional connections and loyalties (Griffin 2007). The death of a fellow student can be a life-altering experience, similar to losing a family member (Neimeyer *et al.* 2008). However, the grief of young adults who are not spouses or cohabitating partners may be overlooked (Doka 1999). The extent of the impact may be minimized because students are often young and there is a perception they will 'get over it'. Neither the level of grief nor the duration of the impact may be fully appreciated by family, friends or university staff. The extent and depth of emotion, as well as the extended nature of grief felt, may even surprise those who are affected.

> Three years on...it still feels part of daily life...too painful to remember...

Identifying who is affected

The key to identifying who is impacted by a student death may depend on the deceased's academic and social connections, face-to-face and online. The impact will also be shaped by how widely the circumstances of the death are known. A suicide may impact on students who did not personally know or have a close relationship with the deceased. Where the student was well known on campus or had a leadership role, the repercussions will be intensified (Levine 2008). Students are often surprised by the intensity of their feelings for someone they did not know personally but who held a recognizable role or status on campus. This can engender a particular kind of guilt that students find hard to comprehend.

> I feel guilty for feeling so much...is that wrong?

Like any bereavement, the experience is shaped by the meaning or closeness of the relationship and the role of the deceased in the bereaved student's life (Servaty-Seib and Taub 2010). Close friends, romantic partners, flatmates, classmates, lab partners, students in the same clubs and societies or sports teams may be impacted in different ways. Zinner (1985) suggests there are 'levels of survivorship', ranging from primary to quaternary depending on the relationship to the deceased. Table 19.1 adapts Zinner's model as a useful framework for identifying students who may be impacted, and Cerel et al.'s (2014) ideas as to the level of the impact. They propose four different levels of impact along a continuum: from exposed to suicide to suicide bereaved long term. Identifying the level of impact as well as the relationship allows for a more targeted response.

Some research suggests what seems intuitive: that closeness to the deceased and level of exposure to the trauma of the death will be directly correlated with more painful experiences of bereavement. For example, following a suicide, flatmates, whether in campus accommodation or in the private rented sector, may require special support (Stanley et al. 2007). This applies particularly where students themselves are involved in the discovery of the body (Parrish and Tunkle 2005) and are required to attend an inquest (Stanley et al. 2007).

> It was awful...[finding him in his bedroom]...I thought I got over this. It comes back. I can still see him there...

Table 19.1: Level of survivorship and level of impact

Level of survivorship	University examples	Level of impact
Primary: present or past significant relationship with the deceased	Romantic partner, close friends / close classmates / close housemates These students / others may or may not have known the deceased was struggling. They may have received final texts / voicemail messages or may have witnessed the suicide	Exposed and affected by the suicide and bereaved short term May be bereaved long term
Secondary: intermediate level of interaction with the deceased – knew the deceased but in relation to specific activities	Members of the same clubs / societies Played a team sport together Lab partner Classmate Housemates / student residence Connected on social media Isolated students who depended on the relationship with the deceased	Exposed and affected by the suicide May be bereaved short term
Tertiary: little or no interaction with the deceased but share meaningful identification and experiences	Vulnerable students struggling with their own mental health issues Students who have experienced previous losses Minority group membership	Exposed and may be affected by the suicide
Quaternary	Classmates of larger classes Other students at the university	Exposed to suicide

While the shock to close friends is easily understandable, the impact on students not closely connected but who played a role in the student's life may not be fully understood by staff. Classmates for instance are not a homogenous group, will not all have the same relationship with the deceased (Dyregrov, Wikander and Vigerust 1999) and may not necessarily be the students who are most affected by the death. Similarly, the loss of a peer can be keenly felt if that peer was present for important routines, such as eating together or going to the library or gym. Such connections may possibly go unrecognized and unacknowledged.

How are students impacted?

Reactions to bereavement may be physical, emotional, cognitive or behavioural and may intensify when the death is sudden or traumatic.

> When he disappeared, I knew he was gone; I was certain; but I kept on searching for him. I was rushing around everywhere and then I'd sob and cry. I felt I shouldn't be so upset...look at his family; they're the ones to be crying!

Shock and disbelief are common initial reactions, followed by emotional distress. Those affected may experience impaired memory and may be unable to manage routine tasks.

Emotional wellbeing

Suicide raises the question 'why?' for all those who knew the person, but particularly for those who were close to the deceased (Stanley *et al.* 2007). In the case of death by suicide, students often engage in an endless search for answers, asking questions such as: 'Could it have been prevented?', 'What might I have done?' and 'Did I miss warning signs?' Feelings of responsibility and guilt can be pervasive (Bell *et al.* 2012).

> I feel so guilty I hadn't been in contact with her...it's just so sad she had everything going for her...I still can't believe she made this decision...I keep thinking maybe I could have done more to prevent her...

> I keep seeing images of her...and thinking about her, I just can't believe it.

Anger towards the individual and feeling rejected or abandoned are also usual, as are feelings of isolation (Grant *et al.* 2013). Some students feel angry that the institution, student services or family did not do more to prevent it (Levine 2008). Others may feel angry at God and feel that religion has little to offer at this time. These questions and feelings can be intense, difficult to process and all-consuming.

> I need to be busy all the time...if I stop, I can't bear the thoughts.

In some circumstances, questioning why the death took place, in combination with the pain of grief, may contribute to or lead to suicidal ideation or suicide (Bell *et al.* 2015).

> Is this just accepted that suicide is part of life...part of student life?

> They tell us to mind our mental health, but if we take time off to see a counsellor, it can be viewed as a sign of weakness.

Students' sense of guilt and anger may be compounded if the deceased communicated something of their suicidal intent to them. In a recent

Irish study (Malone 2013), 70 per cent of young males communicated something about their suicidal intent in the month before they died. Most of these overt or covert disclosures were to young peers or siblings, who may be very distressed that they missed the signs or should have responded differently.

Academic performance

Grieving students may find it hard to concentrate or focus on their academic work. They may stop attending classes or attend sporadically because academic work and exams seem less important, or they avoid learning spaces which remind them of the deceased. Conversely, some students cope by immersing themselves in study (Flynn 2014).

While it has been suggested that bereavement can impact a student's academic performance, which may result in attrition, further studies are required. Servaty-Seib and Hamilton (2006) found that grieving students were at risk of attaining lower GPAs (grade point averages) than their peers during the term in which the bereavement occurred, although this pattern was not as evident in the subsequent term. In Flynn's (2014) study, staff from a particular department reported that the academic results of students bereaved by a sudden death of a fellow student in their final year were not impacted. Staff felt the students were very resilient, although the students reported that they worried about their academic performance and would have liked more support. Staff from other departments reported organizing for students to defer examinations and/or withdraw for the year following deaths of fellow students.

> ...it is good to have people around me who know but sometimes it feels like I am wearing a big sign advertising my grief and sometimes I just can't do any work.

> I can't eat, I can't sleep, I can't do anything.

2. University response to student needs
Key considerations within the HE context

As already illustrated, the responses of students may vary greatly and be complicated by the nature of the death. In responding to the needs of students, universities must consider suicide contagion, partnership with students around their developmental needs and preferences, cultural factors, best practice guidelines and bereavement theory. Each of these will now be explored through the use of key points that can be used to focus the efforts of institutions in developing their response to students' needs.

- *Key point 1: Contagion prevention should be a key aim of any response.* Suicide contagion has been identified as a phenomenon among students (Stanley *et al.* 2007). Levine (2008) suggests an extended focus on suicides could activate emotional distress among those who had previously experienced psychological difficulties, leading to contagion. An Irish study (Malone 2013) suggested that up to 10 per cent of suicides might be part of a cluster and this could be as high as 30–50 per cent in those aged under 21 years. The first suicide in a cluster appears to have a triggering effect on individuals with a pre-existing vulnerability (e.g. depression or history of suicidal behaviour) and among those who have similar characteristics to the person who died (Irish Association of Suicidology and Samaritans 2009). In one study, 10 per cent of young adults reported they had previously attempted to take their own life and 12 per cent had deliberately hurt themselves (Dooley *et al.* 2020). Therefore, contagion prevention should be a key aim of any HE response (see Chapter 9). This aspect needs to focus on individual students, groups and the whole student body. A coordinated team with a compassionate, thorough and non-escalating approach to student needs is the most effective (Levine 2008). The role of social media in contributing to contagion also needs to be considered and addressed in postvention responses, both online and face-to-face (Cimini and Rivero 2013).

- *Key point 2: Response should embody a collaborative partnership model with students.* The suicide of a fellow student can shatter a young adult's sense of invulnerability, their world view and their self-worth (Janoff-Bulman 1992), and may result in an underlying questioning of the meaning of their lives (Neimeyer *et al.* 2008). Students may need help in processing their thoughts and feelings. However, many do not seek help. In a national study of youth mental health in Ireland, 40 per cent said they did not talk to anyone about their problems and 25 per cent said they needed professional support in the last year but hadn't used it (Dooley *et al.* 2020). This may relate to the key developmental task of establishing independence and a perception that they need to solve problems themselves (Stanley *et al.* 2007). Given students' expressed preferences to do certain things themselves, and a desire for support from the university following a student's death (Flynn 2014), the university's response needs to embody a collaborative partnership model with the students to respect their desire for autonomy and their need for support. Students' preferred sources of support are friends (63%) and parents (49%) (Dooley *et al.* 2020), so encouraging them to activate these following a suicide is advisable, as is assisting peers to support other students.

- *Key point 3: Cultural and religious sensitivities of students need to be considered.* For decades, mental illness and suicide were taboo topics in the western world. This has begun to change but we need to be mindful that some students, including international students, may have cultural and religious beliefs which perceive the suicide, and explicit disclosure of a student's death by suicide, as shaming of the individual. This can be very upsetting for them and further complicate their grief response. To ensure that the cultural and religious sensitivities of all students are considered, the membership of the university response team should ideally reflect and be sensitive to the diversity of the student population (Levine 2008).

- *Key point 4: Responses should be timed, tiered and targeted.* Although the death of a fellow student by suicide can be extremely distressing for all concerned, bereavement is increasingly seen as a stressful event which most people have the resilience to manage. Generally, 10–20 per cent of those who are bereaved require clinical interventions (Bonanno 2004). It is thought that the support of family, friends, peers and volunteers helps the majority, while clinical services should be provided for those who request support and those at risk of complicated grief (Schut and Stroebe 2010). Those bereaved by suicide are vulnerable to complicated grief, to suicidal ideation and possibly to suicide (Mitchell *et al.* 2005). Grief is perceived as 'complicated' when the bereaved experience grief-related symptoms which impair functioning for at least six months (Zhang, El-Jawahri and Prigerson 2006). Symptoms include separation distress, loneliness, preoccupation with thoughts of the deceased and symptoms of traumatic distress (Lobb *et al.* 2010).

Best practice guidelines (National Institute for Clinical Excellence 2004) suggest a timed, tiered and targeted response to the bereaved. Adopting these, HEIs would:

- provide information on the process of bereavement and sources of support for all those impacted (within the HEI this needs to be done within two to three weeks of the death, rather than the recommended six to eight weeks)

- harness support of staff and peers

- identify and provide clinical services for those at risk of complicated grief and for those who request it.

- *Key point 5: Response should offer opportunities for appropriate remembrance and connection.* The university response is informed by theories and models of bereavement. Traditional models of bereavement, such as Kübler-Ross's five stage model (Kübler-Ross 1969) and Worden's tasks model (Worden 1982), suggest that the bereaved engage in grief work as a way of processing grief. University responses informed by these models may emphasize the provision of counselling or pastoral support for students. Postmodern theories, like the continuing bonds model (Klass, Silverman and Nickman 1996) and meaning reconstruction model (Neimeyer *et al.* 2010), are less prescriptive about grief work and the need to disengage from the deceased. They emphasize maintaining connections with the deceased through a variety of actions and rituals which affirm the ongoing significance of the deceased in their lives. University responses informed by these models may focus on memorials and/or posthumous award ceremonies. Such initiatives need to be underpinned by an understanding of the unintended part that memorials can potentially play in copycat suicide and suicide contagion. Careful and sensitive consideration of how to honour the loss of a peer and friend without unintentionally glorifying or romanticizing the death is important (see Chapter 23).

Death response plan/team

A proactive university death response plan (DRP) should be capable of focusing on individuals, groups and community needs simultaneously (Cimini and Rivero 2013) and over time. Key objectives might include:

- acknowledging the deceased

- recognizing the loss for students, staff and the university community

- ensuring a compassionate response for those seriously affected by the death

- ensuring a timely, coordinated and consistent response

- harnessing students' support networks

- identifying and reaching out to those requiring assistance and providing a targeted response

- minimizing the risk of suicide contagion

- minimizing the possible negative impact on academic performance and student retention. (Flynn 2019)

Universities which respond most effectively adopt a cross-functional, multicultural death response team (DRT), with a designated leader/ coordinator and assigned roles (Levine 2008; Streufert 2004) which operate from the day of the suicide until after the inquest. The team must communicate across a range of stakeholders internally, and sometimes externally, ensuring staff and students are mobilized and the response is appropriate and meets the needs of all students. In mobilizing staff, the team should be mindful that some will have known the deceased and will themselves be affected (see Chapter 20). The DRT is responsible for identifying impacted students who need support, assigning their care to staff and coordinating delivery.

The HEI should assume a proactive role in the immediate aftermath of a suicide, informing students and contacting individuals affected to offer support, rather than waiting for them to make contact (Stanley *et al.* 2007). Ongoing support should embody a collaborative partnership model with students. This can be done by agreeing tasks to be done by the students immediately, such as identifying the deceased student's university connections, organizing transport to funerals and organizing class or group debriefing meetings which might be facilitated by staff. Subsequently students might be involved in planning memorials, contributing to a review of the university response and suggesting recommendations for policy or practice changes.

Immediate support for 'involved' students

Immediate practical and emotional support is essential for those who were emotionally closest to the deceased and for students involved in any way by proximity to the event and the immediate response (e.g. discovering the deceased's body, calling emergency services). Both groups are likely to be in shock. Stanley *et al.*'s research (2007) indicates it is important that staff assess whether these students are taking on responsibilities which should be held by the HEI, or if they need assistance from student services staff. Some of these students may benefit from 'psychological first aid' (Brymer *et al.* 2006). The literature stresses the importance of student services personnel going to the students to deliver interventions, especially for male students, rather than expecting them to come to counselling services (Norton and Harper 2007). Stanley *et al.* (2007) also found that students in private rented accommodation did not get the same degree of support after a student suicide as those on campus.

Notification of the death/notification meetings for classmates and other students

Classmates and other students who knew the deceased need accurate information, where possible within 24 hours. Social media is often the first source of information today and it is difficult, if not impossible, for institutions to control how the news may initially emerge. Once the university verifies the initial report of a student's death, there remains no substitute for bringing classmates and others together in their discrete groupings and conveying appropriate information face-to-face as soon as is practically possible. This face-to-face contact is key to supporting students emotionally and psychologically, managing misinformation and rumour, and identifying individuals or groups of students who need further intervention. The support of familiar staff who also knew the deceased is important to the students. Informing classes or other groups is therefore best done by a head of school or dean of residence, with the support of chaplains, counsellors or other members of student services familiar with responding to distressed students.

It is crucial for students that the death is acknowledged and not perceived as being 'brushed under the carpet'. This can be difficult to manage given some of the sensitivities that surround suicide. It is recommended that the information given confirms the death, shows that the institution mourns the loss, and gives clear messages encouraging students who may be struggling to reach out to others or to use student services. It is critical to highlight that suicidal thoughts and feelings can be addressed by asking for support and explaining that this is available, and that the university is committed to helping students with their wellbeing and mental health. The devastation a suicide leaves in its wake should be acknowledged, but not dramatized; tone and nuance in the delivery of information matters.

Academic considerations

In the event of the news of a sudden student death becoming known and being verified by the university, it is advised that classes are cancelled for the remainder of the day. Consideration should be given to deferring any immediate academic deadlines with a new submission date issued as soon as possible. Rescheduling of any immediate examinations may need to be considered. Students may benefit from being given the option to sit these later during the current examination period or at the time of the resits, without penalty implications. If bereaved students start missing classes and academic deadlines, it is helpful when academic staff who know them can reach out, discuss what is happening and enquire if they might benefit from a referral to student health or counselling. Some bereaved students may need to defer their annual examinations and/or seek permission to defer their academic year. This may be particularly relevant for students with pre-existing vulnerabilities. A university be-reavement leave policy for students needs to underpin the DRP (Liew and Servaty-Seib 2020).

Out of term

The needs of students must be addressed when a death of a fellow student occurs out of term, despite the logistical challenges this may present. Phone calls, emails and online video sessions over secure plat-forms should be offered by the response team and academic staff known to the students to provide a compassionate and supportive response.

Acknowledgements

Students appreciate it if each lecturer or tutor of a class/lab which the student used to attend acknowledges the death before commencing, even if several months have elapsed since the class last met. This can consist of offering sympathy and/or having a minute's silence in mem-ory of the deceased student. Students notice if no acknowledgement is made; they do not want staff to act 'as if it never happened'. Attendance at funerals, memorial services, presentation of posthumous awards or certificates of attendance at graduation are important acknowledgments of the ongoing significance of the deceased and opportunities for re-membrance and connection.

Information and self-help

Students need information about the bereavement process in general, and specifically about suicide bereavement, as well as details about sources of support and where to go for help. It is advisable that this information be provided to them two to three weeks after the event as they often do not retain such information if it is given at the time of the incident (Flynn 2014). Counselling services should also have this infor-mation readily available on websites. This may help students who may be reluctant to seek help because they feel their issues do not warrant counselling, or are anxious about stigma and possible consequences of disclosing mental health issues on future academic or career prospects (Stanley *et al.* 2007).

Outreach

Those close to the deceased appreciate being asked by staff from time to time how they are doing. They want and expect staff to be made aware of their friend's death and the nature of their relationship (Flynn 2014). These brief conversations with staff show students that their grief is understood, and they provide opportunities for staff to signpost struggling students to services.

Peer support

Peers are the preferred source of support for students, particularly in relation to the death of a friend (Balk 1997). However, students' limited knowledge and understanding of the bereavement process and related skills may restrict their ability to support their peers (Balk 1997, 2011; Fajgenbaum 2007; Griffin 2007; LaGrand 1985). On the other hand, some students may be well placed to offer support. Experience of bereavement can lead to personal growth and increased compassion and empathy (Mathews and Servaty-Seib 2007). Nevertheless, few universities provide peer support programmes for bereaved students (Fajgenbaum 2007). This gap could be addressed with training and the development of specific peer support models, such as the American 'Actively Moving Forward' support network for bereaved students (AMF 2020). To harness peer support, class and students' union representatives should be given a role on the DRT and be invited to attend meetings. Annual bereavement groups for students, facilitated by chaplains and counsellors, are also a useful way of harnessing peer support and they can assist with meaning-making and fostering a connection with lost loved ones (Hedtke 2012).

> It was transformative for a student I was seeing whose grief was unacknowledged by her family...it was validated in the group, many of whom, I think, didn't feel validated in their grief. (Student counsellor)

Timed, tiered and targeted responses

Students experience various levels of emotional distress after a suicide. In the immediate aftermath, some may need individual or group psychological support. It is advisable that this is provided by appropriately trained staff to ensure the interventions contain rather than escalate distress (Levine 2008).

Later, students may want assistance in processing the suicide and its impact on them. Meetings with university chaplains can be supportive, especially for students whose faith is important to them. For some, the level of distress can be considerable: 'unanswered questions and searching for reasons, combined with feelings of personal responsibility and guilt, brings about a torment that cannot be communicated' (Bell et al. 2012, p.63). Using Neimeyer's meaning-making framework (Neimeyer et al. 2010), student counsellors can help students to:

- make sense of the suicide

- express their feelings of guilt or self-blame

- reframe any sense that the suicide wouldn't have happened if they had done something differently

- explore issues of stigma and shame

- explore healthy ways of connecting with the deceased.

They can also develop strategies for managing any painful, overwhelming feelings and thoughts (Bell et al. 2012) and assess for suicidal ideation, intent or potential contagion and activate referrals if multidisciplinary support is required.

Some students may experience prolonged grief disorder, for which a 16-week treatment model such as complicated grief treatment (CGT) is recommended (Shear and Gribbin Bloom 2017). If students report ongoing distress, difficulties with sleeping, eating or studying, or they can't stop thinking about their deceased fellow student, staff are advised to refer students to student health or counselling. While grief is not perceived as complicated until six months after the death, students experiencing these symptoms for more than six to eight weeks would benefit from a referral due to the potential impact on their academic performance, social life and emotional wellbeing.

Conclusion

When a student dies by suicide the lives of many are changed irrevocably, in an instant. This chapter has sought to describe the multifaceted and individual needs of students and to map out a sensitive and considered university response which can go some way to alleviating the pain of bereavement. Every student death is both tragic and unique, and the needs of those who are bereaved will always be complex. It is hoped that the suggestions and interventions outlined may offer a framework for a compassionate and effective response, based on research and best practice which ensure the grief of the bereaved student is acknowledged and their individual needs are met.

Author biography

Dr Deirdre Flynn is Director of the Student Counselling, Student Learning Development and Student2Student Services at Trinity College Dublin, the University of Dublin. Deirdre's doctoral research, 'Experiences of Sudden Student Death: A Narrative Enquiry', focused on the experiences of students, staff and parents of the university's response to student deaths.

References

AMF (2020) [Online]. Accessed on 19/11/20 at: https://healgrief.org/actively-moving-forward/college-student-grief

Balk, D. (1997) Death, bereavement and college students: a descriptive analysis. *Mortality: Promoting the Interdisciplinary Study of Death and Dying 2*, 3, 207–220.

Balk, D. (2008) Grieving: 22 to 30 percent of all college students. *New Directions for Student Services 121*, 5–14.

Balk, D. (2011) *Helping the Bereaved College Student*. New York: Springer Publishing Company.

Bell, J., Stanley, N., Mallon, S. and Manthorpe, J. (2012) Life will never be the same again: examining grief in survivors bereaved by suicide. *Illness, Crisis and Loss 20*, 49–68.

Bell, J., Stanley, N., Mallon, S. and Manthorpe, J. (2015) Insights into the processes of suicide contagion: narratives from young people bereaved by suicide. *Suicidology Online 6*, 43–52.

Bonanno, G. (2004) Loss, trauma and human resilence: have we underestimated the human capacity to thrive after extremely aversive events? *American Psychologist 59*, 1, 20–28.

Brymer, M., Jacobs, A., Layne, C., Pynoos, R. *et al.* (2006) *Psychological First Aid: Field Operations Guide* (2nd edn). National Child Traumatic Stress Network and National Center for PTSD.

Callahan, C. and Fox, E. (2008) Student death protocols: a practitioner's perspective. *New Directions for Student Services 121*, 87–95.

Cerel, J., McIntosh, J.L., Neimeyer, R.A., Maple, M. and Marshall, D. (2014) The continuum of 'survivorship': definitional issues in the aftermath of suicide. *Suicide and Life-Threatening Behavior: The American Association of Suicidology 44*, 591–600.

Cimini, M.D. and Rivero, E.M. (2013) Postsuicide intervention as a prevention tool: developing a comprehensive campus response to suicide and related risk. *New Directions Student Services 141*, 83–96.

Doka, K. (1999) Disenfranchised grief. *Bereavement Care 18*, 3, 37–39.

Dooley, B., O'Connor, C., Fitzergald, A. and O'Reilly, A. (2020) *My World Survey 2: The National Study of Youth Mental Health in Ireland*. Dublin: University College Dublin School of Psychology and Jigsaw, the National Centre for Youth Mental Health.

Dyregrov, A., Wikander, A. and Vigerust, S. (1999) Sudden death of a classmate and friend: adolescent perception of support from their school. *School of Psychology International 20*, 191–208.

Fajgenbaum, D. (2007) College Student Bereavement: University Responses, Programs and Policies and Recommendations for Improvement. Human Science Honours Thesis, Georgetown University.

Flynn, D. (2014) Experiences of Sudden Student Death: A Narrative Inquiry. Ed. D., University of Bristol.

Flynn, D. (2019) Student death and the university response. *University & College Counselling 7*, 4, 24–29.

Grant, A., Haire, J., Biley, F. and Stone, B. (eds) (2013) *Our Encounters with Suicide*. Ross-on-Wye: PCCS Books.

Griffin, W. (2007) Residence Life: Responding to Loss of Life. In R. Cintron, E. Taylor Weathers and K. Garlough (eds) *College Student Death: Guidance for a Caring Campus*. Lanham, MD: University Press of America.

Hedtke, L. (2012) *Bereavement Support Groups: Breathing Life into the Stories of the Dead*. Chargin Falls, OH. Taos Institute Publications.

Irish Association of Suicidology and Samaritans (2009) *Media Guidelines for Reporting Suicide and Self-Harm*. Dublin: Irish Association of Suicidology and Samaritans.

Janoff-Bulman, R. (1992) *Shattered Assumptions: Towards a New Psychology of Trauma*. New York: Free Press.

Klass, D., Silverman, P. and Nickman, S. (1996) *Continuing Bonds: New Understandings of Grief*. Washington, DC: Taylor Francis.

Kübler-Ross, E. (1969) *On Death and Dying*. New York: The Macmillian Company.

LaGrand, L. (1985) College Student Loss and Response. In E. Zinner (ed.) *Coping with Death on Campus*. San Francisco: Jossey-Bass.

Levine, H. (2008) Suicide and its impact on campus. *New Directions for Student Services 121*, 63–76.

Liew, C.H. and Servaty-Seib, H.L. (2020) College students' feedback on a student bereavement leave policy. *Journal of Student Affairs Research and Practice 57*, 1, 55–68.

Lobb, E., Kristjanson, K.J., Aoun, S.M., Monterosso, L., Halkett, G.K.B. and Davies, A. (2010) Predictions of complicated grief: a systemic review of empirical studies. *Death Studies 34*, 673–698.

Malone, K. (2013) *Suicide in Ireland 2003–2008*. Dublin: St Vincents University Hospital, University College Dublin, 3Ts, National Office for Suicide Prevention and the National Lottery.

Mathews, L. and Servaty-Seib, H. (2007) Hardiness and grief in a sample of bereaved college students. *Death Studies 31*, 3, 183–204.

Mitchell, A., Kim, Y., Prigerson, H. and Mortimer, M. (2005) Complicated grief and suicidal ideation in adult survivors of suicide. *Suicide and Life Threatening Behaviour 35*, 498–506.

National Institute for Clinical Excellence (NICE) (2004) *Guidance on Cancer Services: Improving Supportive and Palliative Care for Adults with Cancer.* London: NICE.

Neimeyer, R., Burke, L., Mackay, M. and van Dyke Stringer, J. (2010) Grief therapy and the reconstruction of meaning: from principles to practice. *Journal of Contemporary Psychotherapy 40*, 73–83.

Neimeyer, R., Laurie, A., Mehta, T., Hardison, H. and Currier, J. (2008) Lessons of loss and meaning-making in bereaved college students. *New Directions for Student Services 121*, 27–39.

Norton, K. and Harper, S. (2007) When a Student Athlete Dies: Dealing with Death in College Athletics. In R. Cintron, E. Taylor Weathers and K. Garlough (eds) *College Student Death: Guidance for a Caring Campus.* Lanham, MD: University Press of America.

Owens, J. and Garlough, K. (2007) College Student Death Policies. In R. Cintron, E. Taylor Weathers and K. Garlough (eds) *College Student Death: Guidance for a Caring Campus.* Lanham, MD: University Press of America.

Parrish, M. and Tunkle, J. (2005) Clinical challenges following an adolescent's death by suicide: bereavement issues faced by family, friends, schools, and clinicians. *Clinical Social Work Journal 33*, 81.

Schut, H. and Stroebe, M. (2010) Effects of support counselling and therapy before and after the loss: can we really help bereaved people? *Psychologica Belgica 50*, 89–102.

Servaty-Seib, H.L. and Hamilton, L.A. (2006) Educational performance and persistence of bereaved college students. *Journal of College Student Development 4*, 2, 225–234.

Servaty-Seib, H. and Taub, D. (2010) Bereavement and college students: the role of counselling psychology. *The Counselling Psychologist 38*, 7, 947–975.

Shear, M.K. and Gribbin Bloom, C. (2017) Complicated grief treatment: an evidence-based approach to grief therapy. *Rational-Emotive and Cognitive-Behaviour Therapy 35*, 1, 6–25.

Stanley, N., Mallon, S., Bell, J., Hilton, S. and Manthorpe, J. (2007) *Responses and Prevention in Student Suicide* (RaPSS). Preston: PAPYRUS.

Streufert, B. (2004) Death on campuses: common postvention strategies in higher education. *Death Studies 28*, 151–172.

Worden, W. (1982) *Grief Counselling and Grief Therapy.* New York: Springer Publishing Co.

Zhang, B., El-Jawahri, A. and Prigerson, H. (2006) Update on bereavement research: evidence-based guidelines for the diagnosis and treatment of complicated bereavement. *Journal of Palliative Medicine 9*, 1188–1203.

Zinner, E. (1985) Group Survivorship: A Model and Case Study Application. In E. Zinner (ed.) *Coping with Death on Campus.* San Francisco: Jossey-Bass.

CHAPTER 20

Responding to the Needs of Staff Impacted by a Student Suicide

HILARY CAUSER

Overview

The purpose of this chapter is to:

- explore the experiences of professional workers who are exposed to a death by suicide because of their job role

- report the experiences and needs of staff at two UK universities following a student death by suicide

- provide guidance in responding to staff needs following a student death by suicide.

Introduction

Staff at higher education institutions (HEIs) and further education institutions (FEIs) may be impacted by a student suicide either because they knew the student prior to their death, or because they undertook tasks relating to the suicide in the aftermath. In both instances, the impact may affect staff across a range of departments and job roles. Research estimates that 135 people are impacted to some extent by each death by suicide (Cerel *et al.* 2018). This figure acknowledges that wider networks of people are affected, in addition to bereaved family members and close friends. When a young person dies, the number of people impacted might be higher due to wider social networks in their physical and online communities (Berman 2011).

In the year ending July 2017, at least 95 higher education students in

England and Wales died by suicide (ONS 2018a). It is difficult to know how accurate this figure is, however. Part-time students may be identified as being employed and their death recorded by an occupation other than that of student (Hawton *et al.* 2012; Stanley *et al.* 2009). The use of open or narrative conclusions by coroners' offices may 'hide' some deaths by suicide (Gunnell *et al.* 2013). Lack of clarity around student status at the time of death, particularly if a suicide occurs during a planned leave of absence due to ill health, may exclude the death from the figures (NUS Disabled Students 2016). Therefore, the figure of 95 student deaths by suicide is likely to be an underestimation. Whilst we know that this figure was lower than the age-related general population (Gunnell *et al.* 2020), the most recent available figures show that the rates of death by suicide per 100,000 for 15–19-year-olds increased during the years 2010 to 2017 (ONS 2018b). Consequently, we can tentatively suggest that this annual figure of 95 deaths may also have increased in actual terms. Multiplying those 135 impacted people by the 95 student suicide deaths produces a figure of up to 12,825 people who perceive themselves to be exposed to, affected by or bereaved by a university student death by suicide in England and Wales in just one year. Lack of research in this area means it is not currently known how they may experience the effects of that exposure. For HEIs and FEIs to plan and deliver effective postvention support, they need to know who to support and what their needs are.

To develop an understanding of staff needs, this chapter first presents findings from a systematic review of the experiences of health, social care and education professionals following the death by suicide of a client, service user, patient or school student (Causer *et al.* 2019). It then focuses on the experiences of staff in UK HEIs after a student death by suicide. The qualitative accounts of 19 staff members, across diverse job roles in two UK universities, were subject to a thematic analysis and bring first person experiences to light. Staff members' experiences are revealed and explored within the themes of 'perceptions of impact', 'undertaking tasks', 'perceptions of needs' and 'experiences of support'. The chapter concludes with key points and recommendations that may inform HEIs and FEIs of the kinds of needs that staff may have, and ways of responding to meet those needs and resources that may prove helpful are signposted. The limitations of current knowledge underpinning UK HEI postvention design and delivery are acknowledged.

The experiences of health, social care and education professionals following a death by suicide

There are considerable gaps in our knowledge concerning the impact of death by suicide amongst wider networks, such as people who are affected because of their job role (Causer *et al.* 2019). A review of the literature revealed that there were no published studies that explore postvention in UK HEIs or FEIs, and none that explore the experience of staff members after a student death by suicide (Causer 2020). However, the review identified that there was a small but significant body of qualitative literature that explored the experiences of other professionals following the suicide of a client, patient, service user or school student. Given the similarities in role, the findings are therefore also useful for the HE and FE context. A systematic review undertaken by the author brought that literature together for the first time in the form of a qualitative research synthesis (Causer *et al.* 2019). Three thematic categories that describe practitioner experiences emerged from this synthesis. They were: 'horror, shock and trauma', 'scrutiny judgement and blame' and 'support, learning and living with'.

The category 'horror, shock and trauma' described practitioners' cognitive, emotional, psychological and physiological responses to the suicide death. These included multiple experiences of the horror of suicide, indicators of trauma responses and evidence that different kinds of client/practitioner relationships and roles can impact on the nature of the experience.

'Scrutiny judgement and blame' describes practitioners' processes of examination of the event and of their own role and responsibilities in the context of the event. This category evidences intense and complex processes of self-scrutiny, self-blame and feelings of professional failure. There were also experiences of being blamed by others, of being held to account, and of feeling abandoned by colleagues and managers to process feelings alone.

'Support, learning and living with' describes how practitioners' experiences prior to and after the event shape the choices and strategies they call upon to facilitate a process of recovery, acceptance and moving forward, both personally and professionally. Perceptions of incrimination and absolution were present for practitioners, either in the form of self-blame/scrutiny or in the form of perceived judgement and blame from others.

In conclusion, the review recommended that postvention support is needed for health, social care and education practitioners, and that this support should be contextualized socially, culturally and organizationally so that it is sensitive to individual need (Causer *et al.* 2019). As stated previously, some job roles within HEIs and FEIs share similarities with those of the practitioners studied in this review. It can therefore be suggested that staff working in these areas also require postvention support in relation to the themes identified above. However, other job roles, such as facilities staff or senior managers, vary considerably from those described, and in order to make recommendations in regard to these groups data from a follow-up qualitative survey are now explored.

Staff members' experiences following a student death by suicide in a UK university

To understand the experiences of HEI staff after a student death by suicide, staff members at two UK HEIs participated in a mixed-method research study. The first phase of data collection took the form of an e-survey designed to gather categorical and qualitative data. The aim of the survey was to scope who, amongst HEI staff, perceived themselves to be impacted by a student death by suicide, who undertook tasks related to the suicide, their perceptions of needs and their experiences of support. The findings reported in this chapter were developed through the thematic analysis of qualitative survey data. Nineteen higher education staff members from two UK HEIs responded to the survey (Table 20.1).

Table 20.1: Study participants by gender, job role and site of recruitment

		University 1	University 2
Gender of participants	Male	6	2
	Female	6	5
	Total	12	7
Job-role of participants	Leadership team	1	
	Wellbeing team	4	1
	Chaplaincy	1	
	Security team	1	2
	Housekeeping team	2	
	Academic staff	3	4
	Total	12	7

Perceptions of impact

Seven of the staff members stated in the survey that they felt 'exposed to' a death by suicide, 11 stated they felt 'affected by' the death and one stated they felt 'bereaved' (Causer 2020). This follows other studies that have found perceptions of impact following a death by suicide vary. For example, Cerel *et al.* (2014) developed the continuum of suicide survivorship, which suggests that people impacted following a suicide death may perceive themselves to be 'exposed to', 'affected by' or 'bereaved by' a suicide, where bereavement may be a short- or long-term experience. It is important to note that staff may perceive an impact whether or not they knew the student prior to their death. The level of impact perceived may be unconnected to staff members' job role or the tasks that they performed after the death, suggesting that there may be other individual factors that affect perceptions of impact for staff members.

Survey data also showed that impacts were experienced in different ways. Most staff experienced an emotional response to the death. The most commonly described feelings were sadness or helplessness. There was also a sense of shock and panic about what had happened. Some staff shared that their emotional responses did not emerge until later, as their immediate focus was on undertaking necessary crisis response tasks. Overall, staff accounts expressed the enormity and breadth of impact, with a sense of being 'knocked for six' (HE lecturer), experiences of increased anxiety amongst teams, and a 'profound effect' (senior academic) being felt across the university.

A process of seeking understanding was evident for some staff as they wrestled with a sense of confusion about what had happened. Others searched for explanations and reasons, sometimes engaging in a process of filling in the gaps in their own understanding of events to create a cohesive 'story' that made sense to them:

> I did wonder about the medication that the suicide victim had been on...I wondered if such an apparently random and senseless act might have happened because of a mood disturbance/side effects. (Student support staff)

Part of the 'thinking' work that took place after the suicide was directed towards reflection on the staff member's own role in supporting students, specifically on the question of whether more could have been done:

> I was the personal tutor to the student who died...it was difficult coming

to terms with my thoughts about whether I had done enough to prevent the event. (Lecturer)

For some staff members, such thought processes continued over time. Having experienced one student death by suicide, the fear that it may happen again emanates as an underlying anxiety amongst teams, which may lead to a disproportionate sense of responsibility for ensuring student safety. There appeared to be a lack of strategy for coping with such worries in some staff accounts. A student wellbeing team member expressed a sense of helplessness, stating, 'At times I cross my fingers.'

Ongoing memories, images and flashbacks of the suicide impacted staff across different roles. Some staff held the belief that the memories will persist over time:

> The thoughts take a long time to go away. Even now when I am on the residential site it is always there...so I don't think it ever goes from your mind. (Cleaner)

> I still think about them and the family. It is something I think never leaves you. (Student wellbeing manager)

For some, the impact of the event led to changes in practice, either at an individual level, or within teams. One lecturer, when reflecting on a student suicide, wondered if the timing of student tutorial meetings was inconvenient and had contributed to the student feeling unsupported:

> I invited all my students for individual meetings during a time that was more convenient to them than the one I chose last year. The suicide changed my behaviour. And it has a long-lasting effect. (Lecturer)

STAFF NEEDS

- Staff members' responses to the event may be delayed. Lack of a visible response does not necessarily indicate that the individual is coping well.

- Staff may have previous professional or personal experiences with suicide, sudden death or experience of a recent bereavement. They may also be facing current personal struggles or those of somebody they are close to. Staff may not share these 'private' matters with colleagues or managers.

RESPONDING TO STAFF NEEDS

- Support processes ought to be needs-led and offered individually, at team level, and across all staff groups.

- Consideration should be given to the possibility that personal and 'private' experiences may complicate individual responses and capacities to cope with a suicide at work.

- A formal and constructive information sharing process will provide a forum within which:

  – clarity of explanation around reasons for the death can be offered, or information about the kinds of reasons people die by suicide

  – narratives that dispel any fears of responsibility or harm done can be developed and shared

  – a constructive exploration can be made of what, if anything, could have been done differently prior to and after the death. Such a process may help by focusing on institutional procedures rather than individual decision-making.

Undertaking tasks

To develop a full understanding of the kinds of support needed and which individuals and teams may require support, it is helpful to identify which staff members and teams are involved in responding to a student death by suicide. Staff were asked to describe the kinds of job, role or task that they undertook after a student death by suicide. Sixteen staff members described 54 distinct tasks undertaken between them. These tasks were not evenly distributed. One participant listed 20 unique tasks; others listed just one task. Multiple staff members may be involved in delivering the same or very similar tasks, for instance offering support to other students. The tasks were diverse in nature and function. They are briefly described here within four categories that were developed through a thematic analysis: crisis response tasks, strategic tasks, support tasks, and practical and administrative tasks. Staff accounts illustrated that the tasks varied in complexity and sensitivity, that some tasks were completed immediately whilst others were undertaken later or were ongoing months after the event.

Crisis response tasks included performing cardiopulmonary

resuscitation (CPR), incident response, management and liaison. Staff members such as security officers may be first on the scene, and life-saving might be the first task performed. Facilities teams may also be involved in tasks such as securing the area, moving other students away from the incident and liaising with other professionals such as the emergency services. Staff teams, such as student wellbeing and chaplaincy, take on tasks such as supporting the housemates of the student who has died and ensuring that appropriate information is shared with other students in nearby accommodation.

Strategic tasks are those that include information sharing and gathering, liaison with others, response planning and advising. Some of these tasks take place in the immediate aftermath of the event, for instance gathering information about the student who has died, such as identifying their next of kin, their social networks and whether they were previously known to support services. Other tasks may happen over the following days, such as planning how to inform wider groups like coursemates and providing briefings to university leadership and the executive board. Staff members' expertise was called upon at a strategic level as well as in front line delivery, and in some cases the same staff members who were carrying out crisis response tasks were also taking a lead role in response planning.

Support tasks started in the immediate aftermath of the death and continued in various forms for months or years afterwards. Tasks included supporting students, supporting other members of staff, liaison and support for the family of the student who died, and facilitating opportunities for remembrance. In supporting students, staff provided immediate comprehensive support to the housemates and wider support to the student's coursemates, the student body and to students identified as being vulnerable in the context of suicide. Some of these tasks were ongoing, for instance the creation of a monitoring system to assess the wellbeing of coursemates, or one-to-one check-ins with housemates over the following months. Support of staff affected by the event was in some instances targeted to particular staff groups. This was provided via line management or sometimes 'open door' support. In some instances, the task of supporting other staff created additional tasks for the supporter. This might take the form of extra line management duties or the additional support of staff across other teams. Support of the student's family might be a formal response from senior team members but was also offered through individual initiative. For instance, a lecturer gathered electronic copies of the student's work to send to the parents. Support was also offered at a community level in the form of ritual and remembrance, through the provision of a memorial service, for instance.

Practical and administrative tasks were encountered in supporting the housemates, dealing with the aftermath, supporting the student's family, and in supporting the wider university community. Practical tasks included rehousing the housemates, packing the belongings and cleaning the room of the student who died and arranging student transport to attend the funeral. Administrative tasks might include the updating of records and liaising with local media to ensure sensitive reporting of the event.

STAFF NEEDS

Tasks may be taken on by staff members above and beyond their usual job role. Staff may not highlight the extent of the extra tasks they are performing, which may lead to a sense of being burdened or overworked and feelings of invisibility.

RESPONDING TO STAFF NEEDS

Understanding the tasks undertaken and identifying the staff involved will aid the delivery of targeted support.

Perceived needs

Staff members experienced a range of needs after a student suicide. The majority of participant accounts demonstrated a complex entanglement of emotional responses with the undertaking of tasks within the context of the suicide (Causer 2020). As such, it appeared that needs arise not just from the fact that a student has died by suicide but also from the experience of responding to a student's death by suicide. For some, this led to the challenge of finding space to process their feelings as they first had to respond to the crisis that was unfolding around them:

> I was tearful on the day but then 'just got on with it' because the rest of the cohort were in need of support. (Lecturer)

Some needs arose from the emotional impact of the suicide; feelings such as sadness, tearfulness, anger, confusion and fear generated the need to talk things through and process such feelings. For others, it was the task itself that gave rise to emotional needs, leaving the staff member to grapple with the dilemma between professional responsibilities and self-care:

> Sitting with other people's intense suffering – even as a trained professional – has an emotional impact, but as the 'professional' the expectation is to keep going...but it still has an impact. (Student counsellor)

For one academic, there was a sense of reward from taking on specific tasks:

> The feelings/needs were quite ambivalent around that time – a mixture of sadness but also a sense of doing a worthwhile job. (Senior academic)

The 'doing' of tasks or job roles following a student suicide gave rise to additional needs. For instance, some staff experienced uncertainty about how to approach a task or of their ability to take on a role. As such, advice-seeking or the need for guidance or reassurance from line management was evident. For others, lack of skills created a sense of need:

> As academic staff we have little training in pastoral care, and especially no training or support in how to ensure we look after our own mental health. (Lecturer)

Meeting the needs of others, in turn, meant putting aside or ignoring their own responses as staff juggled to manage priorities and put others before themselves. Some staff, however, found that in responding to the needs of others they were unable to ignore their own needs.

Depending on their job role, some staff members took on a significant additional workload. For instance, staff in student wellbeing or counselling teams found that they needed to clear their diaries to attend to the needs of students and other staff. This gave rise to the need for practical strategies to help them cope with an increased workload and potential overwhelm. The risk that impacts such as sleeplessness, anxiety and depression might affect their capacity to work was also apparent to some and gave rise to the need for support to aid the processing necessary to continue doing their job.

Additional work responsibilities meant additional support was needed in their personal life too. However, for some staff, the ability to switch off the personal and focus on the task in hand appeared to be complete, creating a sense of not having any needs:

> You just do it – you don't think of yourself, you are focused on the students and the family. (Cleaner)

STAFF NEEDS

- The perceived necessity of doing practical and supportive tasks impacts staff members' ability and choices around recognizing and acknowledging their own needs.

- Staff needs extend beyond the emotional. Needs may also arise in connection with delivering tasks and managing workloads.

- Staff members engage in an ongoing process of balancing and managing their own needs alongside meeting the needs of others. Managers and team leaders appear particularly likely to focus on the support of others before themselves.

RESPONDING TO STAFF NEEDS

- A process of checking in with individual staff members and team managers to gain oversight of their experiences should happen immediately and over subsequent weeks.

- Staff engaged in ongoing tasks may require ongoing support.

Experiences of support

Staff accounts evidenced the tendency to put the needs of others and the doing of tasks ahead of meeting their own needs. It is pertinent, therefore, to explore the perceptions that staff members had regarding support. None of the staff accounts articulated a clear description of their support needs. Rather, staff members acknowledged their support needs only when they perceived those needs as being unmet or unseen. For some staff, perceptions of the expectations attached to their roles appeared to shape their experiences:

> ...we are...often expected to be the strong ones in front of students; this can be extremely harrowing without proper support being in place. (Lecturer)

For other staff, a sense of invisibility was evident as they felt that the impact of carrying out challenging tasks went unacknowledged:

> There seemed to be no consideration that staff carrying out the necessary practical things after the suicide might be impacted on and need support. (Team manager)

Some staff members were offered support; others requested it or sought it out independently. Both formal and informal support were accessed. This included support from line managers, via supervision or through utilizing personal networks such as friends and family. Other staff members, however, did not ask for support; it was not always clear whether they felt they needed support. A perception that staff should pro-actively request support presented a barrier for some staff members. For others, though, there was a clear belief that there was no support available:

> There are plenty of promises for support but no actual support – as the saying goes, all talk no action. (Facilities team member)

For some, this presented the contradiction of actively providing support to others but not being offered any for themselves:

> No support was offered to me by the university – on the contrary, I was the one giving support to my team. (Team manager)

There appeared to be little consistency in the experiences of staff members regarding the provision of support. A disparity in the provision of support across staff teams was perceived by some, with the idea that academic staff received greater provision than those in other roles. For other staff additional support was offered from external sources.

Dissatisfaction with their experience of provision of support was expressed by some. This tended to be either in terms of the routes through which support was offered, the timeliness of support, or in terms of the realistic capacity of an HEI to meet the complex needs of staff members following an event such as a suicide death:

> ...the little support given was by under-qualified support members who are trained to deal with students rather than staff; [I] felt we are ignored when it comes to our mental wellbeing. (Facilities team member)

> The 'emotional landscape' after a death by suicide can include anger, blame and guilt, and these are difficult to process and manage in a university setting which isn't set up, really, to deal with them. (Senior academic)

There were others, however, who appeared satisfied with the provision of support that they experienced and were able to describe multiple offers of support to meet a range of needs.

For those who did receive and engage with support services, the experience was once again mixed. Support might come from colleagues in different teams, from line managers, or 'from within our immediate team' (student wellbeing team member). However, it is clear that colleagues or line managers did not always have the capacity to provide the kinds of support that staff felt they needed:

> I have a supportive boss which while reassuring does not stretch to emotional support. (Senior manager)

Whilst some staff members expressed complete satisfaction with their experience of being supported, others experienced dissatisfaction:

> I asked for support but this seemed to be lost in the melee of other things going on at the time. I tried [the online counselling service], which I found unhelpful and actually made things worse. (Lecturer)

Additional avenues of support were sought and utilized. Some staff members called upon self-care strategies like established habits or behaviours, whilst others accessed support via pre-existing networks, highlighting that personal factors may contribute towards staff members' capacity to cope:

> I am lucky – I have a strong family and I am pretty resilient. (Lecturer)

STAFF NEEDS

- Staff may not express their needs nor ask for support. This does not mean that they do not have needs or would not benefit from being offered access to support.

- Staff who undertake crisis response tasks – specifically, staff who discover or are present with the body of a student – may experience trauma responses which give rise to specific support needs.

RESPONDING TO STAFF NEEDS

- Support should take a variety of forms beyond counselling and listening services. Staff welcome support from a range of formal and informal sources from within and beyond their institution.

- Engaging with support providers beyond the HEI may lift the burden from the shoulders of staff members and provide a neutral forum from which support can be offered and accessed.

- Support offered ought to be consistent and inclusive across job roles and staff teams.

Conclusion

It is clear that for these staff members, impact is not dependent upon them knowing or working with the student before their death; neither is impact dependent upon the kinds of tasks that staff members may have undertaken following the death. These accounts demonstrate that there are staff in UK HEIs who require postvention support following a student death by suicide. As such, and in the absence of any other published research (Causer 2020), these accounts offer the beginnings of an evidence base which HEI leaders and policy makers might utilize in reviewing, designing and delivering postvention support offers for HEI staff members who are impacted following a student death by suicide.

Additional resources

- UUK and PAPYRUS (2018) *Suicide-Safer Universities*, www.universitiesuk.ac.uk/policy-and-analysis/reports/ Documents/2018/guidance-for-sector-practitioners-on-preventing-student-suicides.PDF

- PAPYRUS (2018) *Building Suicide-Safer Schools and Colleges: A Guide for Teachers and Staff*, https://papyrus-uk.org/wp-content/ uploads/2018/08/toolkitfinal.pdf

- Samaritans (2021) *Information for University or College Staff*, www.samaritans.org/how-we-can-help/schools/universities/ information-university-or-college-staff

- HEMHA (Higher Education Mental Health Alliance) (2014) *Postvention: A Guide for Response to Suicide on College Campuses*, https://hemha.org/wp-content/uploads/2018/06/jed-hemha-postvention-guide.pdf

- Public Health England (2016) *Support after a Suicide: A Guide to Providing Local Services*, www.gov.uk/government/publications/ support-after-a-suicide-a-guide-to-providing-local-services

- The Workplace Postvention Task Force of the American Association of Suicidology *et al.* (2013) *A Manager's Guide to Suicide Postvention in the Workplace: 10 Action Steps for Dealing with the Aftermath of a Suicide*, https://theactionalliance.org/sites/default/ files/managers-guidebook-to-suicide-postvention-web.pdf

Author biography

Dr Hilary Causer undertook her PhD at the University of Worcester, UK. Her research focused on exploring the experiences of staff at two UK higher education institutions following a student death by suicide. She has published in the *International Journal of Environmental Research and Public Health*. Her research interests extend to include student mental health and wellbeing; workplace wellbeing and cultures; and the social, cultural and political contexts of suicide and mental ill-health.

References

Berman, A.L. (2011) Estimating the population of survivors of suicide: seeking an evidence base. *Suicide and Life-Threatening Behavior 41*, 1, 110–116.

Causer, H. (2020) A Critical Exploration of Staff Experiences and Roles Following a Student Death by Suicide within Two United Kingdom Higher Education Institutions. Unpublished doctoral thesis, University of Worcester.

Causer, H., Muse, K., Smith, J. and Bradley, E. (2019) What is the experience of practitioners in health, education or social care roles following a death by suicide? A qualitative research synthesis. *International Journal of Environmental Research and Public Health 16*, 18, 3293.

Cerel, J., Brown, M.M., Maple, M., Singleton, M. *et al.* (2018) How many people are exposed to suicide? Not six. *Suicide and Life Threatening Behavior 49*, 2, 529–534.

Cerel, J., McIntosh, J.L., Neimeyer, R.A., Maple, M. and Marshall, D. (2014) The continuum of 'survivorship': definitional issues in the aftermath of suicide. *Suicide and Life-Threatening Behavior 44*, 6, 591–600.

Gunnell, D., Bennewith, O., Simkin, S., Cooper, J. *et al.* (2013) Time trends in coroners' use of different verdicts for possible suicides and their impact on officially reported incidence of suicide in England: 1990–2005. *Psychological Medicine 43*, 7, 1415–1422.

Gunnell, D., Caul, S., Appleby, L., John, A. and Hawton, K. (2020) The incidence of suicide in university students in England and Wales 2000/2001–2016/2017: record linkage study. *Journal of Affective Disorders 261*, 113–120.

Hawton, K., Bergen, H., Mahadevan, S., Casey, D. and Simkin, S. (2012) Suicide and deliberate self-harm in Oxford University students over a 30-year period. *Social Psychiatry and Psychiatric Epidemiology 47*, 1, 43–51.

NUS Disabled Students (2016) *Mental Health and Suicide Prevention Guide: An In-Depth Guide for Students' Unions and Student Activists*. London: NUS.

Office for National Statistics (ONS) (2018a) *Estimating Suicide among Higher Education Students, England and Wales: Experimental Statistics*. London: ONS. Accessed on 21/01/20 at: www.ons.gov.uk/peoplepopulationandcommunity/birthsdeathsandmarriages/deaths/articles/estimatingsuicideamonghighereducationstudentsenglandandwalesexperimentalstatistics/2018-06-25

Office for National Statistics (ONS) (2018b) *Suicides in the UK: 2017 Registrations*. Accessed on 21/01/20 at: www.ons.gov.uk/releases/suicidesintheuk2017registrations

Stanley, N., Mallon, S., Bell, J. and Manthorpe, J. (2009) Trapped in transition: findings from a UK study of student suicide. *British Journal of Guidance & Counselling 37*, 4, 419–433.

CHAPTER 21

Understanding and Responding to Bereavement after a Suicide

SHARON MALLON

Overview

This chapter aims to:

- provide an overview of bereavement by suicide, including a discussion of language use when speaking about death by suicide

- allow the reader to reflect on why bereavement by suicide may be different from other forms of bereavement

- discuss the potential impact of an individual death by suicide, and how this might be affected by the HE and FE setting.

Introduction

> ...it's a very difficult, it's a very uncomfortable area for, for society to deal with you know because...it is about how valued people feel in their community and in society, you know. And you know what sort of society are we creating, have we created where...people...have got such a difficulty with it that they're prepared to take their own life. (Jack)

The quote above comes from an interview with an HE student bereaved by the suicide of a close friend. I interviewed him over ten years ago as part of my PhD research. The sentiments shared by Jack and the other young adults I interviewed have stuck with me. Many of us will have experienced the death of a loved one. There is a universality to bereavement; it is rare to reach adulthood without experiencing the loss of someone with whom one had a meaningful relationship. However, as the quote from Jack also indicates, suicide is a unique form of death. It is bound up with issues of rejection, abject and painful misery, as well as self-harm and choice. It cuts to the core of our existence and what it means to be alive, in ways that are rarely acknowledged until one is forced to respond to it, on a personal or professional level, through the death of someone to suicide.

In order to respond sensitively to a suicide that has taken place in HE and FE, it is useful to reflect upon some of these issues. This chapter thus takes a broad approach to the topic of suicide bereavement that is intended to allow the reader to learn about some of the issues that shape the aftermath of a death by suicide. These are closely entwined with the themes that have emerged from the research into bereavement by suicide. The chapter makes use of direct quotes from my doctoral work with students who were bereaved by the suicide of a friend. I also include some of my reflections from working on the RaPSS research study in which I interviewed parents and staff who had experienced the loss to suicide of a young person who was a student (Stanley *et al.* 2007). As the focus of the book is student suicide, the work presented here will focus predominantly on the aftermath of suicide that occurs in young adulthood. However, there are parallels across the experiences of those who are bereaved by suicide at any age.

Suicide is a different type of death: a 'common sense notion'?

Over the past few decades, studies exploring those who have experienced a loss to suicide have increased (Maple *et al.* 2014). During this time, the research evidence on whether suicide bereavement is a distinct or unique form of loss has shown no clear pattern. Some have stated that it is a unique type of bereavement (Clark and Goldney 2002). There is also a discernible trend in the literature which depicts it as being worse than other forms of bereavement, with one study describing this as a 'common sense notion' (Bailley and Kral 1999, p.256). Resolving this debate is beyond the scope of this chapter. In this section, I present a discussion of some of the core themes that, based on my experiences of researching and writing in this area, are helpful to be aware of when responding to a student death by suicide.

Acknowledging our attitude towards death by suicide

Communicating with, and in many cases offering support to, someone who has very recently experienced the death of a loved one through any cause can be daunting. The raw emotions of early grief can be overwhelming. However, the complex emotions that emerge when it appears that the death took place because of an act of self-harm can challenge even the most experienced practitioner or educator. As the quote from Jack included at the outset of this chapter indicated, it raises deep-rooted, often existential, issues. Additionally, some of us may have personal experience of dark times in our own lives when we experienced suicidal thoughts; others may have cared for someone who was suicidal or undertook self-harming actions. The statistics also show that many of us will have experienced the loss of someone we know to suicide. Therefore, before I introduce the literature on suicide bereavement, I encourage the reader to begin by considering their own attitude to the topic and to explore their own reaction to suicide.

Points of reflection

- What personal experiences have you had that may impact on your response to a death by suicide?
- Have you experienced personal loss to suicide, or supported someone through a suicidal crisis?
- How might you best manage these experiences, protecting yourself against harm while also using them to enhance your response?

Suicide as a stigmatized act

You may have found it challenging to think about the reflections above. Even if you consider yourself to be experienced and open minded, suicide is difficult. My experiences of interviewing those bereaved by suicide, and of working more broadly in this area, have shown me that the very idea of death by suicide is a subject which many people struggle to communicate about. This can shape the experiences of those who have been bereaved and those who support them. Considerable efforts have been undertaken to challenge the stigma that surrounds suicide, and these have had some positive consequences, particularly for families and friends left behind. However, those who have been bereaved by suicide continue to report that their experiences are affected by the stigma. For example, they cite an absence of social support as a particular problem (Wertheimer 1991). Additionally, suicide remains an emotionally charged subject. Although the attitude of some religious leaders has eased, many religions continue to prohibit it on moral grounds. Negative stereotypes of suicide also remain prevalent in wider society. Self-preservation is conceptualized as a normative part of human nature (Joiner 2010). Alvarez, writing after the death of his close friend Sylvia Plath, called it a controversial and often taboo area of human behaviour (2002). Similarly, Hewett and Oates (1980, p.11) pointed out that until one is personally affected by these deaths, they are a 'whispered taboo that only happens to other families...'. The taboo nature of suicide can in part be linked to its long history as a prohibited act, both in moral and legal terms. In the UK, suicide is no longer a criminal act. However, this criminal legacy continues to shape the definition of suicide, as will be discussed in the next section.

Suicide as a deliberate act of self-harm

> ...it wasn't an accident, you know the windows are so high up, you know takes some effort to jump out of them, and they'd made them like to stop people jumping out of them, you know, so it was something he definitely wanted to do. (Jennifer)

The procedures by which a death is classified as a suicide can vary from country to country. Until recently in England, the coroner, whose job it is to determine that a death is a suicide, relied upon both the 'intent' with which an act of self-harm was undertaken and the 'intention' with which the individual must have undertaken this action (Atkinson 1978). In this context, 'intent' refers to the determination that the individual deliberately undertook a harmful act, and 'intention' refers to the expectation that death would be the outcome of these actions. Both of these criteria had to be satisfied before the death could be officially and legally recorded as a suicide. This aspect of death by suicide has some important consequences. For example, at the time of writing, public inquests into death by suicide still take place in England and Wales (in Northern Ireland and Scotland, this varies). For some of the bereaved, the public nature of inquest procedures into death by suicide can cause additional distress.

One of the problems with the conventions of intent and intention were that they are closely linked to criminal definitions of human action

(Fletcher 1998), which in turn also accounts for the widespread use of the term 'committed suicide'. Those bereaved by suicide have expressed increasing dissatisfaction with the continued use of this term and its derivations because it draws upon criminal constructions and has consequences for the moral construction of such acts (Hewett and Oates 1980). For these reasons, terms such as 'died by suicide' are preferred (see Beaton, Forster and Maple 2013), while terms such as 'killed himself' should also be avoided because they are perceived as being expressly violent (Szasz 2002).

Above all, when speaking to someone who has been affected by a death that may *appear* to be a suicide, it is important to gain knowledge about what *that* individual's interpretation of the death is. Research involving family members of the deceased has shown that the official and unofficial considerations of a death do not necessarily concur (Mallon and Stanley 2014; Wertheimer 1991). To put it another way, sometimes the family do not accept the coroner's verdict of suicide and, at other times, they consider it to be a suicide even when the coroner has not officially determined that it is so. Consideration of whether the death is a suicide may also vary between different parties who are bereaved. For example, in the RaPSS study, I interviewed a father who thought his daughter had died by suicide, while the mother did not, thinking instead that the medication overdose had been accidental. Therefore, an important step for anyone responding or supporting a death that may be a suicide is to determine how those affected have come to think of the death, bearing in mind that this may also change with time.

Coming to the conclusion that a death is a suicide has important consequences for those who are bereaved (Wertheimer 1991). My own research showed that students came to categorize the death of their friend as a suicide, independently from the coroner's inquest (although sometimes using information gained from it). It also demonstrated that the process by which they did that was not always straightforward. For example, only a minority of students who were close to the person who died accepted the label of suicide. Instead, in most cases they undertook what I described as a 'personal inquest', carefully considering their friend's final thoughts and actions, in order to determine that their friend had deliberately harmed themselves, and to assess whether they meant to end their life (see Mallon and Stanley 2014).

This meant the bereaved were sometimes keen to have details of the specific methods used by their friend to harm themselves. This can be significant for those supporting them, particularly those who are privy to specific and explicit details about the death. They may find themselves invited to engage in an intense discussion of the exact circumstances of the death. While it is important to respond sensitively to such requests, avoiding questions entirely can cause speculation and uncertainty. It is also important to be mindful of the requirements of confidentiality and the deceased family's right to privacy. Crucially, there is also a primary need to prevent any risk of copycat suicide and to be aware that excessive details may inadvertently contribute to additional deaths.

Points of reflection

- Consider briefly the type of language you use when speaking about suicide – if you routinely use terms such as 'committed suicide', practise alternative ways of speaking about these types of death.
- Make sure any policy or guidance your institution has allows for variation in how different bereaved parties may consider the death and is sensitive to accommodate those who do not accept that the death is a suicide, regardless of what the official stance may be.

Suicide as an act that requires an explanation

...I was obviously asking questions, so the first question I asked was 'How?' and then 'Why?' But I didn't know any of them answers... (Sam)

The bereaved may also seek information about the circumstances running up to the death as part of their efforts to answer the 'why' question which often accompanies suicide. Shneidman (1972) reported that the survivor was left with 'a complex of negative feelings and, most importantly, to obsessing about the reasons for his suicidal death' (p.ix). In my research, as indicated in the quote from Sam, for most of the students, the search for an explanation began at the point at which they found out about the death and was closely connected to the deliberate nature of the act of self-harm. In some instances, this search was connected by some of the bereaved to the notion that they considered suicide to be a rejection of life, and therefore a rejection of those who had shared that life. An explanation helped to manage this rejection.

As the following quote from Monica indicates, this search for information sometimes involved approaching other bereaved parties:

> I found out a bit more like from speaking to his girlfriend just because it, I felt quite selfish doing it because obviously she was going through like Hell, but she was the only person that kind of knew anything like none of us, we didn't know anything...I think me and a couple of others just needed to know a bit more... (Monica)

This process of deduction is replicated to some extent in other forms of death. Meaning and meaning reconstruction are recognized as being fundamental tasks of bereavement (Neimeyer 2001). The ability to communicate about the experiences of bereavement plays a crucial role in accepting the death of someone with whom one was close. However, the deduction and communication that takes place after a bereavement experience that follows a suicidal death can be quite specific. Those working with the bereaved may encounter friends and relatives who are involved in a painful and active consideration of the state of mind of the deceased at a time when they were in a state of absolute psychological pain. In my interviews, it was clear that the process of thinking through the thoughts and emotions of their friend at the time of death was one of the most distressing parts of the bereavement experience. Those supporting these students may find it challenging to support such work; they may even find it painful themselves.

When undertaking my research, I frequently met multiple parties who had been bereaved by the same death, and I became aware of confidential details that I was not at liberty to share with all those who had been affected by the same death, but which, in some instances, may have helped further explain the suicide. Over time, these details became painful for me to 'hold', and in some cases I was asked direct questions which I could not openly reply to. It is important in these circumstances that you have a trusted colleague or supervisor with whom you can share any concerns and who can help guide you in any decisions and alleviate the burden of holding such painful details.

Suicide as a preventable death

> ...then I was really tormenting myself and saying to myself 'why haven't I done something?' and I just felt really useless as a person and as a friend. (Grace)

A common part of any grief process is dealing with a sense of helplessness and loss of control over the situation (Attig 2003). In cases of suicide this aspect can be complicated. Prevention handbooks aimed at friends and family advise them of the warning signs and how and when to intervene with young people suspected to be suicidal (Kolehmainen and Handwerk 2008). This gives the impression that suicide is an act that can be predicted, controlled and stopped. It can, therefore, be particularly challenging for those bereaved by suicide as they are faced with a suicide that has not been prevented.

From my interviews, it was clear that one of the most devastating consequences for some of those left behind after a suicide was a feeling that the death may have been prevented from happening. I called it the 'if only' factor. As indicated in the quote from Grace, my experience of interviewing those affected by these deaths was that it emerged in their talk as feelings of guilt and self-reproach. However, in some instances it also included blaming those who were near to the student or those who had a role in supporting them. Blame is rarely expressly mentioned in the literature on suicide bereavement. However, it is a feature of some deaths by suicide. HE and FE staff should be mindful that in some instances a friend or intimate partner or a member of staff may be blamed by some parties for failing to stop the death.

This aspect of the death is particularly challenging for those to whom the student may have confided feelings or thoughts of suicidality. Even if there is no overt blame, some of the bereaved may fear that something they did or didn't do may have contributed to the suicide. This has an additional important consequence for the bereaved. Researchers have established the importance of social networks in bereavement and found that sharing stories with close friends is a useful means of coping (Harvey *et al.* 2003). However, the complexity of information sharing after death by suicide can also mean that the bereaved do not support each other, or that they may not wish to share information about what they do know in relation to the death, for fear of this being highlighted as them having contributed to it or having failed to prevent it.

The consequences of this aspect of suicide are unspeakably tough for all those affected by the loss of a young person. In the RaPSS study, I witnessed how tough it was for family and friends as they struggled to find out and to form an explanation for what had happened. I also saw how those working in support roles attempted to protect the emotional needs of various parties involved, as well as the university's wider reputation. I was continuously mindful of the overwhelming complexity of these emotions and the immense responsibility staff hold in responding sensitively, ensuring the needs of all those involved are met, while not getting drawn into potentially legally and ethically challenging discussions. There are no easy answers, but again my sense was that skilled management of these complex situations required FE and HE professionals to work together. Shutting down the lines of communication entirely rarely worked; however, there were aspects of the death that simply had to remain private. Blame and shame are destructive emotions that no one staff member can manage alone. Again, a trusted confidant who is aware of the details of each unique death is essential to manage and respond to the complex needs of all those involved.

Points of reflection

- Where can you access further information about what your institution's policy is on communication following a death by suicide?
- Identify a trusted supervisor or colleague who can support you in making difficult decisions about sharing of information.

Suicide as an untimely death

A final issue I wish to explore in this section on death by suicide is specific to a death which occurs in youth. Death in young adulthood is regarded as particularly tragic because they are considered to be premature, occurring before the natural fullness of life has been achieved (Finch and Wallis 1993). Consequently, those left behind may also be less prepared for their death. Blauner (1997) claims that society actively values the social importance of younger people. Therefore, the rejection of life by young people who bring about an end to their days is particularly challenging and causes a greater state of social frustration and need for meaning. In addition, young people are likely to be socially active and may be highly involved in society, thus potentially increasing the impact of their death, something we explore in greater detail in the next section.

Impact of death by suicide

So far in this chapter, we have explored some of the broad aspects of death by suicide that can shape the experiences of the bereaved. The consequences of death by suicide are now widely recognized as one of the most pressing public health issues faced by the global community (Cutliffe 2011). The increased awareness of the impact of these tragic deaths has in part come about because of sustained efforts by survivors of suicide, including a number of personalized accounts (see in particular Wertheimer 1991). However, there have also been a number of influential studies which have led to increased awareness of the scale of the impact of these deaths. These will be explored next.

The suicide survivor continuum

Early estimates of the number of those affected were focused on the family and suggested that around six people were affected by each suicide (Shneidman 1972). The impact of death by suicide is now accepted to be much wider than this early estimate and suicide is acknowledged to touch not only family members but also friends, staff and, in some cases, emergency services personnel. Recent research estimates that approximately 60 people are directly affected (Berman 2011), with up to 135 people in wider networks thought to be impacted by each suicide death (Cerel et al. 2019). Given the particularly social nature of student life, it is possible to argue that the number of people affected by the suicide of a student may be significantly higher, but no figures have been located in the literature in relation to this specific group.

In addition to research on numbers impacted, there have been some attempts made to rationalize the 'suicide survivor' spectrum. Although some researchers have suggested that those individuals most closely related to the deceased are likely to be the most adversely affected by the death, others have suggested we should not assume that the consequences of all suicides are the same, or that the level of impact of the death is associated with the closeness of the relationship with the deceased (Jordan and McIntosh 2011). Acknowledgement of the widespread impact of death by suicide is particularly concerning when it is combined with the final aspect of bereavement by suicide considered in this chapter, that of the suicide contagion effect, which is the subject of the next section.

Suicide as a 'contagious' death

> ...you know that it happened to him, it could happen to me, you know because until that happens you don't know, you, it's always something that happens to someone else, but when it happens to a very close, close friend, it suddenly becomes something that becomes possible... (Jack)

Awareness of the 'contagious' nature of suicidal behaviour has been around for some time. One author summed it up thus: 'coping with suicide is coping with death, and although death always takes its toll, suicide extracts even a higher price, threatening the very lives of the living' (Wallace 1973, p.3). This phenomenon is particularly concerning for those working in the HE/FE sector as research has established that there is a relationship between exposure to a suicidal friend and the future risk of suicidal ideation and action in their peers (Melhem *et al.* 2004; Prigerson *et al.* 1999).

From my experience, a potentially concerning feature of this aspect of bereavement is that when interviewing family and friends of those who had died by suicide, I was shocked by how many knew that their experiences of this bereavement now placed them at risk of suicide. This commonly repeated fact can bring about considerable fear to those bereaved by suicide. It is vital that this aspect of bereavement should be accompanied by a sensitive explanation of why this might happen and how it can be protected against. In brief, it should be stressed that while suicide may take place in clusters, it is not inevitable that one suicide leads to another. All those working with the bereaved should be aware of postvention strategies that can help protect the bereaved against a risk of further suicides.

Survivors of suicide

Klass (2003) suggests that meaning-making takes place within a community which recognizes the death and mourns the dead person, while also validating and sharing in the development of a continuing bond with the dead. The term 'survivor of suicide' is frequently used to describe the community of those who have been bereaved by suicide. Wertheimer (1991) suggests 'suicide survivors' emerged as a distinct group during the 1960s. She also suggests that 'it is not uncommon for survivors to state that *only* someone who has also experienced a suicide could understand them or be of any use to them' (p.193, original emphasis). Wertheimer further stated that survivor groups are one of the main sources of specialist help for those bereaved by suicide. At the time of writing, the biggest support organization for those bereaved by suicide in the UK is called Survivors of Bereavement by Suicide (SOBS).[1]

While such groups can quite obviously provide solidarity, my experience of undertaking research interviews with the bereaved has emphasized that survivors of suicide are not a homogenous group and the needs of the bereaved will vary. For example, my interviews with young people found that contact with survivor groups could be overwhelming for them because they were largely made up of parents. In addition, interviews with multiple friends showed that their responses varied greatly, even after the same death. This was, in part, because the nature of the relationship which had been lost varied, and the reaction to the suicide itself varied depending on how much they knew about their friend's state of mind. For example, Jack knew his friend was struggling with his mental health and had helped to support him:

> ...you know, because of how well I knew him and what he'd been through, I think I could understand why he did it you know as soon as I heard... but I think I, I was very kind of there with him, a lot of the time. So I kind of feel like I do understand why it happened. (Jack)

In this case, although Jack felt sad that he had failed to prevent the death, he also could understand that his friend's struggles had led to their death. In other cases, friends expressed more bewilderment and shock.

Conclusion

Death and bereavement are a fundamental and exceptionally painful human experience; this aspect of humanity binds us all. Remembering this can help to empower us, as we attempt to support those bereaved by suicide. Empathy and kindness are at the core of any compassionate response. However, depending on personal and cultural background, individuals will react differently to a loss, and as a consequence, support needs will vary. In addition, as this chapter has examined, there is an increasing awareness of the issues relating to suicide bereavement and the specific support needs of this group. This chapter has highlighted some of the core literature on this issue, entwined with examples from

---

1   https://uksobs.org

interviews undertaken as part of my doctoral work with students bereaved while studying at university. I have also included some of my broader reflections of working and researching in this area, including those based on interviewing family, friends and staff affected by suicide.

It is hoped that having read this chapter, the reader may better understand some of the complexities of bereavement by suicide and how their own reaction, and that of those around them who have been exposed to these tragic deaths, will be shaped by broader issues relating to suicide, death and youth. It is possible, with a sensitive and carefully planned approach, to make a real difference to the bereavement of those affected by a death by suicide. It can prevent further tragedies and help protect the long-term mental health of those affected. However, this is challenging emotional work that requires self-awareness and strong supervisory support.

Author biography

Dr Sharon Mallon is a senior lecturer (Mental Health) at the Open University. She is co-author of the UK's first national qualitative study of student suicide (*RaPSS: Response and Prevention of Student Suicide*). She was also involved in a major study of suicide in Northern Ireland and co-authored the *Understanding Suicide* report.

References

Alvarez, A. (2002) *The Savage God: A Study of Suicide*. London: Bloomsbury Publishing.

Atkinson, J.M. (1978) *Discovering Suicide: Studies in the Social Organisation of Sudden Death*. London: Unwin Brothers.

Attig, T. (2003) Relearning the World. In R.A. Neimeyer (ed.) *Meaning Reconstruction and the Experience of Loss*. Washington, DC: American Psychological Association. pp.36–53.

Bailley, S.E. and Kral, M.J. (1999) Survivors of suicide do grieve differently: empirical support for a common sense proposition. *Suicide & Life-Threatening Behaviour 29*, 256–271.

Beaton, S., Forster, P. and Maple, M. (2013) Suicide and language: why we shouldn't use the 'C' word. *InPsych. 35*, 1, 30–31.

Berman, A. (2011) Estimating the population of survivors of suicide: seeking an evidence base. *Suicide and Life Threatening Behavior 41*, 1, 110–116.

Blauner, B. (1997) *Our Mothers' Spirits: On the Death of Mothers and the Grief of Men: An Anthology*. London: HarperCollins.

Cerel, J., Brown, M., Maple, M. and Singleton, M. (2019) How many people are exposed to suicide? Not six. *Suicide and Life-Threatening Behavior 49*, 2, 529–534.

Clark, S. and Goldney, R.D. (2002) The Impact of Suicide on Relatives and Friends. In K. Hawton and K. Van Heeringen (eds) *The International Handbook of Suicide and Attempted Suicide*. Chichester: John Wiley and Sons. pp.466–484.

Cutliffe, J.R. (2011) Introduction. *Routledge International Handbook of Clinical Suicide Research*. Abingdon: Routledge. p.1.

Finch, J. and Wallis, L. (1993) Death, Inheritance and the Life Course. In D. Clark (ed.) *Sociology of Death*. Oxford: Blackwell. pp.50–68.

Fletcher, G.P. (1998) *Basic Concepts of Criminal Law*. New York: Oxford University Press.

Harvey, J.H., Carlson, H.R., Huff, T.M. and Green, M.A. (2003) Embracing Their Memory. In R.A. Neimeyer (ed.) *Meaning Reconstruction and Experience of Loss*. Washington, DC: American Psychological Association. pp.231–243.

Hewett, J. and Oates, W. (1980) *After Suicide*. Philadelphia: Westminster Press.

Joiner, T. (2010) *Myths about Suicide*. Cambridge, MA: Harvard University Press.

Jordan, J. and McIntosh, J. (2011) The Impact of Suicide on Adults. In J. Jordan and J.McIntosh (eds) *Grief after Suicide*. Hove: Routledge. pp.43–92.

Klass, D. (2003) The Inner Representation of the Dead Child. In R.A. Neimeyer (ed.) *Meaning Reconstruction and the Experience of Loss*. Washington, DC: American Psychological Association. pp.77–94.

Kolehmainen, J. and Handwerk, S. (2008) *Teen Suicide*. Minneapolis: Lerner Publications.

Mallon, S. and Stanley, N. (2014) Creation of a death by suicide: a study of the processes by which the bereaved determine that the death of a friend is suicide. *Crisis 36*, 2, 142–147.

Maple, M., Cerel, J., Jordan, J. and McKay, K. (2014) Uncovering and identifying the missing voices in suicide bereavement. *Suicidology Online 5*, 1, 1–12.

Melhem, N.M., Day, N., Shear, M.K., Day, R., Reynolds, C.F. III and Brent, D. (2004) Traumatic grief among adolescents exposed to a peer's suicide. *American Journal of Psychiatry 161*, 1411–1416.

Neimeyer, R.A. (2001) *Meaning Reconstruction and the Experience of Loss*. Washington, DC: American Psychological Association.

Prigerson, H.G., Bridge, J., Maciejewski, P.K., Beery, L.C. *et al.* (1999) Influence of traumatic grief on suicidal ideation among young adults. *American Journal of Psychiatry 156*, 1994–1995.

Shneidman, E. (1972) Foreword. In A. Cain (ed.) *Survivors of Suicide*. Springfield: Charles C. Thomas. pp.ix–xi.

Stanley, N., Mallon, S., Bell, J. and Manthorpe, J. (2007) *Responses and Prevention in Student Suicide: The RaPSS Study*. Preston: University of Central Lancashire/PAPYRUS.

Szasz, T. (2002) *Fatal Freedom: The Ethics and Politics of Suicide*. New York: Syracuse University Press.

Wallace, S. (1973) *After Suicide*. New York: John Wiley and Sons.

Wertheimer, A. (1991) *A Special Scar*. London: Routledge.

CHAPTER 22

Suicide Postvention in Higher Education Settings

KARL ANDRIESSEN AND KAROLINA KRYSINSKA

Overview

The purpose of this chapter is to provide:

- information on how to respond to a suicide, with regard to students, staff, family and the media

- guidance in developing a comprehensive suicide response plan, suitable for implementation and evaluation.

Introduction

A death by suicide can occur in a variety of ways, ranging from contained situations that impact only on those close to the person, to more public and/or violent deaths that may attract a great deal of attention. This chapter explores how higher education settings, such as universities and colleges, may plan to ensure timely interventions that are appropriate to the circumstances of any suicide. Dealing with the aftermath of a suicide, i.e. postvention, involves caring for those who have been exposed to and affected by the death. By doing so, the response to a death by suicide may also contribute to prevention of adverse psychosocial outcomes and to concerted suicide prevention in the exposed communities (Andriessen 2009).

The chapter addresses a suite of topics and good practices for consideration in a comprehensive suicide response plan. It is based on the literature on suicide bereavement support (e.g. Andriessen, Krysinska and Grad 2017a; Jordan and McIntosh 2011), postvention in higher education (e.g. Leenaars and Leenaars 2011; Meilman and Hall 2006; Streufert 2004), and published suicide postvention guidelines and related resources for higher education settings (Active Minds 2017; Higher Education Mental Health Alliance 2014; PAPYRUS 2018; Samaritans 2016; Universities UK and PAPYRUS 2018). Planning and communication are crucial for a coordinated response. The chapter specifically addresses the formulation of a response plan and team, providing support to students and staff, contacting the family, responding to the wider community and media, and ensuring ongoing support and evaluation of the postvention response.

While this chapter is focused on dealing with a death by suicide, the guidance on how to respond and create a response plan may also be useful in the context of other modes of death. In fact, a central stance of this chapter is that, overall, a suicide death should not be treated differently from other deaths. The primary reason is that treating suicide and loss by suicide differently entails a risk of stigmatization of the bereaved individuals or glorification of suicide, which may increase the risk of imitation (Robinson, Pirkis and O'Connor 2016). Also, as argued by Jordan and McIntosh (2011) and Levine (2008), while a few features may be more pronounced in suicide bereavement (such as feelings of rejection or stigma), all grief processes may share features such as sadness or anger. Integrating a specific suicide response plan within a broader bereavement, health and wellbeing policy may help to sustain provision of adequate responses after suicide (Cusick 2008; Meilman and Hall 2006).

Review of the literature has found that adopting a public health framework for postvention service delivery offers the opportunity to tailor support to bereaved individuals according to the impact of suicide on their lives (Andriessen et al. 2019). This can range from information and awareness-raising to targeting all bereaved individuals, to specialized help for those who experience high levels of grief and symptoms of poor mental health. Such a framework might also align the postvention plan with broader health programmes.

Responding to a suicide in a higher education setting requires a multidisciplinary approach (Cusick 2008). The practice-oriented information in this chapter may help administrators, clinicians, staff members and student representatives in their preparation of a response plan in case a suicide occurs, as well as in delivering support and evaluating the response plan.

Understanding students' grief after suicide

Over the decades, research has increased our knowledge of risk and protective factors of suicidal behaviour, and how people may evolve from thinking about suicide (i.e. suicidal ideation) to behaviour, possibly with a fatal outcome (O'Connor *et al.* 2016). However, despite identifiable commonalities across suicides, each suicide is characterized by its own life history and suicidal process (Sveticic and De Leo 2012). Similarly, each grief process is a unique experience. Individuals who were psychologically close to the deceased person may be more strongly affected than those whose relationships were more distant. Some people may be exposed to a suicide without experiencing an impact on their life, while others feel mildly affected or distressed, and some may experience intense short- or long-term grief reactions (Cerel *et al.* 2014).

Grief is the natural reaction to the death of a close person such as a family member or a friend (Stroebe *et al.* 2008). In a higher education setting, the deceased person could also be, for example, a fellow student, a staff member or supervisor, a roommate or a member of the sports team. All grief, including grief after suicide, may comprise various psychological, physical and behavioural reactions (Andriessen, Krysinska and Grad 2017b; Erlangsen and Pitman 2017). Feelings of sadness, guilt and anger, physical reactions, such as crying, and a wish to be reunited with the deceased person are common grief features (Stroebe *et al.* 2008). Compared to other forms of bereavement, people bereaved by suicide may experience more shock or trauma related to the unexpected or violent nature of the death, and more feelings of abandonment, rejection, shame, perceived stigma and struggles with meaning-making and 'why' questions (Jordan and McIntosh 2011; Pitman *et al.* 2016).

Bereavement in college and university students is not uncommon. Approximately one in four students has lost a family member or a close friend in a given year (Balk, Walker and Baker 2010). However, bereaved students may face particular challenges, especially after a loss by suicide (Battle *et al.* 2013; Fajgenbaum, Chesson and Lanzi 2012; Levine 2008). Unlike dealing with death and bereavement, individuation is a major developmental task for emerging adults, including students (Taub and Servaty-Seib 2008). This entails a psychological process of establishing autonomy and identity separate from parents and other family. Many students also live at a geographical distance from their family and usual support resources. A bereaved student may feel disconnected from others as social life on campus is often 'fun-oriented' (Fajgenbaum *et al.* 2012). In addition, students must deal with academic pressure and often combine study with part-time work (Battle *et al.* 2013; Fajgenbaum *et al.* 2012). A death by suicide may come as a shock, and the bereaved students may receive little social and formal support, which may be due to limited help-seeking and sharing with others, and reluctance of the social network to provide support (Andriessen *et al.* 2017b; Pitman *et al.* 2017). A personal or family history of suicidal behaviour or mental ill health may further compound the students' grief and mental health (Levine 2008). Consequently, administrators and (mental) health professionals in colleges and universities may need to take the lead in developing appropriate support plans (Callahan and Fox 2008; Rickgarn 1996; Servaty-Seib and Taub 2010).

Responding to suicide

The information in this section is based on the available guidelines for higher education settings (Active Minds 2017; Higher Education Mental Health Alliance 2014) and literature on bereavement support in higher education (e.g. Callahan and Fox 2008; Cusick 2008; Hamilton 2008; Leenaars and Leenaars 2011; Streufert 2004).

A suicide response plan and team

A first task is writing a formal suicide response plan. Guidelines can be adapted to the context of the particular institution (see 'Postvention guidelines' below). It is important that the suicide response plan is endorsed by the appropriate authorities within the institution. The response plan should specify tasks and responsibilities: who is doing what and when for whom (e.g. students, parents, staff). It should include resources such as contact details of 1) emergency services (ambulance, police), 2) helplines (Samaritans, Cruse Bereavement Care, PAPYRUS, SHOUT UK crisis text service), 3) service providers on campus and in the community, and 4) teaching and other staff.

Usually, there is a committee or a team that looks after the suicide response plan. There may be different roles within this team, such as a team leader or coordinator, and an assistant or substitute team leader. The multidisciplinary team can comprise various members such as a pro-vice-chancellor/vice-dean, representatives of the health service, the counselling and/or mental health service, pastoral care, campus safety service and student representatives. Team members can be allocated specific tasks within the response plan. As most people have never been prepared to deal with the aftermath of a death by suicide, response team members might benefit from specific training in suicide prevention and bereavement support (McDonnell *et al.* 2020; O'Neill *et al.* 2020).

Activating the response plan

When a suicide or a possible suicide has occurred, the suicide response plan will be activated. The team coordinator will verify the report of the suspected suicide (e.g. from the police) and inform the members of the response team and the designated authority within the institution. Activating the suicide response plan implies adhering to existing protocols regarding a death on the campus. This may include evacuation and fencing of the site and contacting the emergency services. At this stage, it is important to obtain facts about the death (e.g. who, when, where?) and identifying those who may be directly involved, such as witnesses, student peers, staff or family members.

A nominated team member will contact the family as soon as possible to offer condolences and to find out how they want to refer to the death (including dealing with the media). Some families may wish to keep details, including the mode of death, private. Contact with family may also offer opportunities to direct them to support services, to enquire about the funeral, and their stance regarding a possible memorial event on campus (depending on the institution's usual practice after other deaths).

Informing students and staff

The response team will meet to share the facts regarding the death and to gauge the potential impact on students, staff and the campus as a whole. Subsequently, the team will unfold the support as planned in the response plan. Those who potentially may feel highly impacted by the death, such as best friends, housemates, student course peers, witnesses and first responders (e.g. domestic and security staff), personal tutors or supervisors, might be approached and informed individually as they may require individual support by trained or qualified staff such as a mental health professional. Nominated team members will inform students and staff about the facts, whether this will affect the lectures schedule, and about the funeral arrangements. It is advised to maintain daily routines on campus as much as possible. Belongings of the deceased student or staff member should be collected by a nominated team member. On and off campus support resources should be made available to all students and staff. Ongoing daily contact with students and staff may help to create and sustain a supportive environment and may help to detect those who might need help in the aftermath of the suicide.

Team members involved in informing students and staff may use a script to cover the issues that must be addressed. This will include providing students and staff with clear information about the death (within possible legal limits or wishes of the family), while acknowledging the distressing nature of the death and debunking myths about suicide (e.g. romanticizing or glorifying suicide). Discussing details of suicide methods should be avoided and the complex and potentially multiple factors contributing to suicide should be emphasized. It should be made clear where people can find support or resources on or off the campus. Sharing with others, social support and self-care must be encouraged. The harmful potential of rumours and the institution's policy on contacts with media can be clarified. The responsible use of social media should be promoted (Samaritans 2013). While informing students and staff, it is likely that some may have questions and/or be affected by the news. However, it is important to contain emotions during these information sessions; those deeply affected should be referred to an appropriate support service.

Engaging with wider community and media

If the suicide occurred in a public space and/or is likely to attract public and media attention, the institution might consider contacting community response teams (such as suicide bereavement or bereavement services, victim support services) or distributing a communique through their usual communication channels. This external communication should match with information provided to students and staff. It may include condolences to family and the community, information on how the institution is dealing with the suicide, advice on what to do when people are concerned about others, support resources available on campus and in the community, and contact details of the institution's spokesperson.

In public communications, it is crucial to respect the wishes of the family and to adhere to media guidelines for the reporting of suicide (Samaritans 2013). Such guidelines, based on the research regarding risk and protective factors in the reporting of suicide, have become available in several countries.[1] There is also advice for professionals talking with the media on suicide (Mindframe 2020; see also Chapter 23).

Websites and online newsletters may provide an opportunity to present services available to those in need. However, use of the internet and social media may warrant special attention (Thorn *et al.* 2020). For example, in cases where colleges and universities detect inappropriate social media messages from students (or others), they may react by talking directly to the students involved, rather than engaging in online discussions. In line with the overall policy of the institution, students may be allowed to create an online memorial. Such a memorial may facilitate social support and constructive dialogues, while glorification of suicide should be discouraged.

Ensuring ongoing support

A suicide response plan may cater for potentially long-term effects of a suicide. Hence, it is important to remain attentive for signs of distress for more than a year and to be aware of potentially sensitive dates, such as a birthday or anniversary of death, which may trigger grief and adverse mental health reactions. The institution can encourage help-seeking, social support and self-care, both in students and staff, and maintain contact with external services. Contact details of internal (on campus) and external support services for staff and students can be posted on a regular basis. The suicide response plan may routinely include ongoing support for its team members, especially those who are actively involved in supporting students or staff.

Evaluating and integrating the response plan

To evaluate the suicide response plan a few months after a suicide has occurred, it is important that the agendas and decisions of the team meetings (e.g. related to providing support) are recorded. Dates and time of actions and communications with students, staff, family members, media and external services such as police, mental health services or GPs should also be recorded. Feedback from staff members, collected through nominated team members, may also inform the evaluation process of the response team.

---

[1] For example, in the UK, www.samaritans.org/about-samaritans/media-guidelines, in the USA, www.sprc.org/keys-success/safe-messaging-reporting, in Australia, https://mindframe.org.au/industry-hubs/for-media, and internationally, www.iasp.info/media_guidelines.php

While it is crucial to acknowledge the efforts of everyone involved (suicide response team, other staff, students, the institution as a whole and external services) to adequately deal with the impact of a suicide, it is equally important to assess which aspects of the response plan worked, and what could be done better or differently. Evaluation might also look at the training or support needs of members of the response team or others involved in providing support to students or staff. Evaluation may result in a modified suicide response plan, and regular reviews (e.g. annually), even if no suicide has occurred, can keep the plan up to date.

Integration of the suicide response plan in a broader bereavement or health policy will depend on the context of the institution. Tentatively, it could involve mental health awareness training for staff and/or students, and promotion of self-care and social support.

Published postvention guidelines for higher education settings

A review of the peer-reviewed and grey literature and postvention guidelines published since 2014 (Andriessen *et al.* 2019) found three guidelines for colleges and universities (Active Minds 2017; Higher Education Mental Health Alliance 2014; Samaritans 2016). The 'Postvention guidelines' box below summarizes these three guidelines and Table 22.1 at the end of the chapter describes them according to quality criteria derived from the *AGREE II Instrument* (Appraisal of Guidelines for Research and Evaluation II; AGREE Next Steps Consortium 2017).

Postvention guidelines

After a Campus Suicide: A Postvention Guide for Student-Led Responses (Active Minds 2017)

Developed by a non-profit organization supporting mental health awareness and education for students in the USA, these guidelines specifically address students who may play an active role in a postvention response. They explain what students can do after a suicide, provide recommendations for safe communication about suicide among friends, on social media and at public and campus venues, and stress the importance of self-care. The document offers guidance about how to participate in or initiate a response to a student's suicide at a campus and how to connect with university administrators in this task. The document contains examples of safe communications about suicide and a case study of a student mental health advocacy campaign. While the document has many merits, it does not report how it was developed and if the target audience (i.e. students) was involved. A theoretical model of postvention was not included.

Postvention: A Guide for Response to Suicide on College Campuses (Higher Education Mental Health Alliance 2014)

This guideline is intended for use by colleges and universities affected by a suicide death or other crises and/or want to be prepared for such emergencies. It covers topics such as planning a postvention response (e.g. forming a multidisciplinary committee and developing a protocol) and its implementation (contact with clinical services, communication with the media and managing suicide contagion/clusters). It also addresses campus murder-suicides and provides exercises and links to additional online resources. While the guideline seems comprehensive, a theoretical model of postvention was not included.

Help When We Needed It Most: How to Prepare for and Respond to a Suspected Suicide in Schools and Colleges (Samaritans 2016)

This resource is a part of Samaritans' Step by Step service in which trained volunteers (postvention advisors) provide schools, colleges and other youth settings with practical support to prepare for and respond to an attempted or suspected suicide. The Step by Step service responds within 24 hours. The guideline provides advice regarding creating a postvention protocol, breaking the news about the death, handling the media, and contacting and informing the school community in a sensitive and appropriate way. It provides information on how to identify and support vulnerable students, including how to engage them in a conversation, as well as advice regarding memorials and funerals. In addition, the resource provides guidance on how to respond to suspected suicide and a suicide attempt and offers further information and contact details about Samaritans and other sources of support.

Conclusions

Suicide can have a severe and lasting impact on bereaved students, staff members, and the wider higher and further education community. Some bereaved people will be more affected than others and may require long-term support. A timely and well-organized response is possible to alleviate the impact of a death by suicide on a short- and a long-term basis for affected individuals and the whole institution. Therefore, the institution must be prepared and develop a suicide response plan. Because each university or college campus is unique, available evidence- or practice-based guidelines must be tailored to the context of the specific setting and framed within existing health and wellbeing policies, including liaison with internal and external helping resources.

Acknowledgement

Dr Karl Andriessen was supported by a National Health and Medical Research Council (NHMRC) Early Career Fellowship (ECF) (APP1157796) and an Early Career Researcher Grant of The University of Melbourne (ECR1202020).

Author biographies

Dr Karl Andriessen is a Senior Research Fellow and NHMRC ECF in the Centre for Mental Health, School of Population and Global Health, University of Melbourne, Australia. He has a broad interest in suicide prevention research with a major focus on postvention and grief after suicide and other traumatic deaths.

Dr Karolina Krysinska is a research fellow in the Centre for Mental Health, School of Population and Global Health, The University of Melbourne, Australia. She is an experienced research psychologist whose main interest is research in suicide, suicide prevention and postvention.

References

Active Minds (2017) *After a Campus Suicide: A Postvention Guide for Student-Led Responses*. Accessed on 27/01/20 at: www.activeminds.org/programs/after-a-campus-suicide-postvention-guide
AGREE Next Steps Consortium (2017) *AGREE II Instrument*. Accessed on 27/01/20 at: www.agreetrust.org/resource-centre/agree-ii

Andriessen, K. (2009) 'Can postvention be prevention?' *Crisis 30*, 1, 43–47.

Andriessen, K., Krysinska, K. and Grad, O. (eds) (2017a) *Postvention in Action: The International Handbook of Suicide Bereavement Support.* Göttingen/Boston: Hogrefe. https://doi.org/10.1027/00493-000

Andriessen, K., Krysinska, K. and Grad, O. (2017b) 'Current Understandings of Suicide Bereavement.' In K. Andriessen, K. Krysinska and O. Grad (eds) *Postvention in Action: The International Handbook of Suicide Bereavement Support.* Göttingen/Boston: Hogrefe, pp.3–16.

Andriessen, K., Krysinska, K., Kõlves, K. and Reavley, N. (2019) 'Suicide postvention service models and guidelines 2014–2019: a systematic review.' *Frontiers in Psychology 10*, 2677. https://doi.org/10.3389/fpsyg.2019.02677

Balk, D.E., Walker, A.C. and Baker, A. (2010) Prevalence and severity of college student bereavement examined in a randomly selected sample. *Death Studies 34*, 5, 459–468.

Battle, C.L., Greer, J.A., Ortiz-Hernández, S. and Todd, D.M. (2013) Developing and implementing a bereavement support program for college students. *Death Studies 37*, 4, 362–382.

Callahan, C.M. and Fox, E.K. (2008) Student death protocols: a practitioner's perspective. *New Directions for Student Services 121*, 87–95.

Cerel, J., McIntosh, J.L., Neimeyer, R.A., Maple, M. and Marshall, D. (2014) The continuum of 'survivorship': definitional issues in the aftermath of suicide. *Suicide and Life-Threatening Behavior 44*, 6, 591–600.

Cusick, A. (2008) University student death response plans using a structural management approach provide effective coordinated institutional action. *Death Studies 32*, 6, 550–587.

Erlangsen, A. and Pitman, A. (2017) Effects of Suicide Bereavement on Mental and Physical Health. In K. Andriessen, K. Krysinska and O. Grad (eds) *Postvention in Action: The International Handbook of Suicide Bereavement Support.* Göttingen/Boston: Hogrefe. pp.17–26.

Fajgenbaum, D., Chesson, B. and Lanzi, R.G. (2012) Building a network of grief support on college campuses: a national grassroots initiative. *Journal of College Student Psychotherapy 26*, 2, 99–120.

Hamilton, L.A. (2008) Guidelines for death notification in college student populations. *New Directions for Student Services 121*, 77–86.

Higher Education Mental Health Alliance (2014) *Postvention: A Guide for Response to Suicide on College Campuses.* Accessed on 27/01/20 at: https://adaa.org/sites/default/files/postvention_guide-suicide-college.pdf

Jordan, J.R. and McIntosh, J.L. (2011) Is Suicide Bereavement Different? A Framework for Rethinking the Question. In J.R. Jordan and J.L. McIntosh (eds) *Grief After Suicide: Understanding the Consequences and Caring for the Survivors.* New York: Routledge. pp.19–42.

Leenaars, L.S. and Leenaars, A.A. (2011) Suicide Postvention Programs in Colleges and Universities. In D.A. Lamis and D. Lester (eds) *Understanding and Preventing College Student Suicide.* Springfield, IL: Charles C. Thomas Publisher. pp.273–290.

Levine, H. (2008) Suicide and its impact on campus. *New Directions for Student Services 121*, 63–76.

McDonnell, S., Nelson, P.A., Leonard, S., McGale, B. *et al.* (2020) Evaluation of the impact of the PABBS suicide bereavement training on clinicians' knowledge and skills. *Crisis 41*, 351–358.

Meilman, P.W. and Hall, T.M. (2006) Aftermath of tragic events: the development and use of community support meetings on a university campus. *Journal of American College Health 54*, 6, 382–384.

Mindframe (2020) Communicating about suicide. Accessed on 27/01/20 at: https://mindframe.org.au/suicide/communicating-about-suicide

O'Connor, R.C., Cleare, S., Eschle, S., Wetherall, K. and Kirtley, O.J. (2016) The Integrated Motivational–Volitional Model of Suicidal Behavior: An Update. In R.C. O'Connor and J. Pirkis (eds) *The International Handbook of Suicide Prevention*, 2nd edn. Chichester: Wiley-Blackwell. pp.220–240.

O'Neill, J.C., Marraccini, M.E., Bledsoe, S.E., Knotek, S.E. and Tabori, A.V. (2020) Suicide postvention practices in schools: school psychologists' experiences, training, and knowledge. *School Psychology 35*, 1, 61–71.

PAPYRUS (2018) *Building Suicide-Safer Schools and Colleges: A Guide for Teachers and Staff.* Warrington: PAPYRUS.

Pitman, A.L., Osborn, D.P., Rantell, K. and King, M.B. (2016) The stigma perceived by people bereaved by suicide and other sudden deaths: a cross-sectional UK study of 3432 bereaved adults. *Journal of Psychosomatic Research 87*, 22–29.

Pitman, A.L., Rantell, K., Moran, P., Sireling, L. *et al.* (2017) Support received after bereavement by suicide and other sudden deaths: a cross-sectional UK study of 3432 young bereaved adults. *BMJ Open 7*, e014487.

Rickgarn, R.L.V. (1996) The Need for Postvention on College Campuses: A Rationale and Case Study Findings. In C.A. Corr and D.E. Balk (eds) *Handbook of Adolescent Death and Bereavement*. New York: Springer. pp.273–292.

Robinson, J., Pirkis, J. and O'Connor, R.C. (2016) Suicide Clusters. In R.C. O'Connor and J. Pirkis (eds) *The International Handbook of Suicide Prevention*, 2nd edn. Chichester: Wiley-Blackwell. pp.758–774.

Samaritans (2013) *Media Guidelines for Reporting Suicide*. Ewell: Samaritans.

Samaritans (2016) *Help When We Needed It Most: How to Prepare for and Respond to a Suspected Suicide in Schools and Colleges*. Ewell: Samaritans.

Servaty-Seib, H.L. and Taub, D.J. (2010) Bereavement and college students: the role of counseling psychology. *The Counseling Psychologist 38*, 7, 947–975.

Streufert, B.J. (2004) Death on campuses: common postvention strategies in higher education. *Death Studies 28*, 2, 151–172.

Stroebe, M., Hansson, R., Schut, H. and Stroebe, W. (2008) Bereavement Research: Contemporary Perspectives. In M. Stroebe, R.M. Hansson, H. Schut and W. Stroebe (eds) *Handbook of Bereavement Research and Practice: Advances in Theory and Intervention*. Washington, DC: American Psychological Association. pp.3–25.

Sveticic, J. and De Leo, D. (2012) The hypothesis of a continuum in suicidality: a discussion on its validity and practical implications. *Mental Illness 4*, 2, e15.

Taub, D.J. and Servaty-Seib, H.L. (2008) Developmental and contextual perspectives on bereaved college students. *New Directions for Student Services 121*, 15–26.

Thorn, P., Hill, N.T., Lamblin, M., Teh, Z. *et al.* (2020) Developing a suicide prevention social media campaign with young people (the #Chatsafe project): co-design approach. *JMIR Mental Health 7*, 5, e17520.

Universities UK and PAPYRUS (2018) *Suicide-Safer Universities*. London: Universities UK.

Table 22.1: Quality criteria of published postvention guidelines for higher education settings

Title Author Country, Year	Target users	Target population	Objectives described	Development methods described	Target users included in development	Evidence-base described	Theory of postvention described	Key recommendations included	Sample material included	Source
After a Campus Suicide: A Postvention Guide for Student-Led Responses Active Minds USA, 2017	Students leading a campus-wide response to suicide	Schools after a student suicide	Yes	No	Unknown	Yes (literature)	No	Yes	Yes (social media postings)	www.activeminds.org/programs/after-a-campus-suicide-postvention-guide
Postvention: A Guide for Response to Suicide on College Campuses Higher Education Mental Health Alliance USA, 2014	Colleges, universities	Campuses after a death by suicide	Yes	Yes	Yes	Yes (literature, expert review)	No	No	Yes (one sample letter)	https://adaa.org/sites/default/files/postvention_guide-suicide-college.pdf
Help When We Needed It Most: How to Prepare for and Respond to a Suspected Suicide in Schools and Colleges Samaritans UK, 2016	Schools, colleges	Schools, colleges and other youth settings affected by a suspected or attempted suicide	Yes	No	Unknown	Yes (research and best practice)	No	Yes	Yes (language around suicide, helpful phrases)	https://media.samaritans.org/documents/samaritans-help-when-we-needed-it-most.pdf

Based on the criteria of the Appraisal of Guidelines for Research & Evaluation II (AGREE Next Steps Consortium 2017)

CHAPTER 23

Media Portrayal of Suicide

*Who Is Most at Risk and Why – Key Findings
from International Research Evidence*

LORNA FRASER

Overview

This chapter will explain the impact that media portrayals of suicide can have on vulnerable audiences, describe the risks associated with irresponsible coverage on the one hand and the potential benefits of helpful coverage on the other. It will also outline Samaritans' work with UK media to support responsible coverage, pointing out what higher education (HE) and further education (FE) communications staff can do to encourage responsible reporting and where to find resources and information.

Introduction

The impact of media portrayals of suicide is a well-evidenced area of research. Systematic reviews carried out across the world over the last six decades have linked certain types of media reports of suicide with increases in suicidal behaviour. This body of research describes what has become known as the 'Werther effect'. This phenomenon is part of a broader literature that suggests media reports which give detailed descriptions of suicide methods or sensationalize suicide can influence suicidal behaviour among vulnerable people (Pirkis *et al.* 2018; Sisask and Värnik 2012). When a young person dies by suicide the impact can have a devasting ripple effect which can extend far beyond their family and friends; it can increase the risk of suicide contagion among the wider student community, as well as those who knew them (Bilsen 2018; Pitman *et al.* 2015).

During the last decade, a rise in suicide rates and a significant increase in disclosures of mental health problems among the student community has drawn greater media attention to these issues, often with particular scrutiny around potential causes and the provision of support (ONS 2018). Due to the sensitivities associated with media coverage of suicide, while there is clearly a public interest in youth suicides and suicide clusters, it is important that this topic is approached responsibly. Communications staff representing HE and FE institutions should refer to Samaritans' *Media Guidelines for Reporting Suicide* (2020a) and encourage journalists to refer to these guidelines to help ensure news reports are covered responsibly.

This effect of influencing suicide contagion is not limited to mainstream media. It is now recognized it can take place in the online environment and through face-to-face communication within communities (Thomas and Joiner 2016). Great care and sensitivity are therefore required when communicating with students and staff affected by a suicide, including information and messages shared online and via social media. Those who are most affected by this contagious effect through media reporting include young people, people who suffer with mental health problems and people who are bereaved, particularly those who are bereaved by suicide (Gould, Jamieson and Romer 2003; Pirkis and Blood 2001; Sisask and Värnik 2012; Stack 2003; WHO 2017). In addition to being more susceptible to suicide contagion, young people are also more likely than other age groups to be influenced by what they see and hear in the media (Gould *et al.* 2003).

It is important that universities note that the research evidence does not suggest suicide should not be covered in the press, or that we avoid communications in relation to a student death. This may inadvertently stigmatize suicide if treated differently to other student deaths. A smaller body of research, known as the 'Papageno' effect, has linked certain types of media coverage of suicide with falls in suicide rates (Niederkrotenthaler *et al.* 2010). This research has shown that news stories which demonstrate hopeful recovery, such as personal testimonies of those who have sought help and chosen to live rather than make a suicide attempt, can encourage others to seek help. These helpful stories can raise awareness of the issues surrounding suicide, highlight valuable sources of support, encourage people to start conversations if they are concerned about someone they know and encourage those who are struggling to cope to reach out for help, all of which can play a significant role in preventing suicide deaths.

Samaritans' media guidelines: how we work with the press and how we support HE and FE institutions

Due to the sensitivities associated with media coverage of suicide, encouraging responsible reporting is a key component of national suicide prevention strategies, including the cross-government suicide prevention strategy in England and replicated in Northern Ireland, Republic of Ireland and Wales (DHSC 2012 [England]; Department of Health 2019 [NI]; HSE 2015 [Republic of Ireland]; Welsh Government 2015). In Scotland, encouraging responsible media reporting has been recognized as an important area of focus for future suicide prevention strategies, building on existing guidance and good practice (Scottish Government 2018).

Samaritans is the leading advisor on this issue in the UK and is recognized as the expert impartial voice of authority on media coverage of suicide. Our media advice team provides support on a national and local level to the press and other organizations, including FE and HE institutions, with an interest in communicating about this topic. Samaritans first published guidance for media in 1994 and this best practice guide is regularly updated to reflect the latest research evidence. It forms the basis of our advisory work. In a survey carried out by Samaritans in 2019, 98 per cent of journalists and programme makers who responded rated the guidelines as useful. We have also published additional resources covering suicide-related topics including reporting on youth suicides and suicide clusters (Samaritans 2020b), guidance for covering self-harm in the media (Samaritans 2020c) and working with people bereaved by suicide (Samaritans 2020d). These resources have been produced in consultation with journalists and programme-makers, media regulatory bodies, academic experts and people with lived experience of suicide. In addition, Samaritans has a dedicated Media Advisory team offering support to media outlets across the country to help inform responsible coverage.

Our experience in this area has shown that it is critical to work closely with journalists and programme makers, to engage them to support and encourage responsible coverage of suicide. We work closely with media regulators and editorial policy teams to ensure that those who write and administer editorial codes of practice are fully aware of the risks relating to coverage of suicide. Our work helps to ensure that suicide content reaching the public domain is more sensitive and responsible than it would otherwise be, reducing the risk of content having a potentially harmful effect on vulnerable audiences.

Samaritans also provides training to media outlets and others who communicate publicly about suicide, including educational institutions. In our training, we explain some of the context and sensitivities around handling suicidal behaviour in the media, highlighting the main risk areas and how these can be avoided, who is most at risk and why, and what constitutes helpful coverage. We encourage media outlets to use opportunities to remind audiences that help is available and that recovery is possible, through news reports, factual programmes and drama storylines.

Samaritans' work with coroners

Inquests in England and Wales are independent investigations carried out by HM Coroner following a sudden or unexplained death, to determine the cause of death. Inquests are held in a public court setting and journalists can, and do, attend hearings and report on the findings. The extensive level of evidence covered in an inquest, particularly about the specific details of how a person died, can generate problematic news reports. Samaritans has published guidance for coroners to support their dealings with media. We also work with coroners and FE and HE communications teams behind the scenes to help prevent harmful coverage when there are particular concerns about an upcoming inquest. This includes concerns about suicide methods and cases involving a suicide pact or potential cluster. In such cases, we often produce a bespoke confidential media advisory notice, in agreement with the coroner, which is shared with journalists attending the inquest hearing as a reminder to report the case responsibly. Where there are concerns about how an inquest may be covered in the press, FE and HE communications departments can make contact with Samaritans' media advice team for support and to discuss the possibility of briefing journalists.

Samaritans' news monitoring data

Samaritans monitors news reporting of suicide by local and national press on a daily basis, analysing and assessing approximately 6000 print and online articles each year. In cases where news articles contain content which, based on the research evidence, poses a potential risk to vulnerable people (e.g. detailed descriptions of suicide methods), we contact managing editors to raise the concern and request changes to online stories. We limit these contacts to specifically high-risk content because it is important that these approaches remain noted by editors. Frequent contact would become counterproductive by diluting the impact of such interventions. If problematic news reports of suicide are picked up by FE or HE staff, they can contact Samaritans' Media Advisory team in order that appropriate action can be taken.

Our analysis of news reporting in the UK has provided useful data for identifying trends in suicide coverage over time. Here are some points for FE and HE communications staff to be aware of:

- When a young person takes their own life, their age alone can make their story more newsworthy. News reporting of suicides by young people remains disproportionate to the numbers of young people dying by suicide (Marzano 2019; Marzano *et al.* 2018).

- News reports may contain intense speculation of causes for a death – for example, academic pressure and bullying often feature. This can be unhelpful because it may oversimplify the complex nature of suicidal behaviour.

- Stories about young people who have died by suicide are often reported in a more sensational way – for example, with the use of emotive language and images.

- Local newspapers are sometimes approached by bereaved families with the express wish for their loved one to be memorialized in their local press.

- In the aftermath of a young person's suicide there is often a wider community affected by the death and grieving. While it is important for young people to express their grief following such a tragic event, community outpourings of grief can present a unique set of challenges for local journalists. Local press will aim to reflect the community grief, often lifting comments and images shared on social media, including details of memorial events and fundraising campaigns. Such images and comments can unintentionally serve to romanticize a death by suicide.

- Given the increased sensitivities and risks with young audiences, it is important that journalists are encouraged to report youth suicides responsibly, showing the complexity of suicidal behaviour and the impact of the loss. They should remind people that suicide is preventable and include signposting to sources of support for those affected by the death.

- Careful consideration should also be given to the placement of memorials to avoid romanticizing or glorifying a death, including creating a place or object that becomes associated with suicide. Guidance on memorials is listed in 'Useful resources for FE and HE institutions' below.

Briefing the press

When a suicide is particularly high profile or problematic in terms of reporting (e.g. a potential cluster situation), Samaritans will issue a confidential media briefing to editors. The purpose is to give a timely reminder to editors and news teams of the importance of responsible reporting. We restrict publication of our briefings to cases which deem such intervention necessary, and the media is aware that Samaritans will only publish a briefing when there are significant risks relating to how a story is covered. This considered approach ensures that Samaritans' briefings are respected and adhered to. If FE or HE staff have concerns about how a death or potential cluster may be reported in the press, Samaritans can be contacted for advice and support.

An informed collaborative approach

Samaritans works closely with academic experts currently leading research into the effects of media portrayals of suicide. This has helped to ensure it is kept up to date with research evidence. We also work with others who publicly communicate on the topic of suicide. This includes local and national government, health and education sectors, emergency services and many third sector organizations. We encourage FE and HE communications teams to engage with local media to develop good local relationships with journalists to support more informed coverage of mental health and suicide. This work can include:

- FE and HE institutions sharing details of their student mental health and wellbeing services to demonstrate the types of support available to students

- mental health awareness campaigns, highlighting the importance of reaching out for help and the benefits of talking through problems, including speaking to friends and families, as well as more formal support services

- profiling case study stories, such as students who are happy to share their experiences of their mental health problems and how they manage these, which can serve as influential models to others who may be struggling with their mental health

- engaging with local agencies and charities providing mental health care and support services within communities to encourage them to promote their services in the local press.

Samaritans' Media Advisory team is available to offer support with concerns and issues relating to media reporting. If you are aware of an incident or inquest which is likely to generate unhelpful coverage, you can get in touch with their team for advice.

Reporting youth suicides: the risks and how FE and HE institutions can engage local press and encourage responsible reporting

Dealing with media enquiries and ongoing press reporting of an incident involving a student death can add to an extremely difficult situation for staff and students, as well as the bereaved family. At this time, it is important to differentiate between coverage which, based on the evidence, may increase the risk of contagion, and stories, which may cause concern in relation to reputational risk. In times of heightened alarm, these two can become merged.

It can be helpful to have information ready to share with the media, including prepared statements, details of suicide prevention plans that are in place and details of mental health support facilities available to students. It can also be helpful to offer information to help journalists understand the wider context such as issues which may impact on students' mental health more generally (e.g. adjusting to university life and living away from home for the first time) and additional pressures (e.g. social, academic and financial).

Suicide is an extremely complex topic to cover in the press, one which presents a whole set of unique challenges for journalists. Writing a report about a young person who has taken their life is one of the most sensitive issues a journalist will cover and one which often comes with significant personal impact. It helps to consider some of the specific challenges journalists must navigate when reporting on suicides by young people. These include:

- sensitively paying tribute to a person who has died and conveying the grief of a bereaved family

- representing the voice of the community in the aftermath of a suicide, often expressed on social media, while avoiding inadvertently romanticizing or glorifying suicidal behaviour

- representing a range of different perspectives, including those of family, friends and health professionals, while remaining sensitive and avoiding oversimplification of suicidal behaviour

- appropriately raising awareness of the issues which can increase a person's risk of suicide, such as mental illness and alcohol/substance misuse

- covering campaigns or fundraising activity, carried out in relation to a death by suicide

- accurately reporting on the findings from a coroner's investigation.

When preparing stories, reporters must balance reporting on a sensitive and complex issue that is in the public interest while avoiding reports which may encourage imitational suicidal behaviour among vulnerable people. Samaritans encourages journalists to consider the potential impact of news reports on other vulnerable young people who may identify with the circumstances of a person who has died.

We recommend particular care around speculation of causes for a death by suicide. Contagion can be caused by vulnerable people over-identifying with a young person who has died (Pirkis *et al.* 2018). For example, if a death is reported in a way that oversimplifies suicidal behaviour by the suggestion of a single cause (e.g. bullying), the risk of influencing imitational behaviour in others who may be vulnerable can be increased. Others experiencing bullying, who may feel fearful and hopeless about their own situation, may be more vulnerable to suicide contagion and more likely to identify with the person who has died. Journalists should be reminded that suicide is complex and most of the time there is not one event or factor that leads someone to take their own life. It is usually a combination of individual, community and societal factors interacting with each other which contribute to the increased risk of suicide. Anyone can experience thoughts of suicide and everyone is different; what can make suicide feel like an option to one person might be experienced very differently by someone else. It is safer to convey this complexity when covering suicide.

Language and tone are important with young audiences. Samaritans encourages journalists to make sensible judgements and to cover suicide stories sensitively and accurately, avoiding overly emotional and subjective approaches. Particular care should be taken around the inclusion of comments posted on social media sites. These expressions of grief can unintentionally romanticize, or even glorify, suicidal behaviour. Examples include: 'heaven's gained another angel', 'the most beautiful angel in heaven' and 'at peace now'.

It can also be helpful to remind journalists that suicide is preventable. What the wider public hears more commonly about suicidal behaviour tends to relate to deaths, because this is the more likely news story. However, evidence would suggest that far more people survive suicidal feelings and attempts than the number of people who die by suicide. The World Health Organization estimates that for every person who dies by suicide across the world, there may be 20 others who will make an attempt and survive (WHO 2020). While a previous suicide attempt is the most significant risk factor for suicide, most of those who make an attempt on their life will go on to live a perfectly healthy life and are not likely to attempt suicide again (WHO 2020). It can also be helpful to make journalists aware that while student suicides have been on the rise during the last decade, this reflects wider trends among young people and incidence of student suicide is half that of the wider age-adjusted population (Gunnell *et al.* 2020; ONS 2018).

Reporting of suicide clusters

If more than one death should occur within a relatively short space of time and there is thought to be any connection, such as having attended the same university, this can attract huge media interest and generate excessive volumes of news coverage. The media will consider this to be in the public interest and journalists will often approach bereaved families, students, staff and others for comment. Irresponsible media reports of suicide clusters are known to increase the risk of contagion (Sisask and

Värnik 2012). A US study which looked at newspaper reports of suicide clusters in 13–20-year-olds highlights some specific differences in suicide reports which were followed by clusters, compared with isolated/single suicides (Gould *et al.* 2014).

Features of the suicide clusters coverage included:

- the word 'suicide' and details of suicide methods more frequently being included in headlines

- more details about the act of suicide being given

- stories being more likely to be repeated than non-cluster stories

- being more prominent – front page stories.

As a member of FE or HE staff, it can be helpful to remind journalists of the risks associated with media coverage of suicide, particularly with a young audience in mind, and signpost them to Samaritans' media guidelines (Samaritans 2020a) to encourage responsible reporting.

It can also be helpful to give a broader context – for example, reminding journalists that suicide figures in FE and HE are significantly lower than the general population within this age group (ONS 2018). Highlight the importance of encouraging conversations about mental health and signposting to sources of support.

Bereaved families and the media

When possible, it can be helpful to prepare bereaved families and those affected by a suicide for media coverage. While some people are happy to engage with the press to share their story, others can find this too intrusive and prefer to keep their grief private. Some families may find a memorial piece gives comfort, some may want to engage with local press to highlight fundraising or campaign activity, or to highlight relevant issues such as provision of mental health support. It is advisable to point out that local stories may be picked up by the national press and there is no way of controlling the narrative. Samaritans advises journalists to take particular care when approaching bereaved families, friends and witnesses as they may be in shock and traumatized by their loss. Our *Working with People Bereaved by Suicide* (Samaritans 2020d) is a useful guide.

IPSO (Independent Press Standards Organisation), the UK's main regulator for newspapers and magazines, can offer help in these situations. IPSO operates a 24-hour harassment helpline providing support and advice to those who have been affected by a suicide and do not wish to have contact with the press. IPSO can issue a notice to the press advising them not to contact named individuals and can give advice around reporting in relation to the Editors' Code (IPSO 2021).

Public Health England (2019) has also published useful guidance on identifying and responding to suicide clusters covering all practice aspects of responding to these deaths, which includes detailed guidance from Samaritans on dealing with the media.

To summarize, here are some of the key points Samaritans recommends journalists consider when preparing youth suicide stories:

- Remain sensitive to those affected by a death – bereaved family, friends, tutors and the wider student community.

- Avoid giving details of suicide methods.

- Remember that suicide is complex and rarely, if ever, is the result of a single cause.

- Avoid re-publishing photographs of others who have died, as this can suggest unsubstantiated links between the deaths.

- Stick with a factual tone – stories should be as informed as possible, avoiding sensational speculation.

- If publishing a tribute piece, this should be done respectfully, focusing on the tragic loss of life, without inadvertently romanticizing a death.

- Stories should not be given undue prominence – avoid front page/lead stories with dramatic headlines.

- Repeatedly hearing that support services are inadequate may deter some students from seeking help. Remind audiences that suicide is preventable and signpost sources of support to encourage help-seeking.

Staff working in FE and HE communications and press teams can refer to these points when dealing with enquiries from journalists.

Summary

At Samaritans we are aware, from our many years of media advisory work, that journalists and programme makers view mental health and suicide as hugely important public health topics, and recognize their critical responsibility in increasing understanding of these issues. The media can play a significant role in raising awareness of the issues surrounding suicide and supporting national efforts to reduce these deaths. News stories which depict this hopeful recovery can serve as powerful testimonies to others that this is possible and could prevent suicide deaths (Niederkrotenthaler *et al.* 2010).

Increasing public understanding of mental health and suicide prevention, and the importance of talking about them, better enables people to look out for one another. For example, helping people to spot the signs that indicate a person may be struggling to cope could encourage them to reach out and start an important conversation, creating an opportunity to offer support. It is not uncommon for people to feel apprehensive about opening up a conversation with someone they know is going through a difficult time. Some are deterred by fear of saying the wrong thing and potentially making things worse. There are a number of myths that prevail in relation to talking about suicide, including the myth that if you ask a person about suicide, you may plant the idea in their head (Owens and Charles 2017). Avoiding public discussion around this could increase stigma and discourage people from speaking out.

In summary, if approached responsibly, media coverage presents an effective platform for raising awareness of the issues, including how people can be supported, by highlighting:

- the types of problem which may lead a person to become vulnerable to suicide

- the signs which may indicate a person is struggling to cope and may need help (these are published on Samaritans' website)

- hopeful stories of recovery, such as people who have reached a difficult time in their life but have managed to seek help and come through

- the value of starting a conversation if you are concerned about someone – ask if they're OK

- the importance of talking. Life can be tough. At times our emotions can become overwhelming and could lead to suicidal thoughts. Talking can help to see a way through things – whether this is with a family member, a friend, your GP or one of the many helplines offering support

- the reminder to people who may be vulnerable that suicide is preventable; it is not inevitable

- the fact that while a suicidal crisis can feel very intense, these feelings will pass. There is always someone there to help signpost sources of support such as Samaritans' helpline to encourage help.

These are examples of how media coverage can be used to support suicide prevention work.

Useful resources for FE and HE institutions

Samaritans' Media Advisory team offers advice and support with concerns and issues relating to media reporting. If you are aware of an incident or inquest which is likely to generate unhelpful coverage, you can get in touch with their team at mediaadvice@samaritans.org

IPSO (Independent Press Standards Organisation) is the UK's main regulator for newspapers and magazines and operates a 24-hour harassment helpline providing support and advice to those who have been affected by a suicide and do not wish to have contact with the press. IPSO can issue a notice to press not to contact named individuals and can give advice around reporting in relation to the Editors' Code. IPSO can be reached at inquiries@ipso.co.uk

Samaritans' helpline in the UK and ROI provides 24-hour support to anyone who is struggling to cope. People can call Samaritans for free from any phone on 116 123, or email jo@samaritans.org or visit www.samaritans.org to find details of a local branch to speak with someone face to face.

DEAL (Developing Emotional Awareness and Listening) programme for schools provides online resources to teaching staff on helping young people develop emotional resilience, www.samaritans.org/how-we-can-help/schools/deal

'It's Safe to Talk about Suicide' is information for concerned family members and friends produced by Devon County Council, www.devon.gov.uk/care-and-health/factsheet/suicide-prevention

Step by Step guidance service for schools, colleges and higher education institutions provides practical support and advice to help prepare for and recover from a suspected or attempted suicide. This includes free resources for educational professionals which give advice on sensitively communicating about a suicide, sharing information with friends, family, students and staff, and handling media enquiries, www.samaritans. org/how-we-can-help/schools/step-step/step-step-resources

Guidance for working with people bereaved by suicide is available at www.samaritans.org/about-samaritans/media-guidelines/ guidance-working-people-bereaved-suicide

Help is at Hand: Support after Someone May Have Died by Suicide is a resource for those who have been bereaved by suicide and includes a list of helpful organizations, www.gov.uk/government/news/ you-are-not-alone-help-is-at-hand-for-anyone-bereaved-by-suicide

Memorials guidance can be found at 'Memorials information', www. samaritans.org/how-we-can-help/schools/universities/memorials-information and 'Memorials after a suicide: guidelines for schools and families', www.sptsusa.org/wp-content/uploads/2015/05/Memorials_ After_a_Suicide.pdf

Author biography

Lorna Fraser is the Executive Lead for Samaritans' Media Advisory Service providing advice to UK media on the responsible portrayal of suicide and self-harm.

References

Bilsen, J. (2018) Suicide and youth: risk factors. *Frontiers in Psychiatry 9*, 540.

Department of Health [Northern Ireland] (2019) *Protect Life 2: A Strategy for Preventing Suicide and Self Harm in Northern Ireland 2019–2024*. Accessed on 03/04/21 at: www.health-ni. gov.uk/protectlife2

Department of Health and Social Care (2012) Suicide prevention strategy for England. Accessed on 03/04/21 at: www.gov.uk/government/publications/suicide-prevention-strategy-for-england

Gould, M., Jamieson, P. and Romer, D. (2003) Media contagion and suicide among the young. *American Behavioural Scientist 46*, 9, 1269–1284.

Gould, M., Kleinman, M.H., Lake, A.M., Forman, J. and Midle, J.B. (2014) Newspaper coverage of suicide and initiation of suicide clusters in teenagers in the USA, 1988–96: a retrospective, population-based, case-control study. *Lancet Psychiatry 1*, 1, 34–43.

Gunnell, D., Caul, S., Appleby, L., John, A. and Hawton, K. (2020) The incidence of suicide in university students in England and Wales 2000/2001–2016/2017: record linkage study. *Journal of Affective Disorders 261*, 113–120.

HSE (2015) Connecting for Life Goal 1: Improved Understanding. Accessed on 03/04/21 at: www.hse.ie/eng/services/list/4/mental-health-services/connecting-for-life/improved-understanding

Independent Press Standards Organisation (IPSO) (2021) Editors' Code of Practice. Accessed on 01/05/21 at: www.ipso.co.uk/editors-code-of-practice/#ReportingSuicide

Marzano, L. (2019, unpublished) Analysis of Samaritans' media monitoring data.

Marzano, L., Fraser, L., Scally, M., Farley, S. and Hawton, K. (2018) News coverage of suicidal behaviour in the United Kingdom and the Republic of Ireland. *Crisis 39*, 5, 386–396.

Niederkrotenthaler, T., Voracek, M., Herberth, A., Till, B. *et al.* (2010) Role of media reports in completed and prevented suicide: Werther v. Papageno effects. *British Journal of Psychiatry 197*, 3, 234–243.

Office for National Statistics (ONS) (2018) *Estimating Suicide among Higher Education Students, England and Wales: Experimental Statistics.* London: ONS.

Owens, C. and Charles, N. (2017) Development and evaluation of a leaflet for concerned family members and friends: 'It's safe to talk about suicide'. *Health Education Journal 76*, 5, 582–594.

Pirkis, J. and Blood, R.W. (2001) Suicide and the media: part 1: reportage in nonfictional media. *Crisis 22*, 4, 146–154.

Pirkis, J., Blood, W., Sutherland, G. and Currier, D. (2018) *Suicide and the News and Information Media: A Critical Review.* Newcastle, NSW: Mindframe.

Pitman, A.L., Osborn, D.P.J., Rantell, K. and King, M.B. (2015) Bereavement by suicide as a risk factor for suicide attempt: a cross-sectional national UK-wide study of 3432 young bereaved adults. *BMJ Open 6*, 1, https://bmjopen.bmj.com/content/6/1/e009948

Public Health England (2019) Identifying and Responding to Suicide Clusters: A Practice Resource. Accessed on 03/04/21 at: https://assets.publishing.service.gov.uk/government/uploads/system/uploads/attachment_data/file/839621/PHE_Suicide_Cluster_Guide.pdf

Samaritans (2020a) *Media Guidelines for Reporting Suicide.* Ewell: Samaritans. Accessed on 03/04/21 at: www.samaritans.org/about-samaritans/media-guidelines/media-guidelines-reporting-suicide/ samaritans.org

Samaritans (2020b) *Guidance for Reporting on Youth Suicides and Suicide Clusters.* Accessed on 03/04/21 at: www.samaritans.org/about-samaritans/media-guidelines/guidance-covering-youth-suicides-clusters-and-self-harm/guidance-reporting-youth-suicides

Samaritans (2020c) *Guidance for Covering Self-Harm in the Media.* Accessed on 03/04/21 at: www.samaritans.org/about-samaritans/media-guidelines/guidance-covering-youth-suicides-clusters-and-self-harm/guidance-covering-self-harm-media

Samaritans (2020d) *Guidance for Working with People Bereaved by Suicide.* Accessed on 03/04/21 at: www.samaritans.org/about-samaritans/media-guidelines/guidance-working-people-bereaved-suicide

Scottish Government (2018) Suicide Prevention Action Plan: Every Life Matters. Accessed on 03/04/21 at: www.gov.scot/publications/scotlands-suicide-prevention-action-plan-life-matters

Sisask, M. and Värnik, A. (2012) Media roles in suicide prevention: A systematic review. *International Journal of Environmental Research and Public Health 9*, 1231–1238.

Stack, S. (2003) Media coverage as a risk factor in suicide. *Journal of Epidemiology and Community Health 57*, 238–240.

Thomas, E. and Joiner, J. (2016) The clustering and contagion of suicide. *Current Directions in Psychological Science*, https://journals.sagepub.com/doi/10.1111/1467-8721.00021

Welsh Government (2015) *Talk to Me 2: Suicide and Self Harm Prevention Strategy for Wales 2015–2020.* Accessed on 03/04/21 at: https://gov.wales/suicide-and-self-harm-prevention-strategy-2015-2020

World Health Organization (WHO) (2017) Preventing Suicide: A Resource for Media Professionals – Update 2017. Accessed on 03/04/21 at: www.who.int/mental_health/suicide-prevention/resource_booklet_2017/en

World Health Organization (WHO) (2020) Suicide prevention. Accessed on 03/04/21 at: www.who.int/health-topics/suicide#tab=tab_1

Subject Index

Author Index